ARGUING COMPARATIVE POLITICS

Arguing Comparative Politics

ALFRED STEPAN

OXFORD
UNIVERSITY PRESS

OXFORD
UNIVERSITY PRESS

Great Clarendon Street, Oxford OX2 6DP

Oxford University Press is a department of the University of Oxford.
It furthers the University's objective of excellence in research, scholarship,
and education by publishing worldwide in

Oxford New York

Auckland Bangkok Buenos Aires Cape Town Chennai
Dar es Salaam Delhi Hong Kong Istanbul Karachi Kolkata
Kuala Lumpur Madrid Melbourne Mexico City Mumbai Nairobi
São Paulo Shanghai Taipei Tokyo Toronto

Oxford is a registered trade mark of Oxford University Press
in the UK and in certain other countries

Published in the United States
by Oxford University Press Inc., New York

British Library Cataloguing in Publication Data
Data available

Library of Congress Cataloging in Publication Data
Stepan, Alfred C.
Arguing comparative politics / Alfred Stepan.
p.   cm.
Includes bibliographical references and index.
1. Comparative government.   2. Democracy.   I. Title.
JF51.S67 2001   320.3—dc21   00-045291
ISBN 0-19-924270-4 (hbk.)
ISBN 0-19-829997-4 (pbk.)

5 7 9 10 8 6

Typeset by Kolam Information Services Pvt. Ltd., India
Printed in Great Britain
on acid-free paper by
Biddles Ltd.,
www.biddles.co.uk

To
Rocío and Juan Linz

Contents

List of Figures

List of Tables

Introduction

Reflections on "Problem Selection" in Comparative Politics

Scholars in comparative politics, correctly, are increasingly explicit about the methodologies they employ and the quality of the evidence they use. However, as a group we have not written much about how we select the problems we choose to study. This may be because "problem selection" has a personal as well as a professional dimension. The professional dimension is reproducible; the personal dimension is not. But, do we not miss learning something about the scholarly process by our relative silence on the subject of how and why we select the problems to work on that we do?

Surely, in the evolution of our research, problem selection comes first. It is only after such selection that we can formulate hypotheses about the problem; think about which theoretical and methodological approaches are most appropriate; train ourselves, if necessary, in the most powerful research techniques available; and finally design and actually carry out a research. It is precisely the process of chasing the *problem* that normally also leads us to pursue promising leads from other disciplines. It is in this sense that the most fruitful interdisciplinary work is "done under one skull," as Albert O. Hirschman once counseled me.

In fact, I believe *all* aspects of research are, in a fundamental sense, problem driven. It is from this perspective that I am taken aback when, on occasion, I am approached by brilliant doctoral candidates who have spent a great deal of effort mastering a powerful research tool and who then ask me what topics to apply it to. They are starting their research endeavor in the wrong place. I worry whether they will have the passion to sustain an increasingly creative inquiry, in which they continuously, with more power and more focus, go up and down the research ladder in their dissertation, and, with the "enthusiasm and work"

I would like to thank Archie Brown, Juan J. Linz, and Nancy Leys Stepan for their close reading of an early draft of this Introduction, and the Ford Foundation for its support of my research on federalism.

which Max Weber said was necessary to the production of good scholarship, identify and address new problems in their careers.[1]

Professionally, as comparativists we work in "invisible colleges" that include not only our peers throughout the world working on related problems, but also some of our teachers, and many of our research students. Within this "invisible college" some problems emerge as logical next challenges, leading collaborating and competing groups of scholars to work on them intensively. Often the partial resolution of one problem makes apparent a major new research agenda. Let me give a specific example drawn from my own experience. Juan J. Linz and I had worked for over a decade with a group of scholars from Europe, South America, and the United States on the problem of why democracies broke down. Much of the scholarly tradition in this area had focused on the structural and economic factors that contributed to the rise of the powerful, nondemocratic forces of Nazism in German, Fascism in Italy, Falangism in Spain, and Pinochet's dictatorship in Chile. This tradition often left a sense of the inevitability of these democratic breakdowns.

While not rejecting this tradition, Linz and I felt that the literature could be enriched, and breakdowns possibly seen as less overdetermined, if more research attention were given to what we thought were neglected aspects of democratic breakdowns—specifically political factors, especially the contribution to breakdown made by democratic incumbents themselves. In the preface to the 718-page, four-volume work that eventually emerged from this project, *The Breakdown of Democratic Regimes*, Linz and I wrote that: "High priority for further work along these lines should now be given to the analysis of the conditions that lead to the breakdown of authoritarian regimes, to the process of *transition* from authoritarian to democratic regimes, and especially to the political dynamics of the *consolidation* of postauthoritarian democracies."[2]

As soon as we wrote that sentence, we realized we had a huge new research agenda before us. We thus began co-teaching at Yale University what may have been the first university course on the problems of transition to, and consolidation of, democracies. Eighteen years later our book on the subject appeared, *Problems of Democratic Transition and Consolidation: Southern Europe, South America and Post Communist Europe.*[3]

Often the personal aspects of the comparativist's life interrelate with and help direct and redirect this powerful professional dynamic. We often select a problem to work on because we feel deeply uneasy with the classic literature on

---

1. Max Weber, "Science as a Vocation," in *Max Weber: Essays in Sociology*, ed. H. H. Gerth and C. Wright Mills (New York: Oxford University Press, 1958), 136. In the same quotation Weber says that no scholarly work is worth pursuing unless it is "worth being known" and is pursued with "passionate devotion."

2. Juan J. Linz and Alfred Stepan (eds.), *The Breakdown of Democratic Regimes* (Baltimore: Johns Hopkins University Press, 1978), p. x; my italics.

3. (Baltimore: Johns Hopkins University Press, 1996). As I shall explain later, this book in turn yielded a new set of unresolved problems concerning federalism, democracy, and nation that we felt we had to turn our attention to, so another 500-page book looms.

it, especially if the literature seems to be at odds with aspects of the world to which we have been personally exposed, and which affects us deeply. Intellectual and political unease often stir creativity. For example, Lijphart's theory of consociationalism grew out of his concern, as a citizen of the Netherlands doing his doctoral course work at Yale, and reading that cross-cutting cleavages were considered useful, indeed almost necessary, for democracy. He knew that most cleavages in the Netherlands were compounding. He wondered what made democracy nonetheless work in that setting. His personal experience and his scholarship led him to the political concept of "consociationalism."

Linz, as a Spaniard who had been born in Germany, and a good comparativist, felt increasingly uncomfortable with the dominant typology of regimes in the literature, which divided polities into a totalitarian–democratic dichotomy. Spain fit neither type, and in the early 1960s was not in transit to either. Out of his intellectual unease and personal reflection Linz suggested "authoritarianism" as an additional regime type, and stipulated four key dimensions that differentiate an "authoritarian" regime from a "totalitarian" or a "democratic" regime.[4]

Hirschman's unease with overarching ideologies, his ability to doubt existing paradigms of knowledge in a creative fashion, and his profound belief that politics is important has a connection to his experiences as a young Jewish anti-Nazi and anti-Fascist underground activist, in Germany, Italy, and France.[5]

What follows is this Introduction is my attempt to reflect, in a more explicit way than I do in any of the articles themselves, what led me, from a personal and a professional point of view, to the problems they address. Unlike the autobiographical essays by Dahl, Lijphart, and Linz that I cite, my Introduction is not intended as a full autobiographical statement about my life or career as a comparativist. It is simply an attempt to describe some of the choices that went into the specific articles that make up this volume.[6]

4. For illuminating autobiographical articles by Dahl, Linz, and Lijphart concerning the indirect, but powerful, links between their problem selection and aspects of their personal histories, see Hans Daalder (ed.), *Comparative European Politics: The Story of a Profession* (London: Pinter, 1997).

5. See Albert O. Hirschman, *A Propensity to Self-Subversion* (Cambridge, Mass.: Harvard University Press, 1995), esp. the chapter by the same title, "My Father and Weltanschauung, circa 1928," and "Doubt and Antifascist Action in Italy, 1936–1938."

6. I am aware that these explanations will be very incomplete. For example, I have learned an immense amount from, and my own research agenda has been shaped by, the more than twenty-five doctoral dissertations I have worked on which have been published. Also, like fellow comparativists Peter Evans and Philippe Schmitter, I was greatly shaped by the fact that I was fortunate enough to write my dissertation-book on Brazil and become permanently involved—no matter where I was—with this important alternative academic and political tradition. My multiple Oxford experiences, and my career-long friendship and collaboration with Juan J. Linz and many of his associates, meant that the European traditions of comparative politics, political philosophy, and comparative political sociology have influenced me. Other experiences that, as will become apparent, have also influenced my problem selection and probably my style as a researcher and writer were my activities as a foreign correspondent, human rights activist, university rector, and even my active duty military service.

Two last points before I discuss each of the articles individually. Because each argument is best understood within the specific time and context that it was written, I have chosen to make no changes in any text, except for updating editorial references where I had listed a publication as "forthcoming". I also decided, and the editors of Oxford University Press concurred, that it was best to let each piece stand as a self-contained article; thus there is a small amount of repetition between some of the pieces.

I. The State and Society

From the very beginning of my career I have been concerned with the relationship between the state and society. In Part I of this collection I reprint four articles that advance arguments about how we should think about this relationship.

My first argument is with Samuel P. Huntington about "military professionalism" and democratic civilian control. My second argument is with those branches of North American pluralism (and classic Marxism) that virtually deny an independent role for the state. The third article argues that we can and must demonstrate how the degree of nondemocratic state power over civil society is a sociopolitically constructed (and deconstructed) variable. I conclude with an argument about the need in democratization theory and practice for a concept of "political society."

In comparative politics we work within an intellectual tradition, and we turn to the works we have read and the concepts we find in them. However, when we confront them with political and social realities we sometimes realize that they do not fit; indeed, that the concepts obscure or confuse. Then our task is to reformulate them, highlight different dimensions, sometimes introducing new conceptualizations. For me, this means that a concept must be "problematized" and then, after reformulation, used if it shows how a cluster of phenomena cohere in ways not previously seen. For my early work Samuel P. Huntington's concept of military "professionalism" was such a concept.

Huntington's *The Soldier and the State: The Theory and Politics of Civil–Military Relations* had an immense intellectual and political impact on academics and practitioners concerned with civil–military relations.[7] Huntington's central thesis was that it was precisely the increasing "professionalization" of the military that would lead to "objective civilian control."

When I read Huntington's brilliantly written book in 1965, however, it did not match what I knew of the world. After graduation from Oxford in 1960 I did my compulsory military service as an active duty officer in the United States Marine Corps, both in the Caribbean and in Southeast Asia. As a marine, I was

7. (New York: Vintage Books, 1964).

worried about the growing emphasis I saw being given in US military training programs to the putative nation-building role of the military. After the marines, I became a special correspondent for *The Economist* in West Africa and South America. In March 1964 I filed a story, before the military takeover in Brazil, about an impending coup. Later, in what then were democracies in Uruguay, Argentina, and Chile, I sensed the growing centrality of the military in domestic politics. While I was doing Ph.D. course work at Columbia, I was asked to write background analyses about US foreign aid policies to the Latin American military by Senators Robert Kennedy and Frank Church. I was struck with the fact that these senators, implicitly or explicitly, accepted Huntington's analysis of military professionalism. As long as military schooling and promotion patterns were becoming increasingly "professional," the senators saw no problem with expanding the role of the military into areas that I saw as deeply political. I came to the conclusion that it would be analytically and politically useful for me to problematize the "concept of professionalism." I was convinced I could, and should, demonstrate that there was not one model of military professionalism, but two, with diametrically opposed outcomes for civil–military relations. The result was the article "The New Professionalism of Internal Warfare and Military Role Expansion," reprinted here as Chapter 1.

In this article I argued that what I call Huntington's model of "old professionalism of external defence" had five interrelated subarguments: (1) the function of the military is "external defence"; (2) the military skills required are "highly specialized skills incompatible with political skills"; (3) the scope of military action is "restricted"; (4) such professional socialization "renders the military politically neutral"; and (5) the impact on civil military relations "contributes to an apolitical military and civilian control."

On the basis of the research I did for my first book, the understanding I developed while in the military about the impact of "organizational mission," and my analysis of military curricula in a number of countries such as Brazil, Peru, Indonesia, and France during the Algerian war, I developed an alternative analytic model of military professionalism. I called the model "the new professionalism of internal security and national development."[8] My model of military professionalism differed from Huntington's model of military professionalism in that, using the same five variables as Huntington, I built an equally interrelated, but fundamentally opposed, set of arguments. In the new professionalism (1) the function of the military is "primarily internal security"; (2) the military skills required are "highly interrelated political and military skills"; (3) the scope of military professional action is "unrestricted"; (4) professional socialization is such that it "politicizes the military"; and (5) the impact of the new professionalism on civil–military relations is that it "contributes to military political managerialism and role expansion."

8. My first book was *The Military in Politics: Changing Patterns in Brazil* (Princeton: Princeton University Press, 1971).

Note that I did not discard the concept of "military professionalism." I reformulated it into its political and intellectual polar parts. Both the "old professionalism" and the "new professionalism" are empirically researchable if one examines military journals or curricula.[9] The concept of "new professionalism," in fact, shows how a cluster of phenomena cohere in ways not previously seen. It was thus worth problematizing the concept of "military professionalism."

The next article reprinted in this section comes from my book *The State and Society*.[10] This book grew out of the dismay I felt about a theoretical lacuna. I found that many of the most important theoretical writings in politics, pluralist, and Marxist alike, which I read as a postgraduate student at Columbia, and that later I was using as required readings at Yale, where I took up my first post as an assistant professor, assigned very little independent weight to the state. Indeed, at Yale one of my closest and most distinguished colleagues again and again urged me to use the word "government" instead of the word "state."

I felt professionally and personally uneasy with such a political science both as a way to understand US politics, and especially as a template for comparative politics. The military that were leading the highly coercive regimes that I studied in Brazil, Chile, Argentina, and Uruguay certainly seemed to have some interests of their own as organizations. The *nomenklatura* in communist Europe had their own state-bureaucratic interests. Both the military and the *nomenklatura* radically altered possible societal inputs to the state and skewed state outputs. Whether as a writer for *The Economist*, or as a reader of such books as Alexander Gerschenkron's *Economic Backwardness in Historical Perspective*,[11] it was clear to me that in many parts of the world the state itself was producing the means of production in state industries and controlling access to finance in state banks.

Furthermore, the political systems that I knew the best had Roman law or Napoleonic legal codes. Such codes gave the state greater discretionary powers in rule making and rule adjudication than that found in a US style common law system. In some countries noncommon law legal systems coexisted with, and were reinforced by, a normative tradition I call "organic statism." This tradition legitimized, more than a liberal tradition would, the structuring by the state of economic, group, and political relationships, in the name of the organic unity of state and society. For comparative politics, as it was being developed in the

---

9. For example, the political scientist Jorge Rodríguez and I, after a pretest with a different journal, independently classified 396 articles in Peru's most important military journal into four categories. In the language of content analysis, we had a "coefficient of inter-coder reliability" of 89.6 percent. The percentage of new professional articles in Peru went up from 1.7 in 1954–7 to over 50 in 1964–7, the year before the military seized power and attempted to completely restructure Peruvian state and society. For the content analysis, see my *State and Society* (Princeton: Princeton University Press, 1978), 127–36.

10. For details, see n. 9.

11. (Cambridge, Mass.: Harvard University Press, 1966).

United States, to be so influenced by an almost "stateless" perspective seemed to me to be empirically distorting and methodologically disempowering.

In the preface to *The State and Society*, where I developed these themes, I stated that

the state must be considered as something more than the "government". It is the continuous administrative, legal, bureaucratic and coercive systems that attempt not only to structure relations *between* civil society and public authority in a polity but also to structure many crucial relationships *within* civil society as well. Consolidated modern states should be compared not in terms of whether they structure such relationships, but in terms of the degree to which, and the means through which, they do so.

I went on to write that "while almost everywhere the role of the state grew, one of the few places it withered away was in political science."[12]

I decided to directly confront, and attempt to subvert and reverse, the stateless trend in North American political science. I therefore opened the book with "Liberal-Pluralist, Classic Marxist, and 'Organic-Statist' Approaches to the State," which is reprinted here as Chapter 2. This article, and the overall book, which advances and utilizes propositions about such phenomena as the relative possibility of installing "inclusionary corporatism" and/or "exclusionary corporatism," or the different capacity of the same state to control multinational corporations, depending on the characteristics of the industry which gives the state more or less leverage, eventually stamped me as an early "new institutionalist," and led to my association with a later project called *Bringing the State Back In.*[13]

With my book *State and Society* seven years behind me, my contribution to the *Bringing the State Back In* project took as a given that the state was present as a powerful conditioning variable in the polity. In the article for the book, which is Chapter 3 in this section, "State Power and the Strength of Civil Society in the

12. *The State and Society*, pp. xi, 3. I should have written *North American* political science. I may have been particularly sensitive to the statelessness of such North American political science because of my previously mentioned membership in two other invisible colleges (Brazilian and European) where the state never lost its prominence. For example, in a recent book on British politics, each of the three editors in their separate articles argue that the state never disappeared from British political science. See Jack Hayward, Brian Barry, and Archie Brown (eds), *The British Study of Politics in the Twentieth Century* (Oxford: Oxford University Press for the British Academy, 1999), esp. 33, 370, 467.

13. For example, J. March and J. Olsen in their "The New Institutionalism: Organizational Factors in Political Life," *American Political Science Review*; 78 (1984), 734–9, assert that "the new institutionalism insists on a more autonomous role for political institutions" (p. 738). They then cite three works, Peter J. Katzenstein (ed.), *Between Power and Plenty: Foreign Economic Policies of Advanced Industrial States* (Madison: University of Wisconsin Press, 1978), Stephen D. Krasner, *Defending the National Interest: Raw Materials Investments and U.S. Foreign Policy* (Princeton: Princeton University Press, 1978) and Stepan, *State and Society* (1978). Theda Skocpol, in her introduction to P. Evans, D. Rueschmeyer, and T. Skocpol (eds.), *Bringing the State Back In* (Cambridge: Cambridge University Press, 1985), urges that scholars move toward a more relational approach to the study of state capacities, and refers the reader to my *State and Society*, which has "provided an important model for further studies of state capacities in many policy areas" (p. 19).

Southern Cone of Latin America," the problem I set myself, and with which I was very concerned at the time, both as a human rights activist and as an early writer about democratization, was how and why strong nondemocratic state power, *vis-à-vis* democratic forces in civil society, was not a constant, but a variable. I was particularly interested in analysing the comparative capacity for resistance to state power. I therefore took as an analytic "set" the universe of Guillermo O'Donnell's four "bureaucratic-authoritarian" regimes, and explored the conditions under which democratic forces in civil society were most, and least, able to alter the relations of power.

By the time I wrote "Military Politics in Three Polity Arenas: Civil Society, Political Society and the State" (1988), the last article in this section, civil society in countries such as Poland and Brazil had emerged as the "celebrity" of democratization. But there were increasing analytic, political, empirical, and normative distortions unwittingly being generated by the celebration of civil society.[14] Civil society pressures are often crucial for bringing about and pushing "liberalization" forward. However, if our concern is with democratization, a dominant discourse of "civil society against the state" is not only incomplete, it is dangerous. The practitioners and theoreticians of democratization movements needed not only a concept of civil society, but also a concept I called "political society." By "political society" in a democratizing setting I mean that arena in which the polity specifically arranges itself for political contestation, to gain control over public power and the state apparatus. At best, civil society can destroy a nondemocratic regime. However, a full democratic transition must involve political society, and the composition and consolidation of a democratic polity must entail serious thought and action about those core institutions of a democratic political society—political parties, elections, electoral rules, political leadership, intraparty alliances, and legislatures—through which civil society can constitute itself politically to select and monitor democratic government.[15]

II.   Constructing and Deconstructing Polities: Contexts, Capacities, and Identities

If the institutional context is fixed, and the actors and their goals stipulated, an incentive based, often game theoretic, rational choice analysis can be quite

14. For example, such euphoria often leads to an almost complete lack of scholarly and political attention to the "inconvenient fact" that the "military as organization" would still have some power within the state apparatus even after they were no longer the "military as government." Witness Chile more than a decade after Pinochet left the presidency.

15. The phrase "political society" had, of course, been used by other authors, such as Paulo Farneti in his contribution to Linz and Stepan, *The Breakdown of Democratic Regimes*. However, the literature on democratization was being weakened by its lack of specific attention to what I began to call political society in the above sense.

powerful.[16] However, I have often been interested as a comparativist in how new contexts emerge; how new power capacities—particularly those of a democratic opposition—can be developed; how political, national, religious identities are created and/or transformed; how the values attached to destroying or sustaining an institutional context can diverge sharply; and how some political "games"—depending on the context—are possible, and some impossible. The articles in Part II examine the agents, paths, and processes involved in such construction and deconstruction in politics.

From 1976 to 1986 I worked with a group of scholars on the project that eventually led to the four-volume series edited by Guillermo O'Donnell, Philippe C. Schmitter, and Laurence Whitehead *Transitions from Authoritarian Rule.*[17] Much of our discussions were devoted to creating a body of interrelated concepts such as the "liberalization" versus "democratization" distinction. While I was fully engaged with my colleagues in this effort, I felt it would also be useful to call attention to the consequences of "path dependency." Without attempting to make a mutually exclusive and collectively exhaustive selection of paths, I chose eight analytically distinctive, and historically important, paths to redemocratization. My argument in "Paths toward Redemocratization: Theoretical and Comparative Perspectives" (Chapter 5) is that each path taken constructs new *contexts* which in themselves have an independent and different weight on political outcomes. I certainly do not want to imply that the path taken will overdetermine political outcomes for ever. However, I believe that we can, and should, attempt to achieve greater clarity about the particular strengths and weaknesses of each path in relation to the institutionalization of democracy. The article therefore attempts to spell out the theoretically predictable implications each of the eight paths has for reactionary, status quo, progressive, or revolutionary politics.

In 1986 the new democracies of Argentina and Uruguay seemed, to some, on the brink of breakdown. In Chile Pinochet was still in power and activists wondered what type of democracy could be constructed in a post-Pinochet world. It was in this context that Juan J. Linz and I, as the editors of *The Breakdown of Democratic Regimes*, were asked by a group of current and former presidents and political leaders of Latin America, including Raúl Alfonsín and Jimmy Carter, to talk to them about what aspects of the interwar European breakdowns of democracy (and Spain's success in consolidating democracy by the early 1980s) might be most useful for them to think about. The result was "Political Crafting of Democratic Consolidation or Destruction: European and South American Comparisons" (Chapter 6).

16. The problem I explore in my article with Cindy Skach later in this volume (Ch. 12), "Constitutional Frameworks and Democratic Consolidation: Parliamentarianism versus Presidentialism," conforms to all of these assumptions. Therefore, a major part of our inquiry is structured around the comparative analysis of the consequences of different incentive structures.

17. (Baltimore: Johns Hopkins University Press, 1986).

More than any article we have ever written, we believe that it presents, in a compressed form, the political dimension of the breakdown of democracies in interwar Europe. The article documents that the thesis "the Great Depression led to political breakdown and fascism" needs to be strongly qualified when the actual historical record is examined. Germany and Austria were exceptions among the advanced capitalist countries in that "semiloyal" incumbents used the depression to help them craft regime breakdown by allowing them to cast "system blame" on democratic institutions. This was not inevitable. In fact, unemployment in Norway, Denmark, and the Netherlands in the early 1930s was higher than in Germany. However, in all three countries democratic incumbents did not indulge in semiloyal system blame. The incumbents went about politically crafting new forms of stable, broad-based, democratic welfare states. Furthermore, in the West European country where unemployment was the worst, the Netherlands, fascist parties were never able to gain more than 7.9 percent of the vote. We also noted that the "depression equals fascism" argument had an additional historic weakness. The argument that economic depression led to democratic breakdown overlooks the fact that, in the less advanced capitalist countries in Europe, the rise of fascism in Italy in 1922, the emergence of the Primo de Rivera dictatorship in Spain in 1923, and the Polish, Portuguese, and Lithuanian crises of 1926 *preceded* the Great Depression. We also advance arguments about democratic control of violence and constitutional engineering.

"On the Tasks of a Democratic Opposition" (Chapter 7) had a strange career. In fact, it was the first article I wrote for the *Transitions from Authoritarian Rule* project. But some of the scholars in the project who came from countries where the outcome of the struggle for democracy was by no means clear disliked the article intensely. They argued that if they tried to carry out all of the tasks I discuss, they would be destroyed. I later published the piece in the *Journal of Democracy* because I was (and am) convinced that changing the relationships of power from domination by a nondemocratic state to the hegemony of democratic forces requires analytic and political attention to *each* of the five core tasks of the democratic opposition I discuss.[18]

The following article, "Democratic Opposition and Democratization Theory" (Chapter 8), was largely written as a revisionist critique about "pacted transitions." Four-player pacts—involving regime hardliners and regime softliners, and opposition moderates and opposition militants—were increasingly being seen by important scholars in comparative politics as an attractive, and almost a necessary, part of the construction of democratic transitions. But, I believe it is important to point out why, and in what circumstances, there are limits to how one can construct democratic transitions. The article attempts to spell out why, from a theoretical perspective of regime type, in many regimes—

---

18. Paradoxically, this article is not referred to in Linz and Stepan, *Problems of Democratic Transition and Consolidation*, because I did not want to repeat myself. Both of us now feel that this inadvertent decision was a mistake.

"sultanism," "totalitarianism," and "early post-totalitarianism"—four-player games of pacted transitions are impossible.[19] Impossible because all of the players do not, and cannot, exist. How, for example, can a moderate opposition player exist and carry out tactical and strategic bargaining with moderate regime softliners in a sultanistic or a totalitarian regime? The article also contains a revisionist reformulation, grounded in the recent history of countries such as Poland, Hungary, Russian, and China, of the "civil society against the state" literature. I close with a brief discussion of an as yet undertheorized aspect of opposition theory: How are "non-issues" turned into "issues"?

My "Modern Multi-national Democracies: Transcending a Gellnerian Oxymoron" and a related article with Juan J. Linz, "Political Identities and Electoral Sequences: Spain, the Soviet Union, and Yugoslavia" (Chapters 9 and 10) grew out of my experiences in communist, and early postcommunist Europe, where I conducted some research almost every year after 1988 for various projects.[20] Furthermore, I served from 1993 to 1996 as the first rector and president of Central European University (CEU).[21] At the CEU students from all of the twenty-seven countries of postcommunist Europe were actively recruited and robustly present. I accepted the challenge of being the first rector of CEU because it gave me a chance to contribute, as a scholar and as an individual, to three things that interested me greatly: understanding and where possible advancing democracy; understanding and building socially useful institutions; and educational innovation. At this time in history, in this setting, a new problem for me to study was clear—namely, how to reconcile nationalism and democracy, especially in multinational settings.

By 1986, three years before the wall came down in Berlin, two new important bodies of literature were in place that should have allowed activists and analysts to think about the multinationalism–democracy problem creatively. Ernest Gellner had published his classic *Nations and Nationalism* in 1983 and Benedict Anderson's *Imagined Communities* was published in the same year.[22] In 1986 the four volumes of *Transitions from Authoritarian Rule* were published. Rereading these two bodies of literature in Eastern Europe in the early 1990s, what struck me as amazing was that the democratization literature never thematized nationalism as a problem—there is not a single chapter devoted to the theme in the four volumes of the transition project; meanwhile, the nationalism

19. Definitions and discussions of all these terms are found in Ch. 8.

20. Particularly important in my deepening concern with the democracy–multinationalism problem were my public talks and private meetings in Serbia, Croatia, and Slovenia in the months before Croatia and Slovenia declared independence and the civil wars throughout much of Yugoslavia began.

21. CEU had branches in Budapest, Prague, and Warsaw and a partner in Moscow. During this period I was also one of the directors of the Soros Foundation, which was concerned with postcommunist Europe.

22. Ernest Gellner, *Nations and Nationalism* (Oxford: Blackwell, 1983) and Benedict Anderson, *Imagined Communities: Reflections on the Origin and Spread of Nationalism* (London: Verso, 1983).

literature never thematized democracy—in neither Anderson's nor Gellner's book is the word democracy even found in the index.

Since Gellner and I were both at CEU, I approached him to see if we could work together to help overcome this embarrassing parallel play in our "intellectual sandboxes." With his characteristic verve, he immediately said "Yes!" He created the format. I would open with four public lectures on nationalism, which had to include a critique of his work. He would return the favor with four public lectures on democracy and a critique of my work. Amid Serbs, Croatians, Bosnians, and Kosovars from the former Yugoslavia; Estonians and Russians from the former USSR; and Romanians and Hungarians from the former Austro-Hungarian empire, Gellner attended all my lectures, rapidly tapping his cane at points he no doubt disagreed with. Tragically Gellner, at full intellectual and moral force, died suddenly before he presented his critique. I publish my critique of my great colleague knowing that the article and the reader would have been better informed if Gellner had lived to flail me.

The article I wrote with my career-long colleague and friend Juan J. Linz, on political identities and electoral sequences, addresses and documents three themes that I touch on in my Gellner critique. (1) Human beings can have multiple and complementary identities. (2) Identities, because they are to a great extent socially and politically constructed, can change extremely rapidly. (3) Political leadership and political choices (such as the choice to make the first democratically competitive elections polity-wide or regional) can help create multiple and complementary, or polarized and conflictual, political identities. The integrating and disintegrating states of Spain, Yugoslavia, and the USSR made and make all three of these claims painfully clear.

Part II concludes with "The World's Religious Systems and Democracy: Crafting the Twin Tolerations," drawn from a project that I eventually hope to develop into a book with the same title. I have always been interested in religion and politics, even though the theme has not figured prominently in comparative politics, and I myself have not written much on the subject.[23] My attention to the problem of religion and democracy was intensified by my East European experiences.

A key part of the nationalist conflicts in Yugoslavia involved religion. There was constant debate about whether there were cultural and religious boundaries to democracy. Also, on a few occasions, students at CEU asked me if they could take my course on democracy, even though they came from Orthodox Christian or Muslim countries. They worried that their countries did not possess the cultural requisites that much of the social science literature argued were necessary for democracy, and that existed in Western Europe, such as the "separation of church and state," or "secularism." Such conflicts, perceptions,

---

23. For a discussion of this neglect in comparative politics, see Stathis N. Kalyvas, *The Rise of Christian Democracy in Europe* (Ithaca, NY: Cornell University Press, 1996), esp. the introd.

and misperceptions dismayed me, and began to move me toward a new set of problems and arguments.[24]

From different perspectives the eminent political philosopher John Rawls, Samuel P. Huntington, and even the founder of the conflict approach to democratization, Dankwart Rustow, advance arguments that I believe make it difficult to think in creative and possibilistic terms about resolving conflicts between democracy and religion. My article begins with four pervasive "maps of misreadings" of the actual West European experience with religion and democracy. I then apply this revisionist framework to countries where the Confucian, Islamic, and Orthodox Christian presence is strong in the polity.[25] I emerge with strongly non-Rawlsian, non-Huntingtonian, and non-Rustovian arguments about how the twin tolerations have been, or could be, constructed in such societies.

III. The Metaframeworks of Democratic Governance and Democratic States

Part III of this volume features arguments about the "metaframeworks" of democratic institutions. For *democratic governance*, at the highest level of abstraction, there are virtually only three metaframeworks used in modern democracies: presidentialism, parliamentarianism, and semipresidentialism. Each of these three models has different incentive structures and different repertoires of available institutional mechanisms. For *democratic states*, at the highest level of abstraction, there are virtually only two metaframeworks used in modern democracies: unitary states or federal states.[26] In unitary states, as

24. My decision to write on the topic of religion and democracy was, if anything, "overdetermined." I was born and raised a Catholic and my first degree was from the University of Notre Dame. In my readings in history and politics in the late 1960s and early 1970s I frequently came across arguments to the effect that the major reason why countries such as Spain, Portugal, and Latin America had such a poor democratic record was that they were Catholic. In the 1940s and 1950s there was an analogous "Luther to Hitler" literature on Germany. Vatican II developed the democratic content of Catholicism's multivocality. I was convinced that all religions, to some extent, were multivocal and had at least some doctrines or practices that were usable for democracy. My concern with religion and democracy was also shaped by my work with Brian Smith and Scott Mainwaring on their doctoral dissertations, my two-year participation as a member of the American Catholic Bishop's Conference committee concerned with social justice in the world, and my participation, first as a student and later as a professor, in Juan J. Linz's thought provoking courses on religion and politics.

25. Confucianism is more a code of behavior or philosophy than it is a religion. However, the issue of Confucianism figures prominently in the literature on the cultural boundaries to democracy, such as that by Huntington.

26. To be sure, globalization is creating new possibilities for supranational states and subnational states, which analysts should be and are watching closely. However, the concept of modern democracy among large groups of people is mainly concerned with states. The European Union is functionally increasingly federal, but politically confederal

we have seen, key questions concerning how democracy functions often re-volve around whether the demos is mononational or multinational, and if multinational, whether the dominant political elite insists upon pursuing a nation-state building strategy. Federalism raises this and many other questions of equality, efficacy, and liberty. The majority of individuals who live in demo-cracies live in federal systems. Unfortunately, in my judgement, no important political institution has been so undertheorized, and incorrectly theorized, as federalism. What follows are arguments about the three metaframeworks of democratic governance, the two metaframeworks of democratic states, and some arguments about democratic consolidation.[27]

The article "Constitutional Frameworks and Democratic Consolidation: Par-liamentarianism versus Presidentialism" (Chapter 12) grew out of an exchange at a December 1990 meeting in Budapest of the East–South System Transforma-tions Project, which brought together specialists on Eastern Europe, southern Europe, and South America.[28] When we were discussing topics for future research and dividing up our collective work, Adam Przeworski lamented that although there were assertions in the literature about the probable impact of different types of institutional arrangement on democratic consolidation, there was no systematic data available. In his notes about the Budapest meeting Przeworski reiterated that "we seem to know surprisingly little about the effects of the particular institutional arrangements on their effectiveness and their durability. Indeed, the very question whether institutions matter is wide open."

I was shocked by Adam's Przeworksi's assertion and almost immediately said I would, as someone who believes "institutions matter," accept his challenge to provide some concrete data on the problem. I chose to compare the impact of presidentialism and parliamentarianism on democratic consolidation.[29] Cindy Skach and I first constructed two contrasting models for managing democratic

and democratic legitimacy still emanates, to a great extent, from the democratic govern-ments (all unitary or federal) of the fifteen member states.

27. The structure and impact of some of the other indispensable and influential democratic institutions, such as party systems and electoral systems, varies greatly de-pending on each country's choice of metaframework concerning democratic govern-ance, and the metaframework of the democratic state.

28. The collective results of our discussions were eventually published as Adam Prze-worski et al., *Sustainable Democracy* (Cambridge: Cambridge University Press, 1995).

29. The presidentialism–parliamentarianism debate of course has a longer history. In modern comparative politics the argument about the particular vulnerabilities presidentialism creates for the democratic political process began with an "excursus" that Juan J. Linz inserted into Linz and Stepan (eds.), *The Breakdown of Democratic Regimes* after it was already in galleys. Linz's long-circulated "underground classic" on the subject was finally published as "Presidential or Parliamentary Democracy: Does it Make a Difference?," in Juan J. Linz and Arturo Valenzuela (eds.), *The Failure of Presidential Democracy* (Baltimore: Johns Hopkins University Press, 1994). Intellectually and politic-ally I prefer the title of Linz's article to the title of Linz and Valenzuela's edited volume. The Stepan–Skach article attempted to advance the literature toward a series of probabil-istic propositions.

politics, "pure parliamentarianism" and "pure presidentialism."[30] We then advance a number of deductive arguments; i.e., that the incentive systems of pure parliamentarianism are more "coalition requiring" and "coalition sustaining" than pure presidentialism; that pure parliamentarianism, because of its greater coalitional capacities and incentives, can function democratically with a larger number of parties in the political system than can presidentialism; that the institutional repertoire of pure parliamentarianism gives democratic politicians more degrees of freedom to resolve a "crisis of government" before it becomes a "crisis of regime," and thus would be less prone to military coups. We then did a "large *n*" analysis to see if these theoretically derived predictions are empirically supported, and found that they are.[31]

30. Of course, there are numerous subtypes *within* each metaframework. For example, some observers argue that the British model has gone from a "Member of Parliament" driven, to a "Cabinet" driven, to a "prime ministerial" driven, to (with Thatcher and even more Blair) a "presidential" driven, subtype of parliamentarianism. But, if Britain ever adopted a pure proportional representational system, and no party or coalition of parties commanded a stable majority of seats in parliament, the head of government and, indeed, the government, precisely because Britain had a parliamentary and not a presidential metaframework, could be voted out of office by a vote of no confidence. In the presidential metaframework impeachments exist, but votes of no confidence are simply not part of the opposition's political repertoire. In presidential systems there are also crucially important subtypes with important consequences. For example, a two party subtype that regularly produces presidential majorities, and a fragmented multiparty subtype that seldom produces a presidential majority, function quite differently. When I began research for this article, Cindy Skach was in the early stages of her Ph.D. course work at Columbia and she was my research assistant. Her contribution to my research and thinking was so substantial that I invited her to co-author the article. She is now an assistant professor of political science at Harvard.

31. Subsequently, Adam Przeworski, Michael Alvarez, José Antonio Cheibub and Fernando Limongi, on the basis of an analysis of a massive quantitative study, arrived at a similar conclusion. See their "What Makes Democracies Endure?" *Journal of Democracy,* 7 (Jan. 1996), 39–55; see esp. 44–7. Some analysts, of course, argue that the distinction between "presidential" and "parliamentary" systems is not very useful because of the great variety of presidential and parliamentary systems. There are indeed many subtypes of parliamentary and presidential systems, but varieties of "subtype" should not lead us to eliminate distinctions between "types." For example, some excellent scholarship has been done on constitutional engineering proposals to reduce some of the features of presidentialism that might cause problems for democratic governments. They argue that the likelihood of "divided government" can be reduced by concurrent legislative and presidential elections. To avoid a president being elected without a majority, they recommend second round majority runoffs. Very importantly, they recognize that presidentialism has a well documented problem in sustaining democracy in a context where there are a great number of parties, as measured by the Laakso–Taagepera index. They therefore put great emphasis on electoral system changes that might help reduce the effective number of political parties. These include single member district plurality elections or, if proportional representation is used, they urge closed lists, high thresholds, and small district magnitudes. See Matthew Shugart and John Carey, *Presidents and Assemblies: Constitutional Design and Electoral Dynamics* (New York: Cambridge University Press, 1992) and Scott Mainwaring and Matthew Shugart (eds.), *Presidentialism and Democracy in Latin America* (New York: Cambridge University Press, 1997). I want to make three observations about this literature. First, I find substantial merit in almost all of their proposals for ameliorating the problem of a high number of parties in a presidential system. Indeed, for the case of Brazil, which has had over seven "effective political

From a comparative and global perspective, the metaframework of democratic governance that has been least studied is semipresidentialism. Durverger's pioneering work is about semipresidentialism in West European democracies. The fact that semipresidentialism was undertheorized for democratizing countries, and for countries where the political party system was relatively weak, became an increasingly serious intellectual and political lacuna by the late 1980s and early 1990s. Undertheorized or not, the system was diffusing. Sri Lanka had shifted from parliamentarianism to semipresidentialism. Politicians in most of the post-Soviet states, attracted by the demonstration effect of the French Fifth Republic (and the De Gaulle possibility) opted for semipresidentialism. A referendum was held on semipresidentialism in Brazil. As the Pinochet dictatorship came to an end in Chile, semipresidentialism was widely discussed, as it is now in Korea. This climate of opinion contributed to the unique Israeli experiment with a direct election of a prime minister (a system of democratic governance that does not fit into any of the three major constitutional types), and to the current debate about the direct election of the president in Italy.

My political and theoretical unease with semipresidentialism and democratization is that, as a model, semipresidentialism seems to me to have the potential of producing clashes between the dual executive—the president and the prime minister. Analytically, I am convinced that there can be "three positions" in semipresidentialism. Position 1: the president is a leader of a party, or a coalition, with a majority in both houses. Position 2: the president does not have a majority in the parliament, but the prime minister does. Position 3: neither the president nor the prime minister has a majority in the parliament.[32]

Position 1 has the least potential for conflict within the dual executive because the system functions like pure presidentialism without a divided government. Position 2 is potentially more conflictual because the prime minister

---

parties" over the past decade, I am on the record as advancing virtually identical arguments. Second, the proposals seem to me to strengthen, rather than weaken, my argument that presidentialism has a characteristic set of potential institutionally related problems for democratic governance. Third, even if a specific presidential system adopted all the Shugart, Carey, and Mainwaring reforms, that presidential system would still not have available the extra degrees of freedom that are part and parcel of the parliamentary repertoire, such as votes of confidence for presidents, and the ability rapidly to change presidential leadership without elections to avoid a crisis of government becoming a crisis of regime. Such reforms are absolutely beyond the constitutional engineering potential of presidentialism as a metaframework.

32. Max Weber, again in "Science as a Vocation" (p. 138), argues that every academic "'fulfillment' raises new 'questions'; it asks to be 'surpassed' and outdated." In this sense, Suleiman and I are happy to acknowledge that we have been surpassed by the excellent University of Oxford D. Phil. by Cindy Skach: "Semi-Presidentialism and Democracy: Weimar Germany, the French Fifth Republic, and Post-Communist Russia in Comparative Perspective" (1999). Among many other things she has refined what I call Positions 1, 2, and 3 by noting that they are electorally generated subtypes of semipresidentialism.

with a parliamentary majority, *de jure* and *de facto*, should be the head of government, but the president, even though he does not control a majority in the parliament, still has some constitutionally embedded military, intelligence, foreign policy, and decree prerogatives. "Cohabitation" will thus work best if the president loyally accepts that the prime minister has the right to control the government. Not all presidents do. Position 3 is much more fraught with problems for the working of a democratic regime. Neither the president nor the prime minister commands a majority. But the president (particularly in a system that has recently been nondemocratic, and if political parties are weak, and presidential decree making prerogatives are great) can easily take the political system out of the democratic box and rule by decree.

I enlisted my friend and colleague the eminent scholar of French politics Ezra N. Suleiman to help me examine, for comparative purposes, why the French Fifth Republic seems to have avoided most of the potential pitfalls inherent in the metaconstitutional framework of semipresidentialism. A major finding is that France created a whole series of additional political mechanisms that ameliorated these potential problems and helped it stay in Position 1 for virtually every month of its first twenty-six years of semipresidentialism. Furthermore, these same mechanisms have contributed to the fact that throughout its entire duration of more than forty years French semipresidentialism has never been in Position 3.

Russia, from January 1992 to July 1998, in the absence of the specific political mechanisms used in France (and France's historical circumstances), was *never*, even for a month, in Position 1 or Position 2.[33] Many of the non-Baltic post-Soviet countries have semipresidential executives who have taken their countries out of Position 3 into nondemocratic "superpresidentialism." If Brazil, which has extreme scores on the standard political science indicators for number of political parties, electoral volatility, and party proliferation, had adopted semipresidentialism in the 1993 referendum, it probably would have been in Position 3 for almost all of the years since then.[34]

As Juan J. Linz and I neared completion of our book *Problems of Democratic Transition and Consolidation: Southern Europe, South America, and Post-Communist Europe*, we realized that no matter how fascinating we ourselves might find our 486-page book, many people interested in the subject might never read the tome. Thus, when the editors of the *Journal of Democracy* pressed us as members of the editorial board to put down some of our book's essential messages in less than twenty pages, we reluctantly acquiesced and wrote "Toward Consolidated Democracies." In retrospect, we are happy we did.

33. I refer the reader to Skach's Oxford D.Phil. for more comparative analysis and data concerning France and Russia.

34. In sharp contrast, for much of the 1980s and 1990s semipresidentialism in Portugal was normally in Position 1. When the former Socialist Party leader and prime minister Mário Suarez was elected president, a democratically consolidated Portugal *de facto*, and to a lesser extent *de jure*, increasingly moved toward a parliamentary system.

Only *after* putting the book to press, after six years of writing, were some things crystal clear to us. No state, no democracy. Free and fair elections are a necessary, but not sufficient, condition of democracy. A complete "free market" has never existed in a democracy and never can. Modern consolidated democracies require a set of sociopolitically crafted and accepted norms, institutions, and regulations—what we call "economic society"—that mediate between state and market. If a polity has a "usable state" and an "economic society" and rapidly delivers on a basket of democratic political goods, citizens can, and often *do*, rationally accept a massive (but they assume temporary) decline in their basket of economic goods. If there is only one nation in a state, "nation-state building" and "democracy building" are complementary logics. But, in much of the world that is not now democratic, more than one nation exists in the state. In these circumstances nation-state building and democracy building are conflicting logics. However, we document that human beings are capable of multiple and complementary identities. Thus, if political leaders do not socially construct the polarization of political identities, if they help create structures of inclusive citizenship, and deliver a common "roof of rights" for all citizens, loyalty toward what we call a "state-nation" is possible.

Problem selection often grows out of a previous book, especially when the author in the midst of one book is "ambushed" by a new problem. Again and again Linz and I, as we were writing *Problems of Democratic Transition and Consolidation*, were ambushed by federalism. Of the nine states that once made up communist Europe, six were unitary and three were federal. The six unitary states are now five states (East Germany has united with the Federal Republic), while the three federal states—Yugoslavia, USSR, and Czechoslovakia—are now twenty-three independent states and most of postcommunist Europe's ethnocracies and ethnic bloodshed has occurred in these postfederal states. Why? Yet, as we thought about it, it was also clear to us that empirically, if a polity had territorial areas with different dominant languages, and was multinational *and* a democracy, every single one of these polities is now, like Spain, a federation. Why?

Since many of the polities in the world that are by no means consolidated democracies (e.g., Indonesia, Russia, Nigeria), or even democracies at all (e.g. Burma, China, Malaysia), are also multinational, with different languages spoken in different territories, it would appear that it is of the highest priority to think about how federalism, democracy, and multinationalism can cohere. Unfortunately, as I read the comparative politics literature, little of it helped my thinking with this problem. The classic literature on federalism is dominated by one of the great founders of rational choice theory, William Riker. Riker makes no significant distinction between democratic federalism and non-democratic federalism. But the key question now is precisely what is needed to sustain a democratic federation in a multinational setting.

Riker sees *all* enduring federations as emerging out of a voluntary bargain to pool sovereignty by polities all of which have a substantial degree of previous sovereignty. I call this "coming together" federalism; in effect, Riker elevated the model of the United States to a universal. But, Belgium, Spain, and India were originally *unitary states* with multinational populations, states which, in order to facilitate different groups living together democratically in one state, devolved by constitutional means into federations. I call this "holding together" federalism.

Riker also often calls institutions "congealed tastes." He argues that if the individual tastes of the majority of people change, the institutions can change. But, the hardest types of institutional rules to change are those that require the favourable vote of those who benefit by the existing rules. Those federal systems, for example, which give constitutionally embedded special prerogatives, such as the agreement to allow a great overrepresentation in the federation of underpopulated subunits, are such institutions. In new institutionalist terms, federations are particularly "sticky" institutions and particularly "path dependent."

Riker calls US style federalism the model that all other federations aspire to. But, in fact, the United States in comparative terms—partly due to its strong "coming together" state's rights origins—is an extreme "demos constraining" outlier among modern democratic federations.[35] The US model will not be a model for most new federations, especially if they are multinational, because the US federal model is coming together, demos constraining, and constitutionally symmetrical. Many of the possibly new democratic multifederations in the world will be "holding together," "demos enabling" federations with "constitutionally asymmetrical" structures binding together the members of the federation.[36] We must therefore, in our thinking about federalism, go beyond Riker and US federalism. I thus conclude this volume with a conceptual, theoretical, and empirical overview of how we might go forward. My "Toward a New Comparative Politics of Federalism, (Multi) Nationalism, and Democracy: Beyond Rikerian Federalism" spells out a new general approach and applies it to the United States, Germany, Spain, Brazil, and India.[37]

35. For definitions and discussions of all these terms, and for documentation about the outlier status of US federalism, see my "Federalism and Democracy: Beyond the US Model," *Journal of Democracy*, 10 (Fall 1999), 19–34, as well as the article in this volume.
36. For more detail, see ibid.
37. My article on Federalism in this volume will eventually be incorporated into another 500-page book Linz and I are now writing called *Federalism, Democracy and Nation*.

I

The State and Society

ONE

The New Professionalism of Internal Warfare and Military Role Expansion

Since 1964 the Brazilian military establishment has steadily assumed control over a widening area of the country's social and political life. Indeed, there exists the possibility that what we are witnessing in Brazil is the creation of a new political and economic model of authoritarian development. Other contributors to *Authoritarian Brazil* examine the internal workings, policy outputs, and institutionalization possibilities of this model. My focus is on how changing military ideology contributed to the events leading up to the military coup of 1964 and the emergence of the military-bureaucratic and authoritarian-developmentalist components of the model.

In this chapter I argue that what happened in Brazil was, to a significant extent, part of the wider military phenomenon of what I call the "new professionalism of internal security and national development." In analyzing how the ideology of new professionalism arose and how it contributed to the expansion of the military's role in politics, I also endeavor to identify some of the institutional and political variables that are peculiar to Brazil and that help account for some of the special characteristics of the military regime.

Conflicting Paradigms: New Professionalism versus Old Professionalism

In the 1960s, the political roles of the Brazilian and Peruvian military establishments underwent a great expansion. Yet, as measured by a number of indicators, these military establishments are probably the two most professional in

This chapter was first published in Alfred Stepan (ed.), *Authoritarian Brazil: Origins, Policies, and Future* (New Haven: Yale University Press, 1973), 47–65.

Latin America.[1] They have relatively universalistic procedures for the recruitment and promotion of officers, highly structured military schooling programs that prepare officers for passage to the next stage of their careers, highly articulated and well-disseminated military doctrines and well-programmed military-unit training cycles, all coordinated by extensive general staff systems. If there is one central concept of modern civil–military relations, it is the concept of "professionalism." According to this concept, as the professionalism of a military establishment increases along the lines indicated above, the military tends to become less political in its activities. In the case of Brazil, however, professional standards coexisted with increasing politicization in the years leading up to 1964. Thus, either Brazil must be considered a deviant case, or one must suggest an alternative framework that is capable of incorporating Brazil, Peru (where a similar process of professionalization and politicization has been at work), and, I suspect, a number of other countries, such as Indonesia, as the predictable outcome of the new paradigm.

It is the argument of this chapter that the highly bureaucratized, highly schooled, and yet highly politicized armies of Brazil and Peru are best viewed not as lapses from the paradigm of the "old" professionalism, but as one of the logical consequences of the "new" professionalism. To clarify the theoretical and empirical aspects of this assertion, I briefly consider first the components of the old professionalism. Though many aspects of the argument are widely reproduced by writers who have not studied his work, the classic formulation of the argument about military professionalism and its relation to the political activity of the military is Samuel Huntington's. As quoted or paraphrased from his own writings,[2] his argument is as follows:

1. *On the nature of modern warfare and the requisite skills.* Modern warfare demands a highly specialized military; the military cannot master the new skills needed to carry out their tasks while at the same time "remaining competent in many other fields" as well. (*The Soldier*, p. 32.)

2. *On the impact of pursuit of professionalism.* As a result of this specialization, "the vocation of officership absorbs all their energies and furnishes them with all their occupational satisfactions. Officership, in short, is an exclusive role, incompatible with any other significant social or political roles." ("Civilian Control," p. 381.)

3. *On the relationship between political and military spheres.* The functional specialization needed for external defense means that "it became impossible to be an expert in the management of violence for external defense

1. See Alfred Stepan, *The Military in Politics: Changing Patterns in Brazil* (Princeton: Princeton University Press, 1971), chap. 3; and Luigi Einaudi, *The Peruvian Military: A Summary Political Analysis* (Santa Monica: RAND Corporation, RM-6048-RC, May 1969).

2. Samuel P. Huntington, *The Soldier and the State: The Theory and Politics of Civil–Military Relations* (New York: Vintage Books, 1964); idem, "Civilian Control of the Military: A Theoretical Statement," in *Political Behavior: A Reader in Theory and Research*, ed. H. Eulau, S. Eldersveld, and M. Janowitz (New York: Free Press, 1956).

and at the same time to be skilled in either politics and statecraft or the use of force for the maintenance of internal order. The functions of the officer became distinct from those of the politician and policeman." (*The Soldier*, p. 32.)

4. *On the scope of military concern.* "At the broadest level of the relation of the military order to society, the military function is presumed to be a highly specialized one.... A clear distinction in role and function exists between military and civilian leaders." ("Civilian Control," pp. 380–1.)

5. *On the impact of professionalism on military attitudes to politics.* "Civilian control is thus achieved not because the military groups share in the social values and political ideologies of society, but because they are indifferent to such values and ideologies." ("Civilian Control," p. 381.)

6. *On the impact of professionalism on civil–military relations.* "The one prime essential for any system of civilian control is the minimizing of military power. Objective civilian control achieves this reduction by professionalizing the military" and by "confining it to a restricted sphere and rendering it politically sterile and neutral on all issues outside that sphere." (*The Soldier*, p. 84; "Civilian Control," p. 381.)

This argument runs through a large part of American military writing and appears frequently in congressional discussions of the rationale for United States military assistance policies to developing countries. The argument that assistance policies should be given in order to professionalize the military has been rationalized on the grounds that in doing so the United States could help convert traditional, politicized armies into modern, apolitical ones. However, as the extensive quotations from Huntington illustrate, the professionalization thesis was rooted in the assumption that armies develop their professional skills for conventional warfare against foreign armies. In his later writing Huntington has stated that if the focus shifts from interstate conflict to domestic war it will encourage a different pattern of civil–military relations than that expounded in the passages quoted above.[3] Since many later writers have failed to note this qualification, the concept of military professionalism is still widely misunderstood, and it is useful to formulate explicitly the differences between the old professionalism of external warfare and the new professionalism of internal security and national development.

In reality, by the late 1950s and early 1960s, the success of revolutionary warfare techniques against conventional armies in China, Indochina, Algeria, and Cuba led the conventional armies in both the developed and underdeveloped world to turn more attention to devising military and political strategies to combat or prevent domestic revolutionary warfare. In fact, by 1961, the United States military assistance programs to Latin America were largely devoted to exporting doctrines concerned with the military's role in

3. See in particular his "Patterns of Violence in World Politics," in *Changing Patterns of Military Politics*, ed. Samuel P. Huntington (New York: Free Press, 1962), pp. 19–22.

counterinsurgency, civic action and nation building.[4] In Latin America the process by which the military came to define its mission primarily in terms of dealing with threats to internal security was accelerated by the defeat and destruction of the conventional army in Cuba by Castro's guerrilla force. In Brazil and Peru, where the military was highly institutionalized, the perception of the threat to the internal security of the nation and the security of the military itself led to a focusing of energies on the "professionalization" of their approach to internal security. The military institutions began to study such questions as the social and political conditions facilitating the growth of revolutionary protest and to develop doctrines and training techniques to prevent or crush insurgent movements. As a result, these highly professionalized armies became much more concerned with political problems.

Thus there was a dual process at work. Because of their preoccupation with subversion and internal security, many military establishments in Latin America attempted to undertake institutional professionalization and development and were given extensive United States military assistance in doing so. Yet, given the changed political climate, the formulators of United States military assistance programs and the chiefs of many Latin American military establishments now believed that professional military expertise was required in a broader range of fields. Instead of increasing functional specialization, the military began to train their officers to acquire expertise in internal security matters that were defined as embracing all aspects of social, economic, and political life. Instead of the gap between the military and political spheres widening, the new professionalism led to a belief that there was a fundamental interrelationship between the two spheres, with the military playing a key role in interpreting and dealing with domestic political problems owing to its greater technical and professional skills in handling internal security issues.[5] The scope of military concern for, and study of, politics became unrestricted, so that the "new professional" military man was highly politicized.

4. This shift has been well documented. For an overview and a guide to the United States government programs and publications see W. F. Barber and C. N. Ronning, eds., *Internal Security and Military Power: Counterinsurgency and Civic Action in Latin America* (Columbus: Ohio State University Press, 1966). See also M. Francis, "Military Aid to Latin America in the United States Congress," *Journal of Inter- American Studies* 6 (July 1964): 389–401. A strong criticism of this policy from the Latin American perspective is John Saxe-Fernández, *Proyecciones: hemisféricas de la pax Americana* (Lima: IEP ediciones y Campodónico ediciones, 1971).

5. A thorough and brilliant analysis of some psychological and political implications of this type of military ideology of total counterrevolutionary warfare (especially in the context of a weak political system) is Raoul Girardet's discussion of the French army. See his "Problèmes idéologiques et moraux," and "Essai d'interprétation," in *La Crise militaire française, 1945–1962: Aspects sociologiques et idéologiques*, ed. Raoul Girardet (Paris: Librairie Armand Colin, 1964), pp. 151–229.

In the early 1960s the Indonesian army's Staff and Command School formulated a development and security doctrine that was later implemented in large part when the military assumed power in 1965. For the doctrine and an insightful analysis see Guy J. Pauker, *The Indonesian Doctrine of Territorial Warfare and Territorial Management* (Santa Monica: RAND Corporation, RM- 3312-PR, November 1963).

The new professionalism of internal security and national development almost inevitably led to some degree of military role expansion. However, variables stemming from the larger political system in addition to those associated with the military subsystem affect the degree of this role expansion. The weaker the civilian government's own legitimacy and ability to supervise a "peaceful" process of development, the greater the tendency will be for the new professionals to assume control of the government to impose their own view of development on the state.

The old professionalism of external security and the new professionalism of internal security and national development share many external characteristics, especially those of highly developed military schooling systems and elaborate military doctrines. However, the *content* and *consequences* of the two forms of professionalism are quite distinct, as is shown schematically in Table 1.1. It is useful to distinguish the two types of military professionalism for reasons of policy as well as theory. Since 1961, United States military policy toward Latin America has been to encourage the Latin American militaries to assume as their primary role counterinsurgency programs, civic-action and nation-building tasks. This policy has often been defended in the name of helping to create a professional army, and by implication, an apolitical force in the nation. However, in terms of the schema presented in the table, technical and professional specialization of the military in conjunction with doctrines and ideologies of internal security will tend to lead toward military role expansion and "managerialism" in the political sphere.[6]

TABLE 1.1. *Contrasting paradigms: the old professionalism of external defense, the new professionalism of internal security and national development*

	Old professionalism	New professionalism
Function of military	External security	Internal security
Civilian attitudes toward government	Civilians accept legitimacy of government	Segments of society challenge government legitimacy
Military skills required	Highly specialized skills incompatible with political skills	Highly interrelated political and military skills
Scope of military professional action	Restricted	Unrestricted
Impact of professional socialization	Renders the military politically neutral	Politicizes the military
Impact on civil–military relations	Contributes to an apolitical military and civilian control	Contributes to military–political managerialism and role expansion

6. I develop this argument at greater length in my congressional testimony; see U.S. Congress, House of Representatives, *Hearings before the Subcommittee on National Security Policy and Scientific Developments of the Committee on Foreign Affairs on Military Assistance*

It also seems useful to point out for reasons of politics as well as theory that the new professionalism is not only a phenomenon of the developing countries. Some of the key ingredients of the new professionalism were observed in France in the 1950s and played a major role in the civil–military crises there in 1958 and 1961. Even in the United States, the military's development of the new professionalism in the fields of counterinsurgency and civic action has resulted in the development of skills that, though originally developed for export to the developing countries such as Brazil in the early 1960s, were by the late 1960s increasingly called upon within this country. Huntington's view of the old professionalism, where the military was functionally specific and unconcerned with domestic political events, is now less meaningful for this country. The United States Army has increasingly been used to quell riots and given the function of maintaining internal order. Once given this function, the internal logic of the new professionalism comes into play, and the military sets about in a "professional" way to train to perform this function. In the late 1960s, many units such as the crack 82nd Airborne Division spent an increasing amount of their time training how to occupy American cities in case of domestic riots. The next "new professional" question for the United States military was to inquire into the nature of the enemy. This involved the military in a surveillance and intelligence-gathering role within the United States.[7]

New Professionalism in the Brazilian Political Crisis

The processes leading toward the development of the new professionalism were evident in Brazil before 1964. In Brazil, many of the external standards of the old professionalism had greatly increased before this date. The military schooling system was highly evolved. To be eligible for promotion to the rank of general an army line officer was required to graduate from the Military Academy (Academia Militar das Agulhas Negras, AMAN), the Junior Officer's School (Escola de Aperfeiçoamento de Oficiais, EsAO), and the three-year General Staff School (Escola de Comando e Estado Maior do Exército, ECEME), whose written entrance examination is passed by less than a quarter of the applicants. In terms of rank structure, the rank distribution was roughly similar to that of the United States. According to Janowitz, 21.7 percent of officers in the United States Army were colonels or generals in 1950. In 1964, the figure for Brazil was only 14.9 percent.[8]

Training, 91st Cong., 2nd sess., October 6, 7, 8, December 8, 15, 1970, pp. 105–11, 117–29 passim.

7. For a more detailed discussion of these themes, see Bruce Russett and Alfred Stepan, eds., *Military Force and American Society* (New York: Harper & Row, Torchbook, 1973).

8. For documentation see Stepan, *The Military in Politics,* chap. 3.

At the same time, new military institutions were developing in Brazil that were to become centers of the new professionalism. Of prime importance was the Superior War College (Escola Superior de Guerra, ESG) which was formally established by presidential decree under Dutra in 1949. At the time of its founding, the United States played a key role through a military advisory mission that stayed in Brazil from 1948 to 1960. By 1963, the ESG decreed its mission as that of preparing "civilians and the military to perform executive and advisory functions especially in those organs responsible for the formulation, development, planning, and execution of the policies of national security."[9] That the new professionalism of national security as developed at the ESG was very different in conception from that of the old professionalism, which in theory confines military activity to a more restricted sphere, is clear from an examination of the seven academic divisions of the college. These were (1) political affairs, (2) psychological–social affairs, (3) economic affairs, (4) military affairs, (5) logistical and mobilization affairs, (6) intelligence and counter-intelligence, and (7) doctrine and coordination.[10]

One interesting aspect of the new professionalism was its relation with civilians. In the 1950s in Brazil, the participation of civilians became a key aspect of the college's program. Precisely because the military viewed the situation in Brazil as going beyond questions handled by the old professionalism, and because the ESG was to be concerned with all phases of development and national security, it was felt the Brazilian military needed to socialize civilians from such fields as education, industry, communications, and banking into the correct national security perspective. By 1966, in fact, the ESG had graduated men from many of the key sectors of the political and economic power structure in Brazil: by this date, 599 graduates were military officers, 224 were from private industry and commerce, 200 from the major government ministries, 97 from decentralized government agencies, 39 from the federal Congress, 23 were federal or state judges, and 107 were various professionals, such as professors, economists, writers, medical doctors, and Catholic clergy.[11]

By the late 1950s and early 1960s, the ESG had developed its key ideological tenet: the close interrelationship between national security and national development. The doctrines taught at the college emphasized that modern warfare, either conventional or revolutionary, involved the unity, will, and productive capacity of the entire nation.

The low-mobilization, high-control policies of the military governments since 1964 had their intellectual roots in the ESG's doctrine that an effective

9. Decreto No. 53,080, December 4, 1963.
10. Ibid.
11. For a short official history of the ESG see the heavily documented essay by General Augusto Fragoso, written while he was commandant of the school, "A Escola Superior de Guerra (Origen—Finalidade—Evolução)," *Segurança & Desenvolvimento: Revista da Associação dos Diplomados da Escola Superior de Guerra*, ano 18, no. 132 (1969), pp. 7–40. The figures on occupations of graduates were provided by the ESG and reprinted in Glauco Carneiro, "A guerra de 'Sorbonne,'" *O Cruzeiro*, June 24, 1967, p. 20.

policy of national security demands a strong government that can rationally maximize the outputs of the economy and effectively contain manifestations of disunity in the country. The new professionalism contributed to an all-embracing attitude of military managerialism in regard to Brazil's political system. The ideas and suggestions aired at the ESG at least five years before the coup of 1964 ranged from redrawing state boundaries (to eliminate old political forces and restructure the federation along "natural" economic boundaries) to the enforcement of a two-party system.[12] The language in the 1956 ESG lecture quoted below foreshadowed the tone, substance, and rationale of later military government attempts to impose a hierarchical, semicorporatist unity on the Brazilian political system.

We live in a climate of world-wide war that will decide the destiny of Western civilization.

A decentralized system is fundamentally weak in periods of war, which demand a centralized and hierarchic structure. As total war absorbs all people, institutions, wealth, and human and national resources for the attainment of the objectives, it seems certain that centralization and concentration will increase the efficiency and ability of the political and national power.[13]

Though the ESG always concerned itself to some extent with conventional warfare, it became the center of ideological thought concerning counterrevolutionary strategy in Brazil. In early 1959 the chief ideologue of the school, Colonel Golbery, argued that indirect attack from within was a much more real threat to Latin America than direct attack from without:

What is certain is that the greater probability today is limited warfare, localized conflict, and above all indirect Communist aggression, which capitalizes on local discontents, the frustrations of misery and hunger, and just nationalist anxieties. ... Latin America now faces threats more real than at any other time, threats which could result in insurrection, outbursts attempting (though not openly) to implant ... a government favorable to the Communist ideology and constituting a grave and urgent danger to the unity and security of the Americas and the Western world.[14]

It was this perception of threat, in conjunction with the ESG's underlying preference for "ordered politics," that led to their advocacy of the primacy of

12. See, for example, Christovão L. Barros Falção, Capitão-de-mar-e-guerra, *Mobilização no campo econômico*, Curso de Mobilização Nacional, Escola Superior de Guerra, C-03-59; and David Carneiro, *Organização politica do Brasil*, Escola Superior de Guerra, Departamento de Estudos, C-47-59. These and all subsequent ESG documents that I cite I found either in the archive of Castello Branco located in the library of ECEME or in the Biblioteca Nacional. Most ESG documents are still classified by the Brazilian government.

13. Ildefonso Mascarenhas da Silva, *O poder nacional e seus tipos de estructura*, Escola Superior de Guerra, C-20-56, pp. 32–4.

14. Golbery do Couto e Silva, *Geopolitica do Brasil* (Rio de Janeiro: José Olympio, 1967), pp. 198–9 (from a chapter originally written in 1959). This book is based on ESG lectures. The developments in the Cuban revolution in late 1960 and 1961 intensified the ESG fear of the "communist threat."

the politics of national security (implicitly directed by the military) over competitive politics. Golbery contended that in times of severe crises,

the area of politics is permeated . . . by adverse pressures, creating a form of universalization of the factors of security, enlarging the area of the politics of national security to a point where it almost absorbs all the national activities.[15]

It was from this perspective of the relation between internal security and national development that the ESG set about studying all problems viewed as relating to the security issue. Its civil–military, national security elites studied inflation, agrarian reform, banking reform, voting systems, transportation, and education, as well as guerrilla warfare and conventional warfare. In many of these studies, some of the fundamental aspects of Brazilian social and economic organization were depicted as needing change if Brazil were to maintain its internal security.

Initially, these critiques of Brazilian society by military intellectuals seemed academic, and the influence of the ESG's doctrine was not pervasive within the military in the mid-1950s. But by the early 1960s, as the military perceived a deepening crisis in Brazil, the ESG's emphasis on the need for a total development strategy to combat internal subversion found an increasingly receptive audience in the military. Through the military's highly structured and well-developed publication and education systems, the ideology of internal warfare was widely disseminated throughout the officer corps. The ECEME, one of the major institutions of the old professionalism, became a central vehicle for socializing an entire generation of military officers in the internal-warfare doctrines. The training program is three years long, and entrance is highly competitive. Unless an army line officer is graduated from the ECEME he is ineligible for promotion to general, for appointment to the teaching staff of any military school, or to the general staff of any senior command. Thus the ECEME is the central recruitment and socialization institution of the senior army officer corps of the Brazilian army.

An examination of the curriculum of the ECEME shows that, like the ESG, it increasingly became devoted to the doctrines of the new professionalism, with its emphasis on the expanded political, economic, and social roles of a modern army in times of internal-security threats. In the 1956 curriculum, for instance, there were no class hours scheduled on counterguerrilla warfare, internal security, or communism. By 1966, however, the curriculum contained 222 hours on internal security, 129 on irregular warfare, and only 24 hours on the "old" professional military topic of territorial warfare.[16] Through military publications, such as the newsletter *Boletim de Informações*, sent from the Estado Maior

15. Golbery do Couto e Silva, *Planejamento estratégico* (Rio de Janeiro: Biblioteca do Exército Editôra, 1955), pp. 38–9. Most of this book had its origin in lectures originally given at the ESG. The book is one of the major sources for the ideology of the ESG.
16. Based upon my examination of the curriculum of ECEME on file at their library.

to key troop commanders, the content of the new professionalism was systematically disseminated to all army units.[17]

In their studies of the Brazilian political system the new professionals had, since the early 1960s, moved toward the position that (1) numerous aspects of the economic and political structures had to be altered if Brazil were to have internal security and rational economic growth and (2) the civilian politicians were either unable or unwilling to make these changes. By early 1964, through the prism of internal-warfare doctrines of the new professionalism, a substantial part of the Brazilian military establishment perceived the rising strike levels, the inflation rate of over 75 percent, the declining economy, the demands of the Left for a constituent assembly, and the growing indiscipline of the enlisted men as signs that Brazil was entering a stage of subversive warfare.

Moreover, the new professionals had come to believe that, in comparison to the civilian politicians, they now had constructed the correct doctrines of national security and development, possessed the trained cadres to implement these doctrines, and had the institutional force to impose their solution to the crisis in Brazil. Thus, after overthrowing the civilian president in 1964, the Brazilian military did not return power to new civilian groups, as they had in 1930, 1945, 1954, and 1955, but assumed political power themselves for the first time in the century.

Since 1964, the military has frequently been internally divided over specific policies and the problems of succession. Nevertheless, one must not lose sight of the important point that many of the doctrines of internal warfare, formulated originally at the ESG and later institutionalized in the ESG-influenced government of Castello Branco, permeated almost all major military groups in Brazil and were accepted as a basic new fact of political and military life. The central idea developed at the ESG was that development and security issues are inseparable. Even when differences over policies developed between the Castello Branco government and the Costa e Silva government, almost all military officers agreed that since labor, fiscal, educational, and other problems were intrinsic to the security of the nation, it was legitimate and necessary for military men to concern themselves with these areas. From this basic premise came the steady broadening of military jurisdiction over Brazilian life after the military assumed power in 1964, despite the fact that an important faction of the military had hoped to eventually allow the inauguration of liberal political forms.

Even within the military government itself, security matters have been given special prominence. A new agency, the National Information Service (Serviço

17. Ministério da Guerra, Estado Maior do Exército, *Boletim de Informações*. Copies of this are on open file at the Biblioteca do Exército in Rio de Janeiro. Before October 1961 the format was that of a very straightforward review of professional topics and routine surveys of international news. From October 1961 on, the format changed to one much closer to the framework and terminology of the ESG and, most significantly, began to deal with the question of the threat to internal security presented by communism.

Nacional de Informações, SNI), combining the functions of the FBI and CIA in the United States, has been created, and its director has been granted cabinet rank. In 1968 and 1969, national security laws were passed that have greatly increased the role of SNI and other intelligence units. Since 1969, every ministry has had an SNI representative, responsible for ensuring that all policy decisions of the ministry give full consideration to national security issues. Thus the new professionalism of internal warfare and national development contributed to the expansion of the military's role in Brazil that led ultimately to the military's assumption of power in 1964, and afterward to a widening of military control over those aspects of Brazilian life perceived in any way as threatening to the executors of the national security state—that is, the military.

New Professionalism in Peru

The argument that the internal logic of the new professionalism tends to contribute to an extension of the role of the military in politics receives support from a study of the only other country in Latin America to have developed fully an ideology relating internal security to national development and to have institutionalized that ideology within the military. This country is Peru.[18] The grouping of Peru with Brazil may at first seem incongruous because the policies of their military governments have been very different. However, the two countries are strikingly similar when analyzed from the perspective of the central part played by their respective war colleges in the process of military role expansion. In both countries the staffs and students at the war colleges attempted to systematically diagnose their nation's security-development situation. In the end both colleges had forged a doctrine that implicitly "legitimated" long-term military supervision of the development process. Furthermore, in both military establishments there was the belief that the war colleges and general staff schools had trained the cadres capable of administering this military-directed process. Both, in short, are examples of the new professionalism.

In Peru, as in Brazil, reasonably developed standards for the professional officer's education, promotion, and training exist. In Peru, educational performance is central to any officer's advancement. Eighty percent of all division generals on active duty between 1940 and 1965, for instance, had graduated

18. Argentina, which I would rank highest after Brazil and Peru among the countries of Latin America on a rough scale of new professionalism, experienced a military coup in 1966. Analysts specifically pointed to the evolution of a military ideology concerned with internal security and national development as an important factor in the inauguration of the authoritarian military regime. This would be in keeping with the thesis of the present chapter. See Guillermo A. O'Donnell, "Modernización y golpes militares: Teoría, comparaciones e el caso Argentino" (Buenos Aires: Instituto Torcuato Di Tella, Documento de Trabajo, September 1972).

in the top quarter of their military academy class.[19] A comparable figure for generals in the United States Army in Morris Janowitz's 1950 sample was 36.4 percent.[20]

In 1950, the Peruvian military established its own superior war college, called the Center for Higher Military Studies (Centro de Altos Estudios Militares, CAEM). By the late 1950s, CAEM had largely turned its energies to analyzing the nexus between internal security and national development. As in Brazil, the military's assessment of the development process led the Peruvian military officers into political diagnosis, but in the case of Peru their orientation was markedly more nationalistic and antioligarchical in tone. Five years before the Peruvian military assumed power, a CAEM document stated: "So long as Peru does not have programmatic and well organized political parties, the country will continue to be ungovernable.... The sad and desperate truth is that in Peru, the real powers are not the Executive, the Legislature, the Judiciary, or the Electorate, but the latifundists, the exporters, the bankers, and the American [United States] investors."[21]

CAEM studies in the late 1950s and early 1960s diagnosed a number of problems of Peruvian society. Against a background of growing social tensions and political paralysis, the organization of peasants by Hugo Blanco and later the guerrilla outbreak of 1965–6 served to broaden the consensus within the military that direct action was necessary. Though the military defeated the guerrillas in six months, they intensified their investigations of the causes of insurgency. They concluded that rural conditions in Peru were so archaic and unjust that, unless there was a profound change in the rural structure of the country, more guerrilla outbreaks could be expected. The military concluded

19. Luigi Einaudi, *The Peruvian Military*, p. 7. The analysis of Peru owes much to my discussions with Einaudi. We coauthored the monograph *Latin American Institutional Development: Changing Military Perspectives in Peru and Brazil* (Santa Monica: RAND Corporation, R-586-DOS, April 1971), in which Einaudi is primarily responsible for Peru and I am primarily responsible for Brazil.

In 1972, while on a SSRC-ACLS grant I carried out research in Peru and visited CAEM. Although the discussion in this chapter reflects some of the results of this research, extensive analysis and documentation of the material must await a later publication. One particularly relevant finding is based on my study with Jorge Rodríguez of the University of York, England. Of the 404 articles to appear in the *Revista de la Escuela Superior de Guerra* (Peru) from 1954 to 1967, the percentage of articles whose content met our criteria of "new professionalism" increased from virtually zero in 1954–5 to well over 50 percent by 1964.

20. Morris Janowitz, *The Professional Soldier: A Social and Political Portrait* (New York: Free Press, 1960), pp. 134–5.

21. CAEM, *El estado y la política general* (1963), pp. 89, 92, cited in Einaudi and Stepan, *Latin American Institutional Development*. Victor Villanueva, in his important book *El CAEM y la revolución de la fuerza armada* (Lima: IEP ediciones y Campodónico ediciones, 1972), pp. 85–8, notes that while this document was initially released with the approval of the director of CAEM, it was withdrawn due to pressure, Villanueva argues that this document is considerably more nationalistic and concerned with structural change than most CAEM studies in this period. Nonetheless for purposes of our comparison the document reveals a set of concerns very different from those found at the ESG in Brazil.

from their studies that Peru was in a state of "latent insurgency," which could only be corrected, in their view, by a "general policy of economic and social development."[22] In Einaudi's words, "elimination of the latent state of subversion became the primary objective of military action."[23]

The military's analysis of the factors contributing to latent insurgency included elite intransigence, fiscal and technical inefficiencies, and a wide variety of administrative weaknesses traceable to the weakness of the government and the underlying contradictions of the social structure.[24] As in Brazil, the military educational system in Peru had produced a whole cadre of officers with a highly articulated ideology of internal security and national development, and with a new confidence as to the utility of their technocratic and managerial education. These officers feared that the country could evolve into a dangerous state of insecurity if fundamental changes in the polity and economy were not brought about. Like the Brazilian military officers schooled at the ESG, the Peruvian officers trained at CAEM came to the conclusion that civilian governments were incapable of bringing about these changes, and that their own CAEM training in the new professionalism gave them the trained cadres and correct ideology for the task of restructuring the country. This attitude strongly influenced the military's decision to assume and retain political control of the country.

Significantly, in Einaudi's interviews with key Peruvian generals, implicit reference was made to the impact the new professional training has had on military confidence to rule. A former minister of war commented that in the past the military felt culturally inferior and that "when a general met an ambassador, he turned red in the face and trembled." But a leading general in the current regime argued that whereas past military attempts to induce change, such as the regime of Colonel Sánchez Cerro, were doomed to failure because military men were not adequately trained in matters of national development, the present military officers possessed the correct training to be

22. See Peru, Ministerio de Guerra, *Las guerrillas en el Perú y su represión* (Lima, 1966), p. 80. Articles in this vein had been appearing in Peruvian military journals even before the guerrilla movement of 1965–6. See in particular Lieutenant Colonel Enrique Gallegos Venero, "Problemas de la guerra contrarrevolucionaria," *Revista de la Escuela Superior de Guerra*, año 11, no. 2 (1964), pp. 97–106.

23. In Einaudi and Stepan, *Latin American Institutional Development*. A civilian social scientist who has been on the faculty at CAEM since 1959 told the author that from 1959 to 1962 CAEM experienced a phase of radicalization aimed at bureaucratic and organizational reform in Peru and that many of these policies were implemented by the 1962–3 military government. From 1964 to 1968 CAEM underwent a new phase of radicalization, but this time the studies explored and advocated much deeper social and structural changes because of the realization that organizational changes alone had been insufficient to resolve Peru's security and development crisis. Interview with Jorge Bravo Bresani, Lima, June 22, 1972.

24. See Brigadier General E. P. Edgardo Mercado Jarrín, "La política y estrategia militar en la guerra contrasubversiva en la América Latina," *Revista Militar del Perú* (Chorrillos), November–December 1967, pp. 4–33. In many ways this article is a classic example of new professionalism.

successful. He commented: "Sánchez Cerro was alone. I am but one of forty. And behind us comes a generation of still better trained officers ready to carry on should we falter."[25]

Brazil and Peru: Their Contrasting Policies

Peru is relevant for our analysis of Brazil not only because it is an example of the new professionalism, but also because it illustrates that the new professionalism contributes more to the military's general attitude to political action than to specific policies. In the two countries, the new professional military men have chosen quite different paths. Why has this occurred, and what are the chances that the military in Brazil might take a Peruvian turn?

This is not the place for an extensive comparative analysis of the two regimes, but some of the factors contributing to the different policies of the two military regimes should be stated. First was the impact of World War II. During the war, Brazil sent a combat division, the Fôrça Expedicionária Brasileira (FEB), to fight in Italy as allies of the United States. My extensive interviews with many of the key leaders of the 1964 military government in Brazil indicate that some of the distinctive characteristics of the Castello Branco government—its pro-Americanism, its favorable attitude toward foreign capital, its distaste for "excessive" nationalism—had their roots in this experience. The ally relationship also prepared the way for close personal and institutional ties between the United States and the Brazilian military establishment.[26] In this area, Peru has no comparable experience.

A second area of divergence between the two countries involves their superior war colleges. The Brazilian war college was established and largely dominated by veterans of World War II, who saw the college as the place to "institutionalize the learning experience of World War II." When officers training at the ESG were sent abroad, they were normally sent to United States military schools, and this experience reinforced the security emphasis, which had found a place in United States schools. Some of the officers associated with CAEM, however, had direct contacts with French-Catholic reformist priest Lebret or attended United Nations civilian-directed schools in Chile. These experiences reinforced CAEM's emphasis on development and helped cast the school's concern for development in a nationalistic light. At the Brazilian ESG many of those attending the courses were private businessmen, and undoubtedly this contributed to the ESG's bias in favor of capitalism and efficiency. The private civilian industrial sector has never been as heavily represented at CAEM.

25. Einaudi and Stepan, *Latin American Institutional Development*, p. 59.
26. For a more detailed discussion and documentation, see Stepan, *The Military in Politics*, pp. 239–44.

A third factor influencing the direction and content of the military regimes in Brazil and Peru is the size of the private industrial sector. The much larger and more powerful private industrial sector in Brazil conditioned military attitudes by inhibiting the adoption of the Peruvian approach, because the private sector is considered so large, dynamic, and advanced that the military doubts its own ability to run the industrial sector efficiently. Industrialists are therefore viewed as allies in the low-mobilization, high-coercion development model in Brazil. In Peru, on the other hand, the industrial sector is smaller and less dynamic. It appears that in the less developed economy, the scope for military Nasserism is greater and the working-class groups far more amenable to the military nationalist-statist approach.

A final factor to be considered in this chapter is the way in which the nexus between security and development issues was viewed by military officers at the time they seized power. In 1964, military officers in Brazil were primarily concerned with what they viewed as the immediate security threat. In Peru, on the other hand, the defeat of the guerrillas in 1966 gave military officers time to focus almost exclusively on the long-term development aspects of security. The initial acts of the Brazilian military regime after 1964 were consequently largely concerned with repression, which by 1968 had become institutionalized coercion. In Peru, the military government has been largely concerned with nationalism and development and this has meant that significant internal opposition from the Left is absent.

Even this cursory analysis of some of the different historical, institutional, and economic legacies in the two countries helps clarify why the "Peruvian wing" within the Brazilian military has not been able to assume control in Brazil and why it is unlikely to do so in the future. What in fact is the future of the new professionalism in Brazil?

One factor that must be taken into consideration is that in a number of ways the Brazilian military in the 1950s and 1960s was for the first time moving toward becoming a professional *caste*. In the period 1941–3, for instance, sons of military families represented 21.3 percent of all cadets admitted to the military academy. This figure had increased to 34.9 percent by 1962–6. More startling is the fact that, as the military professionalized its educational system, it expanded its military high schools in order to ensure the entry into the military school system of a sufficient number of attractive officer candidates. In 1939, 61.6 percent of all cadets at the military academy had attended civilian high schools. By 1963–6, only 7.6 percent of all cadets had attended civilian high schools. Thus, probably about 90 percent of the present army officers in Brazil entered the military educational system when they were about twelve years old.[27]

Once the military assumed power, the movement toward professional homogeneity was accelerated. About 20 percent of the field grade officers have now

27. The data on social origins and educational background of cadets at the Academia Militar das Agulhas Negras were obtained at the academy by the author.

been purged from the military for ideological deviation. Possession of the "correct" revolutionary mentality is now indispensable for promotion or assignment to a key command. The purging of a significant group of senior officers, together with the purging of politicians, has created an "Argentine" extrication dilemma. The military fears leaving office because of the threat posed by the return to power of previously purged officers and politicians. Institutional factors such as these must be borne in mind in any assessment of the possibility of military rule ending in Brazil.

On the other hand, despite the new professionals' agreement on the inseparability of internal security and national development, the contrast between Peru and Brazil has helped point out that the ideology itself leaves unspecified most concrete policy decisions. Nor can the particular ideological unity of the military help resolve succession crises. In fact, the nine years of Brazilian military rule have gravely injured military unity. The military experienced major internal crises in October 1965, November 1968, and September 1969. "Defense of the military institution" was one of the keys to the new professionals' entry into national politics. If, however, internal disunity increases over policy or succession problems, "defense of the institution" may well be one of the keys to extrication, via a caretaker junta. The military leaders are attempting to institutionalize the system so that levels of coercion and dissent diminish and support rises. The Mexican model of institutionalization is often mentioned by the military. However, the absence of a revolutionary myth in Brazil and the much more advanced state of both the economy and, more importantly, social groups would seem to rule out this possibility.

TWO

Liberal-Pluralist, Classic Marxist, and "Organic-Statist" Approaches to the State

A major, nearly worldwide trend since the 1930s has been the steady growth of the role of the state in political life. In the industrialized world, the emergence of the managerial state to combat the crisis of capitalism during the depression, the widened scope of executive power in World War II, and growing state regulative and welfare functions since the war, have all contributed to the expansion of the state. In the Third World it is even clearer that most development plans call for the state to play a major role in structuring economic and social systems.

Despite this expansion of the declared and undeclared functions of the state, there had been a significant decline in theoretical analyses of the impact of state policies on society. Starting in the mid-1950s, when the field of comparative politics underwent a major period of innovation, it was widely believed by members of the profession that this subfield of political science contained the most important new contributions. When we examine this period of innovation, however, there is a striking preoccupation with the search for the underlying economic, social, and even psychological causes of political behavior. The new approaches in comparative politics in most cases assigned little independent weight to the impact of state policies and political structures on the social system. Without denying the gains to comparative politics made by the move away from a sterile emphasis on descriptive studies of a formal–legal nature, it is clear that a price has been paid, namely a retreat from what should be one of the central concerns of the discipline. While almost everywhere the role of the state grew, one of the few places it withered away was in political science.[1]

1. Indicative of the tone of mainstream North American literature is the fact that when I culled *World Politics* and the *American Political Science Review* for articles on the state in the period 1958–72, the period in which comparative politics underwent intensive reconceptualization, I uncovered only one major article that explicitly attempted a

This chapter was first published in Alfred Stepan, *The State and Society: Peru in Comparative Perspective* (Princeton: Princeton University Press, 1978), 3–45.

The first task of this chapter, therefore, is conceptual, namely to examine what role the state plays in some of the major models used in contemporary political analysis. Is the state analyzed as an independent variable that has an impact on society, or is it treated as a dependent variable? If the latter, what problems for empirical research are presented by such conceptual approaches and what reformulations are indicated?

My second task in this chapter is analytical and empirical. Are there models that emphasize the role of the state that have been neglected by contemporary political science? Can an awareness of these alternative models help overcome some of the major conceptual and empirical lacunae that characterize much work in contemporary political science? And, less generally, are there political systems that have been influenced by these alternative institutional, administrative, and normative models? If so, it might greatly aid the analysis of politics in such societies to incorporate explicitly elements of these models into our research strategies.

I argue that there exists a recognizable strand of political thought, which I call "organic-statist," that runs from Aristotle, through Roman law, natural law, absolutist and modern Catholic social thought. I suggest that organic statism represents powerful philosophical and structural tendencies found throughout Western Europe, and especially in the Iberian countries and their former colonies, where organic statism was never as fully challenged by alternative political models as in the rest of the European cultural area. In addition, I argue that a modern variant of the organic-statist model of society provides a useful analytic framework with which to begin investigating the interrelationship of state and society in one of the more important and original political experiments in modern Latin American history—Peru. But first it is necessary to review the basic assumptions about the role of the state in some of the major models of political life.

I begin with an examination of liberal pluralism and the classical Marxist model of the role of the state in capitalist societies, because in their various guises these two models are the most influential competing methodological paradigms used in contemporary political analysis.[2] As such, I think it is useful to indicate to what extent some of the major lines of development of both of

general theoretical analysis of the state. That article was J. P. Nettl, "The State as a Conceptual Variable," *World Politics* (July 1968). A telling analysis of the reductionist problem in the political development literature is Joseph LaPalombara's review article, "Political Power and Political Development," *Yale Law Journal* (June 1969). A very useful general discussion of three major perspectives on the relationship between state and society is Reinhard Bendix, "Social Stratification and the Political Community," *European Journal of Sociology* (1960). Fortunately in the last few years there has been a renewed attention to the question of the state in social science and this book hopes to contribute to this reassessment.

2. The Leninist model of the state during the dictatorship of the proletariat is of course quite different from the Marxist model of the bourgeois state. In the concluding section of this chapter I contrast organic-statist and Leninist (or more generically "command socialist") models.

these theories treat the political sphere as a dependent variable, and to indicate some of the empirical and conceptual problems created by an excessive reliance on either approach.[3] A brief discussion of these two approaches is an indispensable prelude to a more extensive analysis of the organic-statist approach for two reasons. First, as a body of literature, from the mid-nineteenth century on, much of the corpus of organic-statist writing has been developed and modified in explicit normative opposition to both liberal pluralism and Marxism. It is therefore important to clarify how these three approaches differ on most of the central questions of political philosophy—on the role of the individual, the nature of the political community, the common good, and most importantly, the state. Second, at the empirical level of twentieth-century Latin American politics, the major political leaders who have attempted to impose corporatist variants of the organic-statist vision of politics on their countries have invariably acted as though liberal and Marxist ideologies and structures were the major obstacles in their path. It is therefore imperative from the point of view of the present analysis to consider the interaction of liberalism, Marxism, and organic statism.

A final preliminary note. By no means do I intend to advocate the normative or analytic superiority of the organic-statist model over that of either liberal pluralism or Marxism. I do, however, want to make explicit the analytic implications of the different models. Most models usually fuse normative, descriptive, and methodological components. However, for analytic purposes these components can be separated. That is, in part, models are *normative statements* about what societies should be like. In part they are *empirical descriptions* of how societies are. In part they are *methodological approaches* suggesting what aspects of political life are important to study.

Classical Marxism and liberalism pluralism, in very different ways, contain vivid descriptions of what societies are like empirically that tend to portray the state as a dependent variable. Analysts working with either a classical Marxist or liberal-pluralist vision of the real world tend to use methodological approaches to study political life that, as I will attempt to demonstrate, all too frequently systematically draw attention away from consideration of the state as a possible independent variable. Normatively, both models also contain (for different reasons) negative evaluations of the state. My point in reviewing the literature on Marxism and liberal pluralism is not to dismiss them but rather to underscore characteristic research problems presented by both models and to suggest subthemes within both models that, if recast, are useful for contemporary research into state–society relations.

3. Numerous exceptions exist, even within Marxist and pluralist writings, to this sweeping statement, and this chapter does not intend, or pretend, to be a comprehensive survey of all approaches. Rather I have deliberately focused on major theoretical strands that assign little independent weight to the state because I feel it is intellectually imperative to confront directly the research consequences of these schemes.

Organic statism, in contrast to liberal pluralism and classical Marxism, is seen most importantly as a normative model of the relations between state and society and not primarily as a methodological approach.[4] However, elites in many different societies, and in different historical periods, have used variants of the organic-statist model as a legitimizing formula—or at times even as a guide—for designing institutions, systems, and administrative structures. Where such state-structured interactions have played a role in shaping societies empirically, then the methodological implications are clear, namely, that at a bare minimum we must design research (even where Marxist or pluralist assumptions figure prominently) so that we are able to assess the comparative weight of the state and/or society in determining political outcomes. My own analytic position, which will emerge more clearly as the book unfolds, is that all three approaches are in some basic respects seriously deficient. Liberal pluralism and a major strand of classical Marxism are deficient largely because of their presuppositions of the near autonomy of society, and organic statism because of its presupposition of the near autonomy of the state. I hope that this book will indicate the necessity of greater theoretical integration of the two obviously non-autonomous spheres: state and society.

The Liberal-Pluralist Approach to the State

In the liberal-pluralist approach the main normative, empirical, and methodological concern is with individuals who, pursuing their individual economic and political interests, together make up society. In pluralist theory, individuals may form into groups, but because they all have a variety of interests they tend to associate themselves with numerous and different groups whose interests cross-cut. A methodological and normative assumption among both political and economic thinkers in the liberal-pluralist tradition is that it is undesirable to use the concept of the general good. Instead, individual utility for the constituent members of society is most nearly achieved when individuals are allowed to pursue freely their own economic and political interests.[5]

4. However, at the end of the chapter I recast organic statism so that it can be studied as an abstract model of governance with its own characteristic requirements and predicaments, just as David Apter has performed a similar task for his "secular-libertarian" and "sacred-collectivity" models in *The Politics of Modernization* (Chicago: University of Chicago Press, 1965), 28–36.

5. The literature is far too extensive and too well known to summarize here. Two excellent critical reviews of the literature that develop some of the points only briefly touched on here are Sheldon Wolin's, "Liberalism and the Decline of Political Philosophy," and "The Age of Organization and the Sublimation of Politics," chs. 9 and 10 of his *Politics and Vision: Continuity and Innovation in Western Political Thought* (Boston: Little, Brown, 1960), 286–435. See also Theodore J. Lowi, *The End of Liberalism: Ideology, Policy, and the Crisis of Public Authority* (New York: W. W. Norton, 1969), esp. chs. 1–3. A useful

The normative and empirical distinction between the "collective interest in the common good" and the "sum of individual interests," which in organic statism or in welfare economics going back to Pareto necessitates a major role for the state in the economy, is obliterated in classical liberal economics because of the supposition that the pursuit of individual interests will in itself produce the best good for society.[6] The classic formulation of the "hidden hand" mechanism that produces this harmony of interests is, of course, that of Adam Smith: "Every individual is continually exerting himself to find out the most advantageous employment for whatever capital he can command. It is his own advantage, indeed, and not that of the society, which he has in view. But the study of his own advantage naturally, or rather necessarily, leads him to prefer that employment which is most advantageous to the society."[7]

For the classical liberal theoretician, the hidden hand of the market mechanism itself would appear to perform—and perform better—almost all the functions that in other theories are seen as being performed by the state. The clear injunction was to let society regulate itself without interference. Society was a homeostatic system with only minimal need for a state. Thus Jeremy Bentham argued, "The general rule is, that nothing ought to be done or attempted by government. The motto, or watchword of government, on these occasions, ought to be—Be quiet. . . . With few exceptions, and these not very considerable ones, the attainment of the maximum of enjoyment will be most effectually secured by leaving each individual to pursue his own maximum enjoyment."[8]

Though the role of the state is apparently reduced to a minimum because of the self-regulating market mechanism, it is often lost sight of that Adam Smith, in a much less well-known passage, in fact assigned three distinct duties to the state:

First, the duty of protecting the society from the violence and invasion of other independent societies; secondly, the duty of protecting, as far as possible, every member of the society from the injustice or oppression of every other member of it, or the duty of establishing an exact administration of justice; and, thirdly, the duty of erecting and maintaining certain public works and certain public institutions which it can never be for the interest of any individual, or small number of individuals, to erect and maintain; because the profit could never repay the expense to any individual or small number of individuals, though it may frequently do much more than repay it to a great society.[9]

analysis and anthology of English liberal thought is Alan Bullock and Maurice Shock (eds.), *The Liberal Tradition: From Fox to Keynes* (Oxford: Clarendon Press, 1967).

6. See my discussion of the significance of the common good in organic statism in this chapter. Pareto's distinction between the "utility of the collectivity" and the "utility of the members," and his argument that "far from coinciding these utilities often stand in basic opposition," is found in Vilfredo Pareto, *The Mind and Society: A Treatise in General Sociology* (New York: Dover, 1935), nos. 2110–2128, esp. no. 2115.

7. *The Wealth of Nations*, 2 vols., Everyman (London: Deut, 1910), i. 398.

8. *A Manual of Political Economy*, reproduced in Bullock and Shock (eds.), *The Liberal Tradition*, pp. xxiii–iv, 28–9.

9. *The Wealth of Nations*, ii. 180–1.

The point then, is, not that society is actually self-regulating but that the market mechanism is assumed to be self-regulating *only if* the state provides the indispensable neutral and impartial administrative, institutional, and physical infrastructures for capitalism to function. This is, in fact, quite a large task for the state to perform in any society, and, far from being automatic, its performance requires great political skill and power. When we turn to the task of the late developing countries, the fact that they are follower economies makes many of the indispensable infrastructure expenditures "unprofitable for any individual," and the role of the state more crucial.[10] Since 1964 Brazil, for example, has been widely regarded as following a liberal, market mechanism model of development. Yet Roberto Campos, a chief economic architect of the regime, believed that, in order to make the market mechanism work, large-scale and systematic state investment and intervention was required in almost all facets of the country's economic, and especially social, structures. The last decade of market mechanism rule in Brazil thus not so paradoxically ushered in one of the most important epochs of expansion of the scope of state power in Brazil's history.[11]

Twentieth-century pluralism, especially the group-theory variant whose most noted exponents are Arthur Bentley and David Truman, allows for a more positive role for the state. Nonetheless, it implicitly shares with classical liberalism the presupposition that society is basically self-regulating.[12] The functional equivalent of the market's hidden hand in group theory is competition among groups combined with cross-cutting membership among groups. This is the essential self-regulating principle of group theory. In group theory, as in liberal theory more generally, the analysis begins with a concern with how individuals act: "No individual is wholly absorbed in any group to which he

10. For a seminal discussion of the role of the state in relation to the "timing" of industrialization, see Alexander Gerschenkron, *Economic Backwardness in Historical Perspective: A Book of Essays*, (Cambridge, Mass.: Harvard University Press, 1966), esp. 5–30.

11. Interview with Roberto Campos, minister of planning in the Castello Branco government, in Rio de Janeiro on September 15, 1967. For a detailed analysis of the expansion of the not-so-hidden hand of the state in order to make the market mechanism work, see Thomas Skidmore, "Politics and Economic Policy Making in Authoritarian Brazil, 1937–71," in Alfred Stepan (ed.), *Authoritarian Brazil: Origins, Policies, and Future* (New Heaven: Yale University Press, 1973), 3–46. For a fascinating discussion of how the state created an Adam Smithian "public institution," the stock market, to allow the market mechanism to operate, see David Trubek, "Law, Planning and the Development of the Brazilian Capital Market," *The Bulletin*, nos. 72–3 (Apr. 1971). For a careful analysis of the many aspects of the growth of the role of the state in the Brazilian economy since 1930 see Werner Baer, Issac Kertenetzsky, and Aníbal V. Vitella, "The Changing Role of the State in the Brazilian Economy," *World Development* (Nov. 1973). Also see Werner Baer, Richard Newfarmer and Thomas Trebatt, "On State Capitalism in Brazil: Some New Issues and Questions," *Inter-American Economic Affairs*, 30 (Winter 1976), 63–93.

12. Pluralist group theory is particularly relevant for our analysis because organic statism is also a form of group theory, but one which, as we shall see, has fundamentally different premises. Although I draw somewhat different conclusions, I profited much by reading John F. Witte, "Theories of American Pluralism: The Writings of Arthur F. Bentley, David Truman, and Robert A. Dahl," MS, Yale University, May 17, 1973.

belongs. Only a fraction of his attitudes is expressed through any one such affiliation... An individual generally belongs to several groups—a family, a church, an economic institution, and frequently a very large number of associations, perhaps sixty or seventy for active 'joiners' in our society."[13] After establishing the fact of multiple memberships, the next step in the analysis is to establish their cross-cutting character: "The demands and standards of these various groups may and frequently do come in conflict with one another.... We must start from the fact that the equilibrium of an individual consists of his adjustment in the various institutionalized groups and associations to which he belongs."[14]

In group theory the empirical and methodological consequences of multiple overlapping memberships are many and significant. It is the central argument used to dismiss the class basis of Marxist theory, on the ground that unified class consciousness (whether upper or lower class) is an untenable concept in the face of the fragmenting impact of multiple cross-pressures.[15] Also the central normative role for the state as being functionally necessary for the regulation of conflict, a role found in numerous variants of organic statism, is rejected by group theorists because in group theory conflict regulation is basically an autonomous outcome of the interaction of different groups. Pluralistic group theory sees the multiple cross-pressures in society as performing the function of inducing a tendency toward bargaining and compromise both in the individual and in the individual's groups, which strive to maintain group unity in the midst of cross-pressures. "The heterogeneity of membership that causes internal difficulties in all such groups tempers the claims of an occupational interest through the process of internal compromise and adjustment."[16]

This approach, while plausible in high consensus situations, is less appropriate in societies where cleavages are compounded or in crisis situations where, despite cross-pressures, some pressures assume greater salience in terms of the stakes involved than others. In both the above cases the hypothesized self-regulating process has little behavioral impact and the role of the state apparatus and strategic political elites often becomes crucial in determining the outcome.[17]

Bentley does not really discuss the empirical possibility of the state elite's altering the effective power of potential groups either by using repression to dismantle the organizational capacity of some groups or by seeking to broaden

13. David B. Truman, *The Governmental Process: Political Interests and Public Opinion* (New York: Alfsed A. Knopf, 1951), 157.

14. Ibid. 157, 162.

15. For their arguments rejecting the Marxist concept of class, see Truman, *The Governmental Process*, 165–6, and Arthur Bentley, *The Process of Government: A Study of Social Pressures* (Chicago: University of Chicago Press, 1908), 207–8.

16. Truman, *The Governmental Process*, 166, also 514. Bentley speaks of the "limitless criss-cross of groups"; *The Process of Government*, 206.

17. For an excellent discussion along these lines see Eric A. Nordlinger, *Conflict Regulation in Divided Societies* (Cambridge, Mass.: Centre for International Affairs, Harvard University Press, 1972), esp. 93–101.

the social base for the state elite's programs by organizing from above a group that otherwise would not be able to organize effectively. His assumption is that "when we have a group that participates in the political system we have always another group facing it in the same plane."[18] Truman does not assert that opposing groups are actually organized, but he does place great weight on the fact that all interests are potential interest groups and that, as such, other actual powerful groups will take them into account. Thus the balancing (or repressive) function does not need to be performed by the government because it is the "multiple memberships in potential groups based on widely held and accepted interests that serve as the balance wheel in a going political system like that of the United States."[19] In the writings of Bentley this methodological emphasis on group forces relegates the concept of the "state" to the "intellectual amusements of the past."[20]

As to the government's adding significantly to the sum total of interest group pressures, or being an agent reshaping the balance of forces in society, Bentley rules this out: "the governing body has no value in itself, except as one aspect of the process, and cannot even be adequately described except in terms of the deep-lying interests which function through it."[21] He accepts the idea that the government or the permanent bureaucracy could be considered an interest group, but insists that as such it would have no autonomous interests because its interests would reflect other more fundamental interest groups in society.[22]

Although other variants of contemporary North American political science are not as reductionist as the interest group theorists, there is a widespread tendency to look for the underlying nonpolitical forces in society and to reduce greatly the autonomy of the state or the government. Significantly, in the elaborate Parsonian schema, society, culture, and personality are judged to be

18. Bentley, *The Process of Government*, 220. He presents no convincing evidence for this and does not address the question of comparative power. For a useful corrective to Bentley's approach, see Mancur Olson, Jr., *The Logic of Collective Action: Public Goods and the Theory of Groups*, rev. edn. (New York: Schocken Books, 1971).

19. Truman, *The Governmental Process*, 514. Once again little hard evidence is given to support this proposition and no discussion of the theoretical or normative problem of "non-issues."

20. "The 'State' itself is, to the best of my knowledge and belief, no factor in our investigation," and "The 'idea of the state' has been very prominent, no doubt, among the intellectual amusements of the past, and at particular places and times it has served to help give coherence and pretentious expression to some particular group's activity. But in either case it is too minute a factor to deserve space in a book covering so broad a range as this." Bentley, *The Process of Government*, 263–4.

21. Ibid. 300.

22. Ibid. 290. While his theory is mainly concerned with modern societies, Bentley argues that group theory would hold for all societies, even in the extreme case of absolute despotism. For the despot himself is merely an expression of the underlying balance of forces in society: "When we take such an agency of government as a despotic ruler, we cannot possibly advance to an understanding of him except in terms of the group activities of his society which are most directly represented through him. Always and everywhere our study must be a study of the interests that work through government; otherwise we have not got down to the facts" (pp. 270–1).

worthy of relatively autonomous levels of analysis, but politics is not.[23] Gabriel Almond, in his influential introduction to *The Politics of Developing Areas*, a book that ushered in a decade of new field research, notes that "It was the conviction of the collaborators in this study that . . . the input functions, rather than the output, would be most important in characterizing non-Western political systems, and in discriminating types and stages of political development among them."[24] Later in the same introduction, Almond acknowledges that "While there is justification for having underplayed the governmental structures in this study, their neglect in the development of the theory of the functions of the polity represents a serious shortcoming in the present analysis."[25]

It is safe to say that, despite empirical refinements, there never was a major methodological advance in this approach in regard to the role of public policy or the state, and that, by and large, the prestigious Social Science Research Council Committee on Comparative Politics contributed heavily to the reductionist tendency to look for nonpolitical explanations of political behavior.[26]

Yet another attempt to analyze a total political system is that of David Easton.[27] His systems analysis approach shares an important dimension with Almond's functional approach, namely an elaborate discussion of inputs but a very cursory analysis of the role that the government plays in shaping inputs and generating its own policies or outputs. Easton does not deny that government can play a role in generating inputs, but even here he characteristically redirects attention back to the need to examine the overall cultural, environmental, and social backgrounds of the "gatekeepers" rather than to the black box of government itself.[28]

A research strategy that is limited to the pluralist, interest-group perspective, while it is certainly useful for some problems, all too often takes for granted what it should be demonstrating, namely that a plurality of interests plays a determining role in shaping policy. This implicit assumption often contributes to a systematic neglect both of the state's role in taking independent policy initiatives, and of the impact of state policy on the structure of society,

23. See Talcott Parsons, E. A. Shils *et al.*, *Toward a General Theory of Action* (New York: Horper & Row, 1962), 28–29.

24. Gabriel Almond, "A Functional Approach to Comparative Politics," in Gabriel A. Almond and James S. Coleman (eds.), *The Politics of the Developing Areas* (Princeton: Princeton University Press, 1960), 17. The four input functions were (1) political socialization and recruitment, (2) interest articulation, (3) interest aggregation and (4) political communication. In fact, all four "input functions" may be strongly structured by government policy as I demonstrate in other chapters.

25. Ibid. 55.

26. For an interesting critique along these lines by a prominent member of the SSRC Committee on Comparative Politics, see LaPalombara, "Political Power and Political Development," 1259.

27. He has developed this in various publications. The two most important are his *A Framework for Political Analysis* (New York: Prentice Hall, 1965), and *A Systems Analysis of Political Life* (New York: Wiley, 1965).

28. Easton, *A Systems Analysis of Political Life*, 97–9.

especially on the types of inputs that social groups can in fact make on the state.[29] To cite one obvious example, in many countries trade unions are subject to prohibitions against organization, or at least are restricted to operating within a legal and administrative network of regulations that has a profound impact on how the unions' interests are organized and articulated.[30] A closely related neglected question concerns the role of state policy in creating groups from above and then establishing guidelines on how they can act.

These examples suggest that the neglect of the institutional, class, and ideological context within which interest groups operate is a serious problem. The dominant supposition of group theorists is that interest groups operate in an *unchartered* context. Significantly, Truman quotes approvingly Bentley's summary statement: "The very nature of the group process (which our government shows in a fairly well-developed form) is this, that groups are freely combining, dissolving, and recombining in accordance with their interest lines."[31]

As a description of the real world, this suffers from the obvious limitation that, for most societies throughout most of history, interest groups have not been at liberty to "freely combine." Quite often, as our later discussion of the organic-statist tradition will make clear, they have been very strictly *chartered* by the state in accordance with the state's, and not the groups', "own interest lines." Reliance on a theoretical scheme that posits freely combining interest groups and a passive, neutral state seriously limits the range of cases that can be considered because only with great difficulty can such a perspective deal with such contemporary architectonic party-states as China and the Soviet Union, where the party-based controllers of the state apparatus have clearly been reasonably successful in imposing their ideological and organizational designs on the body politic.[32] It leads also to historical parochialism, because even

29. My specific intention here is to indicate conceptual and empirical lacunae in regard to state policy in pluralist—especially group—theory. There is of course a voluminous literature devoted to general critiques of pluralism. Some of the more prominent attacks are Lowi, *The End of Liberalism*; Peter Bachrach and Morton S. Baratz, "Two Faces of Power," *American Political Science Review* (Dec. 1962); Michael Parenti, "Power and Pluralism: A View from the Bottom," *Journal of Politics* (Aug. 1970); and William E. Connolly (ed.), *The Bias of Pluralism* (New York: Atherton Press, 1967).

30. In the next two chapters of *The State and Society* I document in extensive detail the effective array of corporatist mechanisms the Brazilian and Mexican state elites have constructed to control unions.

31. Truman, *The Governmental Process*, 167, and Bentley, *The Process of Government*, 359.

32. Schurmann's book on China, for example, begins with a clear acknowledgment of the power of the party-state to redesign and rebuild Chinese society: "Chinese communism came to power and created the present People's Republic of China... They have rebuilt a great country, disciplined its people, improved the conditions of life, and laid the foundations for growth... We are concerned with the systematic structures created by these men. Communist China is like a vast building made of different kinds of brick and stone. However it was put together, it stands. What holds it together is ideology and organization." See Franz Schurmann's *Ideology and Organization in Communist China*, 2nd edn., rev. (Berkeley: University of California Press, 1968), 1. For a telling critique of the lack of usefulness of Almond's analytical framework for dealing with contemporary communist regimes, see Robert A. Dowse, "A Functionalist's Logic," *World Politics* (June 1966). This is not to imply, as the literature on totalitarianism had earlier, that attention

though it is clear that a promising area for political development theory lies in longitudinal historical analysis, many of the dominant theoretical schemes, with their view of the state as a dependent variable and their emphasis on relatively free and powerful interest groups, have great difficulty in dealing adequately with major spans of Western political life. For example, in many Greek, Italian Renaissance, and Swiss city-states, the private sphere of interests was relatively small compared to the political sphere in which the government structured activities. The unchartered interest-group focus has even greater limitations as an analytic approach when the task is the study of power in such formative phases of European political history as the Roman Empire, seventeenth-century absolutism, or the two Napoleonic regimes, in all of which there was a major accumulation of power by the state at the expense of interest groups. As we shall see when we analyze the political philosophy and practice of organic statism in Europe, the state placed strict and effective controls on associations. Despite the rejection of some aspects of the organic-statist approach in the absolutist period, it is clear that state control of interest groups was, if anything, intensified.

Another problem for group theory relates to the question of selective access. Even in societies that were once assumed to approximate closely the pluralist political model, such as England or Sweden, the semi-planned nature of the political economy has given rise to a policy consultation stage that has significantly altered the nature of the input process by interest groups. Before new measures (which are increasingly drawn up by government initiative) are formally considered by the legislature, they are systematically vetted by a consultative committee consisting of the ministerial or public agency representatives delegated by the state, the representatives of employee organizations, the representatives of employer organizations, and occasionally a representative of a public interest group.[33] The crucial point is that the state

to groups in strong party states is irrelevant. For an attempt at utilizing "interest group" analysis for the Soviet Union, see H. Gordon Skilling and Franklyn Griffiths (eds.), *Interest Groups in Soviet Politics* (Princeton: Princeton University Press, 1970). The Skilling approach, however, has a serious conceptual weakness: the confusion of "group politics" with "pluralist interest group politics." In fact a strong case could probably be made that the role of groups in Eastern Europe has more in common at the structural level with the organic-statist or corporatist traditions of chartered group politics than it does with the pluralist interest group tradition. One of the few scholars to begin to develop this potentially fruitful line of inquiry into the relationship of groups to the state in communist societies is Andrew C. Janos, "Group Politics in Communist Society: A Second Look at the Pluralist Model," in Samuel P. Huntington and Clement H. Moore (eds.), *Authoritarian Politics in Modern Society: The Dynamics of Established One-Party Systems* (New York: Basic Books, 1970).

33. In Sweden such committees play a central role in the political process. In the 1961–7 period, 60% of the commissioners were civil servants (up from 41% in 1945–54) and the nonconflictual behaviour of the other members is indicated by the fact that three-fourths of all commissions presented unanimous proposals; see Hans Meijer, "Bureaucracy and Policy Formulation in Sweden," *Scandinavian Political Studies*, 4 (1969), 103–16. For an interesting comparative study that makes a strong case that bureaucracies were the "most consistently important" group in shaping welfare policies

plays a central role in determining which groups are represented in this policy process.[34] *Access capability* also has an impact on the strength or weakness of groups. Groups that can demonstrate reasonably good access capability are often in a superior position to maintain or even accrue support from constituents than those that are perceived to be outside this process of consultation. In addition, since group leaders want to maintain their own power and prestige, which often is derived from their membership on such a consultative committee, they often will be tempted to tailor their groups' demands to stay within the general policy framework being pursued by the government.[35] Because the state plays such a pivotal role in agenda setting, access granting, constituency support capability, and interest-group demand formulation, it obviously plays a central part in shaping the input process even in "pluralistic" politics.[36]

Classical Marxist Theory of the State in Capitalist Societies

As in much of liberal-pluralist thought, a main line of argumentation in the classical Marxist theory of bourgeois society treats the state largely as a dependent variable.[37] Since this aspect of Marxist thought has played a preponderant

in Britain and Sweden and that the earlier emergence of certain welfare policies in Sweden than in Britain was due more to variance in state administrative structures than to the power of organized political pressures see, Hugh Heclo, *Modern Social Politics in Britain and Sweden: From Relief to Income Maintenance* (New Haven: Yale University Press, 1974), esp. 42–60, 301–21, quote from p. 301.

34. Joseph LaPalombara discusses the question of "structured access" in his *Interest Groups in Italian Politics* (Princeton: Princeton University Press, 1964), esp. 258–70.

35. This process has not received the attention it deserves. Two seminal works that begin to address the subject are by Samuel H. Beer, *British Politics in the Collectivist Age* (New York: Alfred A. Knopf, 1965), and Stein Rokkan, "Norway: Numerical Democracy and Corporate Pluralism," in Robert A. Dahl (ed.), *Political Opposition in Western Democracies* (New Haven: Yale University Press, 1966), 70–116, esp. 105–10. Significantly, Rokkan cites no English language work that discusses this aspect of Norwegian politics.

36. Philippe C. Schmitter's stimulating "Still the Century of Corporatism?" in Fredrick B. Pike and Thomas Stritch (eds.), *The New Corporatism: Social-Political Structures in the Iberian World* (Notre Dame, Ind.: University of Notre Dame Press, 1974), 85–131, argues—correctly I think—that corporatist structures are becoming more prominent in countries such as Sweden, Switzerland, the Netherlands, Norway, and Denmark. However he argues that such structures have largely emerged from the interest groups themselves—thus his term "societal corporatism"—whereas I attach significant independent weight to the role the state has played in forging such structured interactions.

37. By classical Marxist theory, I mean the theory found in Karl Marx and Frederick Engels. A number of good studies are devoted to this difficult subject. An analysis that places Marx's view of the state within the context of his general philosophy is Shlomo Avineri, *The Social and Political Thought of Karl Marx* (Cambridge: Cambridge University Press, 1968), esp. 17–64. A book that focuses specifically on the political theory of Marx and Engels is Robert Tucker, *The Marxian Revolutionary Idea* (New York: W. W. Norton, 1969), esp. 54–81. See also Ralph Miliband, "Marx and the State," *Socialist Register* (1965),

role in shaping subsequent "economistic" Marxist analyses of the state, I shall treat it first. Later I shall analyze subthemes in Marx's writings concerning hegemonic crises and Bonapartism that, if properly understood, offer rich, nondeterministic, theoretical insights about such crucial questions as the relative autonomy of the state. Unfortunately, Marx died before he was able to begin a full-scale systematic treatment of the state.[38] Nonetheless, he had already written enough about the relation of the state to society for us to discuss certain broad themes. For in fact Marx had always been interested in the question of the state. Significantly, his first major work, the critique of Hegel's *Philosophy of Right* was largely devoted to a criticism of Hegel's view of the state.

In traditional liberal-pluralist thought, the analytical starting point is with the individual, who is seen as acting alone or with other groups of individuals to advance his private interests. Marx rejects the atomistic starting-point of liberal pluralism on the methodological grounds that it is impossible to discuss any individual without at the same time discussing the sum total of the relationships within which individuals are intermeshed.[39] For Marx, the most fundamental of these relationships involves the mode of production, and thus both individualist psychology and individualist politics are rejected. Marx's basic statement of the relationship of politics to economics is found in his famous preface to the *Contribution to the Critique of Political Economy*:

legal relations as well as forms of state are to be grasped neither from themselves nor from the so-called general development of the human mind, but rather have their roots in the material conditions of life.... The anatomy of civil society is to be sought in political economy.... The sum total of these relations of production constitutes the economic structure of society, the real foundation, on which rises a legal and political super-structure and to which correspond definite forms of social consciousness. The mode of production of material life conditions the social, political and intellectual life process in general.[40]

The hidden hand of classical liberalism and the group competition and crosscutting cleavages of pluralism imply there is fruitful competition and a minimum of systematic conflict or coercion. Though there is no sense of the

278–96; John Sanderson, "Marx and Engels on the State," *Western Political Quarterly* (Dec. 1963); John Plamenatz, *German Marxism and Russian Communism* (London: Longman, Green, 1954), 135–64; and the important interpretations by Nicos Poulantzas, *Political Power and Social Classes*, trans. Timothy O'Hagan (London: New Left Books and Sheed & Ward, 1973), and Jean-Claude Girardin, "Sur la théorie marxiste de l'Etat," *Les Temps Modernes* (Sept.–Oct. 1972).

38. For Marx's intention to write such a work, see Karl Marx, "Preface to a Critique of Political Economy," in Karl Marx and Frederick Engels, *Selected Works*, I (Moscow: Foreign Language Publishing House, 1958), 361.

39. See Karl Marx, *The Poverty of Philosophy* (New York: International Publishers, 1963), 33–46. For an analysis of Marx's critique of "atomistic individualism" see Avineri, *The Social and Political Thought of Karl Marx*, 17–18, 33.

40. Marx and Engels, *Selected Works*, I. 362–3. Engels often formulated the relationship of the political superstructure to the economic structure in much less subtle and more deterministic language. See, for example, his prefaces to the German edition (1883) and the English edition (1888) of the *Communist Manifesto*, in *Selected Works*, I. 24, 28.

collective community as such, as there is in organic statism, classical liberal pluralism in theory can result in a contribution to the greatest good of the greatest number. These assumptions are flatly rejected by classical Marxism. Once division of labor occurs, "every form of society has been based ... on the antagonism of oppressing and oppressed classes."[41] Between classes the economic conflict is basically a zero-sum relationship: "Every advance in production is at the same time a retrogression in the condition of the oppressed class, that is, of the great majority. What is a boon for the one is necessarily a bane for the other; each new emancipation of one class always means a new oppression of another class."[42]

Given the fact that the economic structure is the basis for the political superstructure, the liberal assumption that the state will provide neutral procedural guarantees for free political and economic competition is rejected. The state, at least in Engels's formulation, is exclusively the coercive instrument of the dominant class: "The State ... in all typical periods is exclusively the state of the ruling class, and in all cases remains essentially a machine for keeping down the oppressed, exploited class."[43] The famous passage in the Communist Manifesto that "The Executive of the modern state is but a committee for managing the common affairs of the whole bourgeoisie" thus posits a relationship in which the state is the dependent variable and the economic system is the independent variable.[44]

Since for classical Marxism the state originally arose as a necessary means of coercion once division of labor occurred, the state remains as an instrument of oppression until the proletarian revolution eliminates all class distinctions by eliminating capitalism. This can only be accomplished when the proletariat in turn uses the state as a means of repression during the transitional stage of the "dictatorship of the proletariat."[45] Once private ownership is abolished, and class distinctions eventually eliminated, the need for the state as an instrument

41. The *Communist Manifesto*, in Marx and Engels, *Selected Works*, i. 45.

42. Frederick Engels, *The Origin of the Family, Private Property, and the State*, in Marx and Engels, *Selected Works*, ii. 295. This essay is one of the most detailed treatments of the state to be found in the writings of Marx and Engels. All further references to this work refer to the *Selected Works* edition. For Marxist social science, the fact that Engels, not Marx, wrote most extensively on the state was unfortunate because, as noted, Engels's analysis of the relationship of the superstructure to the structure was often presented in much more mechanistic terms than that found in Marx. To this extent my strictures about "classical Marxism" apply more directly to Engels. Nonetheless, since Engels's works had a great influence on Marxist social science, it would be sociologically unacceptable to exclude his works when we are evaluating the legacy of classical Marxism in regard to the analysis of the state.

43. Ibid. 294.

44. Marx and Engels, *Selected Works*, i. 36.

45. On the need for the revolutionary dictatorship of the proletariat, see Karl Marx, *Critique of the Gotha Program*, in *Selected Works*, ii. 30. For Engels's attack on anarchic socialists who would not use authoritarian means to maintain the victorious revolution, see his "On Authority," in *Selected Works*, i. 636–7. Also see V. I. Lenin, "The Immediate Tasks of the Soviet Government," in V. I. Lenin, *Selected Works* (New York: International Publishers, 1971), 420–7.

of class oppression no longer exists. At this stage classical Marxism shares with classical liberalism the assumption that society can essentially be internally self-managed. Emancipated society has the autonomous, noncoercive managerial capacity to regulate itself. In contrast to the basic assumptions of organic statism, the state in pure communism is seen as both functionally unnecessary, and normatively undesirable for society. As Engels said, "The society that will organize production on the basis of a free and equal association of the producers will put the whole machinery of state where it will then belong: into the Museum of Antiquities, by the side of the spinning wheel and the bronze axe."[46]

The above summarizes a main line of argument of the classical Marxist theory of the state under normal conditions. As in classical liberalism, the state apparently does not play a relatively independent role in the political process. Until the classless society comes into being, the state is envisaged as the instrument of coercion of the dominant economic class, and as such, much research that confines itself to the above aspects of the classical Marxist tradition is directed almost exclusively to the underlying economic forces in society. As Nicos Poulantzas, himself a Marxist, laments, "a long Marxist tradition has considered that the State is only a simple tool or instrument manipulated at will by the ruling class."[47] As he acknowledges, this has often led to "economism" which "considers that other levels of social reality, including the State, are simple epiphenomena reducible to the economic 'base'. Thereby a specific study of the State becomes superfluous. Parallel with this, economism considers that every change in the social system happens first of all in the economy and that political action should have the economy as its principal objective. Once again, a specific study of the State is redundant."[48]

Such a methodological orientation leaves so little scope for overall dynamic analysis of situations that a number of neo-Marxists have argued that the treatment of the state is one of the weakest areas in much Marxist social science. As Ralph Miliband notes: "Marxists have made little notable attempt to confront the question of the state in the light of the concrete socio-economic *and* political *and* cultural reality of actual capitalist societies."[49]

However, there are neglected subthemes in Marx and Engels that, if read properly and applied to the special conditions of late developing,

46. Engels, *The Origin of the Family, Private Property, and the State* (New York: International Publishers, 1942), 292. The even more famous passage describing the withering away of the state is found in the second chapter of the third part of Engels's *Anti-Dühring*.
47. Nicos Poulantzas, "The Problem of the Capitalist State," *New Left Review*, no. 58 (Nov.–Dec. 1969), 74.
48. Ibid. 68.
49. See his *The State in Capitalist Society* (New York: Basii Books, 1969), 6, emphasis in the original. He cites a similar judgment made by Paul Sweezy. A major exception that should be made is the work of the Italian Communist party leader and theoretician Antonio Gramsci. His concepts of hegemony and class fractions will be discussed and used in later chapters. Miliband's book and especially Poulantzas's *Political Power and Social Classes* are important attempts to invigorate the Marxist analysis of the state.

dependent-capitalist societies such as those in Latin America, in fact provide much less theoretical foundation for the neglect of the state than do many conventional Marxist interpretations.

Classical Marxist writings give two major qualifications to the description of the state as a dependent variable: the nonhegemonic qualification and the qualification concerning the permanent tendency toward parasitic bureaucratic autonomy. Taken together, these should constitute an impressive a priori theoretical justification for considering the state as a major source of relatively independent political action even within the Marxist model.

Consider first the implications of the hegemony hypothesis. Engels asserts that the state "in all typical periods is exclusively the state of the ruling class." But how typical are "typical" periods? Apparently, for a period to be typical, a hegemonic class must exist. But how often does even Engels consider that there is a situation of class hegemony? His discussion of periods that are not typical merits quotation at length:

> By way of exception, however, periods occur in which the warring classes balance each other so nearly that the state power, as ostensible mediator, acquires, for the moment, a certain degree of independence of both. Such was the absolute monarchy of the seventeenth and eighteenth centuries, which held the balance between the nobility and the class of the burghers; such was the Bonapartism of the First, and still more of the Second French Empire, which played off the proletariat against the bourgeoisie and the bourgeoisie against the proletariat. The latest performance of this kind, in which ruler and ruled appear equally ridiculous, is the new German Empire of the Bismarck nation: here capitalists and workers are balanced against each other and equally cheated for the benefit of the impoverished Prussian cabbage junkers.[50]

Writing toward the end of the nineteenth century, Engels saw, therefore, much of the seventeenth and eighteenth centuries as nonhegemonic, and extensive periods in the nineteenth-century history of the two major European powers as characterized by nonhegemonic class relations.

Whether or not there is a hegemonic class or fraction of a class capable of ruling politically in any given situation is thus not to be assumed. Rather it is to be determined by empirical investigation of the relationship between the economic structure and the class structure and by a detailed analysis of the relationship between class fractions and the control of the state apparatus.[51]

50. Engels, *The Origin of the Family*, 290–1. In *The Civil War in France*, Marx gives a similar explanation of the rise of Bonapartism: "In reality, it was the only form of government possible at a time when the bourgeoisie had already lost, and the working class had not yet acquired, the faculty of ruling the nation," in *Selected Works*, i. 518.

51. The lack of hegemony is not only due to economic equilibrium. In fact Poulantzas argues that, due to the *normal* difficulties preventing the bourgeoisie from achieving sufficient unity to create their own hegemonic political organization, the "relative autonomy of the state" is a constituent feature of capitalism and in this sense Bonapartism is the "religion of the bourgeoisie"; *Political Power and Social Classes*, 281–5. Ralph Miliband, in his "The Capitalist State: Reply to Nicos Poulantzas," *New Left Review*, no. 59 (Jan.–Feb. 1970), 58, argues (correctly I think) that by labeling all capitalist states "Bona-

With reference to Latin America, numerous studies indicate that, within the context of late-industrializing, dependent economies, the national bourgeoisie has not been able to attain a hegemonic situation comparable to that achieved by the bourgeoisie in England, the United States, and some countries in Europe, *nor* has a hegemonic industrial proletariat emerged.

The reasons for the nonhegemonic class situation are complex but interrelated. The high degree of foreign ownership of industry reduces the relative size and power of the national bourgeoisie, while the national bourgeoisie itself often has a variety of credit, ownership, technological, and marketing dependency relationships with international capital. This, plus their frequent status as relatively recent immigrants, puts members of the national bourgeoisie in a weak political position to compete—in a nationalist environment—as an electoral force aiming at hegemonic acceptance for their position. The character of late dependent industrialization that has followed, not preceded, modernization means that, in comparison to Anglo-Saxon patterns, fewer workers are employed in industry at similar stages of development due to capital intensive methods, and the number of urban workers in the tertiary and marginal sectors is much higher. This pattern of industrialization has not been supportive of the consolidation of large, class-conscious, autonomous worker organizations.[52]

If something like this is in fact the case for much of Latin America and other parts of the Third World, then even from a Marxist perspective we should expect the state to play a large role in mediating conflict between nonhegemonic classes, and the question of the relative autonomy of the state apparatus should be central in any research strategy about politics in such systems.

The second major qualification about the state as a dependent variable in classical Marxism comes in the discussion by Marx and Engels of the tendency toward the parasitic autonomy of the bureaucratic apparatus of the state. Throughout their work they argue that, as class conflict intensifies, the repressive apparatus must become larger; this sets into motion a bureaucratic

partist" it is difficult to make the significant distinction between the meaning of "relative autonomy of the state" under fascism and under a social-democratic regime. At the very least, the debate highlights the fact that the creation of political domination via the state apparatus is the result of shifting coalitions of class fractions and that the forging (or nonforging) of a "hegemonic block" is a fit subject for independent analysis, whether by the political scientist, or—as in the case of Gramsci—by the Marxist party theoretician and tactician.

52. For an excellent discussion of the structure and ideology of the bourgeoisie under such conditions, see Fernando Henrique Cardoso, *Ideologías de la burguesía industrial en sociedades dependientes (Argentina y Brasil)* (Mexico: Siglo Veintuno Editors, 1971). For a comparison with the pattern in the United States and Europe see his "The Industrial Elite," in Seymour Martin Lipset and Aldo Solari (eds.), *Elites in Latin America* (New York: Oxford University Press 1967), 94–114. For a brief comparative study of labor in Europe and Latin America see Kenneth Paul Erickson and Patrick V. Peppe, "The Dynamics of Dependency: Industrial Modernization and Tightening Controls Over the Working Class in Brazil and Chile," paper prepared for the Latin American Studies Association, Nov. 1974, and Brian H. Smith and José Luis Rodríguez, "Comparative Working-Class Political Behavior: Chile, France, and Italy," *American Behavioral Scientist* (Sept. 1974).

momentum whereby the state apparatus tends to play roles more self-determining than that envisaged in any mechanistic model of the state as a passive and malleable instrument of class coercion. Indeed, Engels goes so far as to say that this "transformation of the state and the organs of the state from servants of society into masters of society" is "an inevitable transformation in all previous states."[53] The tendency toward relative state autonomy is thus not restricted to nonhegemonic situations. Indeed, Marx and Engels see it as an actual, not latent, tendency in any society where there is a division of labor and therefore the need for a repressive state. The numerous references by Marx and Engels to this phenomenon indicate that they took it seriously. Marx, for example, describes the state apparatus in nineteenth-century France as one in which the state "constantly maintains an immense mass of interests and livelihoods in the most absolute dependence; where the state enmeshes, controls, regulates, superintends and tutors civil society."[54]

If this is such a permanent tendency even under European conditions in a relatively well-developed civil society, one should expect that under twentieth-century Latin American conditions, where the state apparatus is often larger in comparison to civil society than it was in nineteenth-century Europe or North America, and where the state often "enmeshes, controls, regulates, superintends and tutors civil society," the problem would be even more acute.

Even in socialist societies a tendency toward bureaucratic aggrandizement rather than the hoped for withering away of the state is sufficiently prominent that it should be a central question for Marxist scholars.[55] Indeed, a major concern among some Marxists—especially Yugoslav Marxists—is, how to prevent the party-state apparatus from generating a new bureaucratic elite with special privileges that inhibit the evolution toward a more participatory, stateless communist society.[56]

53. Introduction to Marx's *Civil War in France, Selected Works*, i. 484.
54. Karl Marx, *The Eighteenth Brumaire of Louis Bonaparte*, in Marx and Engels, *Selected Works*, i. 284.
55. The League of Communists in Yugoslavia asserted, for example, that "bureaucratism is a great danger to socialism in the transition period," and warned against the tendency "of transforming the state into an all-embracing social force, a force above society which would in fact liquidate the direct social influence of the working masses on the policies of the state leadership—that is, the tendency of state idolatry." See *Yugoslavia's Way: The Program of the League of Communists of Yugoslavia*, translated by Stoyan Pribechevich (New York: All Nations Press, 1958), 117–18. Svetozar Stojanović deals with similar issues in "The Statist Myth of Socialism," in his *Between Ideals and Reality: A Critique of Socialism and its Future*, trans. Gerson S. Sher (New York: Oxford University Press, 1973), 37–75.
56. See, for example, Edvard Kardelj, "The Principal Dilemma: Self-Management or Statism," *Socialist Thought and Practice* (Belgrade) (Oct.–Dec. 1966), and Najdan Pašić, "Dictatorship by the Proletariat or over the Proletariat," *Socialist Thought and Practice* (Oct.–Dec. 1968). Other works by Marxist scholars which stress that the transition from socialism to communism cannot be assumed to be automatic and that it is particularly important for Marxists to analyze the state apparatus in socialist systems are Paul M. Sweezy, "Toward a Program of Studies of the Transition to Socialism," in Paul M. Sweezy and Charles Bettelheim (eds.), *On the Transition to Socialism* (New York: Monthly Review

A correct interpretation of what Marx and Engels say of the role of the state in nonhegemonic situations and of the permanent tendency toward parasitic bureaucratic autonomy means that any Marxist analysis of politics should devote extensive attention to the conditions in which the state acts with a significant degree of autonomy.

In the case of Latin America a number of central research questions flow from this discussion. For example, given a general context of late, dependent modernization that is relatively unsupportive for establishing class hegemony, how was a hegemonic block of class fractions nonetheless constructed in Mexico? The Marxist literature also often speaks of the role the state plays in the "reproduction of the means of production."[57] Analysis of this role as an independent variable becomes even more crucial when the question is that of the initial *production* by the state, rather than the mere *reproduction*, of the social and economic bases of capitalism. In such a case, as in Mexico, the state apparatus plays a central role in creating the political, ideological, and economic infrastructure necessary for the emergence of the national bourgeoisie. This raises extremely complex questions about the lines of domination in the relations between the state elite and the newly created economic elite.

Finally, what are the *limits* of the relative autonomy of the state? How far can a "revolution from above" by a fraction of the state apparatus (for example the military fraction in Peru) go in transforming economic and political structures?

The Organic-Statist Approach to the State[58]

All too often post-World War II political science references to the theory of the organic state are restricted to Hegel or to twentieth-century fascist or totalitarian regimes that proclaimed the supremacy of the state. This association

Press, 1971), 123–35; Herbert Marcuse, "The Dialectic of the Soviet State," in his *Soviet Marxism: A Critical Analysis* (New York: Vintage Books, 1961), 85–103, and the major study by Charles Bettelheim, *Class Struggles in the USSR: First Period; 1917–1923*, trans. Brian Pearce (New York: Monthly Review Press, 1977).

57. See for example the importance Louis Althusser attaches to this point in "Ideology and Ideological State Apparatuses" in his *Lenin and Philosophy and Other Essays* (New York: Monthly Review Press, 1971), 128–36.

58. The term *organic statism* needs some clarification. "Organic" here refers to a normative vision of the political community in which the component parts of society harmoniously combine to enable the full development of man's potential. "Statist" is used because of the assumption in this tradition that such harmony does not occur spontaneously in the process of historical evolution but rather requires power, rational choices, and decisions, and occasional restructuring of civil society by political elites. "Organic" in this context thus is quite different from either the historical organicism of Burke or the monist organicism of Leninism. Even though the word *state* is a relatively modern term, I have used it to capture the sense that the organic unity of civil society is brought about by the architectonic action of public authorities—hence "organic-statism."

contributes to the tendency to dismiss theoretical discussions of the state as belonging to a normatively aberrant and historically brief and closed epoch of political thought. Added to this negative moral and historical perception is a methodological critique. The concept of the state was often dismissed as a reification, as a nonquantifiable, Hegelian or medieval abstraction. Or, if it was acknowledged that the concept could refer to concrete governmental and bureaucratic agencies, the reductionist school of comparative politics tended to relegate the study of the state to the "legal-institutional-descriptive" school of traditional political science. Thus history, ethics, methodology, and scholarly fashion combined virtually to eliminate the state from the central concerns of modern political science.

Fashion and misguided methodology aside, this has been unfortunate. For of course there exists an important non-German approach to the state that greatly predates Hegel, and that, far from being philosophically aberrant, and despite its tendency toward authoritarian political formulas, has been a dominant strand of political thought since the time of Aristotle. Far from being historically closed, moreover, this approach is very much alive as a philosophical and structural influence, especially in southern Europe and the countries of Latin America. This corpus of political thought is not as textually and historically specific as classical Marxism or liberal pluralism. Nonetheless, there is a body of ideas running through Aristotle, Roman law, medieval natural law and into contemporary Catholic social philosophy that together make up what I call the organic-statist tradition of political thought.[59] As in the liberal-pluralist approach, the organic-statist approach has many, sometimes contradictory, variants. But just as a contemporary pluralist can select from Locke, Madison, de Tocqueville, Truman, and common law a reasonably coherent body of ideas stressing individualism, checks and balances, autonomous interest groups, and the central role of social forces, so a twentieth-century political theorist in Latin America can just as easily select out of Aristotle, Roman law, natural law, and the papal encyclicals a cumulative body of ideas stressing the political community, the concession theory of association, and the central role of the state in achieving the common good.[60] Both bodies of ideas have intellectual

59. Most contemporary political theory textbooks are interested in developing the body of ideas that have contributed to what is seen as the main line of historical evolution of the Anglo-Saxon (and to a lesser extent, French) political culture. There is a tendency to neglect the organic-statist tradition or to select out of it those aspects most relevant for the development of the liberal-pluralist tradition or that of its major contemporary opponent, the Marxist tradition. In many undergraduate courses, this means an ungainly leap from Aristotle to Machiavelli, in the process virtually leaving out a major component of the European cultural heritage.

60. Two important caveats: First, just as liberal pluralism has variants that are not in the main line of development, so does organic statism. Twentieth-century fascist and totalitarian movements are extreme variations of the approach. I argue in Chapter 2 of *The State and Society*, however, that in some fundamental ways these deviated from some of the basic ideas of organic statism and should not be considered essential to the model. Second, liberal pluralism and organic statism at times draw upon the same corpus of writing, such as Aristotle, but they select out of the corpus different elements. In the case

coherence and, as Charles W. Anderson has argued, a distinct "basic logic" as "paradigms of social choice."[61]

For liberal pluralism, the starting point is descriptive—the rational self-interest of the individual. For classic Marxism, the starting point is also descriptive—the dominant mode of production and its characteristic form of class struggle. For organic statism, the starting point is normative—the preferred form of political life of man as a member of a community.

From Aristotle to St. Thomas Aquinas to modern papal encyclicals, a central normative theme is that man's nature can only be fulfilled within a community. Thus Aristotle says: "The man who is isolated—who is unable to share in the benefits of political association, or has no need to share because he is already self-sufficient—is no part of the polis, and must therefore be either a beast or a god.... There is therefore an imminent impulse in all men towards an association of this order."[62] For Aristotle a corollary of man's political nature is the naturalness of political institutions. "It is evident that the polis belongs to the class of things that exist by nature, and that man is by nature an animal intended to live in a polis."[63]

A further corollary is that political institutions require order and power. Political authority as a concept is thus perceived as necessary and legitimate in the organic-statist tradition. Aquinas, for example, states that "law must needs concern itself properly with the order directed to universal happiness,"[64] and, "order principally denotes power."[65]

It is from this perspective of man's nature, as requiring for its happiness and fulfillment participation in a well-ordered political community, that Aristotle argued: "The polis is prior in the order of nature to the family and the individual. The reason for this is that the whole is necessarily prior [in

of Roman law, to take an example, liberal pluralism has drawn upon the rational individualistic aspects of the doctrine of contract, while the organic-statist tradition has drawn upon the concession theory and sovereignty doctrines that grant the state authority to define and promote the common good and charter associational groups. In the economic sphere, the liberal-pluralist selection of ideas is supportive of a market based economy, while the organic-statist selection of ideas is supportive of mercantilist economies.

61. He argues that: "A paradigm of public choice specifies the grounds that are appropriate for making claims within a given political order. It tells us about the kinds of arguments that are most likely to appear acceptable to political actors in arriving at policy conclusions. In this sense, it defines... the range of reasons that will be accepted as legitimate in political argument and debate." See his "Public Policy, Pluralism and the Future Evolution of Advanced Industrial Society," paper prepared for the 1973 Annual Meeting of the American Political Science Association, New Orleans, Sept. 4–8.

62. Aristotle, *Politics*, book I, ch. II, sect. 14, 15, pp. 6–7 (all references to Aristotle's *Politics* refer to the Barker translation). One of the key Vatican II documents, *Gaudium et Spes*, reiterated this theme: "by his innermost nature man is a social being, and unless he relates himself to others he can neither live nor develop his potential" (Article 12). Note however the stress is on man as a social being, not a political being.

63. Aristotle, *Politics*, book I, ch. II, sect. 9, p. 5.

64. Aquinas, *Summa Theologiae*, I–II, Question 90, Article 2, p. 612 (Pegis translation).

65. *Summa Theologiae*, III (Suppl.), Question 34, Article I.

nature] to the part. If the whole body be destroyed, there will not be a foot or a hand....'[66]

Taken together, these arguments about the political nature of man, the necessity and legitimacy of power, and the ontological status of the political community, make the role of the state much more functionally central and normatively legitimate in the organic-statist tradition than in either liberal pluralism or the Marxist tradition. However, the differences go even deeper. The Aristotelian, Thomistic, and natural law concept that is central to the organic-statist tradition is that the state has a moral end, it has a moral *telos*. This is a significant difference between organic statism and liberal pluralism. Liberal-pluralist writings stress the neutral procedures of government within which social groups compete to define goals and policies. Organic-statist writings emphasize the ends of government and are less concerned with procedural guarantees. While Aristotle does not deny the utilitarian or instrumental advantages of political life, he always emphasizes that the higher goal is moral. Thus the polis is not merely

an association for residence on a common site, or for the sake of preventing mutual injustices and easing exchange.... But it is the cardinal issue of goodness or badness in the life of the polis which always engages the attention of any state that concerns itself to secure a system of good law well obeyed.... Otherwise, a political association sinks into mere alliance... law becomes a mere covenant... "a guarantor of men's rights against one another"—instead of being, as it should be, a rule of life such as will make the members of a polis good and just.[67]

The moral center of the organic-statist vision is thus not the individual taken by himself but rather the political community whose perfection allows the individual members to fulfill themselves: "The end of the individual is the same as that of the political community... but, even so, the end of the political community is a greater thing to attain and maintain, and a thing more ultimate, than the end of the individual."[68]

The concern for the pursuit of the common good leads to a de-emphasis or rejection of procedural forms and to a rejection of the legitimacy of "private interests" even if these private interests represent the majority: "The true forms of government, therefore, are those in which the one, or the few, or the many, govern with a view to the common interest; but governments which rule with a view to the private interest, whether of the one, or of the few, or of the many, are perversions."[69]

A standard contemporary treatise of Catholic social philosophy characteristically assigns a central role to the common good: "The common good is the prevailing principle that controls any other interest in its order. It is the creative principle, the conserving power of the body politic; it is the final cause of the

66. *Politics*, book I, ch. II, sects. 12 and 13, p. 6.
67. *Politics*, book III, ch. IX, sects. 12 and 8, pp. 118–19.
68. *Ethics*, book I, ch. II, sect. 8 (Barker translation), p. 355.
69. *Politics*, book III, ch. VII, p. 139 (Jowett translation).

state, its intimate end, it and nothing else gives the political, sovereign power its moral authority and legitimacy."[70] It should be noted that this "common good," while by no means intrinsically antidemocratic, lends itself to nonliberal legitimacy formulas in organic statism for two basic reasons. First, it opens the possibility that, since the common good can be known by "right reason," there is no need for a process whereby interest groups express their opinions and preferences in order for the leaders of the state to "know" what the common good is. Second, as the quotation above indicates, the pursuit of the common good (rather than elections or representation by group interests) is the measure by which the legitimacy of the state is evaluated.

This vision of the common good and the organic political community has led in the nineteenth and twentieth centuries to a moral rejection by all variants of organic statism of both liberalism and Marxism. Marxism is rejected in part because its view of class conflict violates the organic-statist ideal of the harmonious community, which is to be constructed by political action. For example, Leo XIII, in *Rerum Novarum*, presents the following argument:

The great mistake made in regard to the matter now under consideration is to take up with the notion that class is naturally hostile to class, and that the wealthy and the workingmen are intended by nature to live in mutual conflict. So irrational and so false is this view, that the direct contrary is the truth. Just as the symmetry of the human frame is the resultant of the disposition of the bodily members, so in a State is it ordained by nature that these two classes should dwell in harmony and agreement, and should, as it were, groove into one another, so as to maintain the balance of the body politic.[71]

The liberal state and classical capitalism are likewise rejected because they lead to abuses and antagonism between classes, and because the state does not

70. Heinrich A. Rommen, *The State in Catholic Social Thought: A Treatise in Political Philosophy* (St Louis: B. Herder Book Co., 1945), 310. For a more extensive discussion, see the chapters "Organic View of the State," and "The State as a Moral Organism." Aquinas, in *Summa Theologiae*, I–II, Question 94, discusses the content of the common good when he analyzes the three ends of Natural Law, which right reason dictates governments should follow. Like Aristotle—but less strongly—he emphasizes that man's nature requires some political participation for fulfillment. However, of course, neither is democratic in a "one-man one-vote" sense, because there is a tension between the claims of political participation and the claims of the more basic principle of the common good.

71. Leo XIII, *Rerum Novarum* (1881), in Anne Freemantle (ed.), *The Papal Encyclicals in their Historical Context* (New York: New American Library, 1963), 174. After Vatican II, the Catholic Church softened substantially its doctrinal criticism of Marxism. Nonetheless, a close reading of recent church documents shows that the preferred social solution still is normally one that eschews both Marxist ideas of class conflict and liberal ideas of unchecked competition in favor of more "communitarian" formulas. Thus in Peru, for example, the current military regime's initial program of imposed structural change in order to bring about a solidarist society with full communal participation was explicitly endorsed by leading church figures as being consistent with "the major new social teaching of the church" (Interview with Bishop Bambarén in Lima, Nov. 12, 1972). The complex relationship of the post-Vatican II church to the organic-statist tradition will be developed further in later chapters. Also see Luigi Einaudi and Alfred Stepan, *Latin American Institutional Development: Changing Military Perspectives in Peru and Brazil* (Santa Monica, Calif.: Rand Corporation, 1971).

play its morally proper role of actively furthering the balance in the body politic by pursuing the common good. Thus, in the same encyclical, Leo XIII writes: "Some remedy must be found, and found quickly, for the misery and wretchedness pressing so heavily and unjustly at this moment on the vast majority of the working classes.... Workingmen have been surrendered, all isolated and helpless, to the hardheartedness of employers and the greed of unchecked competition."[72]

Forty years later, Pius XI, in his *Quadragesimo Anno (On Reconstructing the Social Order)*, commented that Leo XIII, faced with what he perceived as growing class conflict and disintegration of the social order, had

sought no help from either Liberalism or Socialism, for the one had proved that it was utterly unable to solve the social problem aright, and the other, proposing a remedy far worse than the evil itself, would have plunged human society into greater dangers.... With regard to civil authority, Leo XIII, boldly breaking through the confines imposed by Liberalism, fearlessly taught that government must not be thought a mere guardian of law and of good order, but rather must put forth every effort so that through the entire scheme of laws and institutions ... both public and individual well-being may develop spontaneously out of the very structure and administration of the State.[73]

The state in the organic-statist tradition is thus clearly interventionist and strong. However, it is important to understand that a just and stable organic order is not necessarily to be equated with the established order. The concept of the common good, with the moral obligation it imposes on the state to achieve the general welfare, leaves open the possibility that the state can formulate and impose on its own initiative major changes in the established order so as to create a more just society. From Aristotle to Aquinas to modern popes, there is therefore a strong normative tradition in organic-statist political thought in which the state is conceived of as playing a relatively autonomous, architectural role in the polity. A standard contemporary text of Catholic social theory, bearing the papal imprimatur, illustrates how the idea of imposed change and the need to create an organic order are closely interrelated:

A distortion in the social organism may disturb the balanced functioning and welfare of the whole. If this should occur, the supreme protector of the order, whatever its form, the state in that significant sense, has the right and duty to intervene.... Catholic political philosophy is aware ... that the actual *ordo*, through the shielding of vested interests, can become unjust, that the changing circumstances in social and economic life demand the abolition of unintended privileges

---

72. Ibid. 167.

73. Pius XI, *Quadragesimo Anno*, in Freemantle (ed.), *The Papal Encyclicals in their Historical Context*, 229–30. Further evidence of the strong directing role the state should exercise in order to contribute to the organic, harmonious society is found in Pius XII, *Summi Pontificatus (On the Function of the State in the Modern World*, 1939), where he argues "it is the noble prerogative and function of the State to control, aid, and direct the private and individual activities of national life that they converge harmoniously towards the common good." See Freemantle (ed.), *The Papal Encyclicals*, 266.

protected by the existing order; it knows, in other words, that the positive order may contradict the ideal order of peace and justice.

The order of laissez-faire capitalism thus has become unjust, creating unwarranted privileges of vested property rights against unjustly suppressed personal rights of the working classes. Formal right can, under our mode of existence, become material wrong. In these conditions the state needs power and must apply force for the sake of its own end.... *It must forcefully change parts of the actual order which have grown unjust . . . it must use force against the selfish resistance of the privileged interests that range themselves above the new and juster order.*[74]

Some of the paradoxes of contemporary Latin American politics become understandable if one keeps in mind this organic-statist principle, namely that the goal of a stable, organically integrated society might entail radical change in basic structures. The Peruvian military's "radical" land reform was organic-statist in this sense. The military perceived one class, the oligarchical land owners, as contributing to a revolutionary disintegration of society. In an action consistent with the implications of the organic-statist model, the military attempted to use their power to create a new organic relationship among Peruvians. The apparent radicalism of parts of the Catholic Church in Latin America also has strong organic-statist overtones. In 1968, the Latin American Bishops Conference endorsed the view that Latin America found itself in "a situation of injustice which could be termed one of institutionalized violence, because current structures violate fundamental rights creating a situation which demands global, bold, urgent, and profoundly renovating transformation."[75]

Thus in the organic-statist tradition of political thought, despite the concern for stability, there is a justification for rapid structural change and for a strong state that can impose this change. It is necessary, however, to note that two normative principles, in theory at least, are meant to restrict legitimate state action within the limits imposed by the concept of organic unity. The first principle is that, whatever its form, the state must pursue as its end the common good. For Aristotle, a government that did not rule with a view to the common interest was a "perversion." For Aquinas, an unjust law "seems to be no law at all." Consistent with this interpretation is the fact that the most extensive arguments for "tyrannicide" are found in the works of natural law theorists who stress that the ruler must always rule within the limits imposed by natural law.[76]

The second, and historically more important, principle is that, although the state is the most perfect political community, all the component parts

74. Rommen, *The State in Catholic Thought*, 203, 292 (emphasis added).

75. CELAM (Consejo Episcopal Latinoamericano), *Documento Final de la Comisión No. I*, Subcommittee II, sect. III (Bogota, Sept. 1968).

76. The most coherent and explicit development of this theme is found in the work of the 16th-century political theorist Francisco Suárez; see Bernice Hamilton, *Political Thought in Sixteenth-Century Spain: A Study of the Political Ideas of Vitoria, De Soto, Suárez, and Molina* (Oxford: Oxford University Press, 1963), esp. 61–6.

(individual, family, private association) have a proper function of their own within the organic whole. Thus each part has a sphere of natural action that the state should not eliminate. Since the 1930s this concept has been explicitly referred to as "the principle of subsidiarity." A recent restatement by John XXIII shows that it is still meant to be a limiting parameter to what he saw as the necessarily increasing role of the state in the furtherance of the common good:

This intervention of public authorities that encourages, stimulates, regulates, supplements, and complements, is based on the *principle of subsidiarity* as set forth by Pius XI in his Encyclical *Quadragesimo Anno*: "It is a fundamental principle of social philosophy, fixed and unchangeable, that one should not withdraw from individuals and commit to the community what they can accomplish by their own enterprise and industry. So, too, it is an injustice and at the same time a grave evil and a disturbance of right order, to transfer to the larger and higher collectivity functions which can be performed and provided for by lesser and subordinate bodies. Inasmuch as every social activity should, by its very nature, prove a help to members of the body social, it should never destroy or absorb them."[77]

The subsidiarity principle is the central feature that distinguishes the concept of "organic" in the organic-statist model from the concept of "organic" in the Leninist model of "command socialism." In contrast to liberal pluralism, both the organic-statist and Leninist models give an important place to the concept of organic political unity and give the state a major role to perform in achieving such unity. In Lenin's command-socialist model, however, the organic unity can emerge only after the dictatorship of the proletariat has abolished all elements of subsidiarity. For Lenin, "harmonious organization" is the end result of the total penetration and transformation of all units of society.

The resolution adopted by the recent Moscow Congress of the Soviets advanced as the primary task of the moment the establishment of a "harmonious organization," and the tightening of discipline. Everyone now readily "votes for" and "subscribes to" resolutions of this kind; but usually people do not think over the fact that the application of such resolutions calls for coercion—coercion precisely in the form of dictatorship. And yet it would be extremely stupid and absurdly utopian to assume that the transition from capitalism to socialism is possible without coercion and without dictatorship....

The foundation of socialism—calls for absolute and strict *unity of will*, which directs the joint labour of hundreds, thousands and tens of thousands of people.... Revolution demands—precisely in the interests of its development and consolidation, precisely in the interests of socialism—that the people *unquestioningly obey the single will* of the leaders of labour.[78]

---

77. John XXIII, *Mater et Magistra* (*Christianity and Social Progress*, 1961), in Anne Freemantle, (ed.), *The Social Teachings of the Church* (New York: New American Library, 1963), 228–9. In Aristotle and Aquinas there is less emphasis on the rights of the parts against the whole. This emphasis in the modern church is a response to the secular claims of the liberal state and the total penetration claims of Marxism–Leninism.

78. V. I. Lenin, "The Immediate Tasks of Government," in V. I. Lenin, *Selected Works*, 3 vols. (Moscow: Progress Publishers, 1970), 420, 424–5 (emphasis in original).

Such a model of the unified political community is built upon a monist relationship between the party-state and the citizens in which intermediate groups are perceived as serving neither a necessary nor a legitimate function. Thus, in *The State and Revolution*, Lenin argues: "accounting and control—that is the *main* thing required for 'arranging' the smooth working, the correct functioning of the *first phase* of communist society. *All* citizens are transformed here into hired employees of the state, which consists of the armed workers. *All* citizens become employees and workers of a *single* nation-wide state 'syndicate'.... The whole of society will have become a single office and a single factory, with equality of labor and equality of pay."[79]

This distinction between the view of the organic community in command socialism and organic statism is so fundamental that it is one of the distinguishing characteristics of each as an analytic model, as I show in the concluding section of this chapter.

In terms of organic-statist normative theory, we have stated the main concepts: the political nature of man, the goal of the organically related community in which the subsidiary parts play a legitimate and vital role, the state's proper role in interpreting and promoting the common good, and the radical changes the state may legitimately impose to create an organic society. Any political tendency, if it is more than just a body of ideas, is however an amalgam of articulated norms and empirically identifiable sets of structures and practices.

A particularly influential set of structures and practices that are normatively congruent—and, in the Iberic and Latin American countries, historically associated—with the organic-statist tendency is Roman law. For our purposes, the impact of Roman law on interest association is especially salient. The Greek idea that the public common interest should prevail, and that organized private interests should be allowed only the freedom consistent with the organic functioning of society, took on new significance when transferred from the city-state to the context of the bureaucratic-state of the Roman Empire. Here, in the name of organic relationships, the statist element became extremely strong. The core assumption of group pluralists such as Bentley that the polity is composed of groups that are "freely combining, dissolving and recombining in accordance with their interest lines," is normatively and empirically alien to the Roman law "concession theory" of association. In contrast to group-pluralist ideas that interest groups are unchartered, Roman law posited that groups had to be "chartered" by the state. As the German legal historian Rudolph Sohm observed. "With but few exceptions all societies were, on

79. (Moscow: Foreign Language Publishing House, n.d.), 161–2 (emphasis in original). He immediately adds that "this 'factory' discipline... is by no means our ideal, or our ultimate goal. It is but a necessary step for the purpose of thoroughly purging society of all infamies and abominations of capitalist exploitation, and for further progress." After the dictatorship of the proletariat has completed its tasks "then the door will be open for the transition from the first phase of the communist society to its higher phase, and with it to the complete withering away of the state."

principle, prohibited. The law recognized no freedom of association. Only those societies were lawful which owed their existence to lex specialis, or 'privilege.' A lawful society—such was the view taken—cannot be the creation of a private individual; it can only be the creation of the State operating through the medium of a statute."[80]

In exchange for the privilege of official recognition, the association accepted obligations that in essence made it "part of the organization of the State."[81] Emile Durkheim, often mistakenly seen as an advocate of authoritarian corporatism, decried the impact of such controls on the workers' groups in Roman society because, he argued, "they ended by becoming part of the administrative machine. They fulfilled official functions; each occupation was looked upon as a public service whose corresponding corporation had obligations and responsibilities towards the State."[82]

In the late Roman Empire, and later in the Iberian and Latin American countries, this concession theory of interest groups, utilized in the name of organic unity, has given the state an important lever by which to shape the scope and content of demands articulated by interest groups.[83] Indeed, the concession theory also has provided the normative rationale for the complex mechanisms by which the state itself creates and charters interest groups from above, often leaving a structural legacy of high responsiveness on the part of interest groups to demands orginating from the state.[84]

One last historical-empirical note concerning the organic-statist tradition must be added. In the liberal-pluralist tradition, the absolutist period is seen as

80. Rudolph Sohm, *The Institutes: A Textbook of the History and System of Roman Private Law*, trans. J. C. Ledlie, 2nd edn., rev. (Oxford: Clarendon Press, 1901), 198–9.

81. Ibid. 199.

82. Preface to the Second Edition, "Some Notes on Occupational Groups," in Emile Durkheim, *The Division of Labor in Society*, trans. G. Simpson (New York: Free Press, 1964), 8.

83. This will be a major theme that is developed later in the book. For the argument that the establishment of state control of associations in the Roman Empire was motivated by "fears for public order" see W. W. Buckland, *Roman Law and Common Law: A Comparison in Outline* (Cambridge: Cambridge University Press, 1936), 53. For a discussion and documentation of the influence of Roman Law concession theory in Spanish America, see Ronald C. Newton, "On 'Functional Groups,' 'Fragmentation,' and 'Pluralism' in Spanish American Political Society," *Hispanic American Historical Review* (Feb. 1970), esp. 16–17.

84. Note that it is the restrictive chartering by the state rather than its role in association creation that is most analytically relevant for the question of the degree of subsequent autonomy. For example, the state may play a crucial role in the growth of associations, as in the case of the U.S. government's support for union organization given by the Wagner act. But, because the state did not at the same time build in extensive control mechanisms the unions subsequently became relatively autonomous sources of countervailing power. See, for example, J. K. Galbraith, *American Capitalism: The Concept of Countervailing Power*, rev. edn. (London: Hamish Hamilton, 1957), 128, 135–53. Contrast Galbraith's account with that by Kenneth Paul Erickson, "Corporative Controls of Labor in Brazil," paper delivered at 1971 annual meeting of the American Political Science Association, Chicago. The construction of control mechanisms—and the subsequent system-level consequences of these mechanisms—is discussed later in this book in relation to the Vargas and Cárdenas governments.

one of attack on the medieval church and feudal structures, laying the ground-work for the modern liberal constitutional state, which in turn put checks on absolutist power. In Iberian countries and their ex-colonies, however, absolutism, though it existed, was different in two key respects. First, because the Iberian peninsula did not experience the Reformation in full force, in the period of centralizing monarchy an effort was made to reconcile the principles of absolutist statecraft with natural law traditions. Second, because these countries did not fully experience the socioeconomic processes that accompanied the inauguration of the liberal constitutional state, the absolutist legacy in government and bureaucracy further strengthened the statist components of the organic-statist tradition.[85]

Intellectual awareness of organic statism furthers several analytical causes. Roman law and natural law were the predominant ingredients of the intellectual and political heritage of European philosophy since shortly after Christ until at least the sixteenth century. Many of the basic institutions of Western society—legal systems, bureaucracies, interest groups—were for much of modern history decisively shaped by organic statism and to this day, even in the non-Catholic countries of Western Europe, there are still understudied structural legacies. In addition, as one of the classic Western formulations of the relationship between the state and society, this body of ideas remains "available" for use and adaptation everywhere in the western European cultural area. It provides an intellectual framework for understanding movements, legitimacy formulas, administrative devices, and regimes that have been influenced by this tradition of political thought.

The organic-statist model seems to me to be particularly suitable for partial incorporation into analyses of political development when studying the Latin American pattern of development, where, as I have indicated, the strong normative and empirical tradition of government-chartered interest groups contrasts with some of the basic assumptions of pluralist associational patterns, and where the pattern of delayed dependent development has, from a Marxist perspective, contributed to nonhegemonic class relations that often give the state apparatus some autonomy.

My working hypothesis is that many of the political elites in Latin America have in fact responded to their perceptions of impending crises of modernization and control by invoking, in a variety of modern forms, many of the central ideas of the organic-statist, non-liberal, non-Marxist model of state–society relations described here, and have attempted to use the power of the state to forge regimes with marked corporatist characteristics.

85. Sohm comments on the absolutist attitude toward association: "from the sixteenth century onwards the system of absolutist government, with its rigorous control of private life, struck root in Germany as elsewhere. Such a system was obviously quite as hostile to private societies as the Roman monarchy. It refused altogether to recognize the principle of free association, and required the sanction of the State for the formation of any society whatsoever." Sohm, *The Institutes*, 200.

Organic Statism as a Model of Governance

Organic statism as presented thus far in this chapter has coherence as a normative and historical tendency in political theory, as an ideology, and as a description of one possible mode of articulation between society and the state. In this concluding section, I wish to shift from normative, historical and concrete questions of organic statism to consider organic statism more abstractly as a model of governance. We will be particularly interested in two questions: first, how does it compare with other models, such as classic liberalism or "command socialism"?[86] Second, what predicaments, tensions, or inherent contradictions exist within organic statism as a model?

As models of governance, command socialism and classic liberalism seem to arrive at "optimal" solutions by maximizing different principles of coordination. Classic liberalism, in theory, maximizes information, self interest, freedom, and competition to arrive at maximum economic efficiency and political equilibrium. Command socialism, in theory, maximizes control of the economy by state planning and achieves a perfectly integrated, monist political community by eliminating the autonomy of all groups and by building new collectivist values and structures. Organic statism in contrast, as a model of governance, does not maximize any of the polar principles of coordination of the two other modes of articulation between state and society. Such crucial features of organic-statism as the "concession theory" of private associations involve a far more interventionist role for the state in politics than posited in classical liberalism. However the "principle of subsidiarity" posits less penetration of society by the state in organic statism than that posited by command socialism. Organic statism, in theory, accords an important role for the decentralized political participation of semi-autonomous functional groups. This role is absent in the Leninist version of the harmonious organization of the political community in command socialism. The model of organic statism implies "limited pluralism" in the community, while the model of command socialism implies a "monist" community.

In classic liberalism the economic principle of coordination that is maximized is individual competition in the market; in command socialism it is centralized state planning. Organic-statist concepts of the priority of the political community and of the state's responsibility for the common good imply strong constraints on laissez-faire market individualism. However, the principle of subsidiarity implies equally strong limitations on the legitimacy of the state to act as the chief power of the means of production and chief planner of the economy.

---

86. I originally considered classic Marxism as an analytic approach to the state in capitalist societies. However, here I am concerned with the Leninist model of the state as an instrument to forge socialism. To use a more generic term than Leninism, I call such a model "command socialism." I have already considered some of the features of such a model in the extensive quotations from Lenin.

An economic formula congruent with organic statism is thus one in which the state plays a decisive role in constructing the parameters, rules, and infrastructure of a market economy. In addition, the limits to "egoistic individualism" and "state centralism" posited in the model leads to a key role for intermediate self-managing "labor-capital" functional groups that are assumed to be a modern organic-statist industrial formula for arriving at the harmonious integration of the component parts of the economy.

To present graphically the differences between organic statism, command socialism, and classical liberalism as models of governance, we can place each model on a grid, illustrating the means through which political and economic goals are determined. (See Figure 2.1.)

Although no concrete regimes fit these abstract models completely, Apter has shown that, on analytic grounds alone, each of his somewhat similar polar models predictably faces characteristic tensions and predicaments. The predicament of classic liberalism is that some groups in society (including the government "group") may obtain greater political and economic power than others, upsetting the "perfect competition" assumed by the model. The predicament of command socialism is that coercion may become so high, and the flow of information so low, that distortions and irrationality affect both the economic and political system.[87]

Although in theory organic statism may represent a desirable balance between the two poles of classic liberalism and command socialism, in actuality it too contains inherent predicaments as a model. On the one hand, the statist component of the model implies a strong role for the state in structuring

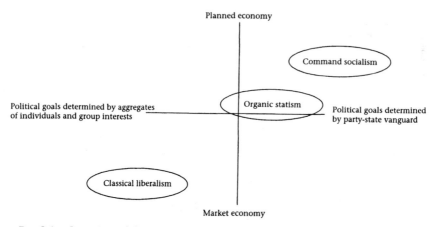

FIG. 2.1. Location of three models in terms of means through which political and economic goals are determined

87. Apter calls his polar models "the secular-liberatarian model" and the "sacred-collectivity model." For his presentation of these models with their characteristic predicaments, see *The Politics of Modernization*, esp. 28–36.

society so that it conforms with the model's assumption of functional parts that are perfectly integrated into a solidaristic whole. The role of the state is to ensure this integration between the parts and the whole. On the other hand, each of the parts is theoretically self-managing, so that there is a high degree of participation within state-chartered, organic structures. The predictable distorting tension in the model is that in the initial construction of the system from above, the state, in order to ensure integration and control, builds such strong control mechanisms into the new state-chartered functional groups that the meaningful participation posited by the model never becomes a reality. In later chapters I discuss numerous examples of concrete corporatist structures imposed from above by the state in which actual autonomy and participation is severely restricted. This, then, is the almost inherent distorting tension in organic statism stemming from the statist component of the model.

The other tension stems from the organic-participatory component of the model. If self-managing groups are in fact allowed to exercise a degree of decentralized autonomy, some groups may acquire political or economic control over others, and this violates the model's presupposition of organic harmony between the different functional groups within society. Thus either self-management and autonomy is allowed and the goal of intergroup balance and harmony is violated, or the state imposes restrictions on self-management and violates the supposition of decentralized group autonomy.[88]

Political elites who attempt to create systems that approximate the organic-statist model commonly come to power, as we shall see, in the context of elite perceptions of crises in pluralist systems and the failure of self-regulating mechanisms. In response to this perceived crisis, the role of the state is broadened and the perceived "responsibility" for the direction of the national economy is shifted from pluralist mechanisms of self-regulation to statist mechanisms. Yet, while the state comes to be considered responsible for the success or failure of the new order, the inherent limitations to state power that are implied in the organic statist model may seriously impede its ability to

---

88. The organic-statist model, purely as a model, faces other logical and empirical problems. First, there are no obvious criteria for assigning exact representational weight to functional groups. Whatever criteria are selected there is the danger of over-enfranchising some functional groups while disenfranchising important nonfunctional groups based on ethnic, religious, linguistic, or regional identities. Second, the model assumes that vertical functional groups are the "natural" organic representational vehicles of modern society. However, in a complex modern society this is probably a more "artificial" representational vehicle than are broader, horizontal parties and movements. Third, multinational corporations challenge the very idea of an organic-statist society, but some of their major structures lie beyond the organizational formulas of organic statism. For a discussion of the first two problems along these lines, see Max Weber's section on "Representation by the Agents of Interest Groups," in Talcott Parsons (ed.), *The Theory of Social and Economic Organizations* (New York: Free Press of Glencoe, 1964), 421–3, and Juan Linz's "Totalitarian and Authoritarian Regimes," in Fred Greenstein and Nelson Polsby (eds.), *Handbook of Political Science*, 9 vols. (Reading, Mass.: Addison Publishing, 1975), iii. 175–441. I discuss the problems presented for the model by multinational corporations in Ch. 7, of *The State and Society*.

achieve success. The new, controlled, functional group process posited by the model may never be brought into being because of the power and autonomy of major groups in society that emerged during the phase of pluralist politics. Short of totalitarian or revolutionary mobilization and penetration, it may be impossible for a state elite to restructure such existing interest groups. But such mobilization and penetration would not only be a violation of the model on theoretical grounds but would also risk alienating the original coalition that supported the state elite on the supposition that limited pluralism would be respected and mass mobilization avoided. The new organic-statist regime may thus be caught in the contradictions that flow from its intermediate position within the full range of alternative models of articulation between state and society.

Apart from this contradiction in the political sphere, organic-statist regimes face a parallel contradiction in the economic sphere. They commonly commit themselves to an intermediate statist model that is "neither capitalist nor communist," by replacing private initiative with overall public regulation in economic life, at the same time retaining the marketplace as the basic mechanism for distributing goods and services. They retain a system that is heavily dependent on entrepreneurial initiative and market flows, while to some extent undermining both. In the economic sphere, as in the political sphere, they may thus face the problems of both of the principal alternative models, while benefiting from the advantages of neither.

Partly because of these inherent tensions in the abstract model of organic statism, in most concrete cases of regimes that initially announce organic-statist principles, there is a political tendency to move toward greater control over groups via manipulative corporatist politics (especially with regard to working class groups) than is theoretically posited in the model, and there is a tendency in economic policy to allow greater entrepreneurial freedom for capitalism than is posited in the model. Such regimes thus become authoritarian-corporatist capitalist regimes.[89]

Yugoslavia acquired added theoretical and political importance because it was an attempt to introduce greater degrees of self-management into the command socialist model. Tanzania became particularly important because of its endeavor to find a formula to reconcile revolutionary power in a one-party state with a significant degree of binding accountability of the rulers to the ruled.[90] Similarly, the Peruvian experiment gained special significance

89. Such concrete regimes are a subtype of Linz's general category of 'authoritarian' as opposed to "democratic" or "totalitarian" regimes, in that they possess *limited*, but not *responsible*, pluralism. For his typological contrast between "democratic," "authoritarian" and "totalitarian" regimes see his initial statement "An Authoritarian Regime: Spain," in Erik Allardt and Stein Rokkan (eds.), *Mass Politics: Studies in Political Sociology* (New York: Free Press, 1970), 251–83, 374–81.

90. For a perceptive analysis of the achievements and limits of Tanzania's 1965 election campaign for posts within the one-party system in which 22 out of 31 party office-holders were unsuccessful and 16 out of 31 MPs lost, see Henry Bienen, *Tanzania: Party*

because it represented an attempt to develop new possibilities, and to resolve some of the central predicaments within a major model of governance—organic statism.

Transformation and Economic Development, expanded ed. (Princeton: Princeton University Press, 1970), 382–405. I discuss self-management in Yugoslavia in ch. 6 of *The State and Society*.

THREE

State Power and the Strength of Civil Society in the Southern Cone of Latin America

Society-centered views of political and economic transformation have never held the unchallenged sway in Latin America that they have in North America. The prevalence of "organic statist" models of society that assume a central and relatively autonomous role for the state has affected both policy makers and social scientists.[1] Beginning in the late 1960s, focus on the state became particularly intense. The erosion of the intellectual credibility of the society-centered "modernization" model of political and economic development coincided with the apparent exhaustion of both industrialization based on import substitution and the associated populist and parliamentary political regimes that were associated with it.[2] The assumptions of modernization theory that liberal democratic regimes would be inexorably produced by the process of industrialization was replaced by a new preoccupation with the ways in which the state apparatus might become a central instrument for both the repression of subordinate classes and the reorientation of the process of industrial development. This new concern is perhaps best exemplified in the seminal work of Guillermo O'Donnell on bureaucratic authoritarian (BA) regimes.[3] A BA regime was associated with (if not necessarily responsible for) an

1. Alfred Stepan, *The State and Society: Peru in Comparative Perspective* (Princeton: Princeton University Press, 1978), ch. 1.
2. See Fernando Henrique Cardoso and Enzo Faletto, *Dependence and Development in Latin America* (Berkeley: University of California Press, 1979).
3. See Guillermo O'Donnell, *Modernization and Bureaucratic Authoritarianism: Studies in South American Politics*, Institute of International Studies, Politics of Modernization Series, no. 9 (Berkeley: University of California press, 1973). See also G. O'Donnell, "Reflections on the Patterns of Change in the Bureaucratic-Authoritarian State," *Latin American Research Review*, 13 (1978), 3–38. He later elaborates what he considers the eight principal characteristics of bureaucratic authoritarianism as a type of authoritarian state in his "Tensions in the Bureaucratic-Authoritarian State and Question of Democracy," in David

This chapter was first published in Peter B. Evans, Dietrich Rueschemeyer, and Theda Skocpol (eds.), *Bringing the State Back in* (Cambridge: Cambridge University Press, 1985), 317–43.

impressive episode of industrialization (in the Brazilian case). Such regimes also proved to be extremely effective at fragmenting, atomizing, and inhibiting potential oppositional collectivities. The initial period of the BA was one in which the civil society lost its capacity to generate new political and economic initiatives while the power of the state grew. Thus, analysis of the actions and initiatives of groups operating within the state apparatus became a central focus of social science research. In my own case, for example, I focused on the military as an institution: first, on the forces that led it to take on the role of military as government and then on the contradictions involved in its attempts to carry out this role while simultaneously maintaining its coherence as an "institution."[4]

Bureaucratic authoritarian regimes are still with us, but if the 1960s was the decade of the exhaustion of the easy stage of import substituting industrialization and parliamentary democracy in the southern cone, the 1980s appears to hold the promise of the "exhaustion" of the BA regime. These regimes are currently beset both by problems of political legitimacy and by an apparent inability to deal with the international economic context of the 1980s. Their difficulties have stimulated new interest in the interaction between civil society and the state in authoritarian contexts. The state itself, the goals of those who control it, the contradictions within it and its continued capacity for repression and economic transformation remain tremendously important. At the same time, however, initiatives for change, insofar as such initiatives exist at all, are coming increasingly from within civil society. The role of the political opposition in shaping the future strategies of the state must be taken more explicitly into account. Likewise, the ways in which state structures and strategies define the options and strategies of the political opposition must be given close attention.

The aim here is to look at the reciprocal relations between the power of the state and the power of civil society. At the grossest level of abstraction there are four possibilities. The first, and most obvious, has already been noted. The growth of state power may be accompanied in zero-sum fashion by a diminution of the power of civil society. It also is possible for the power relations between the state and civil society to be positive-sum. The interaction may also prove to be negative-sum. The state's capacity to structure outcomes may decline while the opposition's capacity to act in concert also declines. Finally, of course, there is the possibility that the power of actors operating outside the state apparatus may grow while that of those working within the state declines.

In this chapter, I explore variations in the power relations between the state and civil society through a consideration of the four countries of the southern cone in Latin American, namely, Chile, Uruguay, Argentina, and Brazil. As a

Coller (ed.), *The New Authoritarianism in Latin America* (Princeton: Princeton University Press, 1979), 291–4.

4. See Alfred Stepan, *The Military in Politics: Changing Patterns in Brazil* (Princeton: Princeton University Press, 1971); Stepan, *The State and Society*.

group they share some important characteristics. In the 1960s or 1970s all four countries witnessed the advent of new, more pervasive forms of authoritarian rule. The new authoritarianism in all four countries followed periods of extensive but faltering industrialization and was installed in an atmosphere of growing class conflict. In each country the bourgeoisie provided the social base for the new authoritarian regimes whose first political acts were the use of the coercive apparatus of the state (located institutionally in the army) to dismantle and disarticulate working class organizations. In all four countries there was a major effort to restructure capitalism, though the concrete means of achieving such restructuring varied greatly from country to country.

All four of these regimes began with periods in which the institutions of civil society were emasculated while the state enhanced its ability to pursue its own goals, but the subsequent history of the relations between the authoritarian state and civil institutions has differed considerably among the four cases.[5] Only in Brazil do we find even a brief positive-sum period in which civil society began to reconstitute its institutions while the state continued to acquire additional capacity. In Chile, eight years of authoritarian rule passed without significant movement out of the initial authoritarian situation; civil society remained debilitated in the face of the strength of the state, though recently there seems to have been some weakening of the relative power of the state. In Uruguay, the initial period was followed by a period of stagnation in which neither the state nor civil society increased its capacity to achieve its goals. Finally, Argentina from 1979 to 1981 moved in the direction of a negative-sum interaction in which the power of civil society and the state declined simultaneously. Only after the defeat in Malvinas did civil institutions begin to recompose themselves, and then in the context of a dramatic decline in the capacity of the military regime.

It is not my purpose in this essay to provide a complete and balanced comparative history for each of the BAs, and thus there is no attempt to make observations at "comparable" moments of each BA. Rather, I am using the four countries to illuminate different dilemmas that the democratic opposition faces in its struggle against quite different BA state alliances. In the discussion that follows I hope to provide some heuristically fruitful suggestions as to the ways in which variations in the nature of the state apparatus and in the structure of civil society have led to such different outcomes in each of the four countries.

By discussing four authoritarian states that share some important characteristics, I also hope to illuminate how the relative autonomy of the authoritarian

---

5. This essay was written originally in the beginning of 1982. The major part of the fieldwork on which it is based was done in 1981 and 1982. Although I have updated the discussion to include some reference to events in 1983, I have left the analysis of the crucial events of 1984 (e.g., the opposition's electoral victory in Uruguay, the massive campaign for direct elections in Brazil, and Alfonsín's removal of recalcitrant members of the higher command in Argentina) for another occasion.

state apparatus is highly fluid and is affected by certain factors. For example, how much direct political (or, in extreme cases, economic) power are the state's bourgeois allies willing to abdicate in a brumairian sense[6] in return for defensive protection? Since coercion is a major component of an exclusionary authoritarian regime such as a BA, why and how can some types of fused or divided power among the chief executive, the three branches of the military, and the major intelligence forces increase or decrease relative state autonomy? How and why can struggles within these elements of the state apparatus create space for the opposition? Since bureaucratic routines and statutes are an important dimension of state control of civil society, is it possible that some routines or statutes adopted for a particular set of state purposes in fact also facilitate new forms of collective action and power creation in civil society?

Growth of State Power and the Decline of Civil Society: Chile, 1973–1981

In 1973–81, in only one of the four authoritarian states in the southern cone, namely, Chile, did state power grow while the power of civil society declined. The possibility of such a trajectory depended on several interrelated factors. First, the intensity of class conflict during the period that preceded the regime made it relatively easy for the regime to gain acceptance of its "project" in the upper and middle classes. Equally important, fear of the possible recomposition of the Marxist opposition helped maintain the internal cohesion of the state apparatus itself. The nature of the state's "project" was also important. By focusing on the problem of domination and carefully designing its efforts at economic transformation so that their primary effect would be to reinforce the project of domination, the Chilean state managed to enhance its power over civil society.

In any regime, but especially in a BA regime, the capacity to lead the regime's political allies depends on the degree to which the regime has both "defensive" and "offensive" projects that potential allies consider to be feasible, crucial for the preservation and advancement of their own interests, and dependent on authoritarian power for their execution. Since coercion is a particularly important part of the regime's power, the degree of internal institutional cohesion of the repressive apparatus is also a key variable. The Chilean regime was strong in all these respects for almost the entire period between 1973 and 1981.

In Chile, the social and institutional groups in control of the state convinced their potential allies that they had a vital "defensive" project (continued

6. Karl Marx, in "The Eighteenth Brumaire," described as one of the characteristics of the Bonapartist regime the abdication by the bourgeoisie of its right to rule in exchange for other kinds of protection by the ensuing strong state. Here, I use the word "brumairian" to evoke the kind of relation described in Marx's essay.

repression of the Marxist Left and its "Kerenskyite" Christian Democratic forms). They also convinced their allies that they had an "offensive" *foundational* project that, if fully implemented by the turn of the century, would restructure Chilean capitalism and civil society so that a stable market economy would emerge, one capable of withstanding the reintroduction of some representative features of government.[7] This "radical" liberal market project included a modified constitution giving the state apparatus residual emergency powers to repress civil society and enforce the economic rules of the game. From 1973 to 1980 both the economic team and the coercive core of the state apparatus demonstrated a surprising degree of internal unity under the leadership of General Pinochet, who showed considerable ability to integrate diverse groups of the power bloc.

The regime's capacity to lead its allies was manifest in the plebiscite called by General Pinochet to ratify the highly authoritarian constitution in September 1980. Among other things, the new constitution called for the beginning of an eight-year "constitutional" term for Pinochet, from 1981 to 1989, with extremely easy procedures for renewing the term for another eight years.

The plebiscite was announced on August 10 and was held on September 10. In the first two weeks following the announcement, virtually all of the more than twenty major producer groups in Chile issued a manifesto urging an affirmative vote to ratify the constitution and paid to have their manifesto published in *El Mercurio*. Most major opposition groups issued manifestos urging a no vote in the plebiscite, and these, too, were published in *El Mercurio*.

Analysis of the newspaper in the thirty days leading up to the plebiscite fails to reveal a single producer group urging a negative vote or even a somewhat qualified yes. The language of the producer groups' manifestos was replete with references to the necessary defensive and offensive tasks of the regime. Most manifestos referred to what were seen to be the chaotic and threatening conditions of 1973 and indicated that a return to such conditions would follow a no vote. In almost all the manifestos it was argued that the social and economic project of the regime constituted a structural attack on the pre-1973 conditions and required a substantially longer period of exceptional rule to make the regime's changes irreversible. Most of the rightist groups in civil society, especially women's organizations and professional associations, remobilized their followers during the plebiscite campaign. Gallup Polls taken before the plebiscite showed that, of seven possible categories of satisfaction with the general direction of the regime's policy, 100 percent of the upper class (but only 45 percent of the middle class) located themselves in the top three categories. The level of upper-class fear was likewise high. In answer to a multiple-choice

---

7. The best overall analysis of the foundational aspirations of the Chilean regime is found in Manuel Antonio Garretón, *El Proceso Político Chileno* (Santiago, Chile: FLACSO, 1983), 131–72. A useful examination of the ideological dimensions of the foundational project in its early phases is found in Tomás Moulián and Pilar Vergara, "Estado, Ideología y Políticas Económicas en Chile: 1973–1978," *Estudios CIEPLAN*, no. 3 (June 1980).

questionnaire by the Gallup Poll of Chile on the consequences of a no vote on the new constitution, 58.8 percent of the upper class (and only 33.2 percent of the middle class) indicated that the worst outcome would result, namely, "return to the year 1973."[8]

The persistence of fear within the upper bourgeoisie was an important element in the bourgeoisie's willingness to accept individual policies that hurt the upper class (there were numerous bankruptcies of domestic firms following the drastic tariff reductions and the decline of consumer purchasing power) but were seen to be the necessary cost of protecting its overall interests. It is impossible to understand the passivity of the industrial fraction of the bourgeoisie in Chile (a passivity that, of course, increased the policy autonomy of the state) outside of the context of fear.

An important indication of the upper bourgeoisie's willingness to abandon some of its independent political instruments for advancing its interests was its closure of the traditional party, the Partido Nacional, in 1973. For almost a decade there was virtually no effort by the high bourgeoisie to create any party mechanism. An interview with the former president of the conservative Partido Nacional during the plebiscite campaign underscores this "Eighteenth Brumaire"—like abdication to the authoritarian state. In answer to a journalist's question as to how he viewed the loss of power of such parties, the former president of the national party said, "I don't regret anything, neither the absence of political parties, nor the absence of parliament for the last seven years, because I believe that the construction of a free society could only have been achieved without them. . . . We were at war and what you have to do in wartime is defend yourself. . . . I simply believe that a government of authority is required for the entire period needed for Chile to be converted into a modern nation."[9]

Turning more explicitly to the issue of the potential for concerted action by opposition groups in civil society, it is clear that this potential is related in part to the internal unity of the state apparatus, the degree of support the state apparatus receives from allies in civil society, and the degree of coercion the state is able and willing to impose on opposition groups. In the case of Chile, as we have just seen, all these factors were such as to make concerted action by the opposition difficult in the 1973–81 period.

Two other factors are important to consider. One is the degree of ideological, class, and party tension *within* the opposition. In Chile, in the period under analysis, these tensions were high. The major components of the party opposition were the Christian Democrats, the Socialists, and the Communists. In democratic Chile, the greatest degree of party polarization occurred during the national elections of 1964 and 1970 and during the congressional elections of 1973. In all three elections the Christian Democrats were on one side, and

---

8. Data supplied by the Gallup Poll of Chile.
9. *El Mercurio*, Aug. 31, 1980, D7.

the Socialists and Communists on the other. At the beginning of the plebiscite campaign, all three parties joined in an informal oppositional alliance, but the history of past party conflict and the different class and ideological bases of the parties made concerted action extremely difficult. Within three weeks, part of the Christian Democratic rank and file, fearful of the consequences of co-operating with the Marxists refused to support the party leader, Eduardo Frei. For his part, Eduardo Frei became engaged in an extremely bitter condemna-tion of what he thought was Communist betrayal of the informal understand-ing. In turn, the Marxist parties were disillusioned by what they viewed as the absence of rewards for their ideologically costly cooperation with the Christian Democrats.[10]

The second factor consists of the structural changes in the political economy and their effect on the capacity of the opposition in civil society to work in concert against the state. The Chilean program of "libertarianism from above" (especially in its halcyon days of 1978–81) was an extreme form of liberal economics imposed by a highly coercive state. Tariffs were reduced to a uni-form 10 percent, robbing the "national industrial bourgeoisie" of protection from imported manufactured goods. One result of the extremely rapid reduc-tion in tariffs was the absolute reduction in the size of the industrial working class.[11] The structural base of potential oppositional collectivities in this very important arena of civil society was thus weakened.

Furthermore, whereas the initial control of working-class collectivities came about by direct coercion by the state, after 1978 there emerged a much more sophisticated attempt at policy-induced structural fragmentation of existing and potential oppositional collectivities. These policies reflected the ideas of Friedrich A. Hayek, the author of *The Road to Serfdom*, and such radical libertar-ian, antistatist, "public-choice" political economists as James Buchanan and Gordon Tullock.[12] In fact, the continuing labeling of the regime's theorists as "Chicago boys" missed important theoretical, historical, and political nu-ances. The Chicago school of economics was most influential in 1973–8. In 1979–81 the "Virginia school" of political economy (Buchanan, Tullock, and to a lesser extent Brunner) had the most impact.[13] The Virginia school was not

10. These observations are based on my interviews with party activists in Chile in June 1981.

11. Overall employment in the industrial sector dropped from a 1974 index of 110.4 to 92 in 1978. Employment in the economically and politically important metallic pro-ducts, machinery, and equipment subsector fell from 117.8 in 1974 to 84.3 in 1978. See Alexandro Foxley, *Latin American Experiments in Neo-Conservative Economics* (Berkeley: University of California Press, 1983), 76.

12. All three were frequent visitors to Chile and were closely associated with the regime's "anticollectivities" think tank, Centro de Estudios Publicos. The first issue of the center's journal, *Estudios Publicos*, was devoted to the theme "Liberty and Leviathan" and featured articles by Buchanan, Tullock, Hayek, Karl Brunner, and Milton Friedman.

13. The Virginia (actually VPI) public-choice school represented a thorough-going critique of what it saw to be the increasing pathological conditions of modern democracy. James M. Buchanan began *The Limits of Liberty: Between Anarchy and Leviathan* (Chicago:

concerned primarily with a general theory of the market. The major preoccupation was with the "marketization" of the state, with turning the state into a firm, and with atomizing civil society into an apolitical market. For their part, the "Santiago boys" went beyond the Virginia school in praxis. They represented a new phase in rightist political economy in the world, in that they actually used their privileged positions in the state apparatus to devise and apply a policy package aimed at dismantling, and then restructuring, civil society in accordance with their radical market views.

Pinochet's Santiago was not going to Washington, London, or Chicago. Reagan's Washington, Thatcher's London, and the University of Chicago economists were going to Santiago to see the future. In the area of social security, the pilgrims envisoned multiple private firms, each advertizing a slightly different program; these programs would virtually assume the resources and the role of the public sector in the social security area. The architect of this plan was quite clear about the political purpose of the new social security system: By setting a single nationwide social security rate, the state provided a systematic incentive for groups in civil society to mobilize collectivities against the state. The intention was to remove this incentive.[14]

The new union code created in 1979 had a similar goal. The intent of the code, according to its author, was to "create rewards and structures that depoliticize automatically" by the systematic insistence on market and individual-choice principles.[15] Thus, the right of any group to form its own union and engage in bargaining was restricted to the plant level, and conflicts were in theory to be resolved by workers and managers without the involvement of the state. Of course, if the market then operated only in a context in which the state apparatus forbade a closed shop, industry wide negotiations, or an active role for union leaders in political parties, the state would hardly be kept out of union life. Nevertheless, by fragmenting union collectivities, by passing large parts of the social security apparatus and public health into the private sector, and by imposing "free-choice antimonopoly rules" on unions and professional associations, the Pinochet state apparatus launched a long-range attack on the organizational potential of the opposition in civil society.

University of Chicago Press, 1975), pp. ix–x, with the following appeal: "When government takes on an independent life of its own, when Leviathan lives and breathes, a whole set of additional control issues come into being ... General escape may be possible only through genuine revolution in constitutional structure, through generalized rewriting of social contract. To expect such a revolution to take place may seem visionary, and in this respect the book may be considered quasi-utopian." Chile became such a "quasi-utopian" experiment. Other important books in this school are that of Richard D. Auster and Morris Silver, *The State as a Firm: Economic Forces in Political Development*, Studies in Public Choice, no. 3, ed. Gordon Tullock (Boston: Martinus Nijhoff, 1979); and the influential early critique by James Buchanan and Gordon Tullock, *The Calculus of Consent: Logical Foundations of Constitutional Democracy* (Ann Arbor: University of Michigan Press, 1962).

14. These comments are based on interviews conducted in Santiago in May 1981.
15. Ibid.

If our focus on the state is the state's share of the economy, the Chilean state can be said to have shrunk. The changes in the role of state enterprises that took place under the Pinochet regime between 1973 and 1981 provide a good example. In sharp contrast to the Brazilian BA model, which involved a dramatic expansion of the role of state enterprises, the Chilean version entailed an equally dramatic reduction in their role. By 1981, state enterprises had been reduced from around 500 to fewer than 20. If, however, our focus is on the role of the state in the domination and imperative coordination of civil society, then in Chile the program of "libertarianism from above" resulted in a "small-state, strong-state" project for the domination of opposition in civil society.[16]

The theory of those in command of the Chilean state in this period might be paraphrased as follows. By eschewing the capacity to produce economic outcomes different from those that flow "naturally" from the operation of the market in a class-divided society, the state may increase its capacity to dominate civil society. One might even go so far as to argue that the Chilean state represents a step beyond Bonapartism. Instead of exchanging the right to rule for the right to make money in the classic Bonapartist transaction, significant fractions of the Chilean bourgeoisie abdicated the right to rule and severely jeopardized their right to make money in the short run in the hope of preserving class privilege in the long run. This is not an unusual occurrence in itself. It characterized, for example, the early period of the Brazilian BA, which was economically difficult for the Brazilian bourgeoisie. What is unusual about the Chilean case is that the state was able to persist in this strategy for almost a decade.

The question raised by the Chilean case, then, was how long the state could continue to find support for a project that stood in objective contradiction to the requirements of local capital accumulation. The fact that it did so for as long as it did must be considered a strong challenge to theories of the "capitalist state." But even the extremities of the Chilean situation seem unlikely to support such a state indefinitely. It might be noted that the first major economic crisis of the Santiago boys' model occurred in November 1981, when three banks came so close to defaulting that the state in violation of its own model, rescued them and imprisoned some officials. The "natural" operation of the market may adversely affect not just the working class but also important segments of the bourgeoisie, especially in a dependent capitalist country.[17] Nonetheless, the Chilean state has been remarkably successful at "turning a deaf ear to the national bourgeoisie."[18]

Clearly, the foundational offensive project of the Chicago, Santiago, and Virginia schools increasingly disintegrated after November 1981, and the range and intensity of oppositional activities increased. However, the state apparatus

16. I owe the "small-state, strong-state" phrase to Manuel Antonio Garretón.
17. See José Pablo Arellano, "De la Liberalización a la Intervención: El Mercado de Capitales en Chile, 1974–83," *Estudios CIEPLAN*, no. 11 (Dec. 1983), 5–49.
18. See O'Donnell, "Reflections on the Patterns of Change."

remained relatively powerful throughout the 1982–3 crises for three reasons. One was the *de facto* unity of command of Pinochet over the army, navy, air force, and intelligence service. No other BA had one-man presidential control over the coercive apparatus remotely comparable to that in Chile. Second was the fact that important sectors of the bourgeoisie, even though they could no longer believe in the offensive project of the authoritarian state or even in Pinochet, still harbored sufficient fear of the Left to be unavailable to the democratic opposition and therefore gave tacit support to the defensive project of the coercive apparatus.[19] The third reason was that there remained major divisions—deeper, as we shall see, than those faced in Brazil, Chile, or Uruguay—within the active opposition itself.

Power Stagnation and Standoff: Uruguay, 1978–1981

Uruguay presents a very different system of power relations between the authoritarian state and civil society. Historians date the installation of the BA regime in Uruguay with the closing of Congress in June 1973. This event, however, only capped a long period of rule by fiat that extended back to 1968. From 1968 until 1978, the state gained power relative to civil society.[20] In fact, in Uruguay the percentage of the population detained for questioning by the police was higher than in any other country of the southern cone, press and intellectual censorship more complete, and repression of guerrillas and labor more severe. Civil society shrank drastically in Uruguay in 1973–8. However, in the three years from 1978 to 1981 there was a noticeable decline in the regime's capacity to lead its original allies in civil society (but absolutely no loss of its capacity to coerce any working-class or leftist opponents), and the opposition began to show greater capacity to formulate an alternative program (though not to challenge the government directly). Why was there this difference between Uruguay and Chile?

I shall start with the "defensive" projects of the regimes. If we contrast Chile and Uruguay before the installation of their respective BA regimes, we see that the Chilean bourgeoisie believed far more strongly than its Uruguayan coun-

19. The Santiago weekly published a poll which indicated that, in answer to the question "What would be the best formula of government to solve the problems of the country?" only 8.5 percent of the upper class selected "the present government of Pinochet" and only 0.7 percent selected "an exclusively military government." However, only 21.7 percent of the upper class said they wanted "a government formed by all the opposition." *Hoy* (Dec. 1983), 12–16.

20. The best general overview of the Uruguay BA is found in Charles Gillespie, "From Suspended Animation to Animated Suspension: Political Parties and the Reconstruction of Democracy in Uruguay," in *Prospects for Democracy: Transitions from Authoritarian Rule*, ed. Guillermo O'Donnell, Phillippe C. Schmitter, and Laurence Whitehead (Baltimore, Md.: Johns Hopkins University Press, forthcoming), vol. ii ch. 8.

terpart that its economic and social survival was threatened. The Chilean bourgeoisie developed numerous vehicles of class mobilization and protection. This element of bourgeois mobilization was virtually absent in Uruguay. In Uruguay, in fact, the military had destroyed the major radical claimants to power, the Tupamaros, months before the military finally closed Parliament and installed the new regime. In sharp contrast to Chile, therefore, the Uruguayan military had a relatively weak "salvationist" relationship to the bourgeoisie when the military closed the classic instrument of the bourgeoisie in Uruguay—Parliament. Since 1975, the Tupamaros have had no visible existence and are simply not a credible threat. Communist-controlled trade unions were certainly a source of resistance to the bourgeoisie and could reappear as a force in some form, but the repression was so massive that the unions did not launch a single important strike for almost a decade.

If we contrast the offensive projects, we see that in Uruguay the state announced an ambitious economic liberalization program that was similar, on paper at least, to that in Chile. In the period from 1978 to 1980 the macroeconomic indicators went in the direction the state planners wanted. The budget, even after the inclusion of the country's capital expenditures, was almost balanced. Inflation was greatly reduced, and, most importantly, the gross domestic product, which had virtually stagnated at 0.3 percent per year from 1961 to 1968, grew at 6.4 percent per year from 1978 to 1980.[21] However, market liberalism as a long-term project that would change the political economy and society lost steam early on.

The less frightened Uruguayan bourgeoisie defended its specific interests much more forcefully than its Chilean counterpart. Thus, the Uruguayan state planners never had the degree of relative autonomy from the Uruguayan bourgeoisie that their counterparts had in Chile. The Uruguayan state planners' lack of autonomy was further diminished by the collegial decision-making formula used by the Uruguayan BA. Virtually all major decisions were made by the Junta de Officiales Generales, which by statute contained all four-star officers from the army, navy, and air force. This decision-making formula was chosen by the military to ensure the participation of all three services, but it engendered significant internal veto power, opened up multiple lobbying points for civil society, and reduced the capacity of the state planners to implement the sweeping policies they proposed on paper. Thus, tariffs, instead of being reduced to a uniform 10 percent as in Chile, were still hovering around 90 percent in Uruguay by 1981. Likewise, although the regime in Uruguay initially made pledges to privatize many state enterprises as in Chile, not a single major state enterprise was abolished. Before 1973 it was rare for the presidency of one of the eight largest state enterprises to be held by a military officer, but after five years of BA rule, it had become the norm for the

21. See the statistical appendix to Luis Macadar, *Uruguay 1974–1980: Un Nuevo Ensayo de Reajuste Económico?* (Montevideo: Ediciones de la Banda Oriental, 1982), esp. 280.

presidencies of the largest state enterprises to be held by active-duty officers. The chief economic architect of the original Uruguayan model acknowledged that the division of power within the state apparatus made the implementation of his privatizing goals unrealistic. As a consequence, he did not make a great effort to push his initial goals. He also judged that the same balance of forces made it unlikely that Uruguay could ever reduce tariffs much below 80 percent. He observed in passing that Uruguay did not have a commanding single figure like Pinochet, but rather that Uruguayan "collegiality slows decision-making and occasionally introduces differences in policy implementation."[22]

By 1980 in Uruguay it was no longer clear that the regime had an unfulfilled sociopolitical offensive project. Offensively and defensively, the regime seemed to have completed its initial agenda. If this is so, on theoretical grounds it would seem that the bourgeoisie would not see a continued need to abdicate to the military the direct articulation of its interests, which would otherwise take place via some representative institutions. This would be even more true if the bourgeoisie had reason to think that the prolongation of a regime of exception might set into motion reactions in civil society that could present long-term threats to its core interests—threats that would be substantially more severe than those presented by the inevitable uncertainities of representative politics. Let us look for evidence related to these issues.

In November 1980 the military government in Uruguay held a plebiscite to ratify a constitution similar to that in Chile. In sharp contrast to the situation in Chile, however, in Uruguay during the campaign, *not one* producer organization issued a manifesto urging a yes vote. Although none issued a manifesto urging a no vote, the lack of active support for the authoritarian state by producer groups was one reason the new constitution was rejected in an election that amazed outsiders.

Although the overlap between producer groups and the group the Gallup Poll of Uruguay calls "upper class" is not exact, the results of the poll were interesting. They indicated that the original allies of the authoritarian regime in Uruguay no longer believed that they could further their interests only within an authoritarian, politically closed system. In May 1980 the Gallup Poll of Uruguay explored opinions about a political opening. Whereas in Chile a large section of the upper class in that year was still certain that a political opening would hurt the economy and set off potentially dangerous conflict, in Uruguay the Gallup Poll revealed a dramatically different response on the part of the urban upper class. By a margin of 2 to 1, upper-class respondents believed that a political opening would speed rather than slow economic recuperation (Table 3.1). Even more significantly, by a margin of 7 to 1, upper-class respondents believed that a political opening would improve rather than worsen tranquility and public order (Table 3.2).[23]

22. Interview with Alejandro Végh Villegas, Montevideo, Mar. 1981.
23. Data obtained at the office of Gallup Uruguay in Montevideo. The office also published a special report on the plebicite, "El Plebiscito Nacional," *Indice Gallup de*

TABLE 3.1. *Public opinion in urban Uruguay concerning the effect of political opening on the economy, May 1980* (%)

	Upper class	Middle class	Lower class
Speed up	35	48	53
Slow down	16	16	12
No effect	28	20	12
No response	14	12	14

Note: The question was worded as follows: "In your judgment, would the reestablishment of political practices—elections, parties, and parliament— speed or slow economic recuperation, or have no effect on recuperation?"

Source: Gallup Poll, Uruguay Indice Gallup de Opinión Politica.

TABLE 3.2. *Public opinion in urban Uruguay concerning the effect of political opening on public order, May 1980* (%)

	Upper class	Middle class	Lower class
Improve	43	37	29
Worsen	6	12	6
No effect	36	37	53
No response	12	10	7

Note: The question was worded as follows: "In your judgment, what would be the immediate effects of a political opening on tranquility and public order?"

Source: Gallup Poll, Uruguay Indice Gallup de Opinión Politica.

Turning to the question of the potential for concerted political opposition in civil society, the contrast between Chile and Uruguay is also striking. The major difference is that the two main political parties in Uruguay, the Blanco and the Colorado parties, are not highly differentiated in terms of programmatic content, ideological discourse, or class composition. Furthermore, between them, the two parties have never received less than 80 percent of the votes cast in any election in the twentieth century. Although the parties have a tradition of intense electoral competition, they also have a history of power sharing that has gone so far as to include some consociational practices. The leadership of the two parties cooperated on the no vote in the plebiscite without any recriminations of the kind that surfaced in the brief attempt at collaboration between the Christian Democrats and the Marxists in Chile.

In fact, the absence of threat and the presence of party alternatives that they found tolerable explained why producer group leaders, in extensive interviews conducted in 1981, voiced the opinion that the return to electoral politics in the near future might be their safest option. In interview after interview, they

Opinión Pública, no. 315 (Jan. 1981); for an excellent analysis of this period, see Luis E. Gonzáles, "Uruguay, 1980–1981: An Unexpected Opening," *Latin American Research Review*, 18 (1983), 63–76.

worried aloud about the risks of a prolonged regime of exception to Uruguay's "safe" party structure. In their opinion, the two traditional parties still retained the allegiance of around 70 to 80 percent of the electorate. Because the regime had no long-range offensive sociopolitical project that seemed attractive or credible, they were afraid that, if there was another decade without party elections, the workers and the Left would seek, and possibly find, other vehicles. For political as well as economic reasons, therefore, the Uruguayan bourgeoisie was becoming less and less willing to abdicate the management of its affairs to the coercive apparatus of the state (the armed forces). In this sense the BA state had lost a significant degree of the autonomy it once had in Uruguay.

However, a close examination of the state–civil society relations in Uruguay during this period illuminates some sobering limitations to oppositional power. First, the upper bourgeoisie, though it did not give active support to the state authoritarian regime, by and large did not join (as many did in Brazil) the active opposition. Second, although the two traditional political parties joined together in opposition on a purely electoral issue, neither party had forged powerful links with the trade unions or attempted to mobilize active resistance to the regime. Thus, the costs of rule for the state apparatus were not very high. There was some division and a major scandal within the army, the key component of the state coercive apparatus, but not enough to shake the military's will or capacity to retain control.

The military did announce an election for 1984. However, on the basis of interviews with the political secretariat of the armed forces, two issues emerged clearly. First, the military did not feel that they were under great pressure from civil society to withdraw from power. In the absence of impelling societal or corporate reasons to withdraw, they prepared a rather elaborate agenda of "participatory prerogatives" for the armed forces in any future democracy. Second, the absence of any effort by the political parties to talk with or organize within the working class weakened Uruguayan civil society, and some key military leaders openly expressed the opinion to me that the barriers to subsequent military reentry and control of the state apparatus were quite low.

Overall, the case of Uruguay reinforces the lessons of the Chilean case regarding the relation between conflicts in civil society and the ability of the state to achieve uncontested domination. The level of class conflict in Uruguay was reduced to the point that the bourgeoisie was no longer willing to give a *carte blanche* to the authoritarian state. Nonetheless, at least until late 1983, elite perceptions of the potential for conflict within civil society were still sufficient to obviate any attempt to build significantly higher barriers to military reentry after the scheduled transfer of state power in 1985.

Decline of State Power and Decline of Civil Society: Argentina, 1978–1981

I shall be even more schematic for Argentina. From 1976 through 1978 the authoritarian regime in Argentina was characterized by four elements that increased state power *vis-à-vis* civil society. First, although Argentina never had the fusion of rule found in Chile (indeed, the regime institutionalized a decision rule whereby virtually all administrative and political units such as provinces, ministries, state enterprises, and even central bank directorates would be allocated one-third to the army, one-third to the navy, and one-third to the air force), there was at least a reasonable degree of harmony between the military as an institution (represented by the junta, which considered itself the ultimate source of authority) and the military as government (represented by the president). Second, the military as an institution and as government used its impressive coercive powers to repress any signs of opposition in civil society and, to a somewhat lesser extent, to support the technocratic team in its economic project, the initial phases of which hurt not only the working class but, with the exception of the financial groups, most sectors of the bourgeoisie. Third, the high bourgeoisie was sufficiently frightened by previous conflict to accept the stated goals (if not yet the actual implementation) of the state program.

In 1980–1, with the exception of the capacity of the state apparatus to coerce the opposition, which remained strong, the situation changed considerably. State power had clearly begun to decline. Critical to this outcome was the growth of contradictions within the state, more precisely between the military as an institution and the military as government. After considerable debate within the military institution, a new military president was selected whose authority was questioned by the military within months of his inauguration. Economic policy indecision, a chaotic series of devaluations, and a dangerous run on reserves cast doubt on the entire economic program. Anyone who analyzed regime power as a capacity not only to coerce but to use the resources of the state apparatus to structure outcomes would have to conclude that in the period 1979–81 there had been a decline in state power.

In contrast, analysis of civil society in Argentina in the period from 1976 to mid-1981 shows that virtually all the components necessary for independent oppositional life in civil society—unions, political parties, and student organization—also declined in power, despite the signs of state decomposition by 1980–1. Certainly, civil society showed few signs of being able to achieve concerted action over an alternative project. Argentina by mid-1981 was a country in which both the state and civil society had experienced major losses of power.

The Argentine case enlarges on the lessons of the Chilean and Uruguayan cases. Conflict within civil society does not by itself provide the preconditions of a growth in state power. In the Argentine case, the absence of cohesion within the heart of the state apparatus had led to a negative-sum game in which the overall capacity to structure either economic or political outcomes, from either inside or outside of the state apparatus, had declined markedly. The Argentine case, even more than the Chilean case, also posed serious problems for conventional theories of the capitalist state. Argentina was a state that was clearly "relatively autonomous" in a society that was clearly capitalist; yet the state was not "organizing capitalist interests" and overcoming problems of capital accumulation, as some theories presuppose.[24] On the contrary, the actions of the state apparatus were a prime factor in the vigorous "underdeveloping" of Argentina, labeled by some the "Bolivianization of Argentina."

The power relations between the authoritarian state and civil society were slowly beginning to change before Malvinas. Beginning in July 1981, the political parties began a public search for a common position called La Multipartidaria Nacional. Indeed, in February 1982, an impressive set of proposals was published in Argentina.[25] The invasion of Malvinas gave the military enormous instant support. However, the unprepared Argentine public reacted with extraordinary revulsion to the news of the military surrender at Malvinas. I attended a number of mass meetings in the after math of the surrender, and charges of cowardice, dishonesty, and incompetence were hurled at the military with a vengeance. The high bourgeoisie, with its extensive ties to English commercial and financial networks, also realized that its alliance with the military was extremely dangerous. For our purposes, however, the most important point is that after Malvinas rapid extrication from state power was seen to be an institutional imperative by many military officers. For example, the vice-director of the Escuela Nacional de Defensa bitterly acknowledged that the parceling out of provinces, ministries, and state enterprises by thirds might possibly have been a way for the military to rule domestically, but Argentina went to war with "three political parties," which were completely unable to perform professionally. He argued that the military had to extricate itself from government, sharply de-emphasize its internal security orientation, and professionalize with a NATO opponent in mind and that democratic parties needed to rule. He stated, "If that option fails, Argentina may face a Russian revolution."[26]

Until Malvinas, fear of Nuremburg-like trials and reprisals was a strong disincentive to military extrication. However, after Malvinas, officers' fear of military and state collapse was so great that it, in fact, made them more willing to accept harder terms from the opposition. This was underscored in an inter-

24. The most influential and provocative argument as to why and how the capitalist state should perform these roles remains the work of Nicos Poulantzas. See, for example, his *Political Power and Social Classes* (London: New Left Books, 1973).

25. *La Propuesta de la Multipartidaria* (Buenos Aires: El Cid Editor, 1982).

26. Interview with the vice-director of the Escuela Nacional de Defensa, Buenos Aires, July 28, 1982.

view with an active-duty brigadier general. In answer to my question as to whether military fear of reprisals would impede extrication, he emphatically shot back, "There *has* to be an exit or we will disintegrate."[27]

State power is relational. The near collapse of the state coercive apparatus increased the relative power of civil society even though many leaders of civil society wanted to contain attacks on the military to give themselves time to reconstitute civil and political society. After the defeat in Malvinas, state power was clearly in disintegration, but civil and political society still faced tough problems of democratic recomposition. Raúl Alfonsín saw the task with startling clarity: "We should not confuse the self-defeat of the regime with the triumph of the democratic forces. The first is happening, the second depends on us."[28]

From Parallel Growth to Conflict: Brazil, 1970–1981

Brazil raises the most theoretically interesting and complex questions of the four cases. Without supplying full documentation, I would like to claim that from 1970 to 1973 both the power of the authoritarian state and the power of the opposition increased. There are two major caveats. Obviously, the power of civil society started its growth from a very low base. The years 1969–70 were the years of maximum repression. In contrast, the power of the state to impose its solution on its allies by 1973 was great, yet already generating contradictions that would later limit state autonomy.

State power grew in the period under consideration under two special conditions. First, in the atmosphere of armed struggle against urban guerillas, the state security apparatus achieved unprecedented independence in its repression of any activity in society believed to be related to "subversion." Second, there was extraordinary economic growth. In the years 1967–70 the gross domestic product (GDP) rose at an average annual rate of 9.3 percent. It had risen by 11.3 percent in 1971, by 10.4 percent in 1972, and by 10.0 percent in 1973. In the same period, the power of the state enterprises at the apex of the economy also grew rapidly. For example, if we rank Brazil's thirty largest non-financial firms by net assets, thirteen of these were public enterprises in 1967, seventeen in 1971, and twenty-three in 1974. Coupled with the rapid growth of the GDP, the state's tax revenues expressed as a percentage of GDP also increased, from 8.4 percent in 1967, to 10.2 percent in 1971, and to 10.8 percent in 1974. The financial role of the state was reinforced still more by the growth of state banks and the state's ability to grant subsidies.[29]

27. Interview, Buenos Aires, July 27, 1983.
28. Letter circulated in Buenos Aires, July 2, 1982.
29. GNP figures based on data in *Economic and Social Progress in Latin America: Annual Report* (Washington, DC: Inter-American Development Bank, 1972), 141; (1973), 145. Tax

Surprisingly, the growth of the state's role in the economy did not damage its relationship with its allies in the private sector. Even though the private sector's share of the gross national product (GNP) declined, attacks on "statism" did not appear because the state gave generous subsidies to the private sector and the private sector experienced high rates of absolute growth. For example, the capital goods and consumer goods sectors, both of which were predominantly private sector-controlled, grew at an annual average rate of 22 percent in the 1969–73 period.[30] The first response of the state apparatus to the oil crisis in 1973 was to centralize decision making even more within the state apparatus and to increase its relative autonomy *vis-à-vis* its allies. Thus, this was a period in which the state appeared to have a "credible, violent enemy" and therefore a continuing defensive project, as well as a credible offensive project.

In what sense can we argue that civil society also gained in power in the same period? Many of the elements that became striking later in the 1970s had their origins in this earlier period. The most important of these was the change within the Catholic church. The church supported the military coup in 1964, but by 1970 the church hierarchy, offended (but not directly affected) by the coercive force of the state's "defensive project," became increasingly critical of human rights violations in Brazil. In the sphere of its internal life, the church had a high degree of autonomy from the state.

The church made particularly good use of this autonomy in the steady development of base community organizations (Comunidades Eclesiais de Base). These base communities did not confront the state directly in the period 1970–3 but began to build up their ideological, human, and organizational resources, resources that eventually could be transferred horizontally from one sphere of civil society to other spheres in which the members of the base communities worked. In the late 1970s, this was an important ingredient in the emergence of stronger urban unions, especially in the critical area of greater São Paulo, and it helps to explain the unprecedented growth of rural unions, which also had a surprising degree of autonomy.

Until the late 1970s, unions had been encapsulated in state-crafted corporatist structures, which reduced the autonomy of worker organizations in civil society. The emergence in this period of a new brand of trade unionism that began to challenge the limits of these structures is seen by a number of labor specialists to have been a vital step in Brazilian labor history. According to José Alvaro Moisés, "It is beyond doubt that from the beginning of the 1970s there began to be developed efforts to create a new structure for representation

revenue figures are based on data in the same series: (1968), 78; (1972), 140; and (1975), 167. Data on state enterprises are found in Thomas J. Trebatt, *Brazil's State-Owned Enterprises: A Case Study of the State as Entrepreneur* (New York: Cambridge University Press, 1983), 59.

30. José Serra, "Three Mistaken Theses Regarding the Connection between Industrialization and Authoritarian Regimes," in Collier (ed.), *The New Authoritarianism*, 121.

of the rank and file factory workers in their unions.... It is now clear that the organizational structure of the new unionism is quite different from the unions of the past."[31]

The growth of the new unionism in the period, like the growth of the church base communities, represented an increase in the autonomous actions of a part of civil society. Like the base communities, the unions did not initially come into direct conflict with the state. This appears to have been because the transformations that were occurring were related primarily to internal organization and ideology and were not immediately reflected in challenges to capital or the state.

By 1973–4, representatives of the new unionism began to negotiate for a series of changes at the factory level. For example, on May 1, 1973, the Metallurgical Federation of São Paulo sent a demand to President Médici for the right to establish factory committees, to negotiate collectively with owners, and to by-pass the state and for greater autonomy from the Ministry of Labor.[32] In fact, before the first wave of strikes in 1978 that brought the unions into direct conflict with the state, the metallurgical unions steadily broadened the scope of their direct, collective negotiations at the factory level.[33]

The emergence of a stronger trade union movement was due not only to changes within the unions themselves, or even within civil society as a whole. It was also, to a significant degree, the unintended consequence of the past actions of the state itself. We have seen how the "success" of the state's defensive project helped generate new forms of church-based opposition in civil society. The success of the "offensive" project also had the unintended consequences of generating new potential for opposition in civil society. The "economic miracle" substantially increased the size of the industrial labor force. Between 1960 and 1970 the number of workers employed in industry grew by 52 percent, and between 1970 and 1974 again by 38 percent.[34] Moreover, the state's policy of relying on multinational corporations and allowing industrial concentration to take its course unimpeded contributed to the tendency of the growth of the working class to concentrate around the city of São Paulo. Industrial growth in itself does not entail a growth in the autonomy of working-class organizations, as the history of Mexican labor illustrates, but the quantitative growth of the Brazilian working class, especially in greater São

31. José Alvaro Moisés, "A Estratégia do Novo Sindicalismo," *Revista de Cultura e Política*, 5/6 (1981), 71. Maria Hermínia Tavares de Aldeida, in her "Tendências Recentes da Negociação Coletiva no Brasil," *Dados* 24 (1981), 160–4, also discusses the period from 1970 to 1973 as one of the germination of the new unionism.

32. See Amaury de Souza and Bolivar Lamounier, "Governo e Sindicatos no Brazil: A Perspectiva dos Anos 80," *Dados*, 24 (1981), 145.

33. See the charts documenting this trend in the article by de Almeida, "Tendências Recentes da Negociação Coletiva," 182–3.

34. See Ronaldo Munck, "The Labor Movement and the Crisis of the Dictatorship in Brazil," in Thomas C. Bruneau and Philippe Faucher (eds.), *Authoritarian Capitalism: Brazil's Contemporary Economic and Political Development* (Boulder, Colo.: Westview Press, 1981), 228.

Paulo, clearly contributed to the generation of the working-class movements that came to be so important in the opposition. Finally, it should be added that in 1976 the minister of labor relaxed the accounting procedures by which the state monitored union funds. In the vast majority of unions this probably meant that the state-approved union officials had access to some discretionary funds for personal and cooptive uses. For his part the minister of labor was able to make an ideological claim that union *abertura* (liberalization) preceded the political *abertura*.[35] For the key São Bernardo union, however, these discretionary funds were actually vitally important in enabling a new generation of unionists like "Lula" to build up the infrastructure that in 1978 helped launch Brazil's first serious strike in a decade.[36] The strategy of the Brazilian state with regard to the working class stands, therefore, in sharp contrast to that of the other BA states, most strikingly to that of Chile.

Those in charge of the Brazilian state also took a very different tack from Pinochet's in their strategy toward Congress, fixed presidential terms, and parties. In order to bolster their ideological claims that the military coup was executed to save democracy, they purged but did not close Congress, they controlled but did not eliminate elections and parties, and they adhered to the existing norms of presidential rotation with fixed terms. All of these initial state decision rules, which in Brazil precluded from the beginning a long-term fusion of power such as Pinochet attained, contributed to a dynamic that increasingly constrained authoritarian state autonomy but that would have been costly (even for the internal unity of the state coercive apparatus) to abrogate.[37] The willingness to tolerate political parties as long as "subversive" individuals were removed probably reflected the generals' prior experience in Brazil in which parties as such were organizationally weak and depended on the charisma of individual leaders or on traditional patronage structures. Parties as organizations were, in short, thought to be much less threatening in Brazil than in Chile. The decision to allow parties to exist at all, however, had unintended consequences for the stability of Brazil's BA regime.

35. "Abertura Sindical Antecede a Política" *Estado de Sao Paulo*, Jan. 1, 1978.
36. Interview with Almir Pazzianotto, the labor lawyer for the Sao Bernardo do Campo Metallurgical Workers' Union, on Aug. 13, 1981, in São Bernardo do Campo. The great increase in the number of rural trade unions in the early 1970s, which remains understudied, was due largely to a small change in the social security law, which presented new legal organizing opportunities for rural workers, opportunities that were rapidly and legally exploited by progressive churches, lawyers, and trade union movements. See Wanderley Guilherme dos Santos, *Cidadania e Justiça* (Rio de Janeiro: Editora Campus, 1979), 35–38, 113–23.
37. Two important articles that explore the constraints on the institutionalization of the autonomous state created by the initial self-proclaimed norms and procedures of the leaders are Juan J. Linz, "The Future of an Authoritarian Situation or the Institutionalization of an Authoritarian Regime: The Case of Brazil," in Alfred Stepan (ed.), *Authoritarian Brazil: Origins, Policies, and Future* (New Haven: Yale University Press, 1973), 233–54; and Bolivar Lamounier, "Authoritarian Brazil Revisitado: O Impacto das Eleições na Abertura Política Brasileira, 1974–1982," paper prepared for a conference, Democratizing Brazil?, Columbia University, New York, Mar. 9–10, 1984.

An official opposition party was created in 1965, only to be weakened with the closing of Congress in 1968. In 1970 the officially sanctioned opposition party, MDB, had very little respect within the Left, and it was not felt to represent in any serious way opposition opinion in civil society. For example, in the city of São Paulo in 1970, blank and defaced ballots were twice as numerous as votes for the MDB. By 1974, however, under conditions of less censorship on television, more open elections, and four years of MDB protest activity in Congress, null and blank votes decreased from 33.7 to 10.9 percent of the votes cast in the national election.[38] In the country as a whole, the MDB won only 39.5 percent of the senate votes in 1970 but 59.1 percent in 1974.[39]

Of course, the election of 1974 falls outside our period of 1970–73 and occurred under conditions of government-initiated liberalization, an initiative that began in the second half of 1974. Nonetheless, the stunning results of the elections can be understood only by realizing that in the period from 1970 to 1973 as a whole, the authoritarian state had failed in its attempt to win ideological hegemony in civil society and that the opposition had made real organizational and ideological gains in their long "war of position" against the BA state. A case can thus be made, I believe, for considering the period from 1970 to 1973 to be one in which both the state and civil society increased their power within the spheres of their major activities.

The following period, from 1974 to 1981, was a very different one. The state's economic strategy remained very similar, but the international context in which it was operating changed dramatically, and the accretionary changes that had occurred in the period 1970–3 began to make themselves felt. By the end of 1973, the urban guerrilla movement had virtually been extinguished as a threat to the bourgeois order and the oil crisis began to curtail the Brazilian economic miracle. Without a credible threat and with technocratic planners having to sail against, rather than with, the prevailing economic winds, two of the major forces that had enhanced the relative autonomy of the state in the period 1969–73 began to flag. The predominant state response to the oil crisis of 1973 was one of (*a*) further grandiose development projects in which state enterprises were programmed to play a major role and (*b*) greater centralization of the economy in the hands of the planning and finance ministries in such areas as price setting, criteria for imports, and special export subsidies. In short, the administration of General Geisel followed in the footsteps of previous military administrations in assuming that a strengthening of the economic role of the state would put the economy back on its trajectory growth, enhance the regime's legitimacy, and reduce its political problems. Unfortunately for Geisel, the state's efforts in the economic sphere did not produce the growth rates of the earlier period; instead, Brazil began to experience slower growth

38. See Bolivar Lamounier, (ed.), *Voto de Desconfiança: Eleições e Mundança Política no Brasil: 1970–1979* (Petrópolis: Editora Vozes, 1980), 72.

39. David V. Fleischer (ed.), *Os Partidos Políticos no Brasil* (Brasília: Editora Universidade Brasília, 1971), i. 222.

and rising debt. Moreover, this time the reaction of the bourgeoisie to the expansion of the state's role was strikingly different. "Antistatism" became a major political issue.

The campaign against "statism" launched by Brazilian business groups in 1975 must be analyzed in a more political context. As we have seen, state enterprises grew at an extremely rapid rate from 1967 to 1973; yet this growth generated little protest. We must therefore qualify the purely doctrinal elements of the antistatist movement that began in 1975. The anti-statist movement is best seen as a movement that began when the state had less disposable surplus to pass on as political and economic subsidies to its domestic allies. In the case of Brazil, by 1975 the state had, with the defeat of the guerrillas, lost its most credible defensive project, and although it had its own offensive project of economic growth, it was not a project that the domestic bourgeoisie would accept *carte blanche*. My interviews in Brazil indicate that Paulista entrepreneurial arguments against statism were arguments not against the state as a producer but rather against the state as a regulator. The antistatist campaign was thus the first clear signal of the declining capacity of the state to lead its allies. By 1978, with the issuing of the famous "Manifesto of the Eight" entrepreneurs, an important fraction of the state's initial allies had in fact joined the movement in civil society for liberalization.

Hand in hand with the growth of political opposition in the bourgeoisie came mounting evidence that the state could not carry out its economic project in the new international context. Inflation, which had been reduced from over 60 percent in 1964 to less than 20 percent in 1972–3, rose again to 29 percent in 1974, 38 percent in 1976, and over 100 percent in 1980. The foreign debt soared from U.S. $12 billion in 1973 to over $70 billion in 1982.[40] With mounting inflation and a severely constraining debt/service ratio, state planners in 1975–6, and again in late 1980, had to abandon key aspects of their development project. From 1974 to 1981, then, we can talk of a significant decline in the state's power to lead its allies and to execute a coherent development project, but unlike Argentina, the state never appeared to be in the process of disintegration, and like Chile and Uruguay, it still retained a high capacity to repress.

Finally, the capacity of civil society to formulate new goals and structure political outcomes, which had been nascent in the earlier period, began to mature. The union movement by 1978 was in a position to organize the most important wave of strikes in over a decade, starting in the most industrialized sector of greater São Paulo and then spreading to much of the southeast and south of Brazil. The ecclesiastical base communities developed in number,

40. *Economic and Social Progress in Latin America: Annual Report* (Washington, DC: Inter-American Development Bank, 1973), 143; (1972), 140; (1974), 209; (1976), 172; and (1980–1), 193. Foreign debt data from *World Debt Tables: External Debt of Developing Countries, 1983–1984 Edition* (Washington, DC: International Bank for Reconstruction and Development, 1984), 166.

fervor, and breadth as they became a major force not only in São Paulo but in the northeast and the north of Brazil as well. The Brazilian Bar Association and the Brazilian Press Association launched sustained campaigns against some of the procedural rules crucial to the autonomy of the authoritarian state. The bar association centered its campaign around demands that the state apparatus adhere to the rule of law and especially habeas corpus. The press association campaigned against state censorship. By a dialectical process of societal demand and state concession, both associations helped to increase the sphere of civil society that was relatively free of direct state repression. In this atmosphere, the number and quality of publications advancing ideas, information, and projects stemming from critical sectors of civil society grew impressively.

The simultaneous development of new organizations and energies in diverse sectors of civil society had a more than additive effect. As developments in each sector progressed, horizontal ties between sectors also grew. As a result of these horizontal ties, changes in each sector helped to speed and reinforce changes in the others.[41]

This "horizontal dimension" is sufficiently critical to the overall growth of the power of civil society to warrant some elaboration. Almost all the sectors in civil society have been helped by the reorientation of the church. The trade union movement has benefited particularly. Union activists stress the extent to which the emergence of a more independent trade union movement in greater São Paulo has been helped by the ecclesiastical base community movements, not because these movements are involved directly in trade union activities (they are not), but because they have helped to nurture a sense of social injustice in community members who are also trade unionists and have convinced them of the need for more participatory organizational styles. In addition, of course, the church has provided concrete assistance by allowing critical union meetings to be held inside local churches.

Unions have also been helped by the increased boldness of the press which has given union positions extensive coverage. It was the press, after all, that made Lula, the new leader of the São Bernardo do Campo metal workers union, a national figure *before* the first major strike. The Brazilian Bar Association's campaign for the legal rights of organizations and individuals, which also came before the strike movement, contributed to undermining the legitimacy of the state's repressive efforts once the strikes began.

The interaction between the revitalization of the press and the emergence of political opposition among industrial elites is particularly interesting. In 1977, despite growing private reservations about the military regime among entrepreneurs, there was no organization or set of publically recognized leaders to transform these sentiments into a politically effective statement. The *Gazeta Mercantil* (Brazil's equivalent of the *Wall Street Journal*) came up with an

41. See Paul Singer and Vinicius Caldeira Brant (eds.), *São Paulo: O Povo em Movimento* (Petrópolis: Vozes/Cebrap, 1982); see also Maria Helena Moreira Alves, *The State and the Opposition in Military Brazil* (Austin: University of Texas Press, forthcoming).

ingenious plan. It sent out a request to 5000 businessmen to choose "the ten most representative spokesmen of the business class."[42] Unlike elections for official business confederations, this "election" included no mechanism for the vetoing of potential candidates by the government. Significantly, almost none of the presidents of existing state-charted business groups were elected. The ten businessmen who were selected, however, became legitimated as public spokesmen for the industrial elite. Eight of them signed the highly critical "Manifesto of the Eight." One of the signers reported to me later: "Once we issued the manifesto, civil society entered right into my office by the window. We received numerous invitations to participate in public forums about Brazil's problems and future with members of the church, trade unions, intellectuals, and students—groups we had almost never worked with before."[43]

Without the growth of horizontal ties within civil society, the kind of political evolution that Brazil experienced would not have been possible. Nonetheless, the state played a central role in setting the conditions that allowed these crucial developments in civil society to take place at all. In fact, it might be argued that the initial decision to allow greater space for organization in civil society was as much as anything else an attempt to resolve certain contradictions within the state apparatus itself.

In 1974, the Geisel regime began to promote an *abertura*. One of the prime architects of this liberalization process, General Golbery, argues that an important motivation for the strategy was that of reducing the autonomy of the secret service apparatus *vis-à-vis* the military as government. During the period of intense fighting against urban guerillas, the Serviço Nacional de Informações (Brazil's peak security organization), along with the individual security forces maintained by each of the three branches of the armed forces, gained a great deal of power. By 1974 the security apparatus had acquired such autonomy and insulation from the regular military that it was perceived to be generating corporate threats to the military as an institution. At least some of those within the military as government wanted to move in the direction of a rule of law in order to reduce the space of "legal exceptionalism" within which the secret service thrived. Liberalization was also seen to be a tactic for generating civil society resources (a freer and more critical press) and movements (protests against torture) that would be useful to the military as government in their "intrastate" effort to gain control of the security forces.[44]

Insofar as the growth of the power of civil society in Brazil served interests within the state apparatus, it was obviously a more robust development, but the nature of the shifting balance of power should not be exaggerated. The state

42. For a discussion of the methodology and results of the elections, see J. P. Martinez, "Os Eleitos pela Empresa Privada Nacional," *Gazeta Mercantil: Balanço Anual*, Sept. 1977, 18–26.
43. Interview with Claudio Bardella, the entrepreneur who received the most votes in the *Gazeta Mercantil* poll, São Paulo, Aug. 21, 1981.
44. Interviews with General Golbery do Couto e Silva, June 16 and July 16, 1982, in Brasilia.

apparatus continued to be very powerful and continued to have a strong interest in domination. For example, in November 1981 the top members of the coercive apparatus determined that they would risk dangerous losses if the rules for the 1982 elections were not changed. President Figueiredo changed them overnight. In the crucial five days after this state fiat, *not one* protest demonstration was held.

In Brazil, as in Uruguay, it was by no means clear that the military was preparing to abdicate. This should not, however, obscure the fact that the evolution of events in Brazil were dramatically different from that in Uruguay. The growth of the power of civil society, fostered in part by state policies, made the tension between the BA regime and the opposition much more dynamic in the Brazilian case. Events subsequent to the period under consideration here, most prominently the elections of 1982, in which the opposition won control of ten states, including the three key states of São Paulo, Rio de Janeiro, and Minas Gerais, and the massive campaigns in 1985 for direct elections, reconfirmed this dynamic.

Unlike Argentina, the Brazilian state in 1982 and 1983 was not threatened with disintegration. The leaders of the state apparatus in 1982 had fewer active supporters and more active opponents in civil society than at any time since the regime began in 1964. Nonetheless, they retained sufficient room for political initiative to make significant changes in the rules of the game for the opposition parties in 1982. Brazil is a clear case in which a lack of civil society support is not a sufficient cause for the military as an institution to yield its share of control over state power. By 1983 it was clear that one of the vital tasks of the democratic opposition would be to forge more organic links between the new organizations in civil society and the political parties. In this way, demands for redemocratization would become a continued social and political force to raise the cost of rule for the authoritarian state apparatus and to present at the same time a clear governing alternative for Brazil's growing political and economic crisis. This happened in 1984 and prepared the way for a candidate of the unified opposition to preside in 1985.

Conclusions

This examination of the variations in relations between the state and civil society in the four BA regimes of the southern cone, however cursory, has suggested several interesting generalizations regarding the way in which the character of the state affects the evolution of opposition politics.

That the state's definition of its "project" affects the possibilities for opposition is clearly evident in the contrast between Chile and Brazil. In Brazil, the BA's appeal to many active supporters came to be based in large part on its association with the improved rate of capital accumulation that characterized

Brazil in the late 1960s and early 1970s. "State strength" was thereby identified in important ways with a capacity for effective economic intervention. Repressive capacity was also important, but it was, in addition, a divisive issue within the state because it implied excessive power in the hands of the security apparatus (relative to the rest of the state apparatus and even to the rest of the military). The Brazilian state's concern with promoting capital accumulation did more than simply leave more space in which the opposition could move without repression. It had the unintended consequence of generating conditions that promoted the development of the structural base of the opposition, most notably in its effects on the growth of the working class in São Paulo.

In Chile, capacity for economic intervention was not simply absent from the regime's definition of state strength; reducing the state's capacity for economic intervention was a positive goal. This did not mean that the state had no impact on the course of economic change. Efforts to extricate the state from the economy had a number of important structural consequences, all of which had the intention of lessening the possibility of mounting a political opposition. One of the most important of these was the reduction in the size of the working class and also its fragmentation through the removal, wherever possible, of suitable targets of economic grievances beyond the level of the firm. In short, until the crisis of the economy in late 1981, the Chilean regime's economic strategy reinforced its strength as an instrument of domination quite independently of the state's (very effective) direct efforts at coercive control.

Looking at Chile and Brazil, it would seem that the "common-sense" hypothesis that state strength defined in economic terms naturally reinforces the state's capacity for the political domination of civil society should be reconsidered. State economic intervention, by politicizing "economistic" issues, may increase the potential for political organization in civil society. Conversely, in the setting of dependent capitalist development, the fight against public sector encroachment may be both antihistorical and antipopular—antihistorical in the sense that it undercuts the belief that continued state presence is an essential component of continued capital accumulation and antipopular in the sense that the major beneficiaries of a reduced public sector role are likely to be a small number of tightly interconnected oligopolists.

The second lesson to be drawn from these four cases involves the importance of the threat of class conflict in creating the conditions for domination of civil society by the state. O'Donnell has already pointed out the importance of this factor,[45] but the analysis presented here reinforces his argument. In Chile, where the possibility for a fundamental reordering of the class structure seemed real to the bourgeoisie, the latter accepted unquestiongly many state policies that were detrimental to its economic interests and acquiesced completely in

---

45. O'Donnell, "Reflections on the Patterns of Change" and "Tensions in the Bureaucratic-Authoritarian State."

the state's project of relatively autonomous domination of the political sphere. In Uruguay and in Argentina (until after Malvinas), fear of opening the door to changes in the class structure kept dominant civilian elites from pressuring more strongly for an opening in the political system. In Brazil, it was only after private elites became convinced that they could manage their economic and political future more effectively within a more open political environment that they began to mount a serious attack on the degree of autonomy that the state had achieved.

Overall, the most important lesson to be derived from these cases may be a methodological one. The power of the state as an actor and institution cannot be analyzed in isolation from an understanding of the nature of the cleavages that rend civil society, on the one hand, or the growth of horizontal ties that bring different sectors of civil society together, on the other hand. At the same time, the evolution of opposition to the state within civil society is shaped by the way in which the state defines its project and by the contradictions and conflicts that emerge inside the state apparatus itself.

FOUR

Military Politics in Three Polity Arenas: Civil Society, Political Society, and the State

The title of this chapter is certainly ponderous, possibly pompous, but unfortunately necessary. The focus throughout this work is on military politics in the polity. I use the word "polity" to call attention to the classic Aristotelian concern with how people organize themselves for collective life in the polis.[1] For a modern polity in the midst of a democratization effort, it is conceptually and politically useful to distinguish three important arenas of the polity: civil society, political society, and the state. Obviously, in any given polity these three arenas expand and shrink at different rates, interpenetrate or even dominate each other, and constantly change.[2]

Very schematically, by "civil society" I mean that arena where manifold social movements (such as neighborhood associations, women's groups, religious groupings, and intellectual currents) and civic organizations from all classes (such as lawyers, journalists, trade unions, and entrepreneurs) attempt to constitute themselves in an ensemble of arrangements so that they can express themselves and advance their interests.

---

1. For Aristotle's argument that there is an "imminent impulse in all men toward an association of this order," see *The Politics*, Book 1, Chapter 1, Sections 6–7, 14–15.

2. Cardoso's article in the companion volume, *Democratizing Brazil*, ed. Alfred Stepan (Oxford: Oxford University Press, 1989), is particularly rich in this respect. He shows how the great growth of the state enterprises has made them in some respects a part of civil society. He is also keenly aware of how civil and political groupings, in order to gain a greater degree of control over the state, must devise new practical and philosophical approaches to democratic collective actions within the state apparatus. Our two approaches are similar but are conducted on different levels of abstraction. One difference is that I insist, for reasons of analysis and political practice, on explicitly treating political society and civil society as distinct categories. He does so implicitly. My analysis in this book consciously sacrifices systematic attention to economic structures, both in order to highlight my discussion of the political aspects of the polity and because of their extensive coverage in the companion volume by Cardoso, Fishlow, Bacha, and Malan.

This chapter was first published in Alfred Stepan, *Rethinking Military Politics: Brazil and the Southern Cone* (Princeton: Princeton University Press, 1988), 3–12.

By "political society" in a democratizing setting I mean that arena in which the polity specifically arranges itself for political contestation to gain control over public power and the state apparatus. At best, civil society can destroy an authoritarian regime. However, a full democratic transition must involve political society, and the composition and consolidation of a democratic polity must entail serious thought and action about those core institutions of a democratic political society—political parties, elections, electoral rules, political leadership, intraparty alliances, and legislatures—through which civil society can constitute itself politically to select and monitor democratic government.

By "the state" I mean something more than "government." It is the continuous administrative, legal, bureaucratic, and coercive system that attempts not only to manage the state apparatus but to structure relations *between* civil and public power and to structure many crucial relationships *within* civil and political society.[3]

In an extreme monist (or what some would call totalitarian) polity, the state eliminates any significant autonomy in political or civil society. In a strong authoritarian regime, political society is frequently absorbed by dominant groups into the state, but civil society characteristically has at least some spheres of autonomy.

I make these distinctions knowing full well that Gramsci, Hegel, Locke, Rousseau, and in the companion volume to this study, *Democratizing Brazil*, Cardoso and Weffort use different definitions. I think, however, that the strongest defense of a definition is its usefulness in analysis, and these working definitions may help illuminate some frequently obscured relationships within a democratizing polity like Brazil. Let us see.

In the democratizing period in Brazil between 1974 and 1985, the most popular topics of systematic, scholarly social science concerned new movements within civil society that presented challenges to the authoritarian state, such as the church, the new unionism, the new entrepreneurs, the press, the Association of Brazilian Lawyers, women's groups, and neighborhood associations. Because the changes in civil society were so significant, interesting, and normatively attractive, scholarly attention in more than fifty published works on these topics is quite understandable.[4] As Cardoso argues, 'In Brazilian political language, everything which was an organized fragment which escaped the immediate control of the authoritarian order was being designated *civil society*. Not rigorously, but effectively, the whole opposition . . . was being described as if it were the movement of Civil Society.'[5]

"Civil society" became the political celebrity of the abertura. Politically the phrase had two tactical advantages in Brazilian discourse. First, because it

---

3. See my discussion in *The State and Society: Peru in Comparative Perspective*, especially the preface.

4. See the ample references in the Keck, Mainwaring, Della Cava, and Alvarez articles in *Democratizing Brazil*.

5. See his article in *Democratizing Brazil*.

explicitly was meant to entail opposition to the regime, the regime found it difficult to appropriate the meaning to its own advantage. Second, it created bonds between groups who in other settings were antagonists: São Paulo entrepreneurs and São Paulo metallurgical workers equally shared in the charismatic legitimacy of being part of the new "civil society."

The intense attention given to "civil" as opposed to "political" society was not without its strategic problems for the democratizing opposition. Important segments within the church and the new labor movement—two key segments of civil society—were deeply suspicious of "intermediaries" and "negotiations." They favored direct participation and articulation of demands, with the ideologically favored groups being "base" organizations. Partisans of this ideological current tended to be deeply suspicious of political parties. Opposition politicians in Congress—many of whom were seen as having been too tame during the pre-abertura period—were held in low esteem, and few organic links were forged between those opposition forces whose ideological and material resources were drawn from the arena of civil society and those opposition forces whose resources and style of action were associated with the arena of political society.

The military regime understood this sharp separation between the two arenas of the opposition and exploited the weakness. Again and again in the late 1970s and early 1980s the military altered the rules of the game for political society (physically and metaphorically isolated in Brasília and surrounded by the state). In this period civil society almost never came to the defense of political society. The regime's strategists were understandably happy with this pattern of behavior of the opposition that supported *liberalization* more than *democratization.*

This is a crucial distinction. In an authoritarian setting, "liberalization" may entail a mix of policy and social changes, such as less censorship of the media, somewhat greater working room for the organization of autonomous working-class activities, the reintroduction of some legal safeguards such as *habeas corpus* for individuals, the releasing of most political prisoners, the return of political exiles, possibly measures for improving the distribution of income, and, most important, the toleration of political opposition. "Democratization" entails liberalization but is a wider and more specifically political concept. Democratization requires open contestation for the right to win control of the government, and this in turn requires free elections, the results of which determine who governs. Using these definitions it is clear there can be liberalization without democratization. Liberalization refers fundamentally to civil society. Democratization involves civil society, but it refers fundamentally to political society.

There were also conceptual and analytical problems with a literature of the democratizing process that focused so heavily on civil society. Most scholars became specialists on the oppositional activity of specific fragments of civil society: base community specialists, new union specialists, specialists on lawyer associations, or the new entrepreneurs. This scholarly focus—though it produced some of the best and most exciting work on social movements anywhere in the world in the period—deflected attention from three important relationships.

First, it tended to leave understudied the immensely complex and innovative *horizontal relations of civil society with itself*, which helped interweave the weft and warp of civil society and give it a more variegated, more resistant fabric.[6]

Second, insufficient analytical attention was given to the problem of how the gap between the opposition based in the civil arena and opposition based in the political arena could be bridged.

Third, there were hundreds of scholarly and newspaper articles with titles such as "Entrepreneurs Against the State," "The Church Against the State," and "Metalworkers Against the State." However, this unidirectional vertical perspective led to a serious neglect, not only of the inter- and intraclass horizontal linkages, but also of the internal contradictions within the state (especially within the military) that led fractions of the state apparatus to seek out (and to tolerate the partial empowerment of) allies within civil society. Thus, even the analysis of the growth of civil society is impoverished if the state's *downward reach* for new allies in civil society is not documented descriptively and incorporated conceptually.[7]

Because civil society was the celebrity of the abertura and the prevailing discourse privileged the dichotomy ("Civil Society versus the State"), activists and scholars alike tended to belittle the role of parties, Congress, and elections, and "political society" was relatively neglected in the literature. Nonetheless, there were at least a score of solid books and articles in addition to a well-conceived collective longitudinal election project that focused precisely on political society in the democratizing period.[8]

Let us now turn to the question of the state, and specifically to the military as a part of the authoritarian state apparatus. As late as mid-1984, although the Brazilian opening was over ten years old, to my knowledge there was not even *one* systematic academic social science monograph or thesis in Portuguese or English, about the military in the period of distensão and abertura.[9]

6. There is a great story waiting to be told. I discuss and document part of this innovative horizontal process in my "State Power and the Strength of Civil Society in the Southern Cone of Latin America" (reproduced as chapter 3 in this volume). The subject, however, deserves book-length treatment.

7. I analyze this "downward reach" in Ch. 3 of *Rethinking Military Politics*.

8. For an analysis of the neglect of political society—especially the role of the opposition in elections—as well as a discussion of the solid literature on parties and elections, see Bolivar Lamounier, "'Authoritarian Brazil' Revisited." La mounier played an important role throughout the democratizing period in developing research and discussion on political society.

9. I called attention to this point in my "O Que Estão Pensando os Militares." The major exception to this neglect is the article by Eliezer Rizzo de Oliveira, "Conflits militaires et décisions sous la présidence du Général Geisel (1974–1979)." Also see Jan Knippers Black, "The Military and Political Decompression in Brazil." There are some

Clearly, both for theoretical and empirical reasons, if the analytic focus is on the transition to democracy—especially a transition that is occurring within the specific context of a military-led authoritarian regime—the military component itself must be studied.

What explains this stunning neglect of the military? Part of the explanation is an understandable fear of repression and censorship. However, it should be noted that this same period saw the publication of numerous detailed accounts of torture in particular, and harshy critical books about the authoritarian regime in general. Certainly, it is also relatively difficult for scholars to do research on the military, especially if they are Brazilian citizens; however, the Brazilian military annually publishes a considerable quantity of documents that merit content analysis and many retired colonels and generals have been surprisingly willing to talk to journalists. Part of the explanation for neglect would seem therefore to be normative disdain for the military as a topic (the obverse of the normative attraction to new groups in civil society). This is a longstanding problem, often referred to as "the liberal bias." It probably merits calling attention once again to Max Weber's eminently sound, if neglected, dictum in his famous essay on science as a vocation, "the primary task of a useful teacher is to teach his students to recognize 'inconvenient' facts—I mean the facts that are inconvenient for their party opinions."[10]

Finally, a significant part of the neglect of the military as a central topic of empirical research, in my judgment, has its origins in theory. The 1970s witnessed a worldwide boom in theoretical writings about the state. Probably the

important comparative reflections in Alexandre de Souza Costa Barros and Edmundo Coelho, "Military Intervention and Withdrawal in South America."

The standard works on the modern Brazilian military focus on the period *before* the abertura. See Alexandre de Souza Costa Barros, "The Brazilian Military: Professional Socialization, Political Performance and State Building"; Edmundo Campus Coelho, *Em Busca de Identidade: O Exército e a Política na Sociedade Brasileira*; Eurico de Lima Figueiredo, *Os Militares e a Democracia: Análise Estrutural da Ideologia do Pres. Castelo Branco*; René Armand Dreifuss, *1964: A Conquista do Estado, Açaõ Política, Poder e Golpe de Classe*; Alfred Stepan, *The Military in Politics*; and Alfred Stepan, "The 'New Professionalism of Internal Warfare and Military Role Expansion.'"

The best systematic, empirically based publication on the security apparatus as it functioned in the abertura period focused exclusively on the military police of São Paulo. See the excellent study by Paulo Sérgio Pinheiro, "Polícia e Crise Política: O Caso das Polícias Militares."

For the military in the abertura period, three books written from a journalistic vantage point provide some of the most important leads and perspectives. See Walder de Góes, *O Brasil do General Geisel: Estudo do Processo de Tomada de Decisão no Regime Militar-Burocrático*; André Gustavo Stumpf and Merval Pereira Filho, *A Segunda Guerra: Sucessão de Geisel*; and Bernardo Kucinski, *Abertura, a História de uma Crise*.

Four works with valuable material on the military in the abertura that appeared in 1983–5 are Maria Helena Moreira Alves, *Estado e Oposição no Brasil (1964–1984)*; René Armand Dreifuss and Otávio Soares Dulci, "As Forças Armadas e a Política"; Walder de Góes, "O Novo Regime Militar no Brasil"; and Wilfred Bacchus, "Long-Term Military Rulership in Brazil: Ideologic Consensus and Dissensus, 1963–1983."

10. Max Weber, "Science as a Vocation," in *From Max Weber: Essays in Sociology*, ed. H. H. Gerth and C. Wright Mills, 147.

single most influential theorist of the state was Poulantzas, an advocate of the "relative autonomy of the state." However, his analysis of the reasons for state autonomy has nothing to do with his analysis of empirically observed dynamics of state bureaucracies, but rather derives from his *functionalist assumption* that such a degree of autonomy is a structural requirement of capital accumulation and domination in an advanced capitalist state.[11] Note how little autonomous power bureaucracies are accorded in his theoretical framework; for him the state is "the site of organization of the dominant class in the relationship to the dominated classes. It is a *site* and a *center* of the exercise of power, but it possesses no power of its own."[12]

Politics and political science are about power. What is particularly revealing about the Poulantzas quotation is that the theoretical logic of his form of diffuse structural determinism conceptually *removes* the military from the exercise of power.[13] This theoretical perspective is misleading. Any military organization is of course affected by the overall balance of class power within which it functions. However, it is also true that any large complex organization has some institutional interests of its own and prerogatives its members seek to advance, as well as some changes or outcomes in the overall political system that it, more than other organizations, particularly fears and thus resists. Complex organizations thus have interests and capacities to advance their interests.

When the unit of analysis is not just a complex organization, but a military organization such as the one found in Brazil from 1964 until 1985—which supplied the bulk of the coercive resources of the state, from whose membership the head of state was selected, and from which a significant portion of the most important state enterprises' and agencies' heads were selected—the requirement to study the specific organizational structures and norms of that military organization is powerful.

The argument becomes overwhelming when we realize that both in 1964 and in 1969–71 there were "Brumairean moments" during which strategic fractions of the bourgeoisie were fearful enough to abdicate, in essence, to the military their claims to rule, in return for the coercive protection they thought only the military could give them.[14] Here the emphasis of Poulantzas is again

---

11. Nicos Poulantzas, especially in his *Political Power and Social Classes*, is primarily a functionalist, notwithstanding the rich problems he raises. For a pointed discussion of the empirical and theoretical questions begged by such functionalism, see Anthony Giddens, *A Contemporary Critique of Historical Materialism*, 214–17; and Douglas C. Bennett and Kenneth E. Sharpe, "The State as Banker and as Entrepreneur: The Last Resort Character of the Mexican State's Economic Intervention, 1917–1970."

12. Nicos Poulantzas, *State, Power, Socialism*, 148. Poulantzas's emphasis.

13. For a brilliant analysis of precisely this problem by a political philosopher, see Stephen Lukes, *Power: A Radical View*, 52–6.

14. Karl Marx, in "The Eighteenth Brumaire of Louis Bonaparte," described as one of the characteristics of the Bonapartist regime the abdication by the bourgeoisie of its right to rule in exchange for other kinds of protection by the ensuing strong state. Here, I use the word "Brumairean" to evoke the kind of relation described in Marx's essay.

misleading. Power does of course diffusely reside in structures, but it can also be actively exercised by individuals controlling complex organizations. Fear may create a social base and the Brumairean moment. But as the São Paulo entrepreneurs learned in the late 1970s, the receding of bourgeois fear does not mean that power once yielded to the military will be given back without a struggle.[15] In the study of the military, as in the study of any other complex organization, we must also bear in mind the ratchet effect of bureaucratic momentum and aggrandizement.

Antonio Gramsci and Max Weber, working from very different theoretical and normative perspectives, both understood the central role of the coercive apparatus in modern, especially authoritarian, states. Gramsci, on various occasions, asserts that "domination" is a function of *hegemony* and *coercion*. He refers in one place to hegemony as "the spontaneous consent given by the great masses of the population to the general direction imposed on social life by the dominant fundamental group."[16] For Gramsci, to the extent that such hegemony does not exist in civil society, compliance is obtained by "the apparatus of state coercive power which 'legally' enforces discipline on those groups who do not 'consent' either actively or passively."[17] In the case of Brazil—especially in the period 1964–74—we are dealing with what O'Donnell calls a "bureaucratic-authoritarian" regime, or what I have called an "exclusionary" authoritarian regime. Whatever it is labeled, the Brazilian authoritarian regime at no time came remotely close to achieving Gramscian hegemony.[18]

Another major conceptual approach to the state, Max Weber's, also put great emphasis on the role of domination and the physical and organizational means of domination. He explicitly says "the state is a relation of men dominating men" and that "organized domination, which calls for continuous administration, requires that human conduct be conditioned to obedience . . . towards those masters who claim to be the bearers of legitimate power. On the other hand, by virtue of this obedience, organized domination requires the control of those material goods which in a given case are necessary for the use of physical violence."[19] In the context of an authoritarian state such as Brazil, a serious reading of Gramsci or Weber would require specific attention to the coercive

15. See Eli Diniz and Renato Boschi, *Empresariado Nacional e Estado no Brasil*; Luis Carlos Bresser Pereira, *O Colapso de uma Aliança de Classes*; and Fernando Henrique Cardoso, "O Papel dos Empresários no Processo de Transição: O Caso Brasileiro."

16. Antonio Gramsci, *Selections from the Prison Notebooks*, ed. Quintin Hoare and Geoffrey Nowell Smith, 12.

17. Ibid.

18. Guillermo O'Donnell, *Modernization and Bureaucratic-Authoritarianism: Studies in South American Politics*; and Stepan, *State and Society*, where, in Chapter 3, I argued that the Mexican authoritarian regime had a substantial degree of Gramscian hegemony and contrasted this sharply with the Brazilian authoritarian regime.

19. See "Politics as a Vocation," in *From Max Weber*, 78, 80. I discuss Weber's theory of the state in my *State and Society*, xi–xiv.

apparatus, that is, the military and the security community. They were, after all, the "inconvenient facts" of the abertura.

However, it is also a theoretical and empirical imperative to then locate this institutional analysis within the larger context of *power as a relationship*. A dynamic, contextually sensitive analysis of the movement from a strong military-led authoritarian regime to the transition to democracy entails the assessment of power relationships between three interactive, but conceptually distinct, arenas of the policy: civil society, political society, and the state. I will attempt to use all these concepts in the ensuing relational analysis of power changes.

II

Constructing and Deconstructing Polities: Contexts, Capacities, and Identities

FIVE

Paths toward Redemocratization: Theoretical and Comparative Considerations

In the course of our three conferences on redemocratization, the editors and I decided it would be useful to attempt to characterize in a systematic (but not ahistorical) manner the major alternative coalitional and institutional paths to redemocratization. What follows is a deliberate effort to use abstract analysis to highlight the political and policy implications of each path, taken by itself. We are of course painfully aware that no path to redemocratization is ever "taken by itself." However, in our efforts to arrive at new synthetic interpretations of redemocratization as an integrated process, we want to avoid undertheorizing the question of the radically different paths available for redemocratization in the modern world and the fact that each path entails a predictable set of possibilities, problems, and constraints.

The tasks of this chapter, then, are conceptual and historical. The goal is to explore the following questions concerning authoritarianism and redemocratization. How should we conceptualize the types of paths by which redemocratization can occur? What are the particular strengths and weaknesses of each path for the institutionalization of political democracy? What theoretically predictable implications does each path have for reactionary, status quo, progressive, or revolutionary policies? What can we learn from the history of the most important cases of redemocratization since World War II? And finally, what insights can we derive from our abstract and historical analysis that will illuminate instances of authoritarianism and redemocratization before us now?

Before I begin the analysis, some caveats are in order. First, some categories established on abstract grounds turn out to have no empirical referents;

This chapter was first published is Guillermo O'Donnell, Philippe C. Schmitter, and Laurence Whitehead (eds.), *Transitions from Authoritarian Rule: Comparative Perspectives* (Baltimore: Johns Hopkins University Press, 1986), 64–84.

nonetheless, by indicating an apparently quite plausible path toward redemocratization, we can expand our conception of the empirically possible, or we can direct our attention to hidden obstacles otherwise not apparent. A second caveat is that any empirical case of redemocratization may well—and almost certainly does—contain features of more than one category. In fact, successful redemocratization, given the built-in limitations of certain paths taken by themselves, may well require the simultaneous pursuit of several paths. Finally, I discuss only what appear to be the most important paths. Logic could derive and history provide examples of many other paths not discussed here. Parsimony and historical complexity rule out a textbook construction of "mutually exclusive and collectively exhaustive" categories. Instead my goal is to be suggestive and at the same time faithful to the realities of authoritarianism and redemocratization in the modern period.

On abstract and historical grounds, we can propose eight particularly plausible and distinctive paths leading to the termination of authoritarian regimes and the process of redemocratization. Obviously, as the rest of this volume makes clear, a complex variety of causes—economic, historical, political, and international—are involved in the outcome of the redemocratization process. Yet it is my contention that the actual route taken toward that redemocratization has an independent weight: serious comparative analysis must attempt the difficult task of isolating and assessing this distinctive contribution.

The first three paths are ones in which warfare and conquest play an integral part in the redemocratization process. The great majority of historical examples of successful redemocratization, most of them European, in fact fall into these first three categories. The balance between prior democratic strength, the political unity and disunity of the conquered country, and the role of external powers in the redemocratization process can be sufficiently different to warrant the identification of three distinct categories: (1) internal restoration after external reconquest; (2) internal reformulation; and (3) externally monitored installation.

For the last three decades, and for the conceivable future, the overwhelming majority of cases of redemocratization have been and will be ones in which sociopolitical forces rather than external military forces play the key role, though international and economic forces, as well as political blocs, play an important role. We can divide these paths toward redemocratization into two general categories. In the first category, the termination of authoritarian regimes and the move toward redemocratization could be initiated by the wielders of authoritarian power themselves. Authoritarian power-holders may attempt to relieve pressure on themselves while at the same time preserving as many of their interests as possible by: (4) redemocratization initiated from within authoritarian regimes. (This important path has three subtypes. Each subtype is differentiated by the distinctive institutional base of the power group within the authoritarian regime that initiates the redemocratization attempt. The initiating group can be drawn from the civilianized political leadership (4*a*), the military-as-government (4*b*), or the military-as-institution which acts against either the military as government or the civilianized political leadership (4*c*).)

In the final category, oppositional forces play the major role in terminating the authoritarian regime and in setting or not setting the framework for redemocratization. The following oppositional routes would seem the most important: (5) society-led regime termination; (6) party pact (with or without consociational elements); (7) organized violent revolt coordinated by democratic reformist parties; and (8) Marxist-led revolutionary war.

Internal Restoration after External Reconquest (1)

Internal restoration after external reconquest means that redemocratization takes place when a functioning democracy that has been conquered in war restores democracy after the conqueror is defeated by external force. Here the key questions seem to be whether the leaders of the original regime are deemed culpable for the conquest, whether there is an issue of collaboration by the democratic leadership, whether a resistance movement unconnected or antagonistic to the defeated democratic leadership becomes a competing center of national identification and authority, and whether, during the occupation, enduring changes occur in the social, economic, and political structures of the country. The more the answer is in the negative for all questions, the more likely it is that the outcome after reconquest will be the restoration of the previous democratic system, with full legal continuities between the old and new democratic regimes. Such restoration would entail few pressures or incentives for major socioeconomic change. The more the answer is positive for these four questions, the less likely it will be that restoration (Path 1) is possible and the more likely that internal reformulation (Path 2) or even externally monitored installation (Path 3) will be the outcome.

The obvious cases that fit Path 1 are the Netherlands, Belgium, Norway, and Denmark. The Netherlands and Norway are in fact cases of perfect fit. In both countries, crown and cabinet went into-exile and there was no hint of the culpability or collaboration of the democratic leadership with the authoritarian conquerors, the Nazis. In both countries, the respective monarchs-in-exile became symbols of national unity and of resistance to the invader; the resistance movements did not challenge the legitimacy of the governments-in-exile, and the conquerors did not succeed in imposing any enduring socioeconomic changes.[1] In both cases, following the defeat of the conqueror,

1. See Sverre Kjelstadli, "The Resistance Movement in Norway and the Allies, 1940–1945," and L. de Jong, "The Dutch Resistance Movement and the Allies, 1940-1945," both in *European Resistance Movements, 1939-1945: Proceedings of the Second International Conference on the History of the Resistance Movements Held at Milan, 26–9 March 1961* (New

there was a complete restoration of the political system, complete legal and institutional continuity with the past democratic system, and no significant restructuring of the socioeconomic system.[2]

Denmark is a more complicated case in that crown and cabinet capitulated to the German "protective occupation" but contined to rule although the Germans controlled the press, radio, and economic policy. At first political leaders attempted to normalize the state of affairs through negotiations with the occupying forces, and relatively free elections were held in spring 1943. However, the growing strength of the resistance and a wave of sabotage led the Germans to demand that the Danish government introduce martial law. This demand was met by a firm rejection which precipitated a *Wehrmacht* assault on the Danish armed forces and the imposition of direct rule. The Danish cabinet retired and neither it nor the king were tarred with collaborationist label nor considered culpable. There was no fundamental questioning of the prevailing democratic structure or socioeconomic order. As in the Netherlands and Norway, no major resistance movement assumed significant claims to autonomy, and after the war there was complete restoration of the *status quo ante*.[3]

Belgium is even more complicated. In Belgium, the cabinet established a government-in-exile in England. However, King Leopold III disobeyed the cabinet's wish and stayed behind in Belgium. During the German occupation, the king did not rule but an ambiguous visit by him to Hitler raised doubts about his personal legitimacy. After reconquest, the Parliament declared Leopold III "unable to reign" but accepted his brother Charles as regent. In 1950, there was a closely fought referendum about Leopold's right to assume the throne. In the aftermath of a divided vote, with the Flemish in favor and the Walloons against, the king, faced with a Socialist-led general strike, assumed the throne briefly and resigned in favor of his son. For our purposes, the point is that neither the constitutional monarchy nor the institutions of democracy were questioned and constitutional and socioeconomic continuity was maintained.[4]

York: Macmillan, 1964). See also Henri Michel, *The Shadow War: European Resistance, 1939–1945* (New York: Harper & Row, 1972), esp. pp. 301–2, 336–8.

2. In Holland, however, the restoration was accompanied by some criticisms to the effect that the prewar political parties had been responsible for the parlous state the armed forces found themselves in on the eve of hostilities. There was also a perceptible shift toward greater secularism in Dutch politics and a nonconfessional Labor party emerged.

3. Per Nutrup, *An Outline of the German Occupation of Denmark, 1940–1945* (Copenhagen: Danish National Museum, 1968) and Henning Poulsen and Marlene Djursaa, "Social Basis of Nazism in Denmark: The DNSAP," in *Who Were the Fascists? Social Roots of European Fascism*, Ed. Stein Ugelvik Larsen, Bernt Hagtvet, and Jan Petter Myklebust (Bergen: Universitetsforlaget, 1980).

4. Michel, *The Shadow War*, pp. 302, 337–8; Val R. Lorwin, "Belgium: Religion, Class, and Language in National Politics," in *Political Oppositions in Western Democracies*, ed. Robert A. Dahl (New Haven: Yale University Press, 1966), pp. 168–9, 177; Jacques Pirenne, *Dossier du Roi Leopold III* (Luxembourg: L'Imprimerie St. Paul, n.d.), and Brian Bond, *France and Belgium, 1939–1940* (London: Davis-Poynter, 1975), pp. 143–57.

Internal Reformulation (2)

In this category redemocratization takes place after a conqueror has been defeated largely because of external force. However, the more internal circumstances cause the previous democratic regime to collapse, or the previous regime is deemed culpable for the conquest, or there is a perception of collaboration, or a powerful resistance movement unconnected or antagonistic to the previous democratic leadership emerges, or profound changes occur during the occupation, then: the more impossible simple restoration of the previous democratic system becomes, and the more likely that redemocratization will entail deep, constitutional reformulation. Further, the more the above factors (collaboration, autonomous resistance, etc.) are positive, the more likely the outcome will be civil war among the competing groups. This path toward redemocratization obviously has much greater potential for political instability than Path 1. It also has much greater potential for rightist reaction or leftist structural change than Path 1. Depending on the outcome of the struggle among the competing groups and classes, there is greater potential for popular forces to gain important changes such as nationalizations, legalization of popular control of unions, or the right to full participation in elections. On the other hand, there is also a greater likelihood that the outcome of the struggle could be repression, the exclusion of groups from the political system, and the denial of their rights to organize; that is, that there will be only partial redemocratization.

The two cases closest to Path 2 are postliberation France and Greece. Italy combines Path 2 and Path 3.

From a formal and legal perspective, the Pétain administration began as a legitimate democratic government. The president of the Republic, Lebrun, made Pétain prime minister on the understanding that he would make peace. However, as Paxton argues, "Vichy was not a band-aid. It was deep surgery. To an extent unique among the occupied nations of Western Europe, France went beyond mere administration during the occupation to carry out a domestic revolution in institutions and values." One could argue then that Vichy France began as a democratic emergency regime but rapidly became an authoritarian one.[5]

The resistance movements, three major groups of heterogeneous political persuasion—radicals, Catholics, Socialists, and Communists—in the South, and the National Front dominated by the Communist party in the North, all acknowledged, to a greater or lesser extent, the leadership of de Gaulle and his Free French forces. All the resistance movements also raised major questions about the culpability, collaboration, and legitimacy of the Vichy government.[6]

5. Robert Owen Paxton, *Vichy France: Old Guard and New Order, 1940–1944* (New York: Knopf, 1972), p. 20; see also Robert Aron, *Histoire des Années 40* (Paris: Librairie Jules Tallander, 1976), vol. 1, pp. 61–226.
6. John F. Sweets, *The Politics of Resistance in France, 1940–1944: A History of the Mouvements Unis de la Résistance* (De Kalb: Northern Illinois University Press, 1976), pp. 33–70, 115–48.

As Paxton demonstrates, France from 1941 to 1944 contained elements of a civil war mixed with a patriotic war.[7] The patriotic war was dominant, however, and the Gaullist forces, working with all the parties contributing to the resistance, and supported by Britain and the United States, reformulated the democratic constitution and founded the Fourth Republic after the war. The regime recognized the de facto configuration of power and the patriotic achievements of the resistance forces. De Gaulle accepted Communist and Socialist control of much of the trade union movement. The Communist party of France (PCF) was able to use the postliberation purges to eliminate opposition in the unions and in the Confédération Générale du Travail (CGT) in particular, and thus establish their overwhelming dominance over that organization.[8] The period 1944–6 also witnessed extensive nationalization of properties owned by collaborators. These included many of the major commercial banks and the major auto producer, Renault. Punitive expropriations were only one feature of the nationalization program as the French state extended its controls over key sectors of the economy, including the mines, electricity, and gas.[9] The French Communist party, though initially hurt by the Nazi-Soviet nonaggression pact of 1939–41, made substantial gains after 1941 because of its role in the resistance.[10] In 1946 the party polled an average of 27.4 percent in the two elections (its previous high had been 15.3 percent) and participated in the government of 1946–7.[11] In France, therefore, the path of redemocratization via reformulation resulted in extensive nationalizations and important organizational gains for the Left, substantially greater gains than occurred in any country following Path 1.

In Greece, by way of contrast, there was a very different constellation of forces, and the outcome, though one of formal redemocratization, was very different. Democracy was reformulated in a more unstable and exclusionary way than in any case following Path 1. Democracy broke down in Greece in 1936 but the authoritarian Metaxas government, though manifesting some sympathy for Fascist styles of government, resisted the Axis powers. After the occupation of Greece in July 1941 by German, Italian, and Bulgarian troops, the king went into exile in England and Egypt. However, the king and his cabinet did not actively support the main resistance movement, which developed into an increasingly autonomous, legitimate, Marxist, and republican force which in fact carried out a program of change in the territory it controlled. With a relative weight much greater than the French resistance movements, with open borders to Marxist partisans in Albania, Yugoslavia, and Bulgaria,

7. Paxton, *Vichy France*, pp. 291–8.
8. Aron, *Histoire des Années 40*, vol. 10, pp. 406–19.
9. Ibid., vol. 9, pp. 16–31.
10. The PCF had two members in de Gaulle's CFLN (National Liberation Committee) as early as 1944, and Communist ministers were also in the Provisional government. See Sweets, *The Politics of Resistance in France*, pp. 115–49.
11. Thomas T. Mackie and Richard Rose, *The International Almanac of Electoral History*, 2d ed. (New York: Facts on File, 1982).

and with no nationalist competitors such as the Gaullists, the Greek resistance movement at liberation had strong military and political claims to participate in, if not to control, Greek national leadership. Domestic power balances completely ruled out Path 1 restoration. However, Churchill and later Truman saw Greece as a key area of struggle against world Communism, and massively backed royalist and conservative forces. The 1944–9 Civil War was waged to determine the terms of constitutional, socioeconomic, and international alignments in Greece. In almost any civil war, regardless of the outcome, the losers lose much beside the war, and the country has normally a weak foundation for a successor democratic regime. In this particular Civil War over 80,000 Greeks were killed and 10 percent of the population were forced to move from their homes. In October 1949, when the remnants of the Democratic army of the resistance fled across the border to Albania, the resulting "democratic reformulation," which grew directly out of the civil war emergency powers, outlawed the Communist party, virtually excluded the Left from employment in the state apparatus, and gave great prerogatives to the Greek army, which was extensively purged of most leftists, republicans, and many centrists. This legacy of exclusion and military prerogatives within a democratic system contributed to the breakdown of democracy in 1967. The authoritarian regime that followed that breakdown was itself terminated in 1974 largely by the "military-as-institution" (Path 4*c*), which nevertheless retained some of the prerogatives of the 1949 reformulation, prerogatives that are being challenged only today by the Socialist government elected in 1981.[12]

Italy from 1943 to 1946 combined elements of Path 2 and Path 3 (externally monitored installation). As Gianfranco Pasquino notes, Mussolini was overthrown not by the allies but by a vote of the Fascist Grand Council on 25 July 1943, a decision that gave authority to the king to dismiss Mussolini from his office of prime minister.[13] The overthrow should also be seen in the context of the successful Allied attack on Sicily, the bombing of Rome, and Mussolini's failure to persuade Hitler to permit Italy to withdraw from the Axis war effort. The armistice signed by the new prime minister, Marshal Badoglio, in September 1943 provoked the full-scale occupation of North and Central Italy by

12. For Greece consult Richard Clogg, *A Short History of Modern Greece* (Cambridge: Cambridge University Press, 1979), pp. 133–226; P. Nikiforos Diamandouros, "Regime Change and the Prospects for Democracy in Greece: 1974–83," in Volume I of this series; George Th. Mavrogordatos, "From Ballots to Bullets: The 1946 Election and Plebiscite as Prelude to Civil War" (Paper presented at the Symposium of the Modern Greek Studies Association on "Greece in the 1940s," 9–12 November 1978, American University, Washington, D.C.); Nicos Mouzelis, "Regime Instability and the State in Peripheral Capitalism: A General Theory and a Case Study of Greece" (Working Paper no. 79, Latin American Program, Wilson Center, Washington, D.C., 1980); and Nicos C. Alivizatos, "The Greek Army in the Late Forties: Towards an Institutional Autonomy," *Journal of the Hellenic Diaspora* 3 (Fall 1978): 37–45.

13. See the excellent chapter by Gianfranco Pasquino, "The Demise of the First Fascist Regime and Italy's Transition to Democracy: 1943–1948," in Volume I of this series.

Germany and the establishment of a puppet state under Mussolini. Italy was not fully liberated until April 1945.[14]

The armed resistance movement played an important role in the struggle against the German military, creating Committees of National Liberation with members from five political parties. In the North, the Left was particularly important. Pasquino notes: "While military actions in the Center and North of Italy were and remained of utmost importance, the resistance movement consistently attempted to create the foundations for a new, democratic, and republican State in the various zones it succeeded in liberating from the Germans."[15] There were thus some ingredients for polarization on the Greek scale, but the actual outcome in Italy was closer to that of France than Greece. Why?

Viewed strategically, the position of the Communist party was weaker in Italy than in Greece. In Greece, the resistance for much of the period between 1942 and 1944 was the strongest anti-Axis military force. In Italy, when the resistance became powerful, the Allies already had a military presence in the South.[16] In addition, the coexistence of four other parties in the Committees of National Liberation meant that the comparative weight of the Italian Communist party (PCI) within the resistance was less than in Greece. Finally, geopolitically, Italian Communistś lacked extensive, open borders with access to Communist partisans as in Greece.

Partly because of this balance of forces, the Soviet Union gave diplomatic recognition to the royalist government under Badoglio in March 1944. Shortly thereafter, Togliatti returned to Italy promising to cooperate with the discredited king and prime minister and to postpone all questions of a social or institutional nature including even an anti-Fascist purge until after the cessation of hostilities. Even after the liberation the PCI used all its influence with the Socialists first to give the cold shoulder to the Action party's call in April 1945 for a revolutionary democratic republic and later, in December 1945, to cooperate with the Christian Democrats in bringing down the Parri administration, which had introduced measures favoring small business and a capital levy as well as stiff prosecutions of Fascists. By 1945, Togliatti could point to the suppression of ELAS in Greece in 1944, the Allied occupation of Northern Italy, and the impossibility of aid from the Red army in diverting the cadres from the revolutionary path.[17] In the judgment of Pasquino, "Togliatti put the Communist party at the service of the national cause: the war of national

14. F. W. Deakin, *The Brutal Friendship: Mussolini, Hitler, and the Fall of Italian Fascism* (New York: Harper & Row, 1962), pp. 419–85.

15. Pasquino, "Demise of the First Fascist Regime," chap. 3 in Volume 1.

16. Armed anti-Fascist parties and organized resistance only began to show their presence to any appreciable extent after September 1943. See Charles F. Delzell, *Mussolini's Enemies: The Italian Anti-Fascist Resistance* (Princeton: Princeton University Press, 1961), pp. 261–314 and Michel, *The Shadow War*, pp. 302–4.

17. See Norman Kogan, *Italy and the Allies* (Cambridge, Mass.: Harvard University Press, 1956) and his *A Political History of Post-War Italy* (London: Pall Mall Press, 1966).

liberation took precedence in his strategy over the goals of sociopolitical reforms."[18] This strategy, unlike that in Greece, precluded any attempt to conquer state power, but, as in France, won for the Left legitimate claims to participate in the postwar political settlement. In the elections of 2 June 1946, the Communists and Socialists helped defeat the system of monarchy in the referendum and on the same day won for themselves 39.6 percent of the seats in the Constituent Assembly which drafted a progressive constitution.[19]

In contrast to France, however, purges of the state apparatus were less widespread and nationalizations were less extensive. It is tempting to assert the explanation that redemocratization in Italy contained an element of Path 3 (externally monitored installation). Certainly Churchill, until his electoral defeat in late 1945, was a strong force for continuity in the Italian state apparatus, and opposed extending participation to the Committees of National Liberation in local governments or factories.[20] However, a number of studies have also argued that neither the Communists nor the Christian Democrats pushed hard for sweeping postwar socioeconomic changes. For both parties, their insertion in the state apparatus and the attainment of a stable postwar institutional arrangement were paramount goals.[21]

Externally Monitored Installation (3)

This category includes cases in which democratic powers defeat an authoritarian regime and play a major role in the formulation and installation of a democratic regime.

The major political weakness of this path toward redemocratization would seem to be its foreign imposition. It would appear to have a problem of legitimacy not found in the first path. However, it does share with the Marxist revolutionary path, described later, the power to dismantle the military and political institutions and other features of the authoritarian state apparatus. Such dismantling removes an important obstacle to redemocratization, an obstacle that looms large in many of the other paths analyzed in this chapter. If the authoritarian regime has been severely discredited, nationalistic

18. Pasquino, "Demise of the First Fascist Regime," chap. 3 in Volume 1.
19. Ibid.
20. Kogan argues that in 1943 the Allies demanded "the provisional abandonment of all goals of social reform for the duration of hostilities.... The preservation of the social structure for its own sake was not the only motive behind Allied demands.... Reform and change would mean political conflict and headaches for Allied administrators. So for immediate, practical reasons the Allies threw their weight behind the status quo." See Kogan, *Italy and the Allies*, pp. 60–1.
21. Pasquino, "Demise of the First Fascist Regime." See also the articles by M. De Cecco, "Economic Policy in the Reconstruction Period, 1945–1951," and B. Salvati, "The Rebirth of Italian Trade Unionism, 1943–1954," in *The Rebirth of Italy, 1943–1950*, ed. S. J. Woolf (New York: Humanities Press, 1972), pp. 156–80, 181–211.

reaction against foreign imposition might be dampened. However, if imposition occurs by capitalist powers, the range of socioeconomic and political changes supported by the monitoring powers will fall within broadly predictable limits.

The purest case of this category is West Germany, followed by Japan.[22] Austria and Italy fall partially into this category, but Austria has elements of the consociational path described later, and Italy, as we have shown, had strong elements of the internal reformulation of Path 2. Rather surprisingly, especially in view of the element of foreign imposition, all four countries that redemocratized by this route have had an unbroken history of democratic rule since World War II. What explains this historical outcome, and why should we be extremely skeptical about the ease with which it could be reproduced?

The historically specific fact of worldwide repugnance against Fascism meant that the defeated regimes had almost no overt domestic political defenders. Also, because all four countries were part of the core of the world capitalist system, even though they had been defeated in the war, the successor democratic systems were the beneficiaries of unprecedented financial support from the United States. The United States emerged from the war as the unchallenged economic, political, and military leader of the world and used these powers—especially after the cold war began in 1947—to create economic and ideological allies against Communism.

The democratic imposition by the United States and other Western powers also helps to account for the consistency of the fundamental outlines of the supported model with the social and economic patterns of the conquering powers, though there were significant social changes and economic reforms during the reconstruction (especially the agrarian reform in Japan).[23]

22. Juan Linz in a commentary on an earlier version of my chapter notes that in Germany "the Allied high command in the western sectors implemented a controlled process of redemocratization defining the rules of the game, the timing of the process, excluding some potential political forces by limiting the number of parties, the *Lizenparteien*, and giving them a series of advantages which would assure the future strengths of some of them, at the same time that they exercised considerable influence on the constitutional framework, imposing their version of federalism and supporting a particular model of social economic organization." See his "The Transition from Authoritarian Regimes to Democratic Political Systems and the Problems of Consolidation of Political Democracy" (Paper prepared for the International Political Science Association, Tokyo Round Table, 29 March–1 April 1982), p. 25.

23. For one of the few comparative analyses of all four cases see Linz, "Transition from Authoritarian Regimes," pp. 23–8. For a standard history of monitored installation in Germany see Hans W. Gatzke, *Germany and the United States: A Special Relationship* (Cambridge, Mass.: Harvard University Press, 1980), pp. 154–78, and Edward N. Peterson, *The American Occupation of Germany: Retreat to Victory* (Detroit: Wayne State University Press, 1977). For a revisionist account, see Bruce Kuklick, *American Policy and the Division of Germany: The Clash with Russia over Reparations* (Ithaca: Cornell University Press, 1972). For Japan see Edwin O. Reischauer, *The United States and Japan* (Cambridge, Mass.: Harvard University Press, 1965), and for a revisionist version see John Dower, *Empire and Aftermath: Yoshida Sigero and the Japanese Experience, 1878–1954* (Cambridge, Mass.: Harvard University Press, 1979).

Despite the concrete outcome in all four of the existing cases, it is virtually impossible—even with the advent of a war—for these conditions to reappear. Given the political and economic evolution of the world system, no single capitalist country today or plausible group of core capitalist countries is ever again likely to have the hegemonic power the United States had in the period immediately after the war. For countries outside the core of capitalism, instead of Marshall Plan integration, there is likely to be a much more complex set of factors, involving nationalism, dependency, North—South and East–West conflicts.

The first three categories are ones in which warfare and conquest played integral parts in redemocratization. The majority of historical examples of successful redemocratization (most of them European) fall into these three categories. The connection between successful redemocratization, World War II, and the legacy of democracy and capitalism is apparent. Equally apparent is that redemocratization today and in the future will almost always occur via very different paths.

Redemocratization Initiated from within the Authoritarian Regime (4)

By this category I do not mean a once-and-for-all decision to devolve power. Such a decision seldom happens. What often does happen, however, is that some major institutional power-holders within the ruling authoritarian coalition perceive that because of changing conditions their long-term interests are best pursued in a context in which authoritarian institutions give way to democratic institutions.

On the surface, it would appear that this path has at least three characteristic constraints and predictable problems that should be given special attention. First, the power-holders can attempt to reverse their initial liberalizing decision if—in Dahlian terms—the opening of the political system contributes to situations in which the costs of toleration are much greater than the costs of repression.[24] Second, the power-holders can attempt to construct formal and informal rules of the game that guarantee their core interests even in the context of the successor democratic regime, and thus yield only a limited democracy.[25] Third, more than in any other path, the security apparatus from the authoritarian regime can attempt to preserve its prerogatives intact.

24. Robert A. Dahl, *Polyarchy: Participation and Opposition* (New Haven: Yale University Press, 1971), p. 15.
25. For the argument that "it is *within the nature of democracy that no one's interests can be guaranteed*" and that "democratic compromise cannot be a substantive compromise; it can only be a contingent institutional compromise," see Adam Przeworski, "Some Problems in the Study of the Transition to Democracy" in this volume. (Emphasis added.)

The path of redemocratization initiated from within the authoritarian regime, however, is quite broad and for analytic and historic purposes it is useful to identify three subtypes, each of which has a somewhat different institutional base.

In any authoritarian regime, the security apparatus and specifically the military play a major role. However, there can be an authoritarian regime in which the political component (civilian or civilianized-military) is dominant over the military-as-institution.[26] In such a case it is possible to have a redemocratization subtype we could call "redemocratization initiated by the civilian or civilianized political leadership." The institutional base of such a redemocratization effort is thus the political leadership of the authoritarian regime.

Another kind of authoritarian regime is one in which a clear military government is the central base of power. If the attempt to redemocratize originates from within such an institutional base, we would call the subtype "redemocratization instituted by the 'military-as-government.'"

Finally there is a case in which the military-as-institution, though at one time a component part of the authoritarian regime, seeks to overthrow either the civilian political leadership or the military-as-government because it comes to believe that the continuation of the authoritarian regime is detrimental to its long-term core institutional interests. I call this subtype "redemocratization led by the 'military-as-institution.'"

In concrete empirical cases these three subtypes may be difficult to disentangle, but there are analytic gains for attempting to distinguish them. For example, in cases in which the institutional base of the redemocratization effort is the civilianized political leadership, there will tend to be a preoccupation on the part of the political leadership with potential vetoes from the military-as-institution and a corresponding preoccupation with obtaining nonmaximalist behavior from the democratic opposition. Likewise, if the institutional base of redemocratization is the military-as-government, the military-as-institution can play an important veto role which predictably can impede, slow, or severely constrain redemocratization. However, if the institutional base of the redemocratization effort is a highly threatened military-as-institution, which for its own preservation thinks it must terminate the authoritarian regime rapidly, there is a potential for a speedier process of redemocratization and greater purges against the authoritarian government than in either of the other two subtypes. Let us therefore examine each of the three major subtypes of redemocratization initiated from within an authoritarian regime.

---

26. Some examples of authoritarian regimes in which the civilian or civilianized military is dominant over the military-as-institution are Spain after the death of Franco, the first Vargas regime in Brazil (1930–45), the Mexican government since the late 1930s, and Turkey in the 1940s.

Redemocratization Initiated by the Civilian or Civilianized Political Leadership (4*a*)

If one accepts as axiomatic that power-holders will retain power unless forced by circumstances to alter the power-sharing formula, then one would predict that (1) the more there are new socioeconomic and political demands from below or from former active supporters, (2) the more there is doubt or conflict about regime legitimacy rules (especially among those who have to enforce obedience), and (3) the more there is the chance that the power-holders will retain and ratify much of their power via competitive elections (or at a minimum be able to remain active in political life), the greater the chance that this path will be initiated and will arrive at redemocratization.[27]

What are the implications of this path for policy and democratic stability? The first point to consider is that even when civilians or civilianized leaders are in control of the state apparatus the military-as-institution is still a factor of significant power. Thus the civilian leadership is most likely to persist in its democratizing initiative (and not to encounter a military reaction) if the democratic opposition tacitly collaborates with the government in creating a peaceful framework for the transition. However, even if the initial transition is successful, much of the coercive apparatus of the authoritarian state will remain intact after the election. There is therefore strong potential for severe constraints against policies that might introduce greater control over the state apparatus via democratic procedures. The stability of the newly democratized regime is particularly vulnerable to an internal coup by the bureaucratic apparatus of the previous authoritarian regime, or an actual coup by the security forces, should members of the coercive apparatus come to believe that democratic procedures are creating security risks.

The clearest case of this path is Spain. A major factor in facilitating the internal transformation of the authoritarian regime was the death in November 1975 of the only chief executive the regime had even known, General Franco, and before that the December 1973 death of the only potential heir apparent. Franco's death inevitably raised fundamental questions about the regime's legitimacy rules even for many of those charged with enforcing obedience. Very important, the pressures of demands from below kept the process of internal transformation of the authoritarian regime going forward. Juan Linz argues that, on the basis of the Spanish case, "the democratic opposition has to be involved in the process. . . . Successful completion requires the cooperation of the democratic opposition."[28] The Spanish opposition at strategic moments

27. For example, in terms of these three factors, the conditions in Egypt and Cuba after Nasser and Castro came to power were such that factor 3 was supportive of a choice for democratization (both Nasser and Castro would have won), but factor 2 pressure was absent in both countries, and in neither country was there significant pressure for democratization from below (factor 1).

28. Linz, "Transition from Authoritarian Regimes," p. 28. In the first version of this chapter I overemphasized the role of the leadership of the authoritarian regime and Linz

shrewdly alternated between pushing and compromising, and the democratizing process went from the initial modest "reform" (*reforma*), initiated by the government, to a reform worked out with the democratic opposition (*reforma-pactada*), to a rupture with the past negotiated with the opposition (*ruptura-pactada*).[29]

This cooperation between the government and the opposition in the transition decreased the chances of a military reaction. Also the agreement of the opposition to the system of electoral laws meant that leaders of the authoritarian regime like Suarez, whose careers had been made almost entirely within the regime's political organization believed they had at least some chance to winning the first election; or, even if they lost, that they would have a chance to continue in political life. Despite these many favorable factors, however, Spanish democracy is fragile, and its fragility is in part a consequence of the path taken to redemocratization. The most sensitive issue is the Basque one. The consolidation of Spanish redemocratization has been greatly complicated because it has involved not only a change to democracy but also a change in the regional nature of the state. The security apparatus was left virtually intact by the transition, and views the Basque conflict as a major threat to order and a threat exacerbated by the style and context of democratic legal and electoral procedures.[30]

At times, Mexican leaders have talked as though they might take the path of internal transformation of the Mexican regime, but in the absence of continuing social pressures delegitimizing the authoritarian framework and pushing the system in the direction of redemocratization, the top political leaders of the party and state bureaucracies limit all such efforts to modest liberalizing measures.[31]

There are elements of internal transformation in Brazil, but ultimately, given the institutional base and the major power-holders in the regime, Brazil does not fit in this category. In Brazil, there are greater social, economic, and political demands for redemocratization from below than in Mexico, and much greater elite dissatisfaction with the original authoritarian formula. However, two factors are substantially less favorable to the path of internal transformation in Brazil than in Spain. The *de facto* executive body in Brazil since 1964 has been the military-as-institution and the leaders have never become "civilian-

---

in the cited manuscript urged a greater attention to the role of the opposition in Spain. I gratefully acknowledge my debt to Linz for this observation.

29. Ibid.

30. Ibid. For the Spanish transition see also José María Maravall and Julián Santamaría, "Political Change in Spain, and the Prospects for Democracy," in Volume 1 of this series; Juan Linz, "Spain and Portugal Critical Choices," in *Western Europe: The Trials of Partnership*, ed. David S. Landes (Lexington, Mass.: Heath, 1977), pp. 237–96, and John F. Coverdale, *The Political Transformation of Spain After Franco* (New York: Praeger, 1979).

31. For an analysis of the aborted movement toward greater democratization in Mexico in the 1970s, see the chapter by Kevin J. Middlebrook, "Political Liberalization in an Authoritarian Regime: The Case of Mexico," in Volume 2 of this series.

ized" as occurred in Mexico under Lázaro Cardenas or in Turkey under Mustafa Kemal.[32] As an institution the Brazilian military has some capacity to renew itself periodically. Unlike Franco, no single military leader provides a self-limiting biological clock. Without such a clock, and with the perception that their chances of winning power in a fully competitive electoral system were much less than in Spain, the military power-holders had every reason to keep the liberalization process just short of democratization for the entire first decade of liberalization (1973–83). Redemocratization in Brazil therefore had to be pursued along additional paths.

Redemocratization Initiated by "Military-as-Government" (4*b*)

In this subpath, the primary drive for regime termination would come from the individual leaders of the military government. Since most modern authoritarian regimes are military regimes, this would seem to be a relatively secure and numerically predominant path. However, the important point to stress here is that if it is not perceived to be in the interests of the military-as-corporate-institution to extricate itself from power, and if there is not a strong societal demand for the termination of the authoritarian regime, this is an extremely precarious path. The redemocratization effort may falter because of military institutional resistance, and no actual transfer of power may occur.

Possibly because of these problems, I know of no pure empirical case in which redemocratization has been achieved by this path alone.[33] Indeed, on theoretical grounds, we can say that, though the leaders of a military government may voluntaristically begin a process of liberalization, the process cannot cross the

32. For a comparative analysis of political institution building that demilitarized the Turkish and Mexican revolutions see Samuel P. Huntington, *Political Order in Changing Societies* (New Haven: Yale University Press, 1968), pp. 255–8. For Atatürk's conscious depoliticization of the army see Dankwart A. Rustow, "The Army and the Founding of the Turkish Republic," *World Politics* 11 (July 1959): 543–52. There is much to learn from Turkey in the 1930s, and 1940s, but it has not been included here because it was a case of first-time democratization, not redemocratization.
33. A borderline case is Turkey in 1961. See Walter F. Weiker, *The Turkish Revolution 1960–1961: Aspects of Military Politics* (Washington, D.C.: Brookings Institution, 1963) and Ergun Ozbudun, *The Role of the Military in Recent Turkish Politics* (Cambridge, Mass.: Harvard University, Center for International Affairs, Occasional Papers in International Affairs, No. 14, November 1966). It falls short of being a pure example because the weightiest element of the "military-as-institution" also urged the extrication from office. Another virtual borderline case of a military-as-government-led redemocratization would be that of Argentine General Aramburu's decision to initiate the process that eventually resulted in the election of Frondizi in 1958. As in Turkey it is not quite a pure case because much of the support also came from the military-as-institution. For a discussion of the Argentine military during this period see Robert A. Potash, *The Army and Politics in Argentina, 1945–1962* (Stanford: Stanford University Press, 1980), pp. 214–71.

threshold of redemocratization without the additional support of societal push or corporate pull. Let us explore the complexities of this assertion by assessing liberalization and democratization in Brazil.

The Brazilian opening began in conditions of voluntaristic fragility. In the months before they assumed office in March 1974, President Ernesto Geisel and his chief ally, General Golbery, the head of the Civil Household, virtually by themselves initiated a controlled series of liberalizing steps which by late 1974 were increasingly turned into liberalizing policies, including a less constricted right to contest elections, less censorship, and fewer arbitrary arrests and tortures. In terms of our eight paths, Brazil is a clear case of liberalization commencing under the aegis of the military-as-government. However, liberalization was sustained and broadened by a complex process involving governmental concessions and societal conquest. Despite the unquestioned growth of the power of civil society, the military-as-institution (particularly the security forces who are now an integral part of the institution) does not yet believe that devolution of power is necessary for the preservation of its institutional interests. Given this perspective, when the security apparatus concluded in November 1981 that the elections scheduled for November 1982 raised the possibility of crossing the threshold from liberalization to redemocratization, the military altered the rules of the political game to complicate this prospect greatly. Because opposition parties had only weak organic connections to the forces of civil society—the lawyers, the base communities, the church, entrepreneurs, and even the new unions—and because the November package did not threaten the fundamental achievements of liberalization (no one was tortured, no censorship was imposed), the parties were unable to rally sufficient support against the new barriers to redemocratization. In the first five days after the passage of the new regulations there was not a single political demonstration against them.[34]

Brazil is a clear example in which lack of support is not a sufficient case for the military-as-institution to yield power. The task of the democratic opposition would seem to be to forge more organic links between the new organizations in civil society and the political parties so that demands for redemocratization become a combined social and political force which raises the cost of rule for the military-as-institution and which presents at the same time a clear governing alternative. Should the strategy lead to success, redemocratization (notwithstanding the origins of liberalization in the military-as-government's policies) would have actually been achieved, not by Path 4*b*, but by a complex series of forces emanating from Paths 4*c*, 5, and 6, involving the calculation of the military-as-institution, the diffuse demands of civil society, and the more politically channeled pressures of the opposition parties.

---

34. See my "O Que Estao Pensando os Militares," *Novos Estudos CEBRAP 2*, no. 2 (July 1983): 2–7 and my "State Power and the Strength of Civil Society in the Southern Cone of Latin America," in *Bringing the State Back In*, ed. Peter Evans, Dietrich Rueschemeyer, and Theda Skocpol (New York: Cambridge University Press, 1985).

Redemocratization Led by "Military-as-Institution" (4c)

In this category, the primary motivation for the termination of the authoritarian regime derives from corporate factors of the military-as-institution.

It is a peculiar category. If the military-as-institution wants to return to democracy in order to protect its fundamental corporate interests, this is an extremely powerful force for the termination of authoritarian rule. In cases in which the military-as-institution sees the leaders of the authoritarian government (be they civilian or military leaders) as carrying out policies that create a crisis for the military-as-institution, it may be willing to sacrifice many of its own fellow officers—especially the leaders of the military-as-government—in order to transcend the crisis and reequilibrate the situation. However, there are also special risks attached to this form of extrication. Unless this path is augmented by other factors such as societal pressure, the military may retain a number of emergency powers. Also, once the crisis is past, there may not be major obstacles to reentry. The institutional factor is so powerful that we should be aware that in cases in which there is military rule, if there is no reason why the military-as-institution feels it is in its interest to relinquish power, redemocratization, short of foreign imposition (Path 3) or opposition-led armed violence (Paths 7 and 8) will almost certainly not occur. I mean to stress that loss of civilian support alone is not enough for the government to fall. Authoritarian regimes, unlike monist regimes, do not have high active support requirements. Apathy and acquiescence will suffice. Loss of civilian support must somehow be transformed into a tangible cost or a direct threat to the military-as-institution.

The two sharpest examples in which perception of intense threat to the military-as-institution played a fundamental role in the termination of authoritarian regimes were Greece in 1973 and Portugal in 1974.[35] The Greek military government was born in 1967 as a colonels'—as opposed to a generals'—coup. But since the generals were never purged, the military government began with a relatively poor base in the military-as-institution. By 1973, the leader of the military government was politically isolated, possibly for this reason, and he became engaged in an extremely risky intervention in Cyprus. This intervention immediately put the military institution under the grave security threat of a war with Turkey, for which it was completely unprepared. Under these circumstances, with an acceptable civilian conservative alternative in former Prime Minister Constantine Karamanlis, the military institution negotiated an extremely rapid extrication. For those officers associated

---

35. There are, of course, a variety of cases. For example, there can be a moderate threat when the military-as-institution withdraws its support from a civilian authoritarian regime (Vargas in 1945) or a greater threat when the military-as-institution, with some civilian support, moves against a civilianized populist military figure who is mobilizing autonomous forces (Perón in 1955).

with the military-as-government, the military-as-institution accepted harsh terms. Over one hundred high-ranking military officers from the military government were still in jail eight years later. The combination of speed and purges would seem to be virtually impossible to achieve in either Paths 4*a* or 4*b*.

However, notwithstanding the unpopularity of the government and the university uprising in 1973, there was not much pressure from society for the military to withdraw from government. Under these conditions, the military-as-institution insisted that the military-as-government withdraw from political power, but retained substantial institutional prerogatives that only began to be challenged by the Socialist coalition elected in 1981. However, the Greek case is important because it illustrates that the rules of the game for extrication can be renegotiated if democracy endures and if a new political force mobilizes new sources of power in the electoral arena.[36]

The other case is Portugal. As a number of authors have documented, the colonial wars in Africa generated a series of what were perceived by Portuguese career officers as increasingly severe problems for their military-as-institution. The length of the war generated manpower shortages at the officer corps level. Conscripted university graduates and sergeants were more frequently made officers, and this practice was resented by the permanent corps of officers. The army, which was closest to the war, also saw the war in the long run as fundamentally unwinnable. The termination of the African colonial war, and of the Portuguese authoritarian government that persisted in waging the war, became a central goal of the Portuguese military institution. The Portuguese case is unusual in two respects. The colonial war radicalized a section of the army, and the Armed Forces Movement played an important role in the initial structure of the state after the overthrow of the authoritarian regime. Even after democratic elections in 1975, 1976, and 1980, the military retained sufficient power to warrant labeling Portugal a "dyarchial" system of government. The Constitution of 1976 gave the military's "Council of the Revolution" *de jure* veto power over the National Assembly in that its members had the power to judge the constitutionality of acts of that elected chamber. In conditions of conflict between the president and the prime minister, latent dual power conflicts in the 1976–82 period could have precipitated a constitutional crisis for Portuguese democracy. The dyarchy ended only in 1982.[37]

The Peruvian case is another example in which corporate, institutional factors in the military played an important role in redemocratization in 1980. As I have argued elsewhere, by 1977 the military-as-institution felt it faced

36. For Greece see Diamandouros, "Regime Change and the Prospects for Democracy in Greece: 1974–83," Clogg, *A Short History of Modern Greece*, and Mouzelis, "Regime Instability and the State in Peripheral Capitalism."

37. For Portugal see Kenneth Maxwell, "Regime Overthrow and the Prospects for Democratic Transition in Portugal" in Volume 1 of this series. See also Antonio Rangel Bandeira, "The Portuguese Armed Forces Movement: Historical Antecedents, Professional Demands, and Class Conflicts," *Politics and Society* 6, no. 1 (1976): 1–56.

external security problems on all its borders with Chile, with Ecuador, and with Bolivia (a Bolivia possibly backed by Brazil). It also felt that it had achieved much of its initial program (settlement of the IPC [International Petroleum Corporation] conflict, some agrarian reform, strengthening of state structures) and that the continuation of the military government created internal conflicts that further aggravated its external security position. More than in Greece or Portugal, societal threats were present in Peru in the form of general strikes and growing pressures from diverse groups and classes for the military to withdraw. In these circumstances, when the Peruvian military withdrew, it retained fewer prerogatives than its Greek or Portuguese counterparts.[38]

In all three cases, external threats played a central role in extrications led by the military-as-institution. Of course, a variety of internal pressures could become contributing factors in a decision by the military-as-institution to relinquish power. The most common of these are policy pressures and divisions that shake the internal unity of the military so that extrication is the safest path to internal cohesion. Sudden internal upheavals often initiate a "return to barracks" movement within the military. Also major reputational or budgetary costs borne by the military-as-institution can erode its support for the military-as-government. In most of these instances of internal pressures, society-initiated demands characteristic of Path 5 are vital.

Society-Led Regime Termination (5)

The key phrase here is "society-led" as opposed to party-, pact-, or revolution-ary-induced transformation of an authoritarian regime. In theory, such a transformation could be brought about by diffuse protests by grassroots organizations, massive but uncoordinated general strikes, and by general withdrawal of support for the government. However, upon closer analysis this is a path toward government change rather than a path toward full redemocratization. The most likely outcome of sharp crises of authoritarian regimes stemming from diffuse pressures and forces in society is either a newly constituted successor authoritarian government, or a caretaker military junta promising

---

38. See Alfred Stepan, *The State and Society: Peru in Comparative Perspective* (Princeton: Princeton University Press, 1978), pp. 298–301. See also the chapter by Julio Cotler, "Military Intervention and Transfer of Power to Civilians in Peru," in Volume 2 of this series. I was in Argentina in July 1982 after the surrender in Malvinas. In interviews with a number of military officers a strong argument repeatedly articulated was that the internal political mission of the military-as-government had made the military incompetent and divided in regard to its central military mission and that the corporate survival of the military-as-institution necessitated that it withdraw from power as soon as possible. As in Greece in 1975, the military's perception of the urgency of the need to extricate from power decreased its will and capacity to resist posttransition reprisals against central members of the military-as-government.

elections in the future.[39] In the latter case, the actual transition involves the extrication by the military-as-institution, and many of the elements of Path 4 obtain. The key factor is that despite societal resistance to authoritarianism, many of the rules of transition are set by the caretaker junta.

On theoretical grounds, therefore, one is tempted to argue that society-led upheavals *by themselves* are virtually incapable of leading to redemocratization but are, nevertheless, often a crucial, or in some cases an indispensable, component to the redemocratization.

Greece in 1973 had elements of this path, led by the student uprising, but the need of the military-as-institution rapidly to alleviate the security crisis with Turkey was the major reason for the rapid redemocratization. Argentina after the massive but uncoordinated revolt in Córdoba in 1969, a revolt that spread quickly to other parts of the country, and Peru after the general strike of 17 July 1977 also fall into this category in some important ways.

The power of civil society to create and channel social pressures is extremely important in successful redemocratization, particularly for all three subtypes of Path 4. Without demands from civil society, in Path 4*a* (redemocratization initiated by civilian or civilianized political leadership) and in Path 4*b* (redemocratization initiated by "military-as-government"), the soft-liners within the authoritarian regime will almost certainly not be able to convince the hard-liners that extrication or redemocratization is an institutional necessity: the best the soft-liners can achieve is liberalization. For Path 4*c* (redemocratization led by "military-as-institution"), the smaller the social pressures, the greater the prerogatives the military can demand in the postextrication period. Finally, for most paths, the politically organized strengths and weaknesses of civil society determine to a large extent the barriers to military reentry in the post-redemocratization period.

Party Pact (With or Without Consociational Elements) (6)

By this category is meant the internal construction of a grand oppositional pact, possibly with some consociational features. The pact members unite to defeat the authoritarian regime and lay the foundation for a successor democratic regime in which power is open to most opposition forces.

In theory, this path, especially in its full-blown consociational form, would appear to be one of great interest for strategies of redemocratization, because it simultaneously addresses two critical issues. First, the construction of such a

---

39. Two cases of society-led regime transition were Iran during the movement against the shah and the French Revolution before Napoleon. Korea during the revolt against General Park was an attempted case but it reverted to a military regime.

pact helps erode the bases of the authoritarian regime, especially if the rationale for the authoritarian regime is that a bloody conflict would ensue in the absence of authoritarianism. Second, it helps lay the foundation for the successor democratic regime with elaborate formulas for power-sharing, mutual vetoes, and grand coalitions.

Despite its apparent attractiveness, a strict consociational path presents several problems of a political nature. Pact *creation* does not necessarily imply pact *maintenance*—pacts can fall apart. Also, even when the pact is maintained, social change may occur and important new groups that were not a part of the original pact will be excluded. This possibility would represent not a case of consociational redemocratization but an example of exclusionary consociational authoritarianism.

When we explore the predictable policy consequences of a strict consociational path toward redemocratization, it should be clear that the "mutual vetoes" and the "purposeful depoliticization" of some major substantive issue areas, which are a part of Arend Lijphart's classic definition of consociationalism, would appear to build in systemic constraints to rapid socioeconomic change. The recognition of such constraints may in turn explain why, if the fundamental conflict in society relates to socioeconomic issues, as opposed to religious, ethnic, or linguistic disputes, it will be difficult for warring classes to walk the consociational path together.

If we start our empirical examination with a reading of Arend Lijphart's *Democracy in Plural Societies: A Comparative Perspective*, we note the rather surprising fact that of the consociational or semiconsociational cases he fully discusses (the Netherlands, Belgium, Austria, Nigeria, Cyprus, Malaysia, and Lebanon), only Austria is a case of redemocratization of an authoritarian regime.[40] All the other cases are of consociationalism first emerging as a conflict regulation device to avoid democratic breakdown or of consociationalism in the process of the decolonization of new states. In the only case of consociationalism emerging for redemocratization, Austria, the defeat of the authoritarian regime is accomplished by foreign powers; this external factor played a role, along with consociationalism, in the creation of democratic institutions. Lijphart mentions Colombia twice in passing, but does not examine it in detail because he claims it is not a plural society. For our purposes, however, both Colombia (1958) and Venezuela (1958) were cases of redemocratization in which party pacts and even some consociational practices—mutual guarantees, vetoes, and purposeful depoliticization—were crucial.[41] Both Venezuela

40. Arend Lijphart, *Democracy in Plural Societies: A Comparative Perspective* (New Haven: Yale University Press, 1977).
41. For the role of party pacts with consociational elements in Colombia see Alexander Wilde, "Conversations among Gentlemen: Oligarchical Democracy in Colombia" in *The Breakdown of Democratic Regimes: Latin America*, ed. Juan J. Linz and Alfred Stepan (Baltimore: Johns Hopkins University Press, 1978), pp. 28–81 and Robert H. Dix, "Consociational Democracy: The Case of Colombia," *Comparative Politics* 12 (April 1980): 303–21. For party pacts in Venezuela see Daniel H. Levine, *Conflict and Political Change in Venezuela*

and Colombia are cases that conform to our theoretical expectation, in that, though pacts for a long time contributed to the stability of political democracy, these same pacts kept socioeconomic change within a narrow range.[42] In Spain, the negotiated agreements on economic policy contained in the Moncloa Pact of 1977 and the consensual working out of the constitution are evidence of the role of party pacts and some consociational practices in the redemocratization process.[43]

Pacts—with or without consociational elements—cannot be created in all political systems. Party pacts by their very nature have two indispensable requirements: first, leaders with the organizational and ideological capacity to negotiate a grand coalition among themselves; second, the allegiance of their political followers to the terms of the pact.

Let us briefly explore the possibilities and problems of party pacts and re-democratization in Chile and Uruguay to show how sharply political systems can vary in regard to these two requirements. In both countries, exclusionary authoritarian regimes came to power in 1973. In both countries, a plebiscite was held in 1980.

For Chile, throughout 1978–80, the original allies and supporters of the authoritarian regime still perceived that the regime had offensive and defensive projects that were desirable and feasible. No process of redemocratization initiated by the power-holders was foreseeable in this period. Some role for an oppositional party pact was seen as a possibility during the 1980 plebiscite. However, the problem of a party pact was clearly one of followers. If the party leaders made a Marxist—Christian Democratic party pact, both ideological components of the pact would have suffered serious erosion of their bases. Much of the Right and even part of the Center of the Christian Democratic party rank and file would probably have shifted to a position of passive support for the authoritarian regime rather than play an active part in a pact with the Marxist parties.[44] Likewise the left wing of the Marxist parties, particularly the Socialists, would probably have rejected party discipline in favor of violent action rather than carry out a pact compromise dictated essentially by the Christian Democrats. Since much of oppositional societal mobilization in Chile in this period was actually party mobilization, societal mobilization

(Princeton: Princeton University Press, 1973) and his "Venezuela since 1958: The Consolidation of Democratic Politics," in *The Breakdown of Democratic Regimes*, ed. Linz and Stepan, pp. 82–109.

42. This statement is the central argument of Terry Karl, "Petroleum and Political Pacts: The Transition to Democracy in Venezuela" in Volume 2 of this series. Jonathan Hartlyn discusses consociational exclusion in his "Consociational Politics in Colombia: Confrontation and Accommodation in Comparative Perspective" (Ph.D. diss., Department of Political Science, Yale University, 1981).

43. See Linz, "The Transition from Authoritarian Regimes to Democratic Political Systems," p. 66.

44. This statement was the reluctant conclusion of a number of senior Christian Democratic leaders, including Eduardo Frei, in interviews with the author in Santiago after the plebiscite.

shared many of the self-isolating, mutually canceling characteristics of party mobilization.

In Uruguay there was much greater potential for a party pact than in Chile. For one thing, in 1978–80 the regime had weaker and less clear-cut offensive and defensive projects than the Chilean regime, and thus its claims to bourgeois support had lost much of their original power. In these circumstances, bourgeois disaffection from pacting parties was less of a potential problem than in Chile. Another crucial variable that differentiated Uruguay from Chile was the class base of the parties. In Uruguay, as in Colombia and Venezuela, the major signatories to any pact would be multiclass parties with a dominant bourgeois ethos. In Chile, the Marxist and the Christian Democratic parties have different class and ideological bases. Finally, unlike Chile, the two major parties in question, the Blancos and the Colorados, had always between them polled over 80 percent of the vote in all national elections in the twentieth century. For all these reasons there is considerably greater potential for a successful party pact path to redemocratization in Uruguay than in Chile.

Yet risks also exist. The very degree of culturally captive voting support the two Uruguayan parties have been able to count upon in the past makes them reluctant in the current authoritarian situation to seek out special support from trade union members. Any party pact must be able to count on both the active support and the mobilization potential of the unions. Without these, even if the military should withdraw from power, the barriers to military recentry would be quite low.[45]

Organized Violent Revolt Co-ordinated by Democratic Reformist Parties (7)

On theoretical grounds this path appears to have a number of advantages for the process of redemocratization. Because the revolt against authoritarianism has a party base, the parties can provide a continuous political direction unavailable to the diffuse society-led path. The political core is also one that is committed to democracy and whose most probable internal political allies will be drawn from democratic forces. If we ask how far this path can go in terms of socioeconomic change, it clearly has greater potential than a party pact with consociational elements because it does not have the mutual vetoes, depoliticization of key issues, and institutionalized power-sharing that are part of the consociational formula. Likewise, the fact that the authoritarian regime has

---

45. I analyze the Uruguayan and Chilean comparison with greater detail and documentation in my "State Power and the Strength of Civil Society in the Southern Cone of Latin America," in *Bringing the State Back In*, ed. Evans, Rueschemeyer, and Skocpol.

been defeated in a political–military struggle gives some scope to the parties to restructure the state apparatus.

This path has predictable constraints, however. The most likely type of reformist parties, in Europe and Latin America at least, are Social Democratic or Christian Democratic parties. The range of international political and economic allies and role models of either type of party keeps socioeconomic change within the boundaries of the international capitalist system. Because Social Democrats, and especially Christian Democrats, do not have a strong tradition of clandestine, violent party activity, the most likely paramilitary formula appears to be one that coopts a wing of the military to its cause of overthrowing the authoritarian government. Even though the military is a junior partner, it still sets limits to the degree to which the military and security apparatus can be dismantled.

Historically, there are no successful examples of this path leading to redemocratization in Europe, Africa, the Middle East, or Asia. In Latin America, the closest case is the 1948 revolt in Costa Rica. Here a Social Democratic "National Liberation Movement" defeated an attempt to disregard election results. This victory, together with the Social Democratic goals of the movement, ushered in a period of important socioeconomic reforms—the complete nationalization of private banks and the nationalization of the oligarchically controlled coffee institute. It also provided the financial and political support to put into practice laws that were on the books but had never been enforced, such as the social security law and the labor code. These reforms were quite extensive by Latin American standards but fully within the parameters of Social Democratic capitalist reforms then developing in Europe. The paramilitary political base also enabled the victors to disband the military forces of the country and to create a smaller but loyal constabulary, which helped the new regime to weather two armed revolts, one supported by Somoza from neighboring Nicaragua. Only in the late 1970s and early 1980s did this formula come under challenge as Costa Rica became engaged in the more polarized revolutionary and counterrevolutionary struggles of Central American ignited by the Nicaraguan Revolution.[46]

46. The Costa Rican case is not a simple case of redemocratization, however. There are numerous ambiguities. For example, despite the government's attempt to annul the presidential election results in 1948 an argument could be made that up to that time Costa Rica did not have a full-blown authoritarian regime, but rather one in which the standards of open electoral contestation had been deteriorating for about eight years. Also the goals of José Figueres, who led the victorious forces in the Civil War, were not simple *restoration* but *reformulation*. In fact he had long urged the need to create a "Second Republic" and had been organizing an armed uprising *before* the presidential electoral fraud. Finally, despite the social reforms that were carried out, Figueres *narrowed* the range of political and legal participation in Costa Rica by outlawing the Communist party and by using a variety of methods virtually to destroy one of Latin America's best organized and most powerful Communist trade union movements, a movement that had originally helped put on the books many of the reforms that Figueres and his followers eventually implemented and claimed for their own. For a book that discusses the broad outlines of the 1948 Civil War and analyzes the ambiguities see John Patrick Bell, *Crisis in Costa Rica: The 1948 Revolution* (Austin: University of Texas Press, 1971). For a more

In Bolivia in 1952 the National Revolutionary Movement (MNR) seized power, dismissed much of the army, and carried out a series of structural reforms, but by 1964 internal divisions, the failure to create political mechanisms for party alternation, and the persistence of economic problems, led to the MNR's increasing reliance on the newly enlarged military, a reliance that ended in the assumption of power by the military and inauguration of a cycle of authoritarianism and revolt that continues to this day.[47]

Venezuela in 1958 was also close to this path but it fell short in two respects. First, a wing of the military was an active junior partner in the party-led revolt and in the transitional democratic government. Second, there were many elements of a consociational pact. In this case, in addition to the two major parties (the Social Democratic Acción Democrática and the Christian Democratic COPEI), the Catholic church, the military-as-institution, and local industrialists participated in the consociational pact of mutual guarantees and vetoes. This overarching coalition, as Terry Karl documents, set limits to socioeconomic change in the postauthoritarian period, limits that were even more severe than in Costa Rica.[48]

Marxist-Led Revolutionary War (8)

This path has the greatest theoretically predictable potential for fundamental socioeconomic change because the revolutionary forces come to power only after defeating the state apparatus and a sector of the social order is displaced without waiting for the results of elections. In theory, the revolutionary forces also have an ideology and a social base supportive of fundamental change.

Theoretically, there can be a space for democratic revolutionary Marxist reconstruction. However, the doctrinal and organizational tradition of revolutionary Leninism, which has been the most effective and prestigious modern revolutionary model, rejects two of the requirements of a minimalist definition of political democracy—the relatively unrestricted right to organize and the relatively unrestricted right to open contestation. The Leninist party model in power therefore virtually precludes the existence of other parties advocating alternative conceptions of society and having a legitimate chance to gain power through electoral means.

Historically, there are many cases—such as China, Yugoslavia, the Soviet Union, Vietnam, and Cuba—in which revolutionary Marxism has overthrown

hagiographic account see Burt H. English, *Liberación Nacional in Costa Rica: The Development of a Political Party in a Transitional Society* (Gainesville: University of Florida Press, 1971).

47. The most complete account of this sad cycle is James M. Malloy, *Bolivia: The Uncompleted Revolution* (Pittsburgh: University of Pittsburgh Press, 1970).

48. See Karl, "Petroleum and Political Pacts."

authoritarian regimes and introduced fundamental change. However, to date there has not yet been even one election with full rights of organization and contestation (and with the right to make the government accountable to the electorate) after a revolutionary Marxist triumph.[49]

Nonetheless, since the 1970s there seems to be greater doctrinal and geopolitical space for this option to be realized than before. There has been greater doctrinal space because the Leninism that dominated revolutionary Marxism from 1917 until the early 1970s began to have serious Marxist critics who drew on Italian Eurocommunism and the antivanguardist critique of democratic centralism, for example, Rosa Luxemburg's and Leon Trotsky's writing against *What Is to Be Done?*, and on some of the participatory themes emerging in Marxism.

There has been greater geopolitical space in the world for democratic revolutionary socialism because neither the functional equivalents of the capitalist encirclement that threatened the Soviet Union after World War I nor the Stalinist encirclement of Eastern Europe after 1945 seemed likely to be repeated. In the multipolar, post-OPEC world since the 1970s, new revolutionary regimes had greater opportunities than before for piecing together aid, trade, and security relationships with a variety of countries.

The country in the world with the greatest opportunity to arrive at revolutionary democratic Marxism was Nicaragua. Given its initial international support from the then financially strong oil powers as politically diverse as Mexico, Libya, and Venezuela, from the ruling Social Democratic party in Germany, good relations with the strong Socialist parties in France and Spain, as well as support from Leninist party systems such as Cuba and the Soviet Union, Nicaragua had the potential to maintain degrees of independence which would have allowed it to construct its own path to democracy within the revolution. International capitalist bankers accepted the new power relations in the region; and, under the aegis of Mexico, and with the initial tolerance of the Carter government, they entered into an unprecedented and creative debt-rescheduling process for the revolutionary government.[50] Domestically, in Nicaragua the participation of the post-Vatican II Catholic church and an important wing of the national bourgeoisie in making the revolution seemed to give the Sandinista regime the possibility of at least a loyal opposition to the construction of democratic revolutionary Marxism.[51]

49. See Alex Pravda, "Elections in Communist Party States," and Juan J. Linz, "Non-Competitive Elections in Europe," both in *Elections without Choice*, ed. Guy Hermet, Richard Rose, and Alain Rouquié (New York: Wiley, 1978), pp. 169–212, 36–65.

50. See Richard Weinert, "The Nicaraguan Debt Re-Negotiation," *Cambridge Journal of Economics* 5, no. 2 (1981): 187–94.

51. For the important role of the domestic bourgeoisie in the struggle against Somoza see Harold Jung, "Behind the Nicaraguan Revolution," *New Left Review* 117 (September–October 1979): 69–90. All the Nicaraguan bishops signed the important statement in support of the then still unresolved revolutionary struggle. See Conferencia Episcopal de Nicaragua, *Mensaje al Pueblo Nicaragüense: Momento Insurreccional, 2 de Junio 1979*. Even more significant was a pastoral letter, again signed by every Nicaraguan bishop, almost

However, the triumph of President Reagan in the United States elections of 1980, the incorporation of El Salvador into the East–West struggle, economic difficulties, and the emergence (in a country without a rich tradition of Marxist debate) of classical Leninism as an important component of the core model of the Sandinista rule of organization have made revolutionary Marxist democracy problematic.

Regardless of the outcome in Nicaragua, some democratic currents within Marxism and new geopolitical realities have created somewhat greater theoretical space for a democratic, revolutionary Marxist alternative. The unfortunate way in which Nicaragua was caught in the East–West conflict reconfirmed capitalist hard-liners and Leninist hard-liners alike in their skepticism about the possibility of democratic revolutionary Marxism.[52]

four months after the revolution was successful, explicitly acknowledging, if a few key safeguards were maintained, a role for the Sandinistas in carrying out the postrevolutionary government. See Carta Pastoral del Episcopado Nicaragüense, *Compromiso Cristiano para Una Nicaragua Nueva* (Managua, 17 November 1979).

52. For a thoughtful discussion of the dilemmas of the Nicaraguan Revolution by an important thinker and participant see Xabier Gorostiaga, "Dilemmas of the Nicaraguan Revolution," in *The Future of Central America: Policy Choices for the U.S. and Mexico.* ed. Richard R. Fagen and Olga Pellicer (Standford: Stanford University Press, 1983), pp. 47–66. See also Richard R. Fagen, "The Nicaraguan Revolution" (Working Paper no. 78, Wilson Center, Latin American Program (Washington, D.C., October 1980).

SIX

Political Crafting of Democratic Consolidation or Destruction: European and South American Comparisons

with Juan J. Linz

Introduction

To what extent can our knowledge about the breakdown of democratic regimes in Europe and Latin America contribute to a better understanding of the conditions under which reborn democracies in Latin America can acquire stability and avoid renewed breakdown? Does our knowledge about past crises in democracies tell us something about the future of democracies? Our answer is a qualified yes. We think that a reading of the work of the many social scientists and historians who have addressed the great theme of democratic stability could help avoid some of the mistakes that in the past have led to the demise of democracy.[1] However, we feel obliged to caution against facile extrapolations from the study of the past. Polities and political actors have to face crises and conflicts as new challenges. As an ancient philosopher said, "We never bathe in the same river twice." We should be conscious that our knowledge of the past is limited, and that it is sometimes selective, particularly when so much of it is derived from the intensive study of a limited number of historically important cases of breakdown and often on an insufficient analysis of those that avoided the drama of democratic breakdown.

More than is commonly deemed to be the case, we think that the difference between political survival or breakdown is a question, as our title implies, of "political crafting." Thus in this essay we will attempt to identify some of the

---

1. See for example the many studies of democratic breakdown and survival in Juan J. Linz and Alfred Stepan, eds., *The Breakdown of Democratic Regimes* (Baltimore and London: Johns Hopkins University Press, 1978).

This chapter was first published in Robert Pastor (ed.), *Democracy in the Americas: Stopping the Pendulum* (New York: Holmer & Meier, 1989). The co-author was Juan J. Linz, the Forward to the book was written by Raúl Alfonsin and Jimmy Carter.

most important dimensions of "crafting" that have contributed to European democratic breakdowns or consolidations.

We believe our conclusions can be of reasonably general theoretical interest to those concerned with the question of democratic breakdown and consolidation. However, the Latin American countries that we have most in mind are those relatively developed countries that have recently had a traumatic experience with bureaucratic-authoritarian regimes and now have fledgling democracies. We refer to Brazil, Argentina, and Uruguay. These are the countries we know best and that we think would benefit most directly from a close comparison with European cases. If democracy were consolidated in these countries this would have a beneficial impact on the even more difficult, more problematic tasks facing many other Latin American countries.[2]

Three sets of questions that emerged from the European struggle for democracy seem to us of particular importance for the current democratizing efforts in Latin America. First, what is the relationship between socioeconomic efficacy and regime legitimacy? Did those democratic regimes that survived major hardships craft their responses to adversity in very different ways from those countries where democracy broke down? How important for democratic survival or breakdown were intervening variables that were primarily political in nature?

Second, how have democracies that have survived or broken down crafted their reactions to nonstate violence and to control of what Max Weber referred to as the state's legitimate monopoly of force? For the purposes of this essay, we think it is especially important to explore how democratic forces might attempt to empower themselves in the major arenas of the polity so as to be able to increase their capacity to control the means of force in society, especially the military.

Third, do some institutional arrangements put greater pressure on democratic governments than others? Could any changes be crafted, such as a shift from presidentialism to parliamentarianism, that might increase the flexibility and crisis-surviving capacity of many Latin American democracies?

Collectively, three sets of problems—worries about the efficacy of the new democracies in the context of the debt crisis, worries about military re-entry into power in the context of still heavily militarized polities, and worries about whether Latin American presidents will be overwhelmed by demands on their resources—contribute to a significant portion of the anxiety about the future of the current redemocratization efforts in Latin America. The tasks facing the new Latin American democracies are undeniably multiple and difficult. Nonetheless, we think that a correct appreciation of these three sets of problems we have chosen to explore can point to areas of choice and possibility that may be of some value to those who would attempt to craft democratic consolidation.

2. For a global review, see Samuel P. Huntington, "Will More Countries Become Democratic?" *Political Science Quarterly* 99 (Summer 1984): 193–218.

Socioeconomic Efficacy and Regime Legitimacy: The Political "Processing of Adversity"

What is the relationship between citizens' perceptions of the socioeconomic efficacy of a democratic regime and their perceptions of the legitimacy of that regime? There is a certain pessimism about this point in the new democracies of Latin America because the region is living through a severe economic crisis and many of the intellectual leaders believe that socioeconomic efficacy and democratic legitimacy are very tightly coupled. While we do believe that in the long run it erodes the accrued political capital of the regime if it is seen as completely incapable of solving major socioeconomic problems—and thus we are very supportive of efforts to solve the debt crises with growth—we believe that perceptions of a regime's socioeconomic efficacy are less tightly coupled to perceptions of a regime's democratic legitimacy than is commonly supposed.

There are a number of theory-based reasons why we would expect democratic legitimacy to be somewhat insulated from perceptions of socioeconomic efficacy. Claims to ruling authority based on democratic procedural origins rather than on governmental performance per se are one insulating factor. The possibility of the democratic alternation of government—the promise of new policies to solve socioeconomic problems—provides another. Another major insulating factor is citizens' perceptions about the past and their worries about the future. Citizens, the high bourgeoisie as well as the working class, care about being protected from personal human rights abuses. A regime in which state behavior is constrained by a rule of law is a vital asset in a new democracy. As long as a democratic regime completely respects the rule of law, this respect can act as an important insulating factor for the regime and one to which citizens can attach an independent value, just as socioeconomic reforms also constitute values in themselves. Indeed the more there is a strongly negative cross-class collective memory about a particularly abusive regime (e.g., Nazi Germany), the more the question of procedural guarantees for personal safety will be a significant value among all classes. In such circumstances, the more that alternative, nondemocratic legitimacy options are not able to dispel serious doubts about their potential respect for personal freedoms, the more the existing democratic regime will be perceived by citizens as the most appropriate (legitimate) political formula for the country. All of the above considerations argue against a tight coupling of a democratic regime's socioeconomic efficacy and its perceived legitimacy. What does the European experience suggest? Let us turn first to post-Franco Spain.

There is absolutely no doubt that the economic situation of Spain deteriorated under democracy. Spanish unemployment in the early 1970s under Franco was one of the lowest in Europe and hovered around 3 percent. With democracy, unemployment rose dramatically. Spain's 20 percent unemployment rate in the mid-1980s was the highest in Western Europe.[3] Economic growth rates, which averaged over 7 percent from 1960 to 1974 and were among the highest in the world, averaged only 1.7 percent between 1975 and 1985.[4]

The "tightly coupled" hypothesis would lead us to predict a corresponding decline in the legitimacy of democracy. What do Spanish public opinion polls indicate? From 1978 through 1983, a poll asked Spaniards whether democracy would enable the problems that have been identified as important by Spaniards to be resolved. (See Table 6.1.) Six years after the death of Franco and the beginning of the Spanish transition and four years after the first democratic election in 1977, negative responses about the efficacy of democracy for solving problems slightly outnumbered positive responses. Belief in the socioeconomic efficacy of democracy had declined by twenty-five points.

How tightly was this dramatic erosion of the belief in the socioeconomic efficacy of democracy tied to beliefs in democracy as the best political formula for Spain? As Table 6.2 demonstrates, the data indicate that for Spanish citizens there was virtually no coupling. Between 1978 and 1983, there was a decline of 5 percent of respondents who indicated that democracy was not the best political system for Spain. More important, affirmative responses that democracy was the best political system for Spain increased by 8 percent.

Clearly in Spain, at least for the short or medium run, other factors besides belief in economic and social efficacy were powerfully affecting citizens' beliefs about the best political formula for the country.

Earlier in this essay we suggested that citizens' evaluations of the specific alternative political formulas of their recent past, or of their plausible future, are a powerful intervening variable. For the Spanish case, despite the 25 percent decline between 1978 and 1981 in the belief in the efficacy of democracy, the politically relevant question was: What available political formula might people want instead of democracy? Here the phrasing of the Spanish question was

TABLE 6.1. *Does democracy allow the resolution of the problems that we as Spaniards face? (%)*

	1978	1980	1981	1982–3	1983
Yes	68	45	43	55	61
No	22	46	45	16	30
Depends			12	21	9
Other, n.a.	10	9	12	8	9
N	5,898	n.a.	1,703	5,463	3,952

Source: See Table 6.2.

3. Banco de Bilbao, Economic Research Department, *Situación: Review of the Spanish Economy*, International Edition, No. 10–11, 1986.
4. Figures are derived from *United Nations Statistical Yearbook*, 1976, 1982, and *Economist* Intelligence Unit, *Quarterly Reports: Spain* (2nd Quarter 1986).

TABLE 6.2. *Democracy is the best political system for a country like ours (%)*

	1978	1980	1981	1982–3	1983
Yes	77	69	81	74	85
No	15	20	13	6	10
Depends				12	
Other, n.a.	8	11	6	7	5
N	5,898	n.a.	1,703	5,463	3,952

Source: National surveys by Data SA, Madrid. For 1978 (July) and 1980 see: J. J. Linz, M. Gómez-Reino, D. Vila and F. A. Orizo, *Informe sociológico sobre el cambio político en España, 1975–1981*, IV Informe FOESSA, vol. I, Fundación FOESSA (Madrid: Euramérica, 1981), 627–9. For 1981, Mar. 4 to 21 (after the Feb. 23 attempted coup), *Cambio, 16*, No. 488 (Apr. 6, 1981), 42–5; for 1982–3, Nov.–Jan. postelection survey with the support of the Volkswagen-Stiftung, unpublished. For the study see J. J. Linz and J. R. Montero, *Crisis y cambio: Electores y partidos en la España de los años ochenta* (Madrid: Centro de Estudios Constitucionales, 1986); for 1983 (Fall) see J. J. Linz, "La sociedad española: presente, pasado y future", in J. J. Linz (ed), *España, un presente para el future*, i: *La sociedad* (Madrid: Instituto de Estudios Económicos, 1984), 57–95; and J. Linz, "Legitimacy of Democracy and the Socioeconomic System," in Mattei Dogan (ed.), *Comparing Pluralist Democracies: Strains on Legitimacy* (Boulder, Colo.: Westview Press, 1988), 65–113.

to the point: "Is democracy the best political system for a country like ours?" A negative answer implied an affirmative response to a different political formula. In the Spanish context the most likely alternative political formula would have been a regime with a strong nondemocratic military component. Unlike in the 1930s, right-wing fascist mobilization was not a real alternative. Neither, given the antiviolence positions of the Spanish people and the Euro-Communist, non-Leninist positions of the Communist Party at the time, was violent revolution a plausible alternative. In fact, of the thirteen countries polled in the European Values Study of 1981, Spain had the highest percentage of people who supported the "gradual reform" option.[5]

But how much legitimacy did Spanish citizens actually accord to what could have appeared to have been the most available alternative ruling formula, military rule? As Table 6.3 makes starkly clear, in the context of four decades of authoritarian rule and a recent coup attempt, a legitimacy formula that entailed military participation in government was an extremely weak competitor to political democracy, notwithstanding the widespread disenchantment with the efficacy of democracy.

What are the implications of the European experience for Latin America? The post-Franco opinion polls and our analysis of interwar Europe lead us to believe

5. See Francisco Andrés Orizo, *España, Entre la Apatía y el Cambio Social* (Madrid: Editorial Mapfre, 1983). For a general discussion of the relationship between the legitimacy accorded to economic systems and to political systems in contemporary Western Europe, see Juan J. Linz, "Legitimacy of Democracy and the Socioeconomic System," in *Comparing Pluralist Democracies: Strains on Legitimacy*, ed. Mattei Dogan (Boulder and London: Westview Press, 1988), pp. 65–113. The data on comparative support for revolution and reform is found on p. 98.

TABLE 6.3.   *At this time, what do you think is best: a government only of the UCD (the unión de Centro Democrático, then the ruling party), a political party coalition, a civil–military government, or a military government? (%) (N = 1703)*

UCD government	27
Coalition government	52
Civil–military government	5
Military government	2
Others (no response, don't know, hard to classify)	14
TOTAL	100

Note: 'En estos momentos, ¿qué cree usted que es el mejor: un gobierno sólo de UCD, un gobierno de coalición entre partidos políticos, un gobierno civico-militar, o un gobierno militar?'

Source: Special poll carried out by Data, SA, Madrid, Spain, between Mar. 4 and 21, 1981 after the putsch attempt of Feb. 23, 1981; unpublished.

that the *political perception of desired alternatives has a greater impact on the survival of democratic regimes than economic and social problems per se.* The economic crisis of the 1930s was felt throughout Europe. For many of the democracies that survived, it was a period of intense and creative political crafting in which new coalitions and new policies were forged. The Netherlands had the highest rate of unemployment in interwar Europe; indeed, thirty thousand Dutch workers went to Germany for employment. But Prime Minister Colijn enlarged the governing coalition to include the Liberals and forged a national crisis cabinet of great longevity. In Sweden, the Saltsjobaden Agreement of 1938 set the basis for the modern social-democratic welfare state, which won acceptance by business and labor. In Belgium, the Rexist facist movement was turned back by a coalition that included Catholic, Liberal and Socialist parties. In the United States the "New Deal" was launched. Based on his major study of the impact of the depression on democracies, Ekkart Zimmermann concludes that in the above cases, "the underlying variable of all these outcomes seems to be the ability of group leaders to come together, form new coalitions, sometimes on the basis of reaffirming older ones (such as in Belgium), and then to settle on how to steer the economy."[6] Zimmerman was particularly concerned in his research design to determine the relative weight of political and

6. Ekkart Zimmermann, "Economic and Political Reactions to World Economic Crises of the 1930s in Six European Countries," paper prepared for the Midwest Political Science Association Convention, Chicago, 10–12 April 1986, p. 51. Other related studies of Zimmerman on this theme are his "The 1930s World Economic Crisis in Six European Countries: A First Report on Causes of Political Instability and Reactions to Crisis" in Paul M. Johnson and W. R. Thompson, eds., *Rhythms in Politics and Economics* (New York: Praeger, 1985), pp. 84–127, and "Government Stability in Six European Countries during the World Economic Crisis of the 1930s: Some Preliminary Considerations," *European Journal of Political Research* 15, no. 1 (1987): 23–52. Also see P. A. Gourevitch, "Breaking with Orthodoxy: The Politics of Economic Policy Responses to the Depression of the 1930s," *International Organization* 38 (1984): 95–129 and M. Weir and T. Skocpol, "State Structures and Social Keynesianism: Responses to the Great Depression in Sweden and the United States," *International Journal of Comparative Sociology* 24 (1983): 4–29.

economic factors in the German and Austrian breakdowns. In the end he assigns greater weight to political factors, especially to what he calls the presence or absence of *system blame*. "In some countries (Germany and Austria) system blame was so widespread that the forces coming to the defense of the democratic polity were already in a minority."[7]

In our judgment, in both Germany and Austria there was more active crafting of democratic destruction than there was crafting of democratic consolidation. The key variable in Germany and Austria was that strong groups on the left and on the right attacked the political regime for political reasons as much as for economic and social reasons.[8] In the German case, the Weimar conservatives saw the alternative to be a nondemocratic monarchy, but they assumed that such a monarchy would be constrained as in the past by the rule of law. However, after Nazi Germany, an entire generation of conservatives and rightists realized that a nondemocratic alternative on the right could be one that entailed absolutely no respect for the rule of law and could possibly put their own lives and personal rights as well as their material interests at stake.

Part of the glue of post-World War II European democracy for the left and right alike is that procedural democracy allowed them to continue to struggle for the advancement of their material interests in a context where there were procedural, constitutional, and legal constraints on government and state behavior. Here we think that Adam Przeworski's widely cited and otherwise insightful discussion of democracy should be refined. Przeworski asserts that "the process of establishing democracy is a process of institutionalizing uncertainty."[9] He is clearly right when he says that democracy presents the permanent opportunity that a party on the right or left could win and implement major changes in laws concerning property and social relations. But democratic governments are constitutional governments and constitutions are not normally changed by simple majorities. Democracy certainly implies long-range "institutionalized uncertainty" about policy alternatives, but it

7. Ekkart Zimmermann, "The World Economic Crisis of the Thirties in Six European Countries: Causes of Political Instability and Reaction to Crisis; A First Report," paper prepared for European Consortium for Political Research, Salzburg, Austria, 13–18 April 1984, p. 43.

8. It should be remembered that Germany and Austria were exceptions among the advanced capitalist democracies. The "Great Depression led to political breakdown and fascism" thesis needs to be strongly qualified when the actual historical record is examined. Unemployment in Norway, Denmark, and the Netherlands in the early thirties was higher than in Germany, but in all three countries democratic governments became more stable and broad-based in the 1930s. In the West European country where unemployment was the worst, the Netherlands, fascist parties were never able to gain more than 7.9 percent of the vote. Also, some important cases of breakdown in the less advanced capitalist countries of Europe, such as the rise of fascism in Italy in 1922, the emergence of the Primo de Rivera dictatorship in Spain in 1923, and the Polish, Portuguese, and Lithuanian crises of 1926, all preceded the Great Depression.

9. See Adam Przeworski, "Some Problems in the Study of the Transition to Democracy," in *Transitions from Authoritarian Rule: Comparative Perspectives*, ed. Guillermo O'Donnell, Philippe C. Schmitter, and Laurence Whitehead (Baltimore and London: Johns Hopkins University Press, 1986), esp. pp. 58–61.

just as strongly implies a system of constitutionally sanctioned procedural guarantees that constrain arbitrary and abusive state behavior.

One of the most interesting and important developments that occurred in Brazil, Uruguay, and Argentina as a result of the massive and unprecedented abuses of state power by the bureaucratic-authoritarian regimes in these states was the increased valorization of democracy as an important end that needed to be protected in and for itself. In the past, a significant part of the left had been ambivalent about democracy and believed that only revolutionary rule could bring about social change. Important parts of the left attached only an instrumental value to democracy. It was a vehicle to be used in pursuit of other goals. The contemporary left, correctly, will not be satisfied with a procedural democracy alone. However, procedural democracy in the 1980s has come to be seen by more and more on the left in Brazil, Uruguay, and Argentina as an indispensible political formula that is a valuable norm in itself and as a political arrangement that offers both protection against state terrorism and some hope of electoral progress toward social and economic democracy.

For Brazil, Argentina, and Uruguay, the contributions by the left in creating a political discourse that validates procedural democracy must be recognized. In this context one of the most destructive things that groups on the right could do to these new prodemocratic values and practices of the left is to encourage forms of force or fraud that do not allow the left the full enjoyment of their rights under the procedural guarantees of democracy.

Much of the bourgeoisie in Brazil, Uruguay, and Argentina emerged from the recent bureaucratic-authoritarian experience with new worries about their ability to control authoritarian regimes. Important sectors of the bourgeoisie had encouraged and strongly supported the overthrow of democratic rule and the advent of military rule. But they learned from personal experience that the state's repressive apparatus was difficult for them to contain. In Argentina many upper-class and middle-class families were drawn into the vortex of indiscriminate and criminal state terrorism against which social contacts and economic influences were powerless.[10]

In Brazil, state terrorism was less salient, but by 1976 many of the most significant Brazilian entrepreneurs were actively struggling to expand their range of influence in the economy and increasingly they began to argue for a political system in which the military's weight was less, and where public policy could be more openly contested and discussed. Notwithstanding the

---

10. The government commission that investigated human rights abuses during the military regime estimated in its report, *Nunca Más*, that over 55 percent of all disappeared persons fell into occupational categories such as white-collar employees, professionals, academics, journalists, and students. See *Nunca Más: Informe de la Comisión Nacional Sobre la Desaparición de Personas*, 10th ed. (Buenos Aires: Editorial Universitaria de Buenos Aires, 1985) pp. 293–9. English translation: *Nunca Más: Report of the Argentine Commission on the Disappeared* (New York: Farrar, Straus and Giroux, 1986). See also Arquidiocese de São Paulo, Brasil, *Nunca Mais*, preface by D. Paulo Evaristo Cardenal Arns (Petrópolis: Editora Vozes, 1985).

uncertainty of democracy that Adam Przeworski correctly stresses, more and more of the bourgeoisie in Brazil decided that in the long run a context in which they could attempt to advance their personal and material interests within a framework of the rule of law and of periodic elections was the system that was most appropriate (legitimate) for them and for Brazil. They had seen that the "Brumairean moment" where they had momentarily abdicated their claims to rule had become praetorian decades. They were also aware that, given the new social forces in Brazil, a new round of authoritarianism might lead to a more dangerous degree of societal conflict and polarization. A political arena could very well emerge in which it would be no means certain that their resources and interests would prevail. Thus in Robert Dahl's terms, for much of the Brazilian bourgeoisie the costs of the repression of democracy now came to be seen as high, and because of the more democratic values on the left, the costs of toleration are now lower.

From the perspective we have just analyzed we believe that reports such as *Nunca Más* in Argentina and *Nunca Mais* in Brazil (reports that have been best sellers in their respective countries) are useful for the consolidation of democracy. These reports have performed an important political task. Groups in civil society, from radicals to conservatives, are increasing their understanding of the potential for criminal, even anarchic, repression by the state apparatus if it is not constrained and if it prescribes to itself a position of complete nonaccountability either to votes or to the law. One of the tasks of the democratic forces is to deepen the collective memory of the reality of these recent authoritarian political pasts. Another task of the democratic forces is to make citizens acutely aware that attacks on the democratic regime could pave the way for an authoritarian political future in which no personal or institutional guarantees against state abuses are ensured.

We also think that the more extensive carrying out and dissemination of political polls could probably serve as a useful check against those who claim that a military regime might be desired by the majority of the people. In Spain, trials of the military leaders of the failed coup in 1981 in which military disputes and goals were made clearly visible to the population, together with the circulation of respected public opinion polls showing that those who wanted military participation in government represented a tiny minority of the population, strengthened the forces working for democratic consolidation.

Control of the Means of Force in Democratic Polities

How should nonstate political violence be handled by the new democracies? Specifically, if political violence occurs, what reaction will minimize the negative consequences for democratic survival and consolidation? More generally, how can the new democratic polities increase their capacity to control, monitor, and manage their own military establishments?[11]

The Management of Nonstate Violence

A widespread worry in Latin America is that the military have a very low tolerance for insurgent violence in a political system. Some argue that it is so important to avoid insurgency that if it occurs, the state should act by whatever means to end it. This often implies giving the military a free hand in the suppression, so that the military cannot blame the government for having prevented them from solving the crisis.

Clearly, guerrilla violence, like economic recession, creates problems for a new democratic regime. However, we believe that as with economic recession, the most important variable is the way the political system processes the facts of guerrilla and political violence.

Once again the Spanish case is illustrative. Table 6.4 shows deaths due to extremists and Basque separatists in the period from 1968 to 1983. We should also note that not one army officer was killed during the Basque insurgency in the 1968–75 Franco period, or in the 1975–7 transition period. But in the postelectoral period of democratic rule between 1978 and 1983, thirty-seven army officers died.[12]

Despite the sharp increase in deaths due to Basque terrorists in the democratic period, the general belief in the legitimacy of democracy in Spain, as we have seen, stayed at a very high level and in fact grew between 1979 and 1983.

Once again the key question is not the undeniable increase in violence, but whether political leaders choose to manipulate the information to the detriment of democracy. In the Spanish case, a complex series of political actions and attitudes helped to minimize the negative consequences of the growing violence by Basque separatists on the new Spanish democracy.

---

11. In our previous studies we have arrived at a number of conclusions that we will simply assert here. State toleration of or ambivalence about paramilitary violence, such as occurred in Weimar Germany or Argentina in the mid-1970s, erodes democratic authority. The responsibility for guaranteeing the peacefulness of the political process is the task of the state, not of uniformed political parties. The police, not the army, is the preferred instrument for the control of domestic violence; the police should have a political not a military chain of command. The temptation for progressive democratic governments to alleviate their anxieties about military loyalty in the face of democratic reforms by encouraging the arming of the government's civilian supporters militarizes the polity and normally destabilizes the chief executive. Democratic governments should consult the military about key decisions concerning law and order, but it is normally a mistake to attempt to generate the military's support by seeking their permission or having them authoritatively share in the decision-making process. It is a mistake because the military often divides over the issues involved and feels co-responsible for the policy. Professional compliance and correct policy distance from inherently controversial tasks becomes difficult.

12. See Ricardo García Damborenea, *La Encruicijada Vasca* (Barcelona: Editorial Argos Vergara, 1984), p. 52.

TABLE 6.4.   *Victims of terrorism in the period 1968–1983*

1. Distribution by months and years

Year	Jan.	Feb.	Mar.	Apr.	May	June	July	Aug.	Sept.	Oct.	Nov.	Dec.	Total
1968					1		1						2
1969			1										1
1970													
1971			1										1
1972							1				1		2
1973			3		1				1			3	8
1974			1	1				12	1			2	17
1975			1	1	3	2	3	4	1	10	1		26
1976	1	2	3	4	3	1			1	5	1		21
1977	10	1	2	1	2	3			2	4	2	1	28
1978	9		10	1	5	6	4	5	4	13	15	13	85
1979	15	10	6	15	21	8	14	6	10	4	6	3	118
1980	13	14	6	7	15	7	9	3	13	15	17	5	124
1981	4	1	5	5	9	7	4			1	2		38
1982	1	2	9	2	3	4	2	2	7	6	3	3	44
1983		5	2	2	5	6	4	1	2	8	4	(4)	(43)
TOTAL	53	35	48	40	67	46	40	23	53	67	52	(34)	558

2. Distribution by historical stages

(1)	General Franco (1968–Nov. 1975)	57
(2)	Period of transition (Dec. 1975–Jun. 1977)	40
(3)	Constituent Assembly period (Jul. 1977–Dec. 1978)	94
(4)	Democracy (from January 1979)	367
	TOTAL	558

Major groups responsible for terrorism (%)

ETA	75.36
GRAPO	11.69
Extreme right	7.01
Others (extreme left, anarchist, international)	5.94

Source: Ministry of the Interior. Reproduced from Ricardo García Damborenea, *La Encruicijada Vasca* (Barcelona: Editorial Argos Vargara, 1985), 51.

Probably the most important fact was that not one single national political party chose to use the deaths associated with the Basque issue to attempt to delegitimize the democratic regime. No major political party manipulated the data to "craft" a democratic breakdown. There was of course a discussion about the best way to handle the Basque violence. However, no party persisted in blaming the various governments for creating the problem. No party claimed that the problem could be handled better outside of a democratic regime. No national party urged that democratic government throw all constitutional constraints aside and allow the army to wage unlimited war against the terrorists and their sympathizers.

In fact the democratic government made a concerted effort to ensure that the state security forces acted legally. The government and the police have made a considerable effort to avoid political deaths. The police, not the army, is implementing antiterrorist operations.[13] Significantly, to date the Spanish military has made no claim that the Basque situation would be better handled if the army were given control.[14]

Very importantly, the overall climate of public opinion in Spain is not supportive of violence. In post-Civil War Spain there is little romanticism about violence. In a public opinion poll that had an eleven-point scale on attitudes toward the Basque insurgents, with zero indicating the most hostile position and ten the most favorable attitude, 99 percent of the Spanish population polled in 1983 located themselves in one of the six most disapproving positions. Even in the Basque country itself, the average support was a low 1.79 on the eleven-point scale and the largest Basque nationalist party, the PNU, was only 1.4.[15]

Italy is another European country where terrorism has continued at a reasonably high level, but where terrorism has not been politically transformed into an issue or manipulated to craft democratic breakdown.[16]

Interwar Austria is the strongest example of the opposite trend, where deaths due to political violence were persistently manipulated to craft political breakdown. Both extremes of the political spectrum used the existence of a high rate of violence to bolster their argument that democracy contributed to, and could not resolve, the question of violence.[17] In both Austria and Germany in the 1920s a very high percentage of political elites and their associated mass movements legitimized violence. This contrasts with the fundamentally different atmosphere of Western Europe in the 1980s, where there is a very low degree of intellectual or popular defense of the use of violence.

In Argentina in the 1970s (and to a lesser extent Brazil and Uruguay in the 1960s and early 1970s) there was a diffuse intellectual and popular legitimization of the use of political violence. Part of the revalorization of democratic procedures has been the corresponding delegitimization of political violence.[18]

---

13. For a more detailed analysis of how the new Spanish democracy handled Basque violence, see Robert P. Clark, *The Basque Insurgents: ETA, 1952–1980* (Madison: University of Wisconsin Press, 1984) esp. pp. 126–39. Also see Christopher Hewitt, *The Effectiveness of Anti-Terrorist Policies* (New York and London: University Press of America, 1984), and Damborenea, *La Encruicijada Vasca.* For an extensive discussion of the Basque question, see Juan Linz, *Conflicto en Euskadi* (Madrid: Espasa Calpe, 1986).

14. For a very incisive analysis of how avoiding political deaths and the strong political control of the state coercive apparatus were crucial to the weathering of a political crisis in France during 1968, see Mattei Dogan, "How Civil War was Avoided in France," *International Political Science Review* 5, 3 (1984): 245–77.

15. See Linz, *Conflicto en Euskadi*, p. 615.

16. An important paper discussing this point is Leonardo Morlino, "Crisis without Breakdown: Italy as a Crucial Case," paper prepared for the International Political Science Association Congress, Rio de Janeiro, 7–11 August 1982.

17. The best study of the question of violence and the deliberate effort to delegitimize the new Austrian democracy is Gerhart Botz, *Krisenzonen einer Demokratie: Gewalt, Streik und Konfliktunterdrückung in Österreich seit 1918* (Frankfurt: Campus Verlag, 1987). See also Gerhart Botz, *Gewalt in der Politik* (München: Wilhem Fink Verlag, 1983).

18. For a discussion of the revalorization of democracy and the delegitimization of violence by a leading theorist of the left, see Francisco Weffort, "Why Democracy?", in

Once again, the recent European effort to avoid political deaths is important to assess. Democratic control of the means of state coercion, rather than abdication to the military, also needs to be studied closely. Democratic control of the military, the police, and the intelligence apparatus, however, requires a major effort by democratic civilians to empower themselves with new knowledge and new institutions so that they can assume effective command of the legitimate use of force by the state. This is not simply a vague injunction. Every part of the polity in the new democracies of Argentina, Uruguay, and Brazil will have to address this task. What could be done by civil society, especially civic groups, and by research institutes? By political society, especially by legislatures? And what could be done at the level of the state by changes in the organization of the executive?[19]

Democratic Management of State Force: The Tasks of Civil Society

Democracy is about an open contest for state power by means of elections and the oversight and control of state power by the representatives of the people. In virtually all polities of the world, and very much so in Latin America, the military are a permanent factor in any calculus of power. Therefore, by definition, civil society must consider how it can make a contribution to the democratic control of military, police, and intelligence systems. It is an obvious point but one that bears repeating that the capacity of the military as a complex institution to develop a consensus for intervention is greatly aided by the extent to which civil society "knocks on the doors" of the barracks. In 1964 in Brazil, and in Chile in 1973, many powerful representatives of civil society— including the church—"knocked on the door" and created the "Brumairean moment." The transitional military governments hoped for by many middle-class and upper-class members of civil society became long-lasting bureaucratic-authoritarian regimes with significant interests of their own. This fundamental point granted, what else is important for civil society to consider?

Turning specifically to the technical capacities of civil society *vis-à-vis* the military, police, and intelligence systems, what could be done that has not already been done in the past? Latin American social scientists have become the leaders of the world social science community in conceptualizing the realities and implications of the new global political economy. They have also done some of the best work in the world on social movements and popular

Democratizing Brazil: Problems of Transition and Consolidation, ed. Alfred Stepan (New York and London: Oxford University Press, 1989), pp. 327–50. Extensive references to the Uruguayan, Argentine, and Brazilian cases are found in Guillermo O'Donnell, Philippe C. Schmitter, and Laurence Whitehead, eds., *Transitions from Authoritarian Rule: Prospects for Democracy*, 4 vols. (Baltimore and London: Johns Hopkins University Press, 1986).

19. The following section draws heavily upon analysis and documentation contained in Alfred Stepan, *Rethinking Military Politics: Brazil and the Southern Cone* (Princeton: Princeton University Press, 1988). We thank Princeton University Press for permission to reuse this material.

culture. However, until recently the formal study of military organizations and international relations—especially geopolitics, and most specifically the study of territorial disputes and military strategy—has been neglected. Those civilians who have concerned themselves with these matters have tended to be professors who attended institutions such as the Escola Superior de Guerra in Brazil or Argentina's Escuela de Defensa Nacional, where the intellectual agenda was set by the military and where, sanctioned by national security doctrines, French, U.S., and Latin American military cold war and internal subversion preoccupations are dominant. This situation has often meant that few members of the democratic opposition in civil society have been specialists on military matters and few wrote alternative geopolitical works. In Argentina especially, this privileged the military's perception of the country's geomilitary problems.

Most major democracies have at least one major civilian-led independent research institute that concentrates on international military politics. In the United States, the Brookings Institution has often supplied authoritative and well-researched expert alternative assessments of military strategy. In England, the International Institute for Strategic Studies performs a comparable function. The creation of such prestigious, independent, and civilian-led institutes would seem to be high on the agenda of civil society. Latin American universities also have not to date routinely incorporated military sociology and geopolitics into their curricula. This is a vital task because in most major democratic politics the newspapers, television networks, and weeklies have military specialists on their staffs. Just as important, the constant academic production of a cadre of citizens who are experts on military questions relating to force structure, organizational style, budgetary affairs, doctrine formation, and the specific details of weapons systems are indispensible for the fulfillment of the military and intelligence oversight functions of political society, especially in the legislative branch.

The Tasks of Political Society

Most major stable democracies have crafted over time permanent standing committees in their legislatures or cabinets that devote themselves exclusively to the routine oversight and monitoring of their country's military and intelligence systems. These committees characteristically have professional staffs who are specialists in matters of military strategy, budgeting, or intelligence. Often these staffs pull their talents both from the ranks of the professional civil service and from the political parties. In Latin American legislatures, such permanent committees with large staffs and independent research capacities often either do not exist or are understaffed and have few resources. What is needed therefore is a deliberate strategy for the empowerment of legislatures to carry out their military and intelligence oversight functions in a routine democratic and legislative fashion.

Military and intelligence officials do occasionally appear before the legislatures in Latin America, but most often this occurs under the circumstances of a special commission of inquiry established to examine a particular controversy. From the perspective of comparative civil–military relations in a democracy, this is a dangerous and ineffective review mechanism for three fundamental reasons. First, precisely because it is *ad hoc* and does not involve a standing committee, legislative leaders are not supported by a cadre of professional staff members with expert knowledge of the intricacies of the field. Second, by its very nature, an *ad hoc* special commission of inquiry occurs in a controversial, conflictual setting that tends to increase the latent paranoia most military organizations throughout the world feel about political "interference" in their professional activities. Thus a primary requirement must be to reduce the atmosphere of an exceptional confrontational inquiry by making the military's appearance before legislative leaders a routine occurrence. Third, if political party leaders know that these permanent standing committees are a routine yet important part of legislative life, some members of all parties will attempt to acquire special expertise in these areas and will be able to conduct or chair these committee meetings in a respectful, but deeply authoritative, manner. The routinization of legislative–military transactions can help reduce mutual fears and ignorance on the part of military leaders and party leaders alike. The self-empowerment of legislatures in national security matters is an imperative and a possible goal.

The Tasks of the State

Working together, political leaders in the legislature and democratic government leaders of the state apparatus can also begin the difficult task of restructuring the military, police, and intelligence systems so they are more consistent with the normal checks and balances of democratic regimes. Without attacking, dismantling, or for the most part demoralizing their intelligence systems, England, France and the United States have crafted mechanisms for the democratic management, monitoring, and oversight of their intelligence systems. In Brazil, even using the existing laws drafted by the previous military regime, the New Republic could eventually demilitarize the four top offices in the Serviço Nacional de Informações (SNI)—none of which are required by law to be occupied by military officers. This would remove the army from direct control of the intelligence system, something many professional officers would welcome because they believe that the SNI collects dossiers on them and heavily influences promotion patterns for reasons that may be extraneous to the officers' own professional capacities, but for reasons that are of direct interest to the SNI's own bureaucratic concerns.

The post-Malvinas concern of Latin America militaries, and especially the military in Brazil, to upgrade their professional capacity for joint operations may present a propitious moment for making changes in the military's representation in democratic governments. The democratic government of Brazil's New Republic has twenty-six ministers, six of whom are active-duty military officers. These cabinet ministers are: the minister of the air force; the minister of the navy; the minister of the army; the director of the SNI; the head of the military household; and, the chief of the Joint General Staff of the Armed Forces. All but the last of these positions are quite important in managing a crisis stemming from Brazilian state politics. Thus even in a democracy the military remains deeply involved in the day-to-day political discussions of Brazil's affairs. This pattern in which the three service chiefs and the intelligence director all have cabinet status is often replicated in other Latin American countries, even under democratic regimes. Such representation is of course to a great extent a direct reflection of the power and capacity of the military in Latin American democracies. To our knowledge, in any given year under nonwartime conditions, normally not even one Western European or North American democracy has even one active-duty military officer with full cabinet status.

Three possible changes that can be initiated within the state apparatus by new democratic leaders are worth serious theoretical and political consideration, and while they would be resisted, they might even present some advantages for the military as an institution and could thus possibly gain some military adherents. First, because of the new appreciation by the military of the importance of an effective joint interservice professional operational capacity—and the military's recognition that historic interservice rivalries make interservice cooperation virtually impossible—it is conceivable that a single civilian minister of defense could replace the traditional ministers of the army, navy, and air force. Politically, this would be the easiest change to implement if some new net resources for joint operations were added to the budget, but Brazil is the only former bureaucratic-authoritarian regime where this is presently possible. Argentina under Alfonsín has recreated a minister of defense, but it was under such confrontational circumstances and in the midst of such a financial crisis that no new resources for joint operations were made available to soften the blow. Second, the intelligence chief could be removed from ministerial status, especially if the institutional power of a monolithic organization such as the SNI in Brazil were divided into separate organizations for external and internal intelligence and if the chief presidential advisor for intelligence did not also command a large operational service. Third, Latin American liberal politicians are deeply suspicious of the idea of an important National Security Council with permanent military representatives. However, if the military representatives have an institutional voice but not institutional command within such an organization, it could in fact strengthen democracy. Precisely because the military constitute a permanent factor of power in all polities, it is better to encapsulate them professionally—but not politically—into the state apparatus.

Military ministers are widely understood in the Latin American military to be political, not professional, appointments to the cabinet. Thus, paradoxically, even with five or six military ministers, the military at times perceive that their enduring professional interests are not represented in the democratic government. Within the state, a paradoxical mix of fewer politically appointed military ministers and more systematic professional incorporation into serious standing national security councils might reduce the military's sense of isolation and create a more effective system of mutual exchange of information and grievances, and thus lessen the tendency for the pendulum to swing violently from radical military aspirations for total control of the state apparatus to liberal civilian fantasies about the total isolation of the military from a modern polity.

Thus, in order to increase its effective control of the military and intelligence systems, any contemporary democratic polity must promote an effort by civil society and political society to empower themselves through improvement of their own capacity for control.

Can the Weight of Democratic Rule be Lightened by New Institutional Arrangements?

A common anxiety that we hear expressed in the new Latin American democracies is that the weight of democratic rule is extremely heavy for the presidency and the cabinet as institutions. While this lamentation is often heard, one seldom hears much discussion of alternative institutional arrangements that might lead toward greater burden-sharing among democrats, toward greater sharing of the responsibility for policy failures and successes, and toward greater flexibility in making coalitional shifts without appealing to nonconstitutional mechanisms.

In this section we will raise such themes because we think that this period of redemocratization and of new constituent assemblies is the right moment to begin serious theoretical and political reflection about what if anything can be done to share the burdens of democratic rule.

Sometimes we are tempted to overemphasize the weaknesses of democracy when confronted with serious problems and crises. There is undoubtedly a certain vulnerability of democratic institutions, due in part to the freedoms created by the state of law, civil liberties, the autonomy of institutions, and the unfettered articulation of interests.

We tend, however, to ignore the advantages of democratic regimes, once they have acquired a certain legitimacy, in confronting difficult or even unsolvable problems. A critical advantage of democracy is that it is possible to distinguish the democratic regime itself from the government of the day. The failure of one government, or of the parties in power at a given moment, does not need to imply the questioning of the type of regime, the constitution, or the legal processes for changing governments. In a democracy one government can be substituted for another without the need to overthrow the institutions or to disrupt the legal order. In a democracy, those dissatisfied with the performance of a particular government or with a particular leadership can within the framework of the institutions find others that might be more successful. The expectation that this will be so gives hope to those who are dissatisfied; a change of government in itself can generate considerable support not only among those who are actively dissatisfied, but also among those who only passively supported the previous government. There is no need for revolutions or coups when people believe in the institutions and in the fairness of the political process, particularly in elections as a method for changing governments. Certainly there will always be small minorities who, knowing that they cannot rally a large number of voters to their support, will turn to violence via terrorism or *pronunciamientos*. The important point, however, is that these attempts are not likely to be successful in a democracy unless there is a much broader basis of support for those engaging in the use of violence. That is why in our model of democratic breakdown we put so much emphasis on the semiloyalty of parties, institutions, or groups, rather than limiting our attention to the antisystem forces. It is painful to remember, but it must be stressed, that strong centrist and center-right elements in civil and political society supported the advent of the bureaucratic-authoritarian regimes in Brazil, Chile, Uruguay, and Argentina.

The possibility of changing governments and leaders without a legitimacy crisis is thus one of the greatest advantages of democracy over most forms of authoritarian rule. That possibility depends fundamentally on the trust of the people in democratic institutions, in the guarantees for political freedoms, in the fairness of electoral process, and in the conviction that those in power will give it up, according to the rules, to others who can be expected to do the same in the future. Both incumbents and the opposition can undermine that trust by their actions and by equivocal statements about their intentions.

In practice the possibility of distinguishing particular governments from the regime becomes more difficult when one party becomes hegemonic, especially if that party creates social conditions that make free competition for the support of the people very difficult. The distinction between the state and society should not be obliterated in a democracy.

The distinction between a government and those exercising temporary authority on the one hand, and the regime on the other hand, is facilitated in parliamentary systems. A vote of no confidence, a break-up of a coalition, or internal conflicts within the governing party can easily lead to a change in government or leaders, and sometimes to a timely dissolution. In a deep crisis, rapidly called elections can give the opposition the chance to govern without a crisis of institutions. This is certainly much more difficult in presidential democracies, where the removal of an incumbent easily becomes a constitutional crisis. Impeachment of a president is a much more traumatic process than the fall of a parliamentary government.[20] The fixed term of office is likely to be more frustrating for the opposition in a presidential system than in a parliamentary system. This potential for greater frustration becomes especially strong if many of the circumstances that made the election of the incumbent possible and his exercise of authority acceptable have changed sharply. In such instances we believe that it is structurally predictable that the opposition in a presidential system is more prone to turn to nondemocratic methods to remove the incumbent from office in order to facilitate a policy realignment than it would be in a parliamentary system. Obviously, parliamentarism has been accused of the opposite danger: the constant overthrowing of governments and discontinuity in government action. Modern constitutionalism, however, has found ways of reducing that danger. It could be argued that the principle of barring reelection so sacred in the political tradition of Latin America and so often violated in practice offers a similar guarantee. We feel, however, that it also has the disadvantage of barring from the continuing exercise of power a leader who might have shown considerable leadership qualities, something that would not be problematic in a parliamentary system, where the same leaders continuously or discontinuously occupy the position of premier.

It might not be an accident that with the exception of the United States, a country that is in so many ways exceptional, almost all stable democracies in the world have been parliamentary democracies. Presidential constitutions have in most of the world not assured stable democracy, and they have easily been converted into authoritarian rule. In fact, the only historically stable purely presidential system in the world exists in the United States. Unfortunately, the presidential example of the United States has always had a great attraction for Latin Americans, although in many respects their polities and social structures have had more similarities with Europe. The success of American presidentialism is based on many institutional and social factors whose combination is not found in one Latin American country: the federal and decentralized government that allows the opposition an important share in power, the separation of powers, the powerful role of the Supreme Court, the sacredness attributed to the Constitution, and the absence of disciplined and ideological parties.[21] Latin Americans, who for so many problems look to

20. For a discussion of how the political process operates under parliamentary as opposed to presidential systems, see Juan J. Linz, "Democracy: Presidential or Parliamentary; Does it Make a Difference?" Paper prepared for the project "The Role of Political Parties in the Return to Democracy in the Southern Cone," sponsored by the Latin American Program of the Woodrow Wilson International Center for Scholars, the Smithsonian Institution, and the World Peace Foundation, July 1985.
21. The very special conditions that have facilitated presidentialism in the United States are the subject of an important work by Fred W. Riggs, "The Survival of Presidentialism in America: Para-constitutional Practices," *International Political Science Review* 9, 4 (October 1988), pp. 247–78.

Europe and who so often reject the American model, might look at European political institutions, especially the classic parliamentary formula or, under exceptional circumstances, a semipresidential formula such as the French Fifth Republic, as alternatives.[22] The Constituent Assembly that was convened in Brazil in 1987, an analogous body that could be convened in Chile after the fall of the dictatorship, and the debate on constitutional reform along French parliamentarian lines presently underway in Argentina could all provide opportunities to explore the comparative advantages of parliamentarianism over presidentialism.[23]

If practitioners and scholars take up this question in greater detail we think it will be particularly useful to attempt to assess how the presidential and parliamentary systems both manage stress. What is the comparative flexibility of these systems to craft solutions to respond to new situations? Unfortunately, we know of no systematic research into comparative political processes under parliamentary and presidential systems.[24]

22. Post World War II Europe has experimented with a variety of formulas that build a presidential component into parliamentary rule. Three studies of this experience are Maurice Duverger, *Echec Au Roi* (Paris: Albin Michel, 1978), his "A New Political System Model: Semi-Presidential Government," *European Journal of Political Research* 8 (1980): 165–87, and Stefano Bartolini, "Sistema Partitico ed Elezione Diretta del Capo dello Stato in Europa," *Revista Italiana di Scienza Politica* 14, 2, (Agosto 1984): 223–44. However, the actual functioning of this institution has not been well studied, except for the important book by Werner Kaltefleiter, *Die Funktionen des Staatsoberhauptes in der parlamentarischen Demokratie* (Köln: Westdeutscher Verlag, 1970).

23. For an extensive discussion of a parliamentary proposal for Chile, see Arturo Valenzuela, "Origins and Characteristics of the Chilean Party System: A Proposal for a Parliamentary Form of Government," Paper prepared for the project "The Role of Political Parties in the Return to Democracy in the Southern Cone," sponsored by the Latin America Program of the Woodrow Wilson International Center for Scholars, the Smithsonian Institution, and the World Peace Foundation, May 1985, Working Papers, 164. In Brazil, Bolivar Lamounier, who has participated in a preparatory commission for the Constituent Assembly, has extensively discussed parliamentary formulas. In Argentina, President Raúl Alfonsín's proposal for territorial and administrative reform suggests combining "elements of our traditional presidential regime with elements of parliamentary systems." See "Argentina: Next, Government by Prime Minister," *Latin American Weekly Report*, 25 April 1986.

24. This is not the appropriate place for a full discussion of semipresidentialism but we would like to register a strong caveat. Among politicians and theorists in Latin America who discuss parliamentarianism, there is frequently an almost automatic preference for semipresidential varieties as opposed to classical parliamentarianism. We do not share this preference. Semipresidentialism works best if a majoritarian party or coalition controls both the presidency and the parliament. Failing this, the tasks of governing in a semipresidential system require higher levels of political skill and greater willingness to compromise than are required in a classic parliamentary system. Semipresidentialism, to a degree impossible in classic parliamentarianism, can produce two democratically legitimated centers of power, a "dual executive" that leaves an ambiguity about who controls the military. The consequences of a "dual executive" in the Weimar Republic during the second presidency of Hindenburg were extremely unfortunate. For an analysis of the exceptional conditions under which a semipresidential system can work well and the unique historical conditions under which it was introduced, see the book by Kaltefleiter.

We think a full-scale research effort could profitably employ four different approaches. The first would be rational choice theory. The second would be comparative historical studies of the political process under a specified number of parliamentary systems and presidential systems. The third approach would be counterfactual analysis of the historical cases presented above in which it would be assumed that the presidential system had been parliamentary and vice versa. The fourth approach would entail extensive use of computer simulations of domestic crisis resolution in parliamentary and presidential systems.

SEVEN

On the Tasks of a Democratic Opposition

While democracy as a form of government has long been a staple concern of social science, the question of the genesis of democracy has been largely neglected. Moreover, until very recently, most studies of the growth of democracy have restricted their focus to its emergence from traditional oligarchies or absolute monarchies over the last two centuries in Europe, or to the problem of democracy in the context of decolonization.

This is unfortunate because much of the current theoretical and political concern with democracy centers on countries that have already had some experience with it, and where what is at stake is not the original establishment of popular government but its restoration as a successor to nontraditional authoritarian regimes. Active democratic opposition movements play a particularly important role in such countries, a role that deserves more sustained attention than it has so far received. Although this essay is based primarily on the experience of authoritarian regimes in countries like Chile, Brazil, Uruguay, South Korea, and the Philippines, I believe that the analysis also applies in substantial part to the recent breakdowns of communist regimes in Eastern Europe, most notably in Poland. What must be studied in all these cases is not merely the final collapse or overthrow of authoritarian regimes, but the incremental process of "authoritarian erosion" and the opposition's contribution to it. This in turn requires a dynamic analysis both of relationships within the authoritarian regime and of the multiple functions or tasks of the opposition.

Although the installation of a democratic regime scarcely heralds the end of political struggle, it does provide a new procedural setting for political life. This setting is not only more just in itself, but in most cases also offers the great masses of the people better opportunities than does authoritarianism to pursue such other goals as economic equality, social justice, and political participation.

In order to understand how a democratic opposition can attenuate the bonds of authoritarianism, we must first consider where the opposition stands in relation to the other components of the regime. Our analysis should emphasize

This chapter was first published in the *Journal of Democracy*, 1/2 (Spring 1990), 41–9.

not governmental *structures* but rather the overall *relationships* of domination. Generally speaking, the principal parties to such relationships are: (1) the core group of regime supporters (who find that their political, economic, or institutional interests are best served under the status quo); (2) the coercive apparatus that maintains the regime in power; (3) the regime's passive supporters; (4) the active opponents of the regime; and, (5) the passive opponents of the regime.

While structural or institutional studies place the coercive elite on center stage, an analysis of power relations within the authoritarian regime gives a fuller picture by examining the interactions among these five groups. The task of the active democratic opposition is to change the relations among all the component parts of the authoritarian system in such a way as to weaken authoritarianism while simultaneously improving the conditions for democratization.

Eroding Authoritarianism

In order to understand how these power relations may change in ways that affect the prospects for a democratic transition, it is useful to consider how each group will tend to perceive its situation and possible courses of action at different stages of authoritarian rule. For illustrative purposes, we will select for comparison two positions from opposite ends of the continuum of changing relationships that characterize authoritarian systems: the first involving a strong regime ruling in an atmosphere of widespread fear, and the second a weakened and eroding regime.

In the first case, the existence of a strong regime will tend to coincide with certain attitudes on the part of both its supporters and its opponents. Its core supporters, for example, will quite likely be gripped by something on the order of a siege mentality. To them, authoritarian rule is a ready help in time of trouble and a shield against clear and present danger. They will think it in their interest actively to help the regime and will not shrink from supporting even harshly repressive measures.

Like the core supporters, the military and security officials who wield the regime's coercive power will tend strongly to identify the interests of their organizations with those of the regime. This group may even conclude that considerations of national security positively require that the armed forces run the government.

Faced with a strong regime enjoying the allegiance of these two formidable groups, the third group—the passive supporters—will submit to authoritarian hegemony. They will remain quiescent and pliable, even to the point of participating in the institutions that serve as the regime's indirect, noncoercive bulwarks. Thus a cohesive and self-confident authoritarianism can enlist numerous middle-class intellectuals, clergymen, journalists, and other professionals on its side.

Among the opposition, the activists will be virtually demobilized by the massive coercion the regime is willing to use against them. The passive opposition is likely to be relatively small in this scenario, and almost certainly will hold itself aloof from those who actively oppose the regime.

In the regime-erosion situation, on the other hand, all these groups will be found thinking and acting differently. With the fear that holds the regime together subsiding, the core group of regime supporters will start to fragment as doubts arise concerning the wisdom and expediency of authoritarian policies. Some core supporters will decide that the perpetuation of authoritarianism is not in their interest, and will go over to passive—or sometimes even active—opposition. Such a shift would reflect their unwillingness to continue abdicating their political power and judgment to the government, and might also signal a newfound appreciation of democracy as a peaceful and predictable method for settling social and political conflicts.

Given the divisions among core supporters—and probably a corresponding resurgence among the active opposition as well—direct physical coercion will become even more important for the maintenance of the regime. But unless the military officers who command the means of coercion perceive severe domestic threats to the military itself, their resolve too may weaken. Some among them will then come to suspect that the continuation of the military-as-government (as in Brazil), or continued military support of an increasingly despised regime (as in Romania), may be inimical to the interests of the military as a national institution.

At these signs of weakening among the forces of authoritarianism, most of the passive supporters will quietly shift to passive opposition. It may also be expected that parts of key groups such as the clergy, the press, and the intellectual classes generally will place themselves under the banner of active opposition. Such passive supporters as do remain will no longer allow themselves to be incorporated into the institutions of the authoritarian regime.

With their ranks bolstered by growing numbers of defectors from authoritarianism, the active regime opponents will find their days of paralysis at an end. They will be able to undertake a broad array of activities to pressure the regime and publicly state their case for change. The passive opposition will grow much larger as people no longer need constantly to fear savage repression. Passive opponents will also lose some of their passivity as they become willing to participate in antiregime actions orchestrated by the active opposition. Under the right conditions, the passive and active opposition will coalesce and expand to the point where the idea of redemocratization wrests hegemony away from authoritarianism.

Although authoritarian regimes may buckle because of external setbacks like military defeat, foreign occupation, or international economic reversals, they are more likely to collapse under the strain of conflicts and contradictions that are purely internal. If it performs its multiple functions well, the active demo-cratic opposition can exacerbate discord among the authoritarians, as well as prepare the indispensable political foundations for a democratic successor regime.

Priorities for the Opposition

What then are the multiple functions or tasks of democratic opposition move-ments in authoritarian regimes? In roughly ascending order of complexity (but not necessarily temporal sequence), the five key opposition functions are: (1) resisting integration into the regime; (2) guarding zones of autonomy against it; (3) disputing its legitimacy; (4) raising the costs of authoritarian rule; and (5) creating a credible democratic alternative. Analytically, the degree to which the opposition can perform these functions is a useful indicator of the severity of authoritarian control. The less the opposition is able to carry out any of these tasks, the more effective the regime's control of the polity is shown to be.

The first of the functions, resistance to integration, is the *sine qua non* for an opposition in the first place. If the cadre of the active opposition allows itself to become effectively demobilized and co-opted into authoritarian institutions, then the active opposition—for the time being at least—will have ceased to exist. On the other hand, if the active opposition maintains some independent ideological, cultural, and above all institutional existence, it will remain able to carry out its other tasks. Indeed, its prospects will be promising, for the total elimination of all opposition requires extremely effective mobilization and the full integration of all institutions and social groups into the structures of the regime, a project of surpassing difficulty at which no modern authoritarian government has ever succeeded.

If the active opposition can remain independent, its next task (in order of survival imperatives) is to encourage the growth of passive opposition. There are two good ways to do this. One is to contest the government's claim to legitimacy. The other and more important way is to maintain some zones of autonomy in which nonregime organizations can operate.

If, for instance, there are political parties or trade unions that predate the authoritarian regime, every effort must be made to sustain them, if necessary from exile (although to be effective, the exiled leaders must maintain national roots). If the coalition of active and passive supporters of the coercive elite is strong, the institutions of civil society most likely to retain some autonomy are those with some claim to extrapolitical legitimacy, such as religious or cultural associations. Religious bodies, especially, can lend tremendous weight to human rights or basic needs claims and can also provide an umbrella under which the active opposition can help furnish community services such as food distribution, health clinics, and missing-persons centers. In Poland, Brazil, and Chile, the Catholic Church played this crucial role.

The more that new or preexisting democratic trade unions, parties, or community movements take root and flourish, the less space is left for the implantation of new-model authoritarian institutions. The larger and stronger these various non-or anti-authoritarian subsystems grow, the more effectively they can perform the other tasks of democratic opposition: contesting the legitimacy of the authoritarian regime, raising the costs of maintaining it, and generally grinding it down while building support for a democratic alternative. This sort of grassroots campaigning to create non-or antiregime subsystems—and not direct assaults on the coercive elite—should be the active opposition's main order of business.

According to the definition given by the Italian Marxist theoretician Antonio Gramsci, a regime has attained *hegemony* when there is "consent given by the great masses of the population to the general direction imposed on social life by the dominant social groups."[1] The more a regime rules by hegemony, the less it has to rely on coercion. The greater the degree of hegemony or tacit consent an authoritarian regime can acquire, the less pressure will be felt by its coercive elite. Hence one of the active opposition's central tasks is to make the costs that the regime's policies impose on society so clear to the initially passive opposition that the achievement of authoritarian hegemony is rendered impossible.

In addition, since the international climate can be a support or an obstacle to an authoritarian regime, the active opposition should appeal to world opinion by documenting and publicizing the regime's most flagrant violations of civilized standards of conduct. If the regime's accession was especially violent (as in Chile in 1973, for instance) and the violence is well documented, this can create well-nigh insurmountable international opprobrium. The stronger such repugnance becomes, the higher the costs of rule mount. The more serious the domestic and international challenges to the legitimacy of the new regime, the greater the likelihood that the coercive elite and its core supporters will be thrown on the defensive and forced to justify their rule as a mere "temporary exception" rendered "indispensable" by the absence of a viable alternative. The "temporary exception" argument plays right into the hands of the democratic opposition by making it more difficult for the regime permanently to institutionalize its rule. The claim to indispensability, on the other hand, presents more of a challenge—but also more of an opportunity—to the active democratic opposition. For the best response to this claim is to create a viable democratic alternative.

Much of the support or acquiescence enjoyed by nontraditional authoritarian regimes comes from passive supporters and passive, demoralized

---

1. Antonio Gramsci, *Selections from the Prison Notebooks*, eds. Quintin Hoare and Geoffrey Nowell Smith (New York: International Publishers Co., 1971), 12; see also pp. 57–9 and 260–1. Gramsci, *The Modern Prince and Other Writings*, trans., Louis Marks (New York: International Publishers Co., 1970), 164–88.

opponents who all believe that the coercive elite is securely in control of the political system. If the active opposition can encourage activities—such as strikes, slowdowns, widespread protests, samizdat style publications, "flying" university classes, and noncooperation generally—that give the lie to this belief, it will have increased the costs of rule yet again.

If such costs are raised high enough, they can rob the government of much of its legitimacy in the eyes of both its active and passive supporters. Some among those active supporters whose adherence springs from their belief in the efficacy of the authoritarian government may shift to merely passive support, either because they have lost confidence in the regime itself or because they find the costs of active identification with an unpopular regime too great. Also, some original active supporters may even make the leap over to passive or even active opposition if they begin to feel that their interests dictate such a move.

The danger lurking in this strategy should be apparent. If the opposition raises the costs of authoritarian rule too high, the coercive elite may lash back with heightened repression. Yet such a backlash would carry its own risks, and the coercive elite must assess the probable net effect on the regime before deciding between suppression and toleration. Under some conditions the coercive elite—especially if its own vital organizational interests are not directly threatened—may opt for toleration. As Robert Dahl has argued, "The likelihood that a government will tolerate an opposition increases as the expected costs of suppression increase."[2]

In most contemporary authoritarian governments, the core of the coercive elite is a military bureaucracy. Although some scholars accord little in the way of independent value to this circumstance, my studies of military organizations in the United States, Peru, and Brazil have led me to conclude otherwise. The internally perceived requirements of complex military bureaucracies, it would seem, do possess a weight and significance all their own. Not surprisingly, this is especially so when the military's vital organizational interests are at stake. The continuation of rule by the "military-as-government" imposes costs on the "military-as-institution." If key officers conclude that these institutional costs outweigh the costs of relinquishing military rule, and if other conditions are right, then—regardless of the interests of the regime's active supporters—the military's withdrawal from power will become a serious possibility. By the same token, intensified repression will grow less likely.

Creating a Democratic Alternative

The redemocratization of an authoritarian regime must combine erosion and construction. The kinds of things that effectively eat away at an authoritarian

2. Robert A. Dahl, *Polyarchy: Participation and Opposition* (New Haven: Yale University Press, 1971), 15.

regime (labor unrest, widespread passive resistance, stubbornly autonomous social groups) are not necessarily the same things needed to lay the procedural foundations for democracy. Indeed, groups such as community-based religious organizations might have developed such independent casts of mind and such maximalist goals that they will balk at integration into broader democratic parties. A crucial task of the active opposition is to integrate as many anti-authoritarian movements as possible into the institutions of the emerging democratic majority. Failure in this task strengthens the authoritarian regime's claim to be the only alternative. If the opposition attends only to the task of erosion, as opposed to that of construction, then the odds are that any future change will merely be a shift from one authoritarian government to another, rather than a change from authoritarianism to democracy.

What type of alternative should the democratic opposition pursue? There is a temptation to respond to this question with calls for a viable shadow government. That temptation should be resisted for two reasons. First, it is likely that the increasing autonomy of subsystems will have enlarged both the number of interests and the means available to advance them. Second, we can also assume that after years of authoritarian rule by a narrow elite, there will be numerous contentious issues of policy to be debated, with a great variety of solutions proposed. Common sense says that under these conditions it will be exceedingly difficult, if not impossible, to get all prodemocratic forces to agree upon the kind of unified, detailed platform that a shadow government would require.

Absent such a platform, of what should the democratic alternative consist? At first, all that would be needed is some kind of broadly agreed-upon formula for the conduct of democratic contestation. A formula like this would serve to begin, not end, peaceful democratic struggles over other issues such as social or economic equality. In effect, a consensus would be reached about the rules of the game, though not about its results.

Focusing on procedure rather than policy serves an important goal of the democratic opposition. Premature wrangling over substantive issues could not only divide democrats, but could do so in a dangerously polarizing fashion. If, for instance, the authoritarian regime were to be so tactically astute as to take up a relatively centrist stance, part of the democratic opposition could well find itself to the right of the government on policy while another part stood to the left. In this case, both poles of the democratic opposition would stand closer—on substantive policy grounds—to the authoritarian regime than to each other. The authoritarians would then enjoy a strategic advantage over their badly divided opponents. If, however, the opposition concentrates on procedure, then all democratic forces can act as one to extract democratic procedural guarantees from the regime.

A broad procedural consensus among all democratic groups would alter the relationships of domination within the authoritarian regime in several crucial ways. The presentation of a clear alternative would undermine one of the authoritarian regime's central self-justifications, namely, its claim to be indispensable.

To the extent that fair democratic procedures would offer guarantees to the former supporters of the authoritarian regime, such procedures would accord them the possibility of continuing to pursue their interests under the new institutional arrangements. Thus, to the extent that the regime's initial supporters come to see democratic contestation as a serious alternative, their fears concerning the costs of democratic reform will diminish. By the same token, the growing power and cohesiveness of the forces of democracy will boost the expected cost of repression, including the prospect that it might ignite a revolutionary upheaval. Should something like this happen, then an important change favoring democratization will have occurred within the authoritarian regime itself. More precisely, the power relations among the regime's five components will have begun to approximate Robert Dahl's axiom: "the more the costs of suppression exceed the costs of toleration, the greater the chance for a competitive regime."[3]

The active supporters of the authoritarian regime and the members of the coercive elite themselves are often the major agents of this change; except in very rare cases of successful democratic revolution, crucial decisions favoring democratization are usually made by those who had previously been counted among the pillars of the authoritarian regime. We have recently seen this in cases such as Spain, Brazil, Chile, South Korea, Poland, and Hungary.

This is not, of course, to say that these decisions will be made gladly, freely, or out of disinterested good will. And there will always be those within the authoritarian regime who will dig in their heels and call for resistance to reform. Intense pressure from below by the active opposition and its allies is almost always the initial reason why liberalization is contemplated. The expected consequences of resisting such pressure figure heavily in the power struggle within the coercive elite and the ranks of its active supporters when they make their final decisions about democratization.

The ways in which democratic opposition movements go about their tasks can and should vary greatly, as prudence and circumstances dictate. Thus the purpose of this essay has not been to set forth a deterministic model describing the manner in which the democratic reform of authoritarian regimes must proceed. My goal, rather, has been a far more modest one. It has been simply to show that a richer understanding of how authoritarian regimes become democratized can be achieved if less attention is paid to the structures forged by the coercive elite, while more is accorded to the relationships of domination that pervade such regimes. In particular, it is important that scholars learn to identify the major parties to these relationships, and to analyze those processes that might serve not only to cut the ground out from under authoritarian modes and orders, but to lay the basis for a securely democratic future.

3. Ibid., 15.

EIGHT

Democratic Opposition and Democratization Theory

About a quarter of a century past the beginning of the "third democratic wave" in politics, what are some of the most important implications to be drawn about the role of the democratic opposition in the processes of democratization, and in new democratic governance? One body of theory concerns "pacted transitions", and another the oppositional role of "civil society against the state". Both bodies of theory, and the empirical evidence brought to bear in them, relate to important processes; but in my view they are in need of substantial revision before they can be incorporated into our new efforts to build a democratic theory of opposition. These revisionist tasks will constitute the main effort of this essay.[1]

However, there are two other concerns which have not yet been extensively documented or theorized. These relate to how, after a democratic transition, the democratic opposition can help consolidate and deepen democracy by turning vital "non-issues" into issues, and by creating new structures of participation, transparency and ultimately of accountability. I will conclude my essay with a brief effort at beginning to address these as yet under-theorized areas.

In a number of the most studied transitions to democracy (Spain, Brazil, Uruguay, Poland and Hungary), a roughly similar pattern emerged in all countries. After the non-democratic regime experienced a combination of internal divisions and growing opposition, softliners from the non-democratic regime held important informal discussions with the moderate democratic opposition. Over time, a "game" emerged in which the regime moderates and the opposition moderates both "used" (and attempted to "constrain") their

1. In this revisionist task I will use and attempt to build upon my recent book with my co-author, Juan J. Linz, *Problems of Democratic Transition and Consolidation: Southern Europe, South America and Post-Communist Europe*, Baltimore and London, Johns Hopkins University Press, 1996. I thank him and Johns Hopkins University Press for permission to use this work extensively.

This chapter was first published in *Government and Opposition*, 32/4 (Autumn 1997), 657–73.

own hardliners. Slowly, in a context where, in a Dahlian sense "the costs of toleration" for the regime seemed to be lower than the "costs of repression", an arrangement arose in which both the regime moderates and the opposition moderates agreed to submit the future question of who had the right to rule to open and relatively, but almost never completely, free electoral contestation.[2] These types of transitions were often called "pacted" transitions and an implicit theory emerged in much of the democratization literature which argued that the opposition's primary function in a non-democratic regime was to negotiate such pacts.

Negotiating "Pacted" Democratic Transitions

I do not want to minimize the importance of such pacts. But if our purpose is to empirically understand the entire universe of successful democratic transitions, failed democratic transitions, regime "collapses" and cases where no democratic transition attempt even started, it is important to stress that pacted transitions have occurred, and I would argue from a theoretical perspective *can only* occur, in a very restricted area of non-democratic regime types. Why?

Pacted transitions of the type I discussed above are in game-theoretical terms a four-player game involving "regime moderates", "regime hardliners", "opposition moderates" and "opposition hardliners".[3] However, two conditions must be satisfied for such a four-player game to be possible in a non-democratic context. The moderate players in the regime must have sufficient autonomy so that they can, over time, conduct strategic as well as tactical negotiations with the players from the moderate opposition. Likewise, the moderates in the opposition need a degree of continued organizational presence, power and followers in the policy to play their part in the negotiation pacts.

While there are often references in the democratization literature to pacts being a key part of most transitions, full four-player pacts are possible in only two of the four most common ideal-typical non-democratic regimes. Analytically and empirically, they are not possible if the polity is close to an ideal-typical totalitarian regime or an ideal-typical sultanistic regime. Four-player pacts are, however, possible in some ideal-typical post-totalitarian regimes (at the

2. See Robert A. Dahl, *Polyarchy: Participation and Opposition*, New Haven, Yale University Press, 1971, p. 15.
3. See Adam Przeworski, "The Games of Transition", in Scott Mainwaring, Guillermo O'Donnell and Samuel Valenzuela (eds), *Issues in Democratic Consolidation*, Notre Dame, Ind., University of Notre Dame Press, 1992, pp. 105–53. For an application of game theory to the Spanish case, see Josep M. Colomer, "Transitions by Agreement: Modeling the Spanish Way", *American Political Science Review*, December 1991, pp. 1283–1302.

"mature" end of the post-totalitarian continuum) and some weakened authoritarian regimes.[4] Let me develop these categorical assertions.

What do I mean by an ideal typical totalitarian regime? If a regime has eliminated almost all pre-existing political, economic and social pluralism, has a unified, articulated, guiding utopian ideology, has intensive and extensive mobilization and has a leadership that rules, often charismatically, with undefined limits and great unpredictability for elites and non-elites alike, then it seems to me that it makes historical and conceptual sense to call this a regime close to an ideal-typical totalitarian type.

If a polity approaches being such a totalitarian ideal type, the two key players for a pacted transition cannot be present. No totalitarian ruler will allow "regime moderates" to exist who have sufficient autonomy to conduct strategies and tactical negotiations with opposition moderates. And just as emphatically, there can be no moderate opposition players with sufficient organizational presence and followers in the polity to have enough power to negotiate their way into a transition pact. At best, therefore, an ideal-typical totalitarian regime is a two-player (non-) game. There is a big player (the hardline maximum leader and his party-state staff) and possibly an underground opposition (half a player?) that can struggle to exist and possibly resist but which has absolutely no capacity to negotiate a pacted transition and, in any case, has no player to negotiate with.

Let us look at the possibility of four-player pacts in sultanistic regimes. A large group of polities, such as Haiti under the Duvaliers, the Dominican Republic under Trujillo, the Central African Republic under Bokassa, the Philippines under Marcos, Iran under the Shah, Romania under Ceauşescu, and North Korea under Kim Il Sung, have had strong tendencies towards an extreme form of patrimonialism that Weber called "sultanism". For Weber:

patrimonialism and, in the extreme case, *sultanism* tend to arise whenever traditional domination develops an administration and a military force which are purely personal instruments of the master... where domination... operates primarily on the basis of discretion, it will be called *sultanism*.. The non-traditional element is not, however, rationalized in impersonal terms, but consists only in the extreme development of the ruler's discretion. It is this which distinguishes it from every form of rational authority.[5]

What Juan J. Linz and I wanted the term sultanism to denote is a generic style of domination and regime rulership that is, as Weber says, an extreme form of patrimonialism. In sultanism, the private and the public are fused, there is a strong tendency towards family power and dynastic succession, there is no

---

4. For a detailed analysis of the "totalitarian", "post-totalitarian", "sultanistic" and "authoritarian" ideal types see Linz and Stepan, *Problems of Democratic Transition and Consolidation*, op. cit., ch. 3.

5. Max Weber, *Economy and Society: An Outline of Interpretive Sociology*, ed. Guenther Roth and Claus Wittich, Berkeley, University of California Press, 1978, Part 1, pp. 231, 232. Italics in the original.

distinction between a state career and personal services to the ruler; there is a lack of rationalized impersonal ideology, economic success depends on the ruler and, most of all, the ruler acts only according to his own unchecked discretion, with no larger impersonal goals for the state.

A regime that approximates the sultanistic ideal type does not have a pacted transition available as a transition path because, as in the totalitarian type, the two moderate players are absent. The essence of the sultanistic ideal type is that the sultan fuses personal and public power. Important figures in the regime are significant not because of any bureaucratic or professional positions they hold, but because of their presence on the personal staff of the sultan. But how can there be room in the "household" staff of the sultan for a moderate player who publicly negotiates the demise of his employer? The other players who never exist in an ideal-type sultanistic regime are moderates from the organized democratic opposition. Neither civil society nor political society has enough autonomy to enable a publicly organized democratic opposition to develop sufficient negotiating capacity for it to be a full player in any pacted transition.[6]

Precisely because pacted transitions are impossible under sultanism and because sultans have no organized party-state and little ideologically augmented compliance, more than any other type of non-democratic regime, they tend to fall to violent opposition. Unless there is strong involvement by a regional democratic hegemon, the outcome of the violent overthrow of sultanism is seldom democratic.[7]

Even "early" post-totalitarian regimes (all of which by definition grew out of and are still relatively close to totalitarian regimes) do not have sufficient diversity and autonomy in the ruling party-state leadership or sufficient strength and autonomy within the democratic opposition to produce all the players needed to conduct successfully a four-player transition game. When an "early" post-totalitarian regime (East Germany in 1989) or a "frozen" post-totalitarian regime (Czechoslovakia from 1968 to 1989) faces a sudden crisis of opposition (in both cases due to a radically changed external context that drastically altered domestic power relations), such a regime is particularly vulnerable to *collapse* if it is not able to repress that opposition, given the early or frozen post-totalitarian regime's limited negotiating capability.

But a wide range of weakened authoritarian regimes such as Spain and Brazil in the mid-1970s, as well as the communist, but *de facto* authoritarian military-led regime of Poland in the late 1980s, and the "mature" post-totalitarian

6. For example, the only Warsaw Pact country in 1988 not to have one opposition samizdat journal published in the country was Romania, a country that combined under Ceauşescu strong sultanistic and totalitarian tendencies.
7. For the special difficulties of a successful democratic transition from a sultanistic regime, see the introductory chapter by H. E. Chehabi and Juan J. Linz in their edited volume in progress, *Sultanistic Regimes*, and Richard Snyder, "Explaining Transitions from Neopatrimonial Dictatorships", *Comparative Politics*, Vol. 24, July 1992, pp. 379–99. Also see Michael Bratton and Nicholas van Walle, "Neopatrimonial Regimes and Political Transition in Africa", *World Politics*, July 1994, pp. 453–89.

regime of Hungary in 1988–9, *can*, and *did*, produce four-player games. Thus, although pacted transitions figure prominently in the democratization literature, classic four-player pacted transitions are in fact available as a transition path only in some already weakened authoritarian regimes and in mature post-totalitarian regimes.

Where does this leave us concerning the function of democratic opposition in non-democratic regimes? If we want a more inclusive conceptual framework than that provided by "pacted transitions", I suggest a "relational approach".

I believe that on theoretical and political grounds it is useful to think of any non-democratic regime as a set of *relationships* of domination. Generally speaking, the principal parties to such relationships are: (1) the core group of regime supporters (who find that their political, economic, social or institutional interests are best served under the status quo); (2) the coercive apparatus that maintains the regime in power; (3) the regime's passive supporters; (4) non-democratic opponents to the regime; (5) the active democratic opponents of the regime; and (6) the passive opponents of the regime. The task of the active democratic opposition is to *change* the relations among all the component parts of the non-democratic regime in such a way as to weaken the regime while simultaneously improving the conditions not just for regime change, but specifically for democratization.[8]

What, then, are the multiple functions or tasks of democratic opposition movements in non-democratic regimes? In roughly ascending order of complexity (but not necessarily temporal sequence), the six key opposition functions are: (1) staying in, or coming into, existence; (2) resisting integration into the regime; (3) guarding zones of autonomy against it; (4) disputing its legitimacy; (5) raising the costs of non-democratic rule; and (6) creating a credible democratic alternative.

The democratization of a non-democratic regime must combine erosion of the old relationships of domination and the construction of a new set of relationships which present such a credible and viable democratic alternative that many of the passive supporters of the non-democratic regime become at least passive supporters of the opposition, and many of the passive supporters of the opposition are transformed into part of the active democratic opposition.

If the democratic opposition keeps up its momentum, and especially if it presents the possibility of a future built around the rule of law, even some of the regime's once core supporters might join the passive opposition.

As the relations of domination increasingly shift (and I have studied how this process has occurred in countries as diverse as Hungary, Chile, Spain and Taiwan), the Dahlian calculus tangibly alters for most groups except the inner core of coercive apparatus. For the vast bulk of the regime's passive, and even

---

8. For a more extensive treatment of this subject, see Alfred Stepan, "On the Tasks of a Democratic Opposition", *Journal of Democracy*, Vol. 1, Spring 1990, pp. 41–9.

some more active supporters, the costs of continued repression may well seem to rise dangerously, at the same time as the costs of tolerating (or passively joining) the democratic opposition decline.

I must stress again that a fundamental part of changing relationships of domination depends on the opposition not only presenting itself as democratic, but also preparing itself for democratic contestation. It must be ready for democratic governance, or to form the loyal opposition. In many countries, such as Spain and Chile, one of the great transformations that occurred in the period of violent repression was that many members of the opposition, particularly on the left, began deeply to internalize democracy as a permanent value in itself and not merely as an instrumental tactic to be used to bring about fundamental change.[9] The democratic left in Spain was thus ready to form the loyal opposition to the first democratically elected prime minister, and in Chile to be a loyal junior partner in the first two post-Pinochet administrations led by the Christian Democratic President.

"Civil society against the State": Some Revisionist Notes

Let us next move from pacted transitions to the role of opposition in civil society. It is fair to say that the idea of civil society emerged from the recent wave of democratization as the celebrity of political theory, especially in countries such as Poland and Brazil. I acknowledge this. However, I also want to note that on political, conceptual and historical grounds, the oppositional role of civil society, as currently formulated, carries with it the potential for making it difficult to construct a political society of the sort necessary for consolidated democracy.[10] I will draw my example from Poland, but much of what I will say applies equally to Brazil.

The general problems of post-communist representation and the authentication and legitimization of political society were compounded and given a distinctive specificity in Poland because of the length and ethos of the opposition campaign. *Civil society*, like many other key political words such as *democracy*, can be used by different theoreticians and different social movements in

9. The revalorization of democracy by the Left produced a rich new genre of writings. For one such example see Francisco Weffort, "Why Democracy?" in Alfred Stepan (ed.), *Democratizing Brazil: Problems of Transition and Consolidation*, New York, Oxford University Press, 1989, pp. 327–50.

10. By *political society* in a democratizing setting I mean that arena in which the polity specifically arranges itself to contest the legitimate right to exercise control over public power and the state apparatus. By *civil society* I refer to that arena of the polity where self-organizing groups, movements and individuals, relatively autonomous from the state, attempt to articulate values, create associations and solidarities, and advance their interests.

different ways.[11] In Poland and in a slightly different way in Brazil, the idea of civil society as opposition developed some very distinctive and politically powerful overtones. In Poland *civil society* referred to the sphere of uncoerced activity not created by the state and virtually independent of the state. Poland was a particularly strong case of the "Civil Society against the State" dichotomy, which had strong cultural roots in the struggle of the nation against foreign-controlled state authority. "Civil Society against the State" was a politically useful concept in the opposition period because it allowed a sharp differentiation between them (the Moscow-dependent party-state) and us (Polish civil society).[12] The language associated with civil society further strengthened the opposition's position against the party-state because it was encoded in a moral discourse of "truth" and the existential claim of "living in truth". This discourse was particularly functional for what was in effect the national liberation movement, which was waged in Poland from 1976 to 1989. In any movement of liberation, an extremely high value is attached to "unity" within the struggle, and the ideas of *compromise* or *internal conflict* are spoken of pejoratively. Given the difficulties of the opposition's struggle against a highly organized state, there was an understandable tactical and strategic need for immediacy, spontaneity and anti-formal modes of operation. Imperceptibly, however, the instrumental aspects of immediacy, spontaneity and anti-formalism became ethical standards of personal and collective behaviour. Taken as a whole, this language and behaviour are what some Polish analysts called "ethical civil society", which no doubt was one of the most powerful and innovative features of the Polish opposition and, ultimately, of the Polish path to democratic transition.[13]

While the idea of ethical civil society contributed to a very powerful politics of opposition, many theorists and practitioners went even further. They were so eager to avoid becoming captured in the routines and lies of the party-state that they elevated the situational ethics of oppositional behaviour into a

---

11. For a discussion of the different meanings of *civil society* in various philosophical approaches and how it began to be used in Eastern Europe, see Jean L. Cohen and Andrew Arato, *Civil Society and Political Theory*, Cambridge, Mass., MIT Press, 1992. For a selection of different approaches and for a good essay on how *civil society* became central to the theory, practice and life of East European opposition movements, see John Keane (ed.), *Civil Society and the State*, London, Verso, 1988. A revisionist critique of *civil society* is now emerging. See e.g., the chapter arguing that civil society was the "last ideology of the old intelligentsia", in Klaus von Beyme, *Systemwechsel in Osteuropa*, Frankfurt am Main, Suhrkamp, 1994, pp. 100–23.

12. By now there is an extensive literature on many aspects of Polish civil society. Some of the best works include Timothy Garton Ash, *The Polish Revolution: Solidarity*, New York, Charles Scribner's Sons, 1983; Jadwiga Staniszkis, *Poland's Self-limiting Revolution*, ed. Jan T. Gross, Princeton, NJ, Princeton University Press, 1984; and Andrzej M. Tymowski, "The Unwanted Social Revolution: From Moral Economy to Liberal Society in Poland (The Social Origin of the Transformation of 1989)", PhD dissertation, Yale University, 1995.

13. The theme of "ethical civil society" is developed in Piotr Ogrodzinski, "The Four Faces of Civil Society", Warsaw, 1991, unpublished manuscript.

general principle of the "politics of anti-politics".[14] This politics of antipolitics entailed the aspiration of creating a sphere of freedom independent of the state.

Unfortunately, Poland's pioneering and heroic path to democratic transition via ethical civil society in opposition inevitably created discourses and practices that, until they can be transformed, will generate systemic problems for the creation of a democratic political society. Ethical civil society may claim to represent "truth", but political society in a consolidated democracy normally represents "interests". In political society the actor is only seldom the "nation", but more routinely "groups". "Internal differences" and "conflict" are no longer to be collectively suppressed, but organizationally represented in political society. Compromise and institutionalization are no longer negative but positive values. Antipolitics is dangerous for democratic politics. In new democracies, the effort should no longer be to live parallel to state power but to monitor, achieve and direct state power. In fact, most of the values and language of ethical civil society that were so functional to the tasks of opposition are dysfunctional for a political society in a consolidated democracy (see Table 8.1).[15]

TABLE 8.1. *The contrasting language of "ethical civil society in opposition" and "political society in a consolidated democracy"*

Value or attitude	Ethical civil society in opposition	Political society in a consolidated democracy
Basis of action	Ethics of truth	Interests
Actors	The ethical nation	Groups
Attitude towards "internal differences"	Viewed pejoratively	Accepted as normal
Attitude towards "internal conflict" within democratic community	Effort to repress	Effort to organize, aggregate and represent
Attitude towards "compromise"	Negative	Positive
Attitude towards routinized institutions	Negative	Positive
Attitude towards "antipolitics"	Positive	Negative
Attitude towards "state"	Operate outside it	Strive to direct it

Source: This table is reproduced from Linz and Stepan, *Problems of Democratic Transition and Consolidation*, op. cit., p. 272.

14. David Ost argues that a significant part of the Polish opposition "rejected the state not just because it could not win there, but also because it did not want to sin there . . . This opposition did not want to possess power so much as to abolish it . . . So 'anti-politics' is not just the necessary rejection of the state, but also the deliberate rejection of the state, the belief that what is essential to a just order is not a benign government and good people in power, but rather a vital, active, aware, self-governing and creative society". David Ost, *Solidarity and the Politics of Anti-Politics: Opposition and Reform in Poland since 1988*, Philadelphia, Temple University Press, 1990, p. 2.
15. On the collapse of Solidarity as a political force and the eventual weakening of the civil society in Poland, see the two articles by Aleksander Smolar, who played a key role in "civil society in opposition" and later was involved in the difficult task of building an

I do not want to be misunderstood. Properly understood, a robust civil society is indispensable for democratization. But democratic theorists and activists should not create false contradictions between civil society and political society. Democratic consolidation obviously needs both strong civil society and political society. I have talked about a potential danger of some types of civil society rhetoric. But one finds equally dangerous ideas and action emanating from some groups in political society. All too often some democratic leaders in political society argue that civil society, having played its historic role, should be demobilized so as to allow for the development of normal democratic politics. Such an argument is bad democratic theory and bad democratic practice. A robust civil society, with the capacity to generate political alternatives and to monitor government and state, can help transitions to their completion, help to consolidate and help to deepen democracy. At all stages of the democratization process, therefore, a lively and independent civil society is invaluable.

Another revisionist, or better, cautionary, note about "Civil Society against the State" is that it may so restrict our "gaze" that we overlook how some eventually important opposition groups may have actually emerged not *against* the state but from *within* the state. In fact, the theoretical optic, "Civil Society against the State", will lead to a very partial history of recent democratic opposition.

Poland was clearly a case of Civil Society against the State. Unfortunately, the drama of Poland has led to an underanalysis of Hungary. Few analysts of 1989 recognize that the decision to have multi-party competitive elections was actually made a few months *earlier* in Hungary than in Poland. Also, Poland's elections in 1989 were in fact not a free contestation. At the "pacted transition" conducted around the Polish Round Table, the Communist Party and its Peasant Party allies were in effect guaranteed 65 per cent of the seats in the lower house because only 35 per cent of the seats would be open to free and competitive contestation. In Hungary the Communist Party agreed to free elections with no guarantees for the number of seats they would have. How did Hungary arrive at such a result? Did something happen *inside* the party-state that contributed to this result?

A Hong Kong-based Chinese social scientist (not blinded by Poland and no doubt thinking about what could emerge in China) was the first to see correctly and to conceptualize an important feature of the Hungarian process.[16] He

effective political society in such a context. See his "A Communist Comeback? The Dissolution of Solidarity", *Journal of Democracy*, Vol. 5, No. 1, January 1994, pp. 70–84; and his "Civil Society after Communism: From Opposition to Atomization", *Journal of Democracy*, Vol. 7, No. 1, January 1996, pp. 24–38.

16. For his argument that the sharp "civil society versus the state" dichotomy is empirically a rare exception in communist systems and that the norm is infiltration and manipulation of the party-state by counterforces or reformists within the state, see X. L. Deng, "Institutional Amphibiousness and the Transition from Communism: The Case of China", *British Journal of Political Science*, Vol. 24, July 1994, pp. 293–318.

makes the point that it is impossible to understand the Hungarian transition without understanding the key role of what he called "amphibians". The reform factions in the Hungarian Communist Party (who became the "regime moderate" players) were informally connected—via amphibians—to groups who themselves eventually became the "moderate opposition" players in the regime. The amphibians were never systematically against the state. Indeed, they were often located *inside* state planning and social studies institutes. From these state institutes the amphibians increasingly provided data, analysis and ideologies that turned out to be useful in making regime moderates the most powerful faction inside the regime. Amphibians also helped to make democratic opposition moderates increasingly credible, informed and legitimate critics of the regime.[17] Given the important role amphibians played in helping to constitute both regime and opposition moderates, any analysis that leaves amphibians out of the story of how the Hungarian democratic opposition was able to arrive at a four-player game, and to *win* the four-player game, without making *any* of the concessions of the sort made in Poland, Brazil, and Uruguay, is damagingly incomplete.[18]

One last cautionary note about the excessive use of the "Civil Society against the State" optic is that it misses the downward reach by one part of the state to get civil society allies in its struggle against its opponents within the state. The fact that these allies eventually turned into effective opposition should not prevent us from recognizing the facilitating role played by the state in their emergence.

In fact, two of the most consequential opposition movements in recent politics emerged owing to intra-state conflicts. One faction within the state attempted to increase its intra-state power resources by actively facilitating the

17. Some of Hungary's most important and influential analysts who are now seen as sociologically part of the historical movement of the opposition were in fact for much of the 1970s and early 1980s occupying key administrative and/or advisory positions inside the state and should technically be seen as "amphibians". If we accept Deng's terminology, one of the most influential "amphibians" was János Kornai, who "reframed" existing concepts of what was likely and unlikely in the area of economic reforms. Much of the argumentation and documentation in his classic book, *The Socialist System: The Political Economy of Socialism*, Princeton, Princeton University Press, 1992, about the limits of market reform with a state led by a communist party were widely circulated among communist party officials for a decade before 1989 and contributed to making some party leaders "moderates"; and eventually, to making the "moderate players", the dominant player within the regime.

18. For good studies of the fifteen-year dynamic process of regime concessions and oppositional conquests, see Robert M. Jenkins, "Movements into Parties: The Historical Transformation of the Hungarian Opposition", Program on Central and Eastern Europe, Working Papers Series, No. 25, Harvard University, 1993; Gábor Halmas, "Representation and Civil Society in Hungary: The Recodification of the Right of Assembly and Association", *Law and Policy*, Vol. 13, April 1991, pp. 135–47; George Schopflin, Rudolf Tökós and Ivan Völgyes, "Leadership Change and Crisis in Hungary", *Problems of Communism*, September–October 1988; and two articles by Anna Seleny, "Hidden Enterprise and Property Rights Reform in Socialist Hungary", *Law and Policy*, 13 April 1991, and "Constructing the Discourse of Transformation: Hungary, 1979–82", *East European Politics and Societies*, Vol. 8, No. 3, 1994, pp. 439–66.

emergence of previously marginalized groups. In both cases the activation of these new groups by the state contributed to a complex dynamic of regime concession and societal conquest that eventually led to greatly empowered oppositional forces.

In Brazil, the key architect of the Brazilian opening in 1973–4, General Golbery do Couto e Silva, in a series of five interviews explicitly told me that he helped to initiate a liberalization process in 1973 because he had been worried about the growing autonomy of the security forces. Golbery was convinced that his challengers in the state thrived in an atmosphere of "darkness and torture". Whatever Golbery felt about secrecy and torture in the formative stages of the military regime in 1964–9, by 1973 he no longer felt they were necessary. All effective opposition had been crushed. In 1973, Golbery actually "courted" four or five of Brazil's major editors. He told them that while he could not guarantee that they would not occasionally be censured, he encouraged them to try to expand the limits of the possible by publishing some articles about abuses by the security apparatus. Golbery also met privately with a number of key Roman Catholic cardinals and told them they had a common enemy—the increasingly dangerous and autonomous coercive apparatus. He asked the cardinals to attend the upcoming inauguration of General Ernesto Geisel, who had agreed with Golbery to attempt a reform. He encouraged them to continue with their criticism of torture. Eventually, Brazil's press and Catholic Church emerged as key actors in the opposition's push to go beyond liberalization to democratization.[19]

In the USSR one of Gorbechev's most important political allies concerning Glasnost was Aleksander Yakovlev. In an interview with me in Moscow in October 1989, Yakovlev stressed that he had advocated the upcoming competitive elections in the Republics as a way of marginalizing opposition from the nomenklatura. The elections in the Republics of course contributed to the creation of new agendas and new ethnic-based power groups in the USSR, and an entirely new structuring of effective, if not always democratic, opposition.[20]

Let me now conclude by briefly turning to the areas where, in my introductory remarks, I said that the literature was as yet quite thin: issue creation and the social construction of processes of democratic accountability.

19. For these interviews and a more extensive analysis and documentation, see my chapter "Abertura: Intra-State Conflicts and the Courtship Society", in *Rethinking Military Politics: Brazil and the Southern Cone*, Princeton, Princeton University Press, 1988, pp. 30–44. Also see my article "State Power and the Strength of Civil Society in the Southern Cone of Latin America", in Peter B. Evans, Dietrich Rueschemeyer and Theda Skocpol (eds), *Bringing the State Back In*, Cambridge, Cambridge University Press, 1985, pp. 317–46.

20. For this interview and an analysis of the unforeseen consequences of elections in the Republics, see Linz and Stepan, *Problems of Democratic Transition and Consolidation*, ch. 19. Also see our article "Political Identities and Electoral Sequences: Spain, the Soviet Union, and Yugoslavia"; see Ch. 10.

Turning Non-issues into Issues: or How to Reverse the Presumption of Impunity

Much of the classic literature on opposition focuses on "political society", that is, groups such as parties, or decisional arenas such as legislatures, and how such parties or legislatures process the most salient agenda items. But recent experiences of democratization underline the importance of also studying how opposition groups in civil society can themselves create new agenda items, and especially turn non-issues into issues. In many of the transitions, particularly pacted transitions, key groups of the old regime, especially the military, simply withdrew into the state, where they still have substantial prerogatives. Quite often the former opposition implicitly adheres to their presumption of the impunity relating to their past violations of human rights. From a rational-choice perspective, the incentives for the democratic parties are often to play within the structure of the game whose parameters have been set by the relations of power at the end of the transition, that is, to accept the presumption of impunity. Occasionally, however, oppositional forces in civil society can alter the parameters of the political game and thereby create a new incentive structure.

An example of the potential of an opposition group to reconfigure political space in such a way so as to make a potential non-issue a salient issue is the case of the "Mothers of the Disappeared [Disaparecidos]" in Argentina. After the defeat of the junta in the Falklands-Malvinas, it was widely assumed that the Peronist Party would win elections if the military left office. The Peronists did not want to antagonize the military and rallies were held in which the Peronists kept the issue of the 8,000 people who had "disappeared" in the "dirty war" waged by the military off the agenda. However, the Mothers of the Disappeared took to infiltrating such rallies one by one, placing whites scarves on their heads and chanting: "los disaparecidos! los disaparecidos! los disparecidos!" The moral force of such protests was so strong that Raúl Alfonsín, the not yet leader of the Peronists' largest party competitor, the Radical Party, decided to base his bid for party leadership, and eventually for presidential leadership, on his ability to reverse the presumption of impunity. When he became president, he held the first successful, legally correct, trials in Latin American history against a former military government for crimes against human rights. But it was the "Mothers of the Disappeared" who had started the transformation of political space. In so doing, they transformed the incentive structure. In this new context political actors such as Alfonsín were able to seek and win office by turning the non-issue of impunity into the most salient issue.[21]

21. Indeed Aryeh Neier, in his forthcoming book on trials for crimes against humanity, argues that the first major advance against impunity since the Nuremberg Trials was probably in Argentina and that this had a direct influence on the Tribunal in The Hague for crimes against humanity committed in Bosnia and Rwanda, and the trials in South Korea which led to the conviction and imprisonment of the last two military presidents.

Creating Societal Structures of Transparency and Accountability: or How to Make Corruption Less Likely

Corruption has become one of the most eroding features of many potentially democratizing countries. It is especially a problem in countries such as Russia where the party-state imploded and where the combination of a weak state and rapid, but poorly regulated, privatization opens up many opportunities for public and private corruption.

Since the problem of corruption is so endemic and there is still little good news in this area, I want to close this short essay with some tentative reflections about a still relatively undocumented attempt to contain corruption in Brazil. The experiments do not involve an opposition in any classical sense. Rather, they involve some effort by reformers in the state apparatus to encourage groups in society to organize themselves in such a way that they become an effective structural opposition to corruption.

The experiment in Brazil began in the area of education. The essence of the experiment is that communities which are to receive a fixed amount of money (say the equivalent of £25,000) from the federal government or the state government, are asked to form councils composed of parents of schoolchildren, teachers, students over the age of eighteen, and representatives of nongovernmental organizations (NGOs). Members of the council must discuss spending priorities for their local schools among themselves and eventually before the wider community. Some decisions are quite simple, but nonetheless fundamental, in a country like Brazil where corruption is structurally embedded and where income distribution is possibly the worst in the world.

The council and the community might decide that every schoolchild is entitled to a hot lunch, and that every schoolchild is also entitled to three books. The council and the community may also arrive at making a collective decision to construct a basic computer lab and to pay a young specialist in the community to teach volunteer classes of children on Saturdays. The council and the community may also make negative decisions. They may decide that there is no need to buy a car for the school authorities from the limited funds that they have been allocated.

How the communities receive this money is a crucial part of the social construction of opposition to corruption. Different communities organize transactions in different ways but in general the more public the transfer of money to the council, the better it seems to be because it allows for a receipt of the money in a community setting. It also structures a process whereby individuals who are known in the community publicly reaffirm the purposes for which the money is to be used or not to be used.

In theoretical terms, there are important normative and institutional dimensions of such a simple public ceremony. *Normatively*, it enables a rededication of the council and the community to producing commonly agreed upon collective goods. *Institutionally*, it reduces the likelihood of corruption for three interrelated reasons. The community as a whole has participated in creating a system in which: (1) the transfer of public funds to their community is legitimized by widespread local demand; (2) the public transfer of money is to individuals who personally pledge themselves to carry out these tasks; and (3) the public receipt of the money allows the presumption of routinized corruption to be replaced by the presumption of routinized responsibility.

Normatively and institutionally, the key concepts characterizing the above process are classic principles of democratic theory: "participation", "transparency" and "accountability". In short, the social creation of a community structure of "opposition" to corruption.[22]

22. The efficaciousness of these socially engineered structures of opposition to corruption have already had some "demonstration effects". The World Bank has begun to re-evaluate its system for loans and grants in the area of regional environmental projects. The chief World Bank official in charge of such loans in Brasília told me in December 1996 that until they began to emulate Brazil's education experiment it was difficult for the World Bank to account for even 50% of its dispersed funds, but that with the new system of "participation", "transparency" and "accountability", in a new forest project the World Bank was funding, it could account for over 90% of the dispersed funds. Just as important, the project was achieving most of its social and economic objectives. An excellent economist of the Albert O. Hirschman school, Judith Tendler, has published a book that addresses such issues. See her *Good Government in the Tropics*, Baltimore and London, Johns Hopkins University Press, 1996.

NINE

Modern Multinational Democracies: Transcending a Gellnerian Oxymoron

Introduction

By 1986, three years before the walls came down, two new important bodies of literature were in place that should have helped us to think carefully about the difficult relationship between democratization and nationalism. Ernest Gellner published his magisterial *Nations and Nationalism* in 1983, the same year that saw the publication of another modern classic on nationalism, Benedict Anderson's *Imagined Communities: Reflections on the Origin and Spread of Nationalism.*[1]

By 1986 the four volume work edited by Guillermo O'Donnell, Phillipe C. Schmitter, and Laurence Whitehead *Transitions from Authoritarian Rule* was released and immediately created the field of "transitology."[2]

What now strikes me as amazing is that these two bodies of literature, which in retrospect should have learned so much from each other, were virtually separate and noncommunicating discourses. In the four volumes on democratic transitions nationalism is never thematized as a major issue, or even given one separate chapter. Indeed, the word "nationalism" only appears in the index of one of the four volumes, that on southern Europe, and the reader is only refered to one page on Spain, one page on Portugal, and two pages on

---

1. See Ernest Gellner, *Nations and Nationalism* (Oxford: Blackwell, 1983); and Benedict Anderson, *Imagined Communities: Reflections on the Origin and Spread of Nationalism* (London: New Left Books, 1983).
2. See Guillermo O'Donnell, Philippe C. Schmitter, and Laurence Whitehead (eds.), *Transitions from Authoritarian Rule: Prospects for Democracy* (Baltimore: Johns Hopkins University Press, 1986). The four paperback volumes, published separately, were devoted to general theoretical concerns, southern Europe, Latin America, and comparative perspectives.

This chapter was first published in John A. Hall (ed.), *The State of the Nation: Ernest Gellner and the Theory of Nationalism* (Cambridge: Cambridge University Press, 1998), 219–39.

Greece. The name of Ernest Gellner does not appear in the index of any of the four volumes, nor does the name of Benedict Anderson. As the author of one of the comparative papers in this series, I of course must share responsibility for the oversight.

For their part, on the other hand, neither Gellner in *Nations and Nationalism*, nor Anderson in *Imagined Communities*, in any way thematizes democracy, and indeed the word does not enter into the index of either book.[3]

In my judgement two of the most urgent problems facing modern democratic theorists and practitioners are how to reconcile nationalism and democracy, especially in multiethnic settings, and how to improve the quality of consolidated democracies. This essay is devoted to the first question, but it has implications for the second. Obviously, if we are to make advances concerning the first question, then the two previously noncommunicating discourses must come into constant dialogue with one another.

As an analyst of democratization, and as the first rector of Central European University (CEU), I mentioned this problem of our noncommunicating discourses, and the opportunity to contribute to overcoming it, to Ernest Gellner, the founder of CEU's Program on Nationalism. With his characteristic collegial generosity and energy he immediately accepted the challenge to bring the discourses together. He attended a series of four lectures I gave in CEU Prague on the relationship of democratization to nationalism, and personally typed eight pages of suggestions in 1994 on an early draft of what is now a book Juan Linz and I co-authored on the problems of democratization.[4]

Gellner agreed to a Festschrift for his seventieth birthday, but only if I as rector guaranteed that it would not take the form of "boring praise" of a silent scholar. He wanted equal time to reply to every paper. He urged me to be critical, but he warned me that he would respond in kind. Obviously, my attempt to relate democratization to Gellner's thoughts on nationalism is only a shadow of what it could have been had Gellner lived to flail me.

---

3. Gellner's central preoccupation in *Nations and Nationalism* is with the relationship of the emergence of nationalism to the advent of industrialization. In private correspondence with me he said that he saw democratization as a complicated offshoot of industrialization. Obviously, in the overall corpus of his work, especially in one of his last books, *Conditions of Liberty: Civil Society and its Rivals* (London: Hamish Hamilton, 1994), he is concerned with democratic practices. *Conditions of Liberty* will be the main focus of my comments in this essay.

4. See Juan J. Linz and Alfred Stepan, *Problems of Democratic Transition and Consolidation: Southern Europe, South America and Post-Communist Europe* (Baltimore: Johns Hopkins University Press, 1996), particularly chs. 2, 6, 19, and 20, which relate to some of the themes of this essay. Also see our joint article "Political Identities and Electoral Sequences: Spain, the Soviet Union and Yugoslavia," *Daedalus*, 121/2 (Spring 1992), 123–40; Linz's "De la crisis de un Estado unitario al Estado de las autonomías," in Fernando Fernández Rodríguez (ed.), *La España de las autonomías* (Madrid: Instituto de Estudios de Administración Local, 1985), 527–672; his "State Building and Nation Building," *European Review*, 1 (1993), 355–69; and my "When Democracy and the Nation-State are Competing Logics: Reflections on Estonia," *European Journal of Sociology*, 35 (1994), 127–41.

Let us now turn explicitly to what Gellner says, and does not say, about the relationship of nationalism and democracy in his last great book, *Conditions of Liberty: Civil Society and its Rivals*.

Gellner's Bounded World of Nation-States

Ernest Gellner stated his functionalist argument for "one nation one state" especially forcefully in *Conditions of Liberty:*

the new imperative of cultural homogeneity...is the very essence of nationalism...for the first time in world history a High Culture...becomes the pervasive and operational culture of an entire society...The state has not merely the monopoly of legitimate violence, but also of the accreditation of educational qualification. So the marriage of state and culture takes place, and we find ourselves in the Age of Nationalism...For the average person, the limits of his culture are...the limits of his employability, social acceptability, dignity, effective participation and citizenship.[5]

But what happens if there are one or more conscious nations in the territory, nations which do not partake of this state–culture congruence? Gellner, as always, was direct: "Under the new social regime, this [condition] becomes increasingly uncomfortable. Men then had two options, if they were to diminish such discomfort: they could change their own culture, or they could change the nature of the political unit."[6]

Gellner did not really develop the full implications of the above assertions, but for the sake of even more brutal clarity I shall call the major cultural change option *assimilation*, and the major political change option *boundary change*. In this essay I will explore what implications Gellner's argument properly has, and does not properly have, for the crafting of multinational democracies.

Later in the book Gellner, in his brilliant and sweeping way, used the metaphor of marriage to discuss the four time zones, as he conceived them, of Europe. For Gellner, in Time Zone I, encompassing roughly the Atlantic coast of Europe (Ireland and parts of northern Spain being the major exceptions), historically strong dynastic states correlated with high cultural areas. According to him, "If nationalism requires the marriage of state and culture, then in this zone the couple had been cohabiting long before their union was acclaimed by nationalist Manifest Destiny...History had made a present to nationalism..."[7]

Time Zone II, to the east, was different. It was an area of "quite exceptional political fragmentation," but "was exceedingly well-equipped with preexisting, codified, normative High Cultures."[8] Thus, for Gellner, in what is

---

5. Gellner, *Conditions of Liberty*, 105–8.
6. Ibid. 108. 7. Ibid. 113. 8. Ibid. 114.

now Germany and Italy there was some—but not great—need for state building, because "An existing High Culture had to be endowed with a political roof worthy of it and capable of giving it shelter. It took a certain amount of military and diplomatic activity, but not much else."[9]

In Time Zone III, most of which is now central and eastern Europe, no dominant states existed. This time zone "presented the greatest problems from the viewpoint of the implementation of the nationalist principal of *one culture, one state*."[10] For Gellner, "If the eventual units were to be compact and reasonably homogeneous, more had to be done: many, many people had to be either assimilated, or expelled or killed."[11]

In Gellner's view, the path in the tsarist empire, which concerns his Time Zone IV, was roughly similar to that in Time Zone III until what he calls the "Leninist Umma" emerged. Then "The new ideocracy and the institutions it spawned controlled the entire territory with ease, and obliged its inhabitants to proclaim that their nationalist aspirations were satisfied. This fiction was maintained well into the 1980s..."[12]

Gellner argued that the postcommunist situation in most of the former Soviet Union was even more complicated than in Time Zone III because not only was it an area "Where neither the political bridegroom nor the cultural bride was available for the required marriage of nation state and national culture, but where the search for them was delayed by seventy or forty years of Bolshevik ideocracy..."[13] It is this special context, according to Gellner, that explains why the economic and political aspects of civil society in postcommunist Europe are difficult to bring into being, while "ethnically based and defined associations appear to be capable of almost immediate formation and firm as well as rapid crystallization."[14]

Where does *Conditions of Liberty* leave democratization crafters and/or theorists interested in the prospects of democratization outside of territories that are actually a part of, or analogous to, Time Zones I and II? The central implication of *Conditions of Liberty* is that if a single high culture, and a state broadly supportive of that culture, do not coexist in one territory, the crafting of a democracy will be substantially more difficult than if they do. Unfortunately for those like myself who personally value the quality of life in a culturally diverse society, the existing empirical evidence would seem to indicate that Gellner's argument is justified.

We should also note for the record that some of the world's most influential liberal and democratic theorists can be seen to be in fundamental agreement with Gellner. For John Stuart Mill, for instance, it was almost axiomatic that "free institutions are next to impossible in a country made up of different nationalities. Among a people without fellow-feelings, especially if they read and speak different languages, the united public opinion necessary to the

9. Ibid. 115. 10. Ibid. 11. Ibid. 116.
12. Ibid. 117. 13. Ibid. 123. 14. Ibid. 126.

working of representative institutions cannot exist...."[15] In our own time Dankwart Rustow, the seminal founder of the dynamic conflict approach to modern democratization theory, argues that his model of democratization "starts with a single background condition—national unity... National unity ... must precede all the other phases of democratization."[16] The leading American theorist of pluralism and democracy Robert A. Dahl does not argue that multinational democracies are impossible, but he does suggest that if there is no clarity about which groups or individuals are members of a political community, "we cannot solve the problems of the scope and domain of democratic units from within democratic theory. Like the majority principle, the democratic process presupposes a unit."[17] The contemporary Oxford political philosopher David Miller argues on grounds of quasi-Humean moral sentiments that "democratic states that have successfully pursued policies aiming at social justice have a unifying identity." Miller goes on to suggest that a high degree of trust and solidarity are necessary for democratic redistributive policies, and "for that reason socialists should be more strongly committed than classical liberals to the nation-state as an institution..." For Miller the positive consequences of solidarity and cultural homogeneity are such that "political authorities are likely to function most effectively when they embrace just a single national community."[18]

What can democratic theorists and practitioners learn from Gellner, and where, why, and how must we attempt to go beyond him?

In my judgement the legitimate insight that Gellner makes, and that in different ways is implicit in the work of Mill, Rustow, and Dahl, is that if there is only one homogeneous high culture in the territory, and the vast majority of long-term residents identify with that culture, *and* that culture has a supportive state, many of the problems that will *normally* appear in the effort to democratize a multinational community are simply *not* on the agenda in such "one nation one state" polities. On balance, David Miller's book is probably also right that national homogeneity may make certain statewide policies concerning social justice more politically feasible than in a multinational, multicultural polity. But let us return to Gellner's time zones. How far will they take us, even metaphorically? First, we must recognize the well-documented fact that there are very few states in the entire world that are relatively homogeneous nation-states and approximate Gellner's Time Zone I.[19] But the evidence from

15. See John Stuart Mill, *Considerations on Representative Government* (1861), from *Utilitarianism, On Liberty, Considerations on Representative Government*, ed. Geraint Williams (London: Everyman, 1993), 396.

16. Dankwart Rustow, "Transitions to Democracy: Toward a Dynamic Model," *Comparative Politics* (Apr. 1970), 350–1.

17. Robert A. Dahl, *Democracy and its Critics* (New Haven: Yale University Press, 1989), 207.

18. David Miller, *On Nationality* (Oxford: Oxford University Press, 1995), quotations from pp. 90–3.

19. In the early 1970s Walker Conner calculated that only twelve of the world's 132 states that were in existence were "essentially homogeneous from an ethnic viewpoint."

those that did begin their democratic process in Time Zone I supports Gellner's thesis.

For those territories that are analogous to Gellner's Time Zone I, whatever other problems they had or have, they did *not* have to manage the culture–state incongruence problem. Japan is the clearest example. Long before any Western polity, Japan had culture–state congruence. Portugal, as Western Europe's longest-standing dictatorship, faced many problems when it began its democratization process in 1974. However, because it was one of the world's oldest and most homogeneous nation-states, culture–state incongruence was not an issue, notwithstanding the return of an overseas population proportionately five times greater than that which France had to absorb after Algeria.

Democratization in Greece and South Korea was somewhat more analogous to Time Zone II than to Time Zone III because these countries had relatively homogeneous high cultures. Of course, at various times in their history they had some Time Zone III qualities because their high common culture lacked a political roof due to the existence of foreign rule or occupation. However, when Greece and South Korea began their democratization processes in the 1970s and 1980s, respectively, they conformed to what Gellner would label Time Zone II. Though the Diaspora in Greece, and the geopolitics of "two Koreas," presented some congruence problems, these problems complicated, but ultimately did not prevent, democratization.

Some parts of the world's map are of course more culturally homogeneous in the 1980s than they were in the 1930s, but in Poland and in Czechoslovakia this was "helped" first by Nazi genocide of Jewish and Gypsy minorities and later by the Soviet-backed expulsion of the Germans, an expulsion which the Allies accepted. As the millennium turns, Croatia is now nearly homogeneous, but at the cost of ethnic cleansing and the creation of an ethnocracy. These are not usable templates for the practice and theory of democracy.

The hard reality is that, in the vast majority of the world's countries that are not now democratic, homogeneous high cultures do not coexist within one state. Thus, if we want to avoid ethnic cleansing, if Time Zone I territories cover little of the planet, and if much of the world is in Time Zones III or IV, what is left in the Gellnerian world to produce culture–state congruence in a democratic way? According to Gellner, there are only two options: changing the political boundaries democratically, or voluntary and democratic cultural assimilation. Unfortunately, probably neither route can expand democratic boundaries in the world very much. Why?

See Conner, "Nation-Building or Nation-Destroying," *World Politics*, 24 (1972), 320. For later discussions using somewhat different criteria that also arrived at very low estimates of the number of true nation-states in the world, see Hakan Wiberg, "Self-Determination as an International Issue," in Iaonna M. Lewis (ed.), *Nationalism and Self-Determination in the Horn of Africa* (London: Ithaca Press, 1983); George Thomas Kurian, *The New Book of World Ranking* (New York: Facts on File, 1991); and the various articles brought together in Walker Conner, *Ethnonationalism: The Quest for Understanding* (Princeton: Princeton University Press, 1994).

In principle there is no democratic reason to oppose the democratic division of one state into two or more states. However, a democratic division is facilitated greatly if the groups to be divided live in relatively clearly demarcated cultural zones. The Czech and Slovak parts of Czechoslovakia satisfied this criterion. But in many countries redrawing of the boundaries to produce culture–state congruence is simply not an available democratic option. For example, in Latvia Russian is the dominant language in the seven largest cities; in India the 115 million Muslims are found in numerous parts of the federation; in the Ukraine and Estonia, though major concentrations of Russian speakers are indeed clustered on the borders with Russia, the inescapable reality is also that the capitals of Ukraine (Kiev) and Estonia (Tallinn) are located in the centers of the countries and are culturally and linguistically *de facto* multinational.

Gellner's second option involves consensual change in cultures so as to produce a culture–state congruence. This is of course conceivable for many individuals, and if voluntarily done, does not involve a violation of individual rights. However, for entire cultural communities, such as Muslims in Orthodox Christian or Hindu cultures, or working class Russophones in linguistically distant cultures such as Estonia, cultural assimilation may not be desired, or even if desired, may be extremely difficult to achieve in less than two or three generations.

The historical question of assimilation in some Time Zone I or Time Zone II states probably needs to be reexamined with greater care. In some countries with a high codified culture (such as France, Germany, and Italy) Gellner certainly understates the statecraft and power involved when, in a casual aside, he writes that congruence only entailed "a certain amount of military and diplomatic activity, but not much else."[20] Near cultural homogenization in France was in fact, as Eugene Weber has so meticulously documented, the result of the assiduous combination of state sanctions and inducements concerning language, dress, education, and military service.[21]

Could such state sanctions be democratically and effectively used in many Time Zone III or IV areas to produce congruence via voluntary cultural assimilation? Given the significant technological changes that have occurred since the late nineteenth century state-induced homogenization processes so well described by Eugene Weber, and the analytically distinct but related emergence of what Charles Taylor calls the "politics of recognition," there are grounds for thinking such processes are now less available.[22] Most of the world's minorities can keep in cultural contact with their home cultures via radio, cassettes, and

20. Gellner, *Conditions of Liberty*, 115.

21. Eugene Weber, *Peasants into Frenchmen: The Modernization of Rural France, 1870–1914* (Stanford, Calif.: Standford University Press, 1976).

22. For the argument that the recognition of difference is a growing claim in the contemporary theory and practice of democracy, see Charles Taylor, "The Politics of Recognition," in Amy Gutmann (ed.), *Multiculturalism and the "Politics of Recognition"* (Princeton: Princeton University Press, 1992), 25–73.

cheap air travel to a vastly greater extent than was possible a hundred years ago. Also, due to advances in literacy and communications, more minority communities have semiprofessional "cultural carriers," in the Weberian sense of *Träger*, than a hundred years ago. Normative changes in the form of increased desire for cultural autonomy in some minority (especially Muslim) communities—contested by rising antiforeign sentiments in the majority cultures that reduces the integrating capacity that in theory the majority culture would like—probably have contributed to greater cultural will, and greater cultural capacity, for minorities to resist cultural assimilation.

Furthermore, the original territorial *source* of immigration (e.g., Sudan or Guatemala) and the *location* of emigration (e.g., to Britain or to the United States) are becoming "deterritorialized." For reasons of sociology, politics, and even census recording, new identities (given or adopted) and new communities (e.g., "Muslims" in Britain, "Latinos" in the United States) are emerging with at least some of the affective power previously associated only with nationalism.[23]

My point is that voluntary cultural assimilation into the dominant host culture is in many parts of the world now more complex and problematic than it was in the nineteenth and early twentieth centuries. If I am right in these reflections, cultural congruence via minority community choice and/or via state inducements are, not surprisingly, a waning, rather than a growing, force in our globalizing societies.

Living Democratically Outside of Nation-States

An urgent question for democratic theorists and practitioners concerns whether there is anything that can be done to improve the chances of successful democratic consolidation in polities that are actually multinational. This is a huge and complicated question, but in order to focus the debate on the possibility of multinational democracies, I will make two sets of simplifying assumptions to start our analysis.

The first is that we are talking about a polis that does not now have culture–state congruence (i.e., there are at least two self-conscious cultures or nationalities in the territory), and for which voluntary and effective minority cultural assimilation to the dominant culture in the middle range, say twenty-five years, seems extremely unlikely, and where peaceful democratic secession is virtually impossible. This is where our reflections about Gellner's argument,

23. See e.g. the interesting discussion of the "deterritorialization" of ethnicity in Dale F. Eickelman and James Piscatori, *Muslim Politics* (Princeton: Princeton University Press, 1996), esp. the final two chapters. Also see Rubén G. Rumbaut, "The Americans: Latin American and Caribbean Peoples in the United States," in Alfred Stepan (ed.), *Americas: New Interpretative Essays* (Oxford: Oxford University Press, 1992), 275–307.

and our assessment of contemporary polities, leave us in many countries in the world.

The second set of assumptions is that, for whatever reasons (their current democratic values, their desire to join a prestigious international organization that only admits democracies, or simply out of fear of dangerous ethnic or cultural conflict if a democratic future can not be crafted), at least some important policy making leaders from the dominant culture or nation, and of the nondominant cultures or nations, want the polis to become a consolidated democracy or to remain a consolidated democracy.[24]

For those interested in polities which meet the above assumptions, three connected but analytically distinct clusters of practices and concepts should be on the political and/or research agenda. First, we must analyze how the policies of nation-state building, and the policies of democracy building, are in such a polity conflicting logics. Second, we should explore how to contribute to the construction of complementary identities. Third, we have to search for political formulas that do what many liberal democratic theorists argue is dangerous, or even impossible: create policies that reconcile group rights and individual rights.

Crafting Integration and Difference into Democratic Institutions

For Rogers Brubaker, leaders who pursue nation-state policies assume that the state is *of* and *for* the dominant cultural nation.[25] If there is only one culturally conscious demos in the polity, nation-state building and democracy building are, as David Miller would argue, mutually reinforcing political logics. But, if there are two or more culturally conscious demoi in the polity, nation building policies *of* and *for* the dominant nation would imply restricted citizenship, or at least unequal citizenship, for many of the long-standing minority residents in the state. Formally, and prudentially therefore, in multinational or multicultural polities nation-state building policies and democracy building policies are conflicting political logics. Would-be democracy crafters in such a polity have to recognize this political reality and search for an alternative set of policies to that of a "nation-state."

If the goal is to further advance toward democratic consolidation in a multinational polity, leaders of political and civil society will have to explore a range of state and governmental institutions that encourage political integration and

24. In some polities of course there is not a significant set of such leaders, and until something happens to change that, democracy is not on the agenda in such a polity.

25. See Rogers Brubaker, *Nationalism Reframed: Nationhood and the National Question in the New Europe* (Cambridge: Cambridge University Press, 1996).

loyalty toward the democratic regime, while simultaneously guaranteeing the right of minorities to organize and express cultural and national differences.

In cultural areas like schools, and access to radio or the media, some politically crafted power sharing institutional formats and practices that Arend Lijphart calls "consociational" are almost certainly called for in multiethnic democracies.[26] Nonterritorial forms of representation need to be explored much more carefully.[27]

If the choice is between parliamentary and presidential systems, the "non-winner take all" aspects of parliamentarianism, and parliamentarianism's greater "coalition requiring" and "coalition sustaining" properties, are worth serious consideration.[28] Electoral systems should also be studied thoughtfully for their impact on minority representation; in general we can say that proportional representation systems are better at representing minorities than are strong majoritarian formulas such as "first past the post" in large single member districts.

Among the forms of territorial representation that are particularly important to consider if groups are spatially concentrated in a multinational polity is federalism. Unfortunately, there is virtually no modern high-quality comparative research on the relationship between democracy and federalism so we must have a brief excursus on this topic.

Excursus on Federalism and Institutional Choice in Multinational Polities

Postcommunist Europe points out the need to be careful about federalism. If one excludes the case of "one nation in two states" in Germany, then we can say

26. See Arend Lijphart, "Consociational Democracy," *World Politics*, 21 (Oct. 1968–July 1969), 207–25; *Democracies: Majoritarian and Consensus Patterns of Government in Twenty-One Countries* (New Haven: Yale University Press, 1984); and "The Puzzle of Indian Democracy: A Consociational Interpretation," *American Political Science Review*, 902 (June 1996), 258–68.

27. Alternative solutions to territorial autonomy as a means of conflict resolution are beginning to receive scholarly attention, but remain undertheorized. One useful work is John Coakley, "Approaches to the Resolution of Ethnic Conflict: The Strategy of Non-Territorial Autonomy," *International Political Science Review*, 153 (1994), 297–314.

28. One of the earliest theoretical writings on this question is Juan J. Linz's "Excursus on Presidential and Parliamentary Democracy," in Juan J. Linz and Alfred Stepan (eds.), *The Breakdown of Democratic Regimes: Crisis, Breakdown, Re-equilibration* (Baltimore: Johns Hopkins University Press, 1978), 71–4, which ignited subsequent debate and quests for data to substantiate the claims regarding parliamentarianism's properties. See in particular the two volume work edited by Juan J. Linz and Arturo Valenzuela *The Failure of Presidential Democracy* (Baltimore: Johns Hopkins University Press, 1994); and Alfred Stepan and Cindy Skach, "Constitutional Frameworks and Democratic Consolidation: Parliamentarism versus Presidentialism," *World Politics*, 461 (Oct. 1993), 1–22; repr. as Ch. 12 in this volume.

that there were eight European states with communist political systems. Five of these were unitary states (Hungary, Poland, Romania, Albania, and Bulgaria). Three were federal states (USSR, Yugoslavia, and Czechoslovakia). Seven years after the "annus miraculous" of 1989 the five unitary states remain five unitary states. But, the three federal states have fragmented into twenty-two states.

Clearly, federal systems must be crafted carefully, or instead of attenuating the problems of multinationality, they can aggravate them. For the cases of the three European communist federal ruptures, one of the major causes was that none of these federal systems was designed to operate in a context where competitive democratic elections were decisive. They only worked as long as the centralized party-state played the major coordinating role.

In the standard literature on federal systems often no distinction is made between democratic and nondemocratic federal systems.[29] For modern democratic theorists this makes such literature of limited value. If federalism is to be a useful concept to employ in the comparative analysis of democratization, we will have to restate what should be the minimal requirements of democratic federalism. Democratic political systems probably should not be called federal systems unless they meet two criteria. First, within the state there must exist some territorial political subunits whose electorate is exclusively drawn from citizens of the subunit *and* which have areas of legal and policy making autonomy and sovereignty that is constitutionally guaranteed.[30] Second, there must be a statewide political unit which contains at least one chamber elected by the statewide population, and which has some law and policy making areas that are constitutionally guaranteed to fall within the sovereignty of this state-wide body.

Two conclusions immediately flow from these criteria. If the subunits do not in theory and practice have at least one significant policy making area where they are relatively autonomous *vis-à-vis* the center, then the political system is *de facto* centralized. But, if the center does not have a policy making area or areas where it is relatively autonomous to make policy, the political system is not a federal system but a confederation or even only an alliance.

If one accepts these arguments, it also follows that in a robust democratic federal political system the more the citizens feel a sense of separate allegiance to two democratically legitimated sovereignties, each with its constitutionally guaranteed scope of action, the more democratically secure the federation.

---

29. See e.g. the classic studies by William H. Riker, *Federalism: Origins, Operation, Significance* (Boston: Little Brown, 1964); and his "Federalism," in Fred I. Greenstein and Nelson W. Polsby (eds.), *Handbook of Political Science*, v: *Governmental Institutions and Processes* (Reading: Addison-Wesley, 1975), 93–172. For Riker, the United States, Canada, Yugoslavia, and the USSR all fit the criteria of federal systems. Indeed, according to Riker, the United States and Yugoslavia fit the same subtype, "centralized federation." See "Federalism," 101.

30. Robert A. Dahl, in a short but classic discussion of a federal systems in a democracy, uses the phrase "constitutionally privileged." See his *Democracy, Liberty and Equality* (Oslo: Norwegian University Press, 1986), esp. 114–26.

Ideally, therefore, citizens within a democratic federation should have *dual* but *complementary* political identities. This is so because, as citizens of a territorial subunit, if they and their elected leaders of the subunit do not feel that the center provides some goods, security, or identities that they consider valuable, and which are *not* available from the subunit alone, then their loyalty to the center will be weak. Potentially they will provide a constituency for the politics of secession. At the very least, they might provide a constituency for a politics of alienation, or a sense of exploitation, neither of which will help democratic consolidation. Likewise, if many citizens of the federal state and leaders of the center feel that the federal system entails few benefits, but imposes many political and economic costs, *and* that the costs of intervention (or encouraged exit) are relatively low, the democratic federation will be endangered.

Federalism is an attractive formula for some types of multinational polities, but the politics of building and maintaining dual and complementary identities needs more thought and research.

The most widely known example, and emulated model, of democratic federalism is that crafted in 1786 in Philadelphia. But the American model has two major characteristics that are not essential to democratic federalism and should be open to debate, negotiation, and challenge. Both characteristics concern the second chamber. All modern democratic federations have second chambers. The rationale of such second chambers is that they pay particular attention to issues of special relevance to the subunits of the federation. Not as a point of principle, but rather as a part of the historical "grand compromise" between the big and small states, the representatives of the big states in 1787 made two major concessions which violated formal democratic equality. First, they gave the small states equal representation, or more accurately, *massive overrepresentation*. Second, with less awareness of the implications, they made the *policy scope* of both houses basically the same. These two decisions that I will call "disproportionate representation" but "symmetrical scope" are a fundamental part of the US formula. But should they necessarily be a part of modern democratic federalism?

How disproportionate is the US Senate? When Robert Dahl did the calculation of the United States in the 1950s, he came to the conclusion that "an average vote cast in Nevada has eighty-five times as much weight as an average vote cast in New York, other things being equal."[31]

In 1988, after twenty-one years of direct military rule, a Brazilian constituent assembly, following almost two years of intense debate and discussion, created what was thought to be a very democratic constitution. However, almost no discussion was devoted to the Senate.[32] Following Dahl's logic, I have to assert

31. Robert A. Dahl, *A Preface to Democratic Theory* (Chicago: University of Chicago Press, 1956), 116.
32. See Scott Mainwaring, *Rethinking Party Systems in the Third Wave of Democratization: The Care of Brazil* (Stanford, Calif.: Stanford University Press, 1999), esp. ch. 9.

that an average vote cast in Roraima has 144 times as much weight in producing a Brazilian senator as a vote cast in São Paulo, other things being equal.[33]

Such massive overrepresentation is not a necessary feature of democratic federalism. If an ethnic or cultural minority in a federation was overrepresented by such a drastic number in the upper chamber, and if the chamber had a scope equal to that of the more democratically elected house, this would almost certainly create problems of allegiance to the federation by some leaders at the center. There can be, and there is, a great degree of variation in the representation formulas in the second chamber of democratic federal systems. The democratic federal system with the least overrepresentation is Belgium, with a Gini Index of Inequality coefficient of representation of only 0.015.[34] Germany is 0.32. But the United States has a Gini-coefficient of representation in the second chamber of 0.49, and Brazil 0.52.[35]

To compound the democratic inequalities introduced by the US model, we have only to look at the policy scope of the second chamber. The US model, as I have mentioned, gives the second chamber *symmetrical scope* with the first chamber. The first chamber in the US follows a principle of reapportionment every ten years in order to approach perfect equality of representation. The reapportionment is based on a census taken at the end of each decade. What *is* important theoretically and politically, especially given our concern with multinational federations, is that the second chamber has a special role to play in all areas of fundamental importance to the federation. In a multinational federation issues of special interest to the minority cultures and nations such as language, religion, education, and citizenship should fall within the areas where they can vote and indeed exercise possibly an absolute, but normally a relative, overridable veto requiring a special majority of the lower house. However, it is important to insist that neither democratic theory nor modern democratic practice requires that a chamber with massive disproportionality be given symmetry of scope with the near perfectly proportional chamber. For example, I have not seen a serious charge that the second chamber in Germany, the Bundesrat, is treated unfairly or undemocratically because of its delimited scope. The more proportional first chamber, the Bundestag, which represents all the voters in the states of Germany, has the exclusive power to elect and dismiss the chancellor. Germany's famous "constructive vote of no confidence" is only voted in the lower chamber. Likewise, the second chamber only has special veto powers in areas concerning half of the bills, all of which are of special interest to the *Länder*.

33. See Ch. 15, "Toward a New Comparative Politics of Federalism, (Multi) Nationalism, and Democracy: Beyond Rikerian Federalism", esp. Table 15.3.
34. The Gini Index of Inequality simply measures the degree of inequality among variables, where an index value of zero denotes complete equality and an index value approaching the theoretical maximum of 1.0 denotes complete inequality (which would mean here that one state has all the representatives). See Lijphart, *Democracies*, 173–5.
35. See Ch. 15, Table 15.3.

This difference in scope between the US model and what eventually became the German federal model was absolutely understood—and resisted—by the American Occupation authorities during the drafting of the Bonn constitution. According to the eminent scholar of political institutions Herman Finer, the Americans had been strongly "convinced of the desirability of a *weak* federal authority. They were persuaded by the kind of arguments for federalism and the separation of powers needed in the nascent U.S.A. in 1788, namely, to keep government weak for the sake of a *durable* and *democratic* (that is, atomized) system. This caused the S.P.D. [the German Social Democratic Party] to go into opposition." Eventually the SPD prevailed over American objections and "secured that, broadly speaking, the second chamber should not be of the dominant state-powerful type over the lower chamber."[36]

So German federalism is less disproportionate than US federalism, and less symmetrical in scope than US federalism. On both dimensions, therefore, German federalism is more formally (and I believe substantively) democratic.[37]

Does the fact that US federalism entails both of these democratic shortcomings make any difference? For the most widely cited author on modern federalism, William Riker, it does not matter very much because "If we understand ... that states are agents of the society in just the same way as any government, the worst one could expect of them is minor perversities, no matter how pronounced the federalism."[38] Indeed, elsewhere Riker even asserts that "federalism makes no particular difference to public policy."[39] These assertions simply do not hold up to close scrutiny.

The potential for blockage of the majority by a very small minority, about something that has *nothing* to do with a federal policy issue *per se*, is actually immense. Robert Dahl captures this succinctly:

The eight largest states with 54 percent of the voters have the same number of votes in the Senate as the eight smallest with less than 3 percent of the voters. A majority of votes in the Senate can be cast by Senators representing less than 15 percent of the voters. Thus a policy preferred by the representatives of 85 percent of the voters could be vetoed by the representatives of 15 percent of the voters.[40]

In newly democratizing Brazil the actual figures are even worse. Moreover, the relatively oligarchic small states in the north are often in a blocking position on federationwide issues concerning, for example, higher standards

36. See Herman Finer, *Governments of Greater European Powers: A Comparative Study of the Governments and Political Culture of Great Britain, France, Germany, and the Soviet Union* (London: Methuen, 1956), quotation from p. 690; emphasis in the original.

37. On German federalism, and more specifically on the German constitutional concept known as *Bundestreue* (often translated as "federal trust" or "comity"), see Bertus de Villiers, *Bundestreue: The Soul of an Intergovernmental Partnership: Comparative Analysis of the Principles Underlying Bundestreue in the Federal Republic of Germany, Switzerland and Belgium*, Konrad-Adenauer Stiftung Occasional Papers (Johannesburg: RSA, Mar. 1995).

38. See Riker, "Federalism," quotation from p. 147.

39. Ibid. 143.

40. See Dahl, *A Preface to Democratic Theory*, 116.

of treatment toward indigenous peoples, or higher standards *vis-à-vis* the environment.

In Brazil under the reform president Fernando Henrique Cardoso (1995–present) the difficulty of implementing a policy agenda is substantially, but by no means exclusively, due to the narrow voter base and wide policy scope of the Senate, a Senate which has exercised its blocking powers in such a way as to hinder efforts to enforce the efficacy and legitimacy of Brazil's new democracy.

In a multinational democracy the strains on efficacy and legitimacy, for reasons that we have already mentioned, are likely to be particularly high. Federalism, especially if the policy scope of the upper house is wide enough to have a major say on issues of particular importance to regional minorities, can help engender identification with the center. Likewise, if the cost of federalism, in terms of disproportional weight on policy areas of legitimate interest to *all* members of the federation, is reduced by narrowing the policy scope of the second chamber, the potential for disaffection of the center will be diminished, and center leaders are more likely to accept the necessary costs of the federal democratic bargain. If approached in this way, a balanced democratic federalism in a multinational polity can help integrate citizens into the political regime while constitutionally privileging a degree of subunit autonomy and difference.

Multiple and Complementary Identities in a Multinational Democracy

So far I have argued that democratic federalism entails two constitutionally guaranteed areas of relative policy making autonomy, and that the legitimacy of such systems is enhanced to the degree to which citizens in the federation have a fairly high degree of multiple and complementary identities. This argument calls for explicit discussion of the phrase "political identities."

Linz and I have discussed how many writings on nationalism focus on "primordial" identities and the need for people to choose between mutually exclusive identities. However, *our* research into political identities has shown two things. First, political identities are not fixed or primordial in the *Oxford English Dictionary* sense of "pertaining to, or existing at (or from) the very beginning; first in time, earliest, original, primitive, primeval." Rather, they are highly changeable and socially constructed. Second, if nationalist politicians, by the atmosphere they create (or social scientists and census takers with their crude dichotomous categories), do not force polarization, many people may prefer to claim multiple and complementary identities. In fact, along with a common political "roof" of state protected rights for inclusive and equal citizenship, the human capacity for multiple and complementary identities is precisely one of the key factors that makes democracy in multinational states possible. Because political identities are not fixed and permanent, the quality of democratic leadership is particularly important. Multiple and complementary political identities can be nurtured by political leadership. So can polar and conflictual political identities. Before the conscious use of ethnic cleansing as a strategy to construct nation-states in Bosnia-Hercegovina, Sarajevo was a multinational urban area, whose citizens had multiple identities and one of the highest rates of interfaith marriages of any city in the world. Sadly, we know how such multiple and complementary identities can be eroded. Yet, building on my joint work with Juan Linz, let me show how multiple and complementary identities can be socially constructed in a nurturing and highly interactive way.

In the first four years after the death of Franco sentiments in favor of independence virtually doubled in the Basque Country, and tripled in Catalonia. However, after a sequence of statewide elections for a constituent assembly, consensual crafting of a constitution, a referendum on the constitution, negotiations between elected officials from the center and the regions concerning devolution of power to the regions, a referendum in Catalonia and the Basque Country to approve the parameters of such devolution, and the subsequent implementation of Spain's new federal system of *autonomías*, sentiment in favor of independence declined sharply. Indeed, three years after the consensual creation of Spain's new federal system, of five possible identities that respondents in a 1982 survey could choose from ("Catalan," "more Catalan than Spanish," "equally Catalan and Spanish," "more Spanish than Catalan," and "Spanish"), the modal self-identification chosen was "equally Catalan and Spanish." Even when one breaks down the survey respondents to "both parents born in Catalonia," or "neither parent born in Catalonia," the modal category among both groups of respondents was "equally Catalan and Spanish." In another survey among Catalans, 82 percent were "proud to be Catalan," 73 percent were "proud to be Spanish," and 83 percent were also in favor of "unification of Europe via the European Community."[41]

The best proof is an existence proof. Clearly the data from Spain and Catalonia prove three things:

1. Political identities are not permanent but can be highly changeable and socially constructed.

2. Human beings are capable of multiple and complementary identities.

3. People can simultaneously identify with, and give loyalty to, different types of complementary political sovereignties. In Catalonia the evidence indicates that citizens were strongly and positively identified with a national subunit of a federation (Catalonia), the state of the multinational federation (Spain), and a potential suprastate confederation (the European Union).

41. For these surveys, see Table 10.1.

Let us go to a more difficult case of multiple and complementary identities—that of Russophones in Estonia. Many ethnic Estonian political leaders would like Estonia to be a nation-state—to be, to use Rogers Brubaker's phrase, *of* and *for* ethnic Estonians. However, at independence less than 65 percent of the long-term residents of Estonia were "ethnic Estonians." Indeed, about 35 percent were Russophones. Less than 5 percent of the Russophones had any plans to leave Estonia voluntarily. One should also note that there was great linguistic distance between Estonian and Russian, and that many of the Russophones were adults in industrial or manual labor jobs. Thus, on linguistic grounds alone, I would argue that the Russophone population in Estonia was absolutely *culturally unassimilable* into a democratic nation-state for one or two generations. However, I would also argue, on the basis of numerous different indicators, that the Russophone population in Estonia could be almost immediately *politically integratable* as loyal citizens within a democratic state if a "roof of rights" were to be extended over their heads. Why?[42]

While it is true that the vast majority of Russophone adults who were born in Estonia never learned Estonian, the political context after independence changed drastically. Since over 90 percent of the Russophones are making no plans to leave Estonia, their children's life chances will be significantly improved if they learn Estonian in school (and presumably learn Russian at least in their homes). The critical piece of evidence that supports the thesis that Russophones want to broaden the cultural and employment portfolio of their children is the following evidence from a work in progress by David Laitin. In answer to a question whether the best future for Russians in Estonia was to assimilate, only 7.9 percent of the Russophones said "yes." Attitudes like this of course would be pointed out as evidence by some nationalist ethnic Estonian politicians as supporting their argument that such Russophones should not be citizens. However, 58 per cent of the Russian respondents agreed with the statement that all permanent residents should be fluent in Estonian. Given the difficulty for a Russophone adult to learn Estonian, this strikes me as high, but no doubt would still be unacceptably low for an Estonian nation-state advocate. But for me the key Russophone response was in answer to the question whether Estonian should be a compulsory subject in schools: 95.8 percent of the Russophones agreed.[43]

Crafting democracy is probably more about attitudes toward the future than behavior in the past. The Russophones' answer to the question concerning the

42. For a much more extensive argument concerning Latvia, Lithuania, and Estonia, see ibid., chs. 2 and 20.

43. The details of these surveys are taken from David Laitin's presentation to the Centre for the Study of Nationalism Seminar honoring Ernest Gellner, Central European University, Prague, Dec. 1995. Full details will be published in a forthcoming book, but see his paper "Identity in Formation: The Russian Speaking Nationality in the Post-Soviet Diaspora," Paper prepared for the 1994 Annual Meeting of the American Political Science Association, New York, Sept. 1–4, 1994.

status of the Estonian language in schools indicates that they accept the *authority* of the Estonian state to demand that their children learn Estonian. This means that within two generations, if the Estonian state provides adequate language facilities, the overwhelming majority of Russophones under 40 will also be Estonian speakers. They will have the ability, and probably the propensity, to have dual and complementary political identities. They will probably still not be "ethnic Estonian," but they might well be loyal citizens of Estonia and identify with the "state-nation" of Estonia.

Transcending the Individual Rights versus Group Rights Tension

An assumption of many thinkers in the liberal tradition is that all rights are *individual* and *universal*. This assumption should properly be seen as a normative preference. Advocates of such a liberal approach are prone to see any deviation from individualism and universalism with suspicion.[44]

Thinkers associated with the liberal tradition of rights are particularly skeptical of group rights, and thus, at least implicitly, of many of the "consociational practices" that I and thinkers such as Arend Lijphart believe could be used to craft democracy in a multinational polity.

As a student of the historical development of democracies, and as an empirical democratic theorist, let me conclude this essay with four observations about what I think could be, and at times actually have been, democratic "group specific rights," to use Will Kymlicka's phrase.

First, individuals are indeed the primary bearers of rights and no group right should violate individual rights in a democratic polity. In our example of a democratic multinational federal state, this means that something like a bill of individual rights should be a property of the federal center and that any laws and social policies that violate this statewide bill of individual rights must fall outside the constitutionally guaranteed policy scope of subunits.

Second, while individual rights are universal, it is simply bad history to argue that in actual democracies *all* rights have been universal. Frequently, the struggle to reconcile the imperatives of political integration *and* to recognize the legitimate imperatives of cultural difference has meant according group specific rights such as those given to the Maori in New Zealand, to Spanish speakers in Puerto Rico, to religious and language culture councils in Belgium, and to Muslim family courts in India.[45] The key point is that it is the obligation of the democratic state to ensure that no group specific right violates universal

44. For an excellent discussion of this tradition and its discomfort with "group rights," see Will Kymlicka, *Multicultural Citizenship: A Liberal Theory of Minority Rights* (Oxford: Clarendon Press, 1995), esp. ch. 4.
45. See ibid.; Lijphart, *Democracies*, and "The Puzzle of Indian Democracy."

individual rights. As long as this political condition obtains, there is no contradiction between individual rights and group specific rights.

Third, while individuals are the bearers of rights, there may well be concrete moments in the crafting of a democracy where individuals cannot develop and exercise their full rights until they are active members of a group that struggles for some collective goods common to most members of the group.[46] Some of the cases I have discussed in this essay illustrate this point. If Catalans (who under Franco were not allowed to organize Catalan organizations or to have Catalan language radio and television programs) had not been given some group specific rights, it is not clear that they could have developed as individual democratic activists. It was partially the group rights won by Catalans that contributed to them having the power to argue, vote, and negotiate for a form of devolution and power sharing in the newly constructed Spanish federation. Many of the individuals' multiple and complementary political identities I have discussed emerged after some collective goods had been won by Catalan groups.

In Estonia, after an initial period when some ethnic nationalists tried to freeze Russophones out of politics and to argue against their right to organize and have Russian television channels, the recognized group right of Russophones to organize was crucial in helping some Russophones to participate as individuals (and as members of groups) in Estonian political life. As I have already suggested, effective individual rights for Russians may well only be won initially in a context of groups. Indeed, if compulsory language education in Estonian goes forward with the active assent of the organized Russian community, and if more extensive rights of national citizenship is won (partly due to the Russophone group struggles), then one could expect more extensive individual rights for more long-term residents. Such a process could also contribute to deepening the loyalty of Russophones to the state that gave them a roof of rights over their heads. If all this occurs, the incidence of multiple and complementary identities among what is now the Russophone community will grow.

Fourth, the types of group specific rights I have discussed in the three points above may not be consistent with some nineteenth century tenets of Anglo-Saxon liberal democracy, or the French idea of citizenship in a nation-state, but they are consistent with a polity in which group rights do not violate individual rights and where effective democratic citizenship and loyalty is broadened. They are in fact one of the few ways to craft democracy in the more difficult and more populous world than that found in Gellner's Time Zones I and II.

46. An elegant development of this argument is found in Joseph Raz, *The Morality of Freedom* (Oxford: Oxford University Press, 1986), esp. chs. 8 and 10; and his *Ethics in the Public Domain: Essays in the Morality of Law and Politics* (Oxford: Clarendon Press, 1994), esp. preface and chs. 1, 6, and 8.

TEN

Political Identities and Electoral Sequences: Spain, the Soviet Union, and Yugoslavia

with Juan J. Linz

When thinking about transitions to democracy we tend to assume that what is challenged is the nondemocratic regime and that with democracy a new legitimate system is established. However, in many countries the crisis of the nondemocratic regime is also intermixed with profound differences about what should actually constitute the "state." Some political activists simultaneously challenge the old nondemocratic regime and the existing territorial state itself. A "stateness" problem may be said to exist when a significant proportion of the population does not accept the boundaries of the territorial state (whether constituted democratically or not) as a legitimate political unit to which they owe obedience.

The new literature on democratic transitions did not give much thought or attention to this stateness problem, because most of it focused on transitions in Southern Europe and Latin America, where the challenge of competing nationalisms within one territorial state was on the whole not a salient issue.[1] Even the competing Catalán and Basque nationalisms in Spain barely entered the theoretical literature, possibly because the legitimacy of Spanish stateness was managed with reasonable success.

The neglect in the literature of the question of the legitimacy of the state is unfortunate because this variable, while not always of great importance for nondemocratic polities, is of fundamental theoretical and political importance for democracy.[2] In fact, agreements about stateness are *prior* to agreements

---

1. For example, the most influential study of democratic transitions is the four-volume work edited by Guillermo O'Donnell, Phillipe C. Schmitter, and Laurence Whitehead, *Transitions from Authoritarian Rule* (Baltimore and London: Johns Hopkins University Press, 1986), which is devoted entirely to Southern Europe and Latin America and contains virtually no discussion of "stateness" problems.

2. In fact possibly as much as a third of the countries past and present, where democratization has been on the agenda, have had to grapple with some form of the stateness problem. Some of the major categories of the stateness problem are: (1) "Divided states,"

This chapter was first published in *Daedalus*, 121/2 (Spring 1992), 123–39.

about democracy. Such agreements are not necessarily prior for a nondemocratic system. A nondemocratic system may be able to impose acquiescence over large groups of people for long periods of time without threatening the coherence of the state. In a nondemocratic system, the fact that central authority is not derived and maintained by free electoral competition means that separatist or irredentist aspirations, if they exist, are not routinely appealed to in the course of normal politics and can be suppressed. In sharp contrast, the very definition of a democracy involves agreement by the citizens of a territory, however specified, on the procedures to generate a government that can make legitimate claims on their obedience. Therefore, if a significant group of people does not accept claims on its obedience as legitimate, because the people do not want to be a part of this political unit, however constituted or reconstituted, this presents a serious problem for democratic transition and even more serious problems for democratic consolidation.[3]

The degree to which inhabitants accept the domain and scope of a territorial unit as an appropriate entity to make legitimate decisions about its possible future restructuring is thus a key variable for democratic theory. The hypothesis that derives from this therefore is: the greater the percentage of people in a given territory who feel that they do not want to be members of that territorial unit, however it may be reconstituted, the more difficult it will be to consolidate a single democracy within that unit.

Note that we do not consider that "feelings" about territorial appropriateness are immutable. Rather, we believe that such feelings are to a significant

where democracy was, or is, made more difficult due to security claims, e.g., Taiwan and South Korea; (2) "Nonsovereign states," where democracy is precluded because the community does not have control over its sovereignty and the community will be transferred to a larger polity, e.g., Hong Kong; (3) "States which want to join other states and are precluded by the international system from doing so," e.g., Austria after World War I, which wanted to join Germany; (4) "Irredentist polities," which are subject to violence by groups who want to unite all their ethnic community outside their existing boundary into their state, e.g., the interwar Bulgarian conflicts over Macedonian irredentism, and the Sudetan problem in Czechoslovakia in the 1930s; (5) "Wealthy minority ethnic groups" who want to secede, e.g., the Biafran Civil War in Nigeria; (6) "Poorer ethnic regions" which want to secede, because they believe their rights and economy will be improved in an independent state, e.g., Bangladesh and possibly Slovakia. Many more categories could be added to the list of stateness problems.

3. The classic statement of this problem is by Robert A. Dahl: "We cannot solve the problem of the proper scope and domain of democratic units from within democratic theory. Like the majority principle, the democratic process presupposes a proper unit. *The criteria of the democratic process presuppose the rightfulness of the unit itself.*" See his *Democracy and its Critics* (New Haven and London: Yale University Press, 1989), 207. Emphasis in the original. After a visit to the Soviet Union, Dahl amplified his thoughts on this theme in "Democracy, Majority Rule, and Gorbachev's Referendum," *Dissent* (Fall 1991): 491–6. We do not believe that Dahl's important observation would mean that stateness problems are always unsolvable. Rather, complex negotiations, pacts, and possibly territorial realignments and consociational agreements are often necessary before the majority formula will be accepted as legitimately binding. As Dahl argues, simple insistence on the majority formula *per se* will not do until the appropriateness of the unit is established.

extent socially and politically constructed. Elements of the social and political process itself—such as the way in which the fears of minorities are, or are not, addressed can be crucial. Indeed, our thesis is that the sequence of elections, *per se*, can help construct or dissolve identities. For example, in multinational polities, if all-union elections are held first, there are strong incentives for political activists to create all-union parties, and an all-union agenda. Winners of such all-union elections will have enhanced all-union legitimacy, or at least enhanced legitimacy as a body that can make binding decisions about the future of the union. In contrast, if in multinational polities the first elections are regional, we believe that there will be strong incentives for political contestation to focus on antistate ethnic issues and that the day after the regional elections the legitimacy of the state will be weaker.

We also do not believe that democratic theory should, implicitly or explicitly, have a strong commitment to territorial largeness or territorial integrity in themselves. Democratic theory and democratic practice should have some space for peaceful negotiated secession. The problem we are addressing here is: what are the chances that a given territorial unit can build a single consolidated democracy within that unit, and if it cannot, what are the chances that negotiated secession will be peaceful and not further complicate the building of democracies in the successor states?

While we treat the theme of stateness in much greater detail elsewhere, in this brief essay we will simply explore how the sequence of elections in itself can play an important role in transforming identities and helping integrate or disintegrate states, especially in highly heterogeneous multinational or multicultural polities.[4]

Democratization, "All-Union" Elections, and State-Integrating Politics: Spain

It is now becoming fashionable to see the Spanish consolidation as being almost overdetermined due to its supportive socioeconomic and geopolitical context. We believe that such an unexamined opinion not only leads to a

---

4. "Stateness" is one of the eight key variables we explore in a book we are completing, entitled *Problems of Democratic Transition and Consolidation: Eastern Europe, Southern Europe and Latin America*. Many of the definitions and assertions we make in this essay are developed and documented in much greater detail in that book. While in this essay we will consider only the historical cases of Spain, Yugoslavia, and the Soviet Union, we believe that our argument about electoral sequence has strong theoretical and political implications for other heterogeneous countries that have not started efforts to democratize. Indonesia is a strong case in point. Indonesia, for example, with its multiethnic, multicultural, and multi-island composition, should be wary of any process of democratization that does not create a fully democratic center as a first step.

serious misinterpretation of the actual process of democratic consolidation in Spain, but contributes to the dangerous lack of theoretical attention to relationships between democratic transition, stateness, and electoral sequence. Spain began the process of democratization with the potential for a dangerous stateness problem. The most important indicator of this danger is that while not one army officer was killed during the Basque insurgency in 1968–75 under Franco, or in the 1975–7 transition period, in the postelectoral period of democratic rule between 1978 and 1983, thirty-seven army officers died due to Basque nationalist violence.[5] Surprisingly, despite the deaths of military officers and the inevitable difficulties of creating Spain's quasi-federal state, *none* of the important unionwide interest groups or parties engaged in *system blame*. Adversity was not deliberately used either to delegitimate the fledgling democratic regime or the new constitutional structures that departed from Spain's traditional unitary state organization. In our judgment much of the reason for this lack of system blame was due to Spain's all-union elections.

Elections, especially "founding elections," help create agendas, actors, organizations, and most importantly, legitimacy and power. One of our major arguments is that if a country has a stateness problem, it makes a critical difference whether the first elections are unionwide or regional. In Spain the first elections were unionwide. We believe that they helped transcend Spain's stateness problem. The first post-Franco vote was a referendum to approve a "law *for* political reform," a law that received 94.2 percent approval.[6] This law committed the government not to any details of political reform, but to a process of clear *democratization*, not just *liberalization*.[7]

The second key vote, June 15, 1977, was also not merely about liberalization but about democratization; it was a unionwide general election to select deputies who would create a government and draft the new constitution. Because of the statewide stakes involved, four unionwide parties conducted a unionwide

5. Ricardo García Damborenea, *La Encruicijada Vasca* (Barcelona: Editorial Argos Vergara, 1984), 52.

6. On the "Law *for* Political Reform" see Pablo Lucas Verdú, *La Octava Ley Fundamental*, with a foreward by Enrique Tierno (Madrid: Tecnos, 1976), and Antonio Hernández Gil, *El cambio político español y la Constitución* (Barcelona: Planeta, 1981).

7. Analysts and activists alike must be aware of the difference between *liberalization* and *democratization*. In a nondemocratic setting, "liberalization" may entail a mix of policy and social changes, such as less censorship of the media, somewhat greater space for the organization of autonomous working-class activities, the introduction of some legal safeguards such as habeas corpus, the releasing of most political prisoners, the return of political exiles, possibly measures for improving the distribution of income, and, most important, the toleration of political opposition. "Democratization" entails liberalization but is a wider and more specifically political concept. Democratization requires open contestation for the right to win control of the government, and this in turn absolutely requires free statewide elections, the results of which determine who governs. With the use of these definitions, it is clear there can be liberalization without democratization. Liberalization refers fundamentally to civil society. Democratization involves civil society, but it refers fundamentally to political society. Democratic transitions clearly relate to democratization, not merely liberalization.

campaign around unionwide themes, winning 319 of the 350 seats.[8] Just as importantly, the statewide parties campaigned very hard in areas where the potential for secession was greatest and the history of antisystem sentiment was most deeply rooted—the Catalán and Basque regions. While strong Catalán and Basque nationalist parties did emerge, the four unionwide parties and their regional affiliates won 67.7 percent of the vote in Catalonia, and 51.4 percent of the vote in the Basque Country.[9]

The deputies and government produced by this statewide election engaged in prolonged public and private negotiations over the constitution and over how to proceed on the stateness issue. A consensual constitution was finally supported in Parliament by the four major parties and the major Catalán nationalist party; 258 of the 274 members voting gave it their approval. Spain's third unionwide vote then followed, namely a referendum on the constitution, which was approved by 87.8 percent of the voters on December 6, 1978. In Catalonia the constitution was approved by 90.4 percent of the voters. In the Basque Country 68.8 percent of those who voted approved the constitution, but voter turnout was only 45.5 percent, which was below the Spanish and Catalán level of 67 percent.

Strengthened and legitimated by these three elections, the unionwide government and Parliament began negotiations in earnest over the devolution of power with the provisional Catalán and Basque authorities created after the first all-union legislative elections in 1977. Surrounded by intense controversy, the negotiators eventually crafted a system by which Spain would change its historically centralized state structure for a new decentralized one characterized by an unprecedented devolution of power to the peripheral nationalist constituencies. These negotiated agreements over regional autonomy (the Statutes of Autonomy) were submitted to Basque and Catalán voters in October, 1979. The Catalán statute was approved by 87.9 percent and the Basque statute by 90.3 percent of those who voted in the regions.[10] The largest and oldest Basque nationalist party (the PNV), which had urged a boycott of the constitution, adjusted to the new political situation and urged approval of the Statute of Autonomy.[11]

---

8. For the organization and development of statewide parties, and the importance of the general election in transforming the agendas of these parties, see Richard Gunther, Giacomo Sani, and Goldie Shabad, *Spain After Franco: The Making of a Competitive Party System* (Berkeley: University of California Press, 1988), 37–177. The results of the 1977 election are found on page 38.

9. Ibid., 311.

10. See Juan J. Linz, "De la crisis de un Estado unitario al Estado de las Autonomías," in Fernando Fernández Rodríguez, *La España de las Autonomías* (Madrid: Instituto de Estudios de Administración Local, 1985), 527–672, and Juan J. Linz *Conflicto en Euskadi* (Madrid: Espasa Calpe, 1986). On the negotiation of the Basque Statute of Autonomy, see the account by two journalists, Kepa Bordegarai and Robert Pastor, *Estatuto Vasco* (San Sebastian: Ediciones Vascas, 1979), passim.

11. Some extreme separatist groups continued to boycott the vote on autonomy, and the overall voter turnout was 13 percent lower than the Spanish average on the

We believe that if the first elections in Spain had been regional, rather than unionwide, the incentives for the creation of all-union parties and an all-union agenda would have been greatly reduced. Consequently, the statewide parties and their affiliates would have received fewer votes.[12] We also believe that if the first elections had been on the regional level, ethnic issues would have assumed a much more substantial and divisive role in the electoral campaign than they actually did, and that the nationalist parties and their affiliates would have been more extreme. Strengthened nationalist parties would have gravely complicated the stateness problem in Spain. Relations between the military and the democratizing forces of the central government would almost certainly have been put under greater strain. In a context of heightened stateness conflict, the coup coalition—defeated by the king's personal intervention on February 23, 1982—would probably have emerged earlier, with greater force against a divided and less legitimate government, and might well have triumphed. The democratic transition in Spain certainly began under favorable conditions, but the clear commitment to democratization and unionwide elections strengthened the legitimacy claims of the central government, helped forge links between political society and civil society, and contributed to a new constitutionally sanctioned relationship between Spain's peripheral nationalisms and the central government.

Most importantly, all-union elections restructured stateness identities in ways that were supportive of multiple identities and democracy in Spain. In the new democratic Spain *complementary multiple identities* have emerged. We can see this most clearly in the case of Catalonia. Catalans are now more content with their status as Catalans in that they now have political and cultural control over education, television and radio, and indeed over most of the areas where Catalán nationalism had been most repressed in the past. Catalans also participate as a "supranational" regional group in the European Community, a body which in some important respects is a "community of regions" as much as a "community of states." Finally, in this new context, Catalans to a greater extent than ever before accept their identity as members of the Spanish state. The overwhelming percentage of all Catalans are "proud" to be "Catalán," "proud" to be "Spanish," and very supportive of joining an integrated European political community. The sequence of elections in Spain helped constitute these mutually supportive legal and affective memberships in substate ("Catalán"), state ("Spanish"), and suprastate ("European Community") polities. Table 10.1 shows these complementary multiple identities very clearly.

constitutional reform; nevertheless, the voter turnout of 54 percent was still politically significant.

12. Even when stateness issues are not salient, regional parties in Spain tend to poll 15–25 percent better in regional elections than they do in all-union elections.

TABLE 10.1. *National identities in Catalonia (%)*

	Catalans	All Spain
"Proud to be Spanish"	73	85
"Proud to be Catalán"	82	n.a.
In favor of the unification of Europe via the European Community	83	76

Sources: The statistics on pride were compiled from Francisco Andrés Orizo and Alejandro Sánchez Fernández, *El Sistema de Valors dels Catalans* (Barcelona: Institut Catalá d' Estudis Mediterranis, 1991), p. 207.

The Statistics on the question of European unification are from Los Españoles ante el Segundo aniversario de la firma del Tratado Adhesión de España a la comunidad Europea (Madrid: Centro de Investigaciones Sociológicas, April, 1988, p. 53

The Basque Country presents a more complex political picture. There is still routine Basque separatist violence, but we believe the overall political situation has been ameliorated by the sequence of elections we have described. Indeed, the Basque Country is a particularly dramatic example of how elections can structure identities and delegitimate certain types of antistate violence.

While the support for membership in a unified Europe is high, the citizens in the Basque Country are 40 percent less "proud" to be Spanish than the national average, and about 30 percent less "proud" to be Spanish than the Catalans. See Table 10.2.

Let us now focus explicitly on the question of how identities can be constructed by political processes. Between 1977 and 1979 the most heated question in Spanish politics concerned the relationship of peripheral nationalisms to the unitary Spanish state. In this two-year period the percentage of the population in the Basque Country who said they wanted to be independent *doubled*, to represent virtually a third of the entire population. Starting from a smaller base, proindependent sentiment *tripled* in Catalonia in the same period. Obviously, if these trends had continued for a few more years there would have been a severe crisis of stateness in Spain. However, once there had been a referendum on the Statutes of Autonomy, and governments had been established with Basque and Catalán nationalist parties in office, sentiment for independence began to decline. See Figure 10.1.

TABLE 10.2. *National identities in the Basque Country (%).*

	Basque Country	All Spain
"Proud to be Spanish"	44	85
"Proud to be Basque"	69	n.a.
In favor of the unification of Europe via the European Community	74	76

Source: Same as Table 10.1.

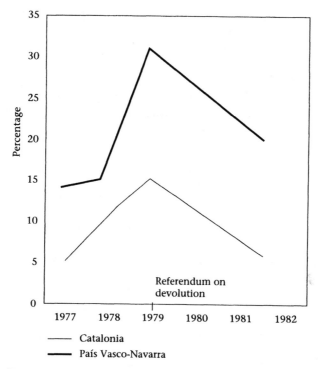

Fig. 10.1.   Percentage of the population wanting independence in Catalonia and País Vasco-Navarra before and after the 1979 referendum on devolution of power to the autonomías.

Source: Juan J. Linz, "De la crisis de un Estado unitario al Estado de las autonomías," in Fernándo Rodríguez, *La España de las Autonomías* (Madrid: Instituto de Estudios de Administración Local, 1985), 587

Assassinations, kidnapping, and terrorism by proindependence groups in the Basque Country still continued after the referendum, but their political significance changed dramatically. In 1979, before the referendum, only 5 percent of the Basque population who were polled labeled terrorists "common criminals" and only 8 percent called them "deranged." However, three years after the referendum the general population assigned much more prejorative identities to terrorists, and by so doing began to marginalize them politically; 29 percent now called them "criminals," and 29 percent said they were "deranged." Most importantly, the same "identity delegitimation" occurred among those who were voters for the largest Basque nationalist party (the PNV). In 1979 only 6 percent of PNV supporters said terrorists were "criminals" and only 12 percent said they were "deranged." In 1983 the percentages were 27 percent and 30 percent respectively.[13] Although political killings continue

13. Juan J. Linz, *Conflicto en Euskadi*, 698.

in the Basque Country, they no longer threaten to bring down the democratic government. The crisis of Spanish stateness has been contained, largely because of the choice of electoral sequence.

Liberalization, Regional Elections, and State-Disintegrating Politics: The Soviet Union and Yugoslavia

Even with extremely skillful handling, the stateness problem in the Soviet Union and Yugoslavia would have been much more difficult than in Spain.[14] This said, the actual policies followed in both countries were virtually the *optimal* sequence to be followed *if* one wanted to disintegrate the state and heighten ethnic conflict.[15] The contrast with Spain is illustrative.

The first important point to stress is that in neither the Soviet Union nor Yugoslavia was there ever a clear commitment to *democratization* as we have defined the term. Certainly in the Soviet Union, *perestroika*, and especially *glasnost*, had strong liberalizing dimensions. In the Soviet Union liberalization contributed to democratizing pressures from below, but in neither the Soviet Union nor Yugoslavia was there ever a commitment by central authorities to submit all-union power to democratization.

In both countries elections were allowed, but in both countries the most democratic and contested elections were for regional power. The point is clearest in Yugoslavia, where competitive all-union elections were simply never held in the post-World War II period. Republic elections were held in Yugoslavia in the summer and fall of 1990 and, not surprisingly, ethnic issues became of paramount concern. The situation in the Soviet Union is somewhat more complicated. The first elections in the Soviet Union were indeed all-union

14. We believe that the problem of the Baltic countries—due to the compounding resentments stemming from their previous status as independent states, their recent and forceful absorption into the USSR, their comparatively greater wealth, and their religious and linguistic differences—was insolvable. It could possibly have been better handled by Gorbachev making an announcement that he recognized the illegitimacy of the secret pact between Hitler and Stalin and holding a referendum on the fiftieth anniversary of that pact which asked the population of the Baltic countries whether they wanted to join the Soviet Union voluntarily. Had they voted not to join the Soviet Union (as they probably would have), a peaceful and rapid split might have been arranged with full citizenship rights for all.

15. The case of electoral sequence in Czechoslovakia also merits attention. Federal and republic elections were held on the same day in Czechoslovakia, so the direct effect of electoral sequence is difficult to discern. However, most ideological and organizational activity was at the republic, rather than the all-union, level. Indeed, of the eleven parties that gained seats in the all-union parliament, only one, the former Czechoslovak Communist Party, had representatives from both republics. The Czechoslovak "founding election" paid almost no ideological or organizational attention to the formation of all-union parties.

elections for the Congress of Peoples' Deputies in March 1989. However, these elections had many limitations. They were not multiparty, so democratic political society in the real sense could not develop. Also one-third of the seats in the 2,250 member Congress of Peoples' Deputies were set aside for the Communist Party and its affiliated organizations and did not face popular ratification. Furthermore, the nomination process allowed many Communist Party-dominated local electoral commissions to pack meetings with their supporters and thus control the nominating process. In many districts, all the candidates to emerge from the local electoral commissions were Communist Party supporters. Indeed, in one-quarter of the contests only a single candidate emerged from the local electoral commission. In this context many opposition candidates fell by the wayside.

The highly selective 2,250-member Congress of Peoples' Deputies that emerged from this process became the electoral college for indirect election to the Supreme Soviet. This indirect method of selection further weakened the electoral credibility of the upper—and more powerful—house and produced numerous inequities. For example, Boris Yeltsin won his seat in Moscow with 89 percent of the popular vote, but was initially denied a seat in the Supreme Soviet until one member offered to step down in his favor. Other less prominent deputies were not so lucky. Thus, though the first elections in the Soviet Union *were* all-union, the proposition holds: the most important and contested elections in both the Soviet Union and Yugoslavia were not at the all-union, but at the republic, level.

Cognizant of the shortcomings of the all-union electoral law, republic parliaments drafted legislation that avoided many of the practices which had helped to discredit the all-union parliament. Election rules varied somewhat across republics, but in general they allowed republic-level actors to make a greater claim to legitimacy than their all-union counterparts. Each republic discarded guaranteed seats for the Communist Party and Communist Party-dominated public organizations. Voters in most republics, the major exception being Russia, elected deputies directly to the upper house of parliament. Inequities did occur in elections to republic parliaments, especially in Central Asia, and in the area of the rights of ethnic minorities. Yet, on the whole, deputies from republic Supreme Soviets could not only claim to be the defenders of ethnic interests; they could also make a stronger claim to legitimacy than USSR Supreme Soviet deputies.

Before analyzing these elections, let us say a word about the post-totalitarian regime type.[16] A key aspect of a totalitarian regime is that independent pre-existing parties and labor, business, and religious organizations have been subject to extensive campaigns of elimination or subjugation. Even in the

---

16. The question of the implications of prior regime type for the *paths* of democratic transition, and the *tasks* of democratic consolidation, is treated in detail in Chapter 4 of our forthcoming book *Problems of Democratic Transition and Consolidation: Southern Europe, South America, and Post-communist Europe.*

most mature post-totalitarian regime, independent parties are not allowed space to compete for control of the government, because the Communist Party is officially accorded the "leading role" in the Communist Party-state. The landscape of civil society is very flat. All-union independent organizations are virtually nonexistent. In all post-totalitarian polities the relative flatness of the landscape of civil society has created problems for politicians, because it is hard to represent amorphous groups. Even after liberalization the articulation of interests based on wealth, ideology, or property relations has been strikingly less than we find in many authoritarian regimes.[17] However, politicians are specialists in mobilizing hopes and grievances. In the context of post-totalitarianism's flattened landscape the easiest hopes and grievances for politicians to mobilize relate to ethnicity. The region's two most multinational states—the Soviet Union and Yugoslavia—predictably were the sites of the most extreme manifestation of this general phenomenon.

We have said that elections can create agendas, can create actors, can reconstruct identities, help legitimate and delegitimate claims to obedience, and create power. The regional elections in the USSR and Yugoslavia did all these things. In Spain the process set in motion by all-union general elections reconstituted stateness on even firmer grounds. The regional elections in the USSR and Yugoslavia did the opposite. The following series of quotes from reports written by teams of electoral observers associated with the Helsinki Commission capture the extent to which the process of republic electoral campaigns—in the context of the Soviet multinational state, which had never submitted itself to an all-union election—contributed to the disintegration of the state:

Moldavia (Election: February 25, 1990)

The election campaign pointed up the necessity for every movement vying for power in the republic to develop a program for sovereignty, the minimum demand in Moldavia.... Whether Moscow has to deal directly with a Popular-Front dominated Moldavian Supreme Soviet, or work through Party First Secretary Lucinski is irrelevant, for it will be faced almost immediately with a demand to make good on the republic's demand for sovereignty.[18]

---

17. For example, when East Europeans were asked "Your country has many problems to solve. Of those conflicts listed on this card, tell me, please, which do you consider very important, somewhat important, of little importance or not at all important," the most commonly articulated conflict involved nationalism. "Conflicts between nationalists and the rest of the country" were mentioned as "very important" by 50 percent in the Ukraine, 39 percent in Czechoslovakia, 29 percent in Estonia, and 27 percent in Lithuania. In contrast, problems between "those with money and those without" were mentioned as very important by only 36, 25, 23, and 24 percent of respondents respectively. See László Bruszt and János Simon, *Political Culture: Political and Economical Orientations in Central and Eastern Europe During the Transition to Democracy, 1990–91, The Codebook* (Budapest: Erasmus Foundation, December, 1991), 37–9.

18. *Elections in the Baltic States and the Soviet Republics*, compiled by the staff of the Commission on Security and Cooperation in Europe (Washington, D.C., December, 1990), 89.

Ukraine (Election: March 18, 1990)

The Democratic Bloc of opposition groups, formed to contest the election, successfully focused the campaign on voters' concerns, inducing the Communist Party candidates often to follow suit. High on voters' lists were greater political autonomy, national and cultural issues.[19]

Increasing demands for the use of the Ukrainian language resulted in an important Ukrainian SSR Supreme Soviet decree stipulating that as of January 1, 1990, Ukrainian is the state language of the republic, while Russian is to be used for communication between nationality groups.... Long suppressed national feelings are now sweeping [through] the Ukrainian population.[20]

It is likely that there will be even greater progress for Ukrainian self-determination leading to independence.[21]

Georgia (Election: October 28, 1990)

By election day, all contending parties—including the Georgian Communist Party—advocated independence.[22]

In an effort to shore up its nationalist credentials, the Georgian Communist Party platform demands guarantees for Georgia's territorial integrity, the introduction of Georgian citizenship ... proclaiming that Georgian citizens should only perform military service inside the republic.[23]

The nationalist theme of the election not only exacerbated relations with the center, but nationalist outbidding in Georgia, as in many other republics, worsened relations with minority groups in the republics and eroded a core component of future democratization—full citizenship rights for all inhabitants regardless of ethnicity. The election observer team noted that in Georgia:

The eventual winner, Gamsakhurdia, made many statements that have alarmed non-Georgians. In June 1990, for example, he called mixed marriages "fatal to the Georgian family and the Georgian language".[24]

Fearing for their national rights in an independent Georgia, some non-Georgian groups have attempted to protect themselves.... the Abkhaz Autonomous Republic and the Southern Ossetian Autonomous Oblast declared sovereignty in August and September, 1990, respectively.[25]

The result of the regional elections in the USSR and Yugoslavia, in the absence of prior freely contested all-union democratic elections, contributed to five interrelated and compounding state-disintegrating dynamics.

First, virtually the day after the regional elections, the statewide legitimacy of the central government was damaged because the nationalist regional forces could make a stronger claim to democratic legitimacy via elections.[26]

---

19. Ibid., 115.   20. Ibid., 119.   21. Ibid., 135.
22. Ibid., 165.   23. Ibid., 170.   24. Ibid., 169.   25. Ibid., 165–6.
26. An important indicator of the erosion of stateness is the sharp drop in citizens who answered the unionwide military draft. By the end of the 1990 draft, quota fulfillment in

Second, in no republic in the Soviet Union or Yugoslavia did a new union-wide political organization emerge from the elections that was in any sense a counterweight to local nationalism.

Third, in the process of the elections, political identities in the USSR and in Yugoslavia became more narrow, compounding, exclusive, and unsupportive of participation in a potentially all-union democratic entity. In Spain during and after the electoral processes political identities had become more multiple, cross cutting, inclusive, and supportive of participation in a reconstituted Spanish democratic state.

Fourth, in many republics such as Georgia, Azerbaijan, Serbia, and Croatia the prospect of ethnic warfare has led presidents to repress dissenting voices within their core ethnic groups and to show greater intolerance toward minority groups.

Fifth, the crisis of stateness and the resulting crisis of governability blocked the formulation and implementation of economic policy. The cataclysmic political collapse of any central or coordinating authority preceded and created the economic crisis, not vice-versa.[27]

Let us conclude our discussion of the consequences of electoral sequence with the prophetic words of a Soviet social scientist writing before the coup and well before the *de jure* disintegration of the Soviet state. He captured the degree to which the regional elections had already contributed to de facto state disintegration: "Local elections contributed to the process of the shift of rhetoric of nationalist movements from 'civic' to 'ethnic'.... The 'war of laws' and 'parade of sovereignties' followed inevitably after republic and local elections.... The crisis of power in the center of the Union and the process of ungovernability increased enormously."[28]

Latvia was 39.5 percent, in Lithuania 35.9 percent, in Armenia 22.5 percent, and in Georgia 18.5 percent. By mid-1991, these figures had declined to 30.8 percent for Latvia, 12.4 percent for Lithuania, 16.4 percent for Armenia, and 8.2 percent for Georgia. Most importantly, by mid-1991 Moscow itself had only fulfilled half its quota for this six-month period. See Stephen Foye, "Student Deferments and Military Manpower Shortages," *Report on the USSR* (August 2, 1991), 5–8.

27. The "state" in the Weberian sense (as the collapse of the all-union draft shows) had disintegrated in the Soviet Union even before the failed coup attempt of August 1991, a coup whose trigger was the desperate effort of some elements within the all-union forces of the Party, the KGB, and the military to block the implementation of the 9 + 1 Treaty which would have given a *de jure* status to the de facto fragmentation.

28. Andranik Migranian, "The End of Perestroika's Romantic Stage," unpublished paper, Moscow, July 1991, 7.

ELEVEN

The World's Religious Systems and Democracy: Crafting the "Twin Tolerations"

Are all, or only some, of the world's religious systems politically compatible with democracy? This is, of course, one of the largest, most important, and intensely debated questions of our times. Illuminating, or at times obfuscating, contributions to this question have been made by practitioners and theoreticians of politics, as well as by philosophers, historians, and sociologists of religion. In this essay my attempt to contribute to this debate will be from the perspective of comparative politics. More specifically, as a specialist in political institutions and democratization, I intend to ask three cumulatively related questions, the answers to which, in my judgement, will give analysts and practitioners increased cognitive control over this critical issue.

First, what are the minimal core institutional and political requirements a polity must satisfy before it can be considered a democracy; and, building on this analysis, what can we then infer about the need for the "twin tolerations," that is, what are the minimal boundaries of freedom of action that must somehow be crafted for political institutions *vis-à-vis* religious authorities, and for religious individuals and groups *vis-à-vis* political institutions?

Second, how have a set of long-standing democracies—the fifteen countries in the European Union—actually met these minimal boundary requirements and what influential "maps of misreading" of the West European experience with religion and democracy should we beware of?

Third, on the basis of our answers to the first two questions, what do they imply, and not imply, for polities heavily influenced by religious traditions such as Confucianism, Islam, and Orthodox Christianity, traditions that some analysts, starting from a civilizational, as opposed to an institutional, perspective see as presenting major obstacles to democracy?[1]

---

1. Confucianism is actually a cultural and philosophical tradition, not a religious tradition, in that it is "this worldly" rather than "other worldly" and has no priests or church. Nonetheless, many observers, from Max Weber to Samuel P. Huntington, treat

Before I begin addressing these three questions, let me briefly give some quotations from an exceedingly influential civilizational perspective which represents a major competing perspective to the more institutional approach I propose in this essay.

Huntington's Religious–Civilizational Approach to Democracy

In his analysis of the emergence of modernity and democracy in the West, Samuel P. Huntington, in *The Clash of Civilizations and the Remaking of the Modern World*, gives primacy of place to Christianity as the distinctive positive influence in the making of Western civilization: "Western Christianity is historically the single most important characteristic of Western civilization."[2] For Huntington, Western culture's key contribution has been the separation of church and state. "God and Caesar, church and state, spiritual and temporal authority, have been a prevailing dualism in Western culture."[3] He immediately contrasts Western Christianity to other major religious systems in the world: "In Islam, God is Caesar; in [Confucianism] Caesar is God; in Orthodoxy, God is Caesar's junior partner."[4] After advancing an argument of how "kin cultures" increasingly support each other in "civilizational fault line" conflicts, and developing a scenario of a religiously driven World War III, Huntington warns: "The underlying problem for the West is not Islamic fundamentalism. It is Islam."[5] About Confucianism and democracy he asserts that contemporary China's "Confucian heritage, with its emphasis on authority, order, hierarchy, and supremacy of the collectivity over the individual creates

it as one of the world's major religious-civilizational traditions and I will do so in this essay.

2. (New York: Simon & Schuster, 1996), 70.

3. The phrase "have been a prevailing dualism in Western Culture" is problematic for at least two reasons. First, the phrase is ahistorical. Religious officials often violated dualism (e.g. Calvinism and Catholicism with theocracies and/or inquisitions) and political officials often violated dualism (e.g. in Anglicanism when Henry VIII created and dominated the "official Church of England" for reasons of state, or personal desires to divorce, or in Lutheranism, especially in the north German princely states, where caesaropapist state domination was the price paid for geopolitical religious protection. Second, the phrase averts attention away from precisely what most needs to be analyzed; i.e., how was toleration politically and socially constructed in contexts where intolerance had been the norm.

4. Ibid. Because Huntington discusses the special problems presented for democracy by Confucionism, Islam, and Orthodoxy, this essay will be limited to these three cases. However, Hinduism, Buddhism, and Judaism raise virtually all the issues discussed in this essay. Their treatment will have to await what I hope will eventually be a book on this topic. However, I will briefly indicate some of the currently most salient religion–state issues in Hinduism and Judaism, in India and Israel respectively, in the conclusion of this essay.

5. Ibid. 217.

obstacles to democratization."[6] Elsewhere, when he discusses postcommunist Europe, he says, "The central dividing line" in Europe after the cold war "is now the line separating the people of Western Christianity, on the one hand, from Muslim and Orthodox people on the other."[7] He asks rhetorically and answers rhetorically: "Where does Europe end? Europe ends where Western Christianity ends and Islam and Orthodoxy begin."[8] For Huntington, civilizations, not states, are now the key agents, and he argues that due to the growing importance of "kin cultures" and "civilizational fault-line conflicts" the world's religious civilizations are increasingly unitary, conflictual, and change resistant.[9] Clearly a central thrust of Huntington's message is that democracy not only emerged *first* from within Western civilization but that the other great religious civilizations of the world lack the unique bundle of cultural characterizations necessary to support a Western style democracy.

If we approach democracy in the world from a core institutionalist perspective, do we arrive at a comparably pessimistic view of the probable cultural boundaries of democracy, or do we arrive at a more politically possibilistic view?

Core Institutional Requirements for Democracy and for Religious Groups in a Democracy

All important theorists of democratization accept that a necessary condition for completing a successful transition to democracy (and many transitions fail) is free and contested elections of the sort discussed by Robert A. Dahl in his classic book *Polyarchy*. For Dahl some requirements for a democracy among a large number of people are the opportunity to formulate preferences, to signify preferences, and to have these preferences weighed adequately in the conduct of government. For these conditions to be satisifed Dahl argues that eight

6. Ibid. 238. The relative weight of the more recent Marxist–Leninist–Maoist party-state tradition, the first two thirds of which are "Western" in origin, in comparison to the relative weight of the more historically distant Confucian tradition, is not analyzed.

7. Ibid. 28.

8. Ibid. 158. Thus, for Huntington it follows that in his proposed new world order the list of countries that he suggests be added to the core organizations of Western Christianity, the European Union and NATO, includes only Western Christian countries. Indeed, while he acknowledges that classical Greece played a role in the development of Western civilization, he nonetheless argues that modern Greece is an increasingly disruptive anomaly, "the Orthodox outsider in Western institutions" (Ibid. 162).

9. Kin cultures, in fact, for reasons of state, still often diverge during geopolitical–military conflicts. For example, during the Serbian–NATO–Kosovo crisis, in predominantly Orthodox Bulgaria, and in predominantly Orthodox Romania, the key agents were not kin cultures, but state elites. State officials in Bulgaria and Romania, partly in the hope of improving their chances of eventually joining NATO and the European Union, gave valuable access to their airspace, as well as their political support, for the NATO attack on Orthodox Serbia.

institutional guarantees are required: (1) freedom to form and join organizations; (2) freedom of expression; (3) the right to vote; (4) eligibility for public office; (5) the right of political leaders to compete for support and votes; (6) alternative sources of information; (7) free and fair elections; and (8) institutions for making government policies depend on votes and other expressions of preference.[10]

My colleague Juan J. Linz and I accept the eight Dahlian institutional guarantees as a necessary but not as a sufficient condition of democracy. Not sufficient, because no matter how free and fair the elections, and no matter how large the majority of the government, the political society produced by such an election must write a constitution that itself is democratic in that it respects fundamental liberties which include, among other things, considerable protections for minority rights. Furthermore, the democratically elected government must rule within the boundaries of the constitution, and be bound by the law and a complex set of vertical and horizontal institutions which help to ensure accountability.

If we combine the Dahl and the Linz–Stepan criteria it should be clear that democracy should not be considered consolidated in a country unless, among other things, there is the opportunity for the development of a robust and critical civil society that helps check the state and constantly generates alternatives. For such civil society alternatives to be aggregated and implemented, political society, especially parties, should be allowed unfettered relations with civil society.

Democracy is a system of conflict regulation that allows open competition over values and goals that citizens want to advance. In the strict democratic sense this means that as long as groups do not use violence, do not violate the rights of other citizens, and advance their interests within the rules of the democratic game, *all* groups are granted the right to advance their interests, both in civil society, and in political society. This is the minimal institutional statement of what democratic politics entails and does not entail. No more, no less.[11]

Building upon this core institutional "threshold" approach to democracy, what does this imply about religion, politics, democracy, and the "twin tolerations"? Specifically, what are the necessary boundaries of freedom for elected governments from religious groups, and for religious individuals and groups from government?

The key area of autonomy that must be established for democratic institutions is that the institutions that emanate from democratic procedures should

10. See Robert A. Dahl, *Polyarchy: Participation and Opposition* (New Haven: Yale University Press, 1971), 1–3.
11. For a much more extensive discussion and for references concerning these additional criteria, see Juan J. Linz and Alfred Stepan, *Problems of Democratic Transition and Consolidation: Southern Europe, South America and Post-Communist Europe* (Baltimore: Johns Hopkins University Press, 1996), ch. 1. Also see our "Toward Consolidated Democracies," ch. 14 in this volume.

be able, within the bounds of the constitution and human rights, to generate policies. Religious institutions should not have constitutionally privileged prerogatives which allow them authoritatively to mandate public policy to democratically elected governments.

The key area of autonomy—from the government or even from other religions—that must be established for religious freedom is that individuals and religious communities, consistent with our core institutional definition of democracy, must have complete freedom to worship privately. More: as individuals and groups, they should also be able to publicaly advance their values in civil society, and to sponsor organizations and movements in political society, as long as their public advancement of these beliefs does not impinge negatively on the liberties of other citizens, or violate democracy and the law, by violence. This core institutional approach to democracy necessarily implies that no group in civil society—including religious groups—can a priori be prohibited from forming a political party. Constraints on political parties may only be imposed *after* that party, by its actions, violates democracy. The judgement as to whether or not a party violates democracy should be decided not by parties in the government but by the courts.[12]

Within this broad framework of minimal freedom for the democratic state, and the minimal religious freedoms of citizens, it would appear, from a purely theoretical perspective, that there can be an extraordinarily broad range of concrete patterns of religion–state relations in political systems that would meet our minimal definition of a democracy.

Let us explore this analytic argument by moving to our second question; empirically, what are the actual patterns of religion–state relations in long-standing democracies? How have the "twin tolerations" of freedom for democratically elected governments, and freedom for religious organizations in civil and political society, actually been socially and politically constructed in specific democratic polities?

Western Christianity and Democracy: Maps of Misreading?

How should one read the "lessons" of the historical relationships between Western Christianity and democracy? In this section I want to call particular attention to four possible "maps of misreading." First, *empirically* we should beware of simple assertions about the actual existence of "separation of church and state" or the necessity of "secularism." Second, *doctrinally* we should beware of assuming that any of the world's religious systems are univocally

---

12. A formal written statement of the parties' statutes that advocates violence could legitimately be construed by the courts as an "action."

democratic or nondemocratic. Third, *methodologically* we should beware of what I will call the "fallacy of unique founding conditions." Fourth, *normatively* we should beware of the liberal injunction, famously argued by the most influential contemporary political philosopher in the English language, John Rawls, to "take the truths of religion off the political agenda."[13]

Separation of Church and State? Secularism? Some Empirical Caveats.

Quite frequently analysts, when they are discussing the prospects for democracy in non-Western, "non-Christian" civilizations assume, as shown in the quotes from Samuel Huntington, that a separation of church and state and secularism are core features not only of Western democracy, but of democracy itself. For such analysts, a religious system such as Orthodox Christianity—where there is often an established church—poses major problems for the consolidation of democracy. Similarly, if an Islamic based party comes to power in a country such as Turkey in 1996, there are frequent references to the threat this presents to Western style secular democracy. Indeed, military encroachments on the autonomy of the democratically elected government in Turkey were frequently seen as an unfortunate necessity to protect secular democracy. Are these correct readings, or dangerous misreadings, of the lessons of the relationship of church and state in Western democracy?

To answer this question, let us do an empirical analysis of the degree to which there is an actual separation of church and state in Western democracies. Let us take a specific set of Western countries, all of which for the last decade have satisfied Robert A. Dahl's necessary requirements of the eight institutional guarantees, and the additional conditions for a democracy that Juan J. Linz and I have stipulated. The set I will examine is the fifteen countries that belong to European Union, all of which meet the core institutional requirements for a democracy I have discussed and have socially and politically constructed the twin tolerations.[14]

13. John Rawls, *Political Liberalism* (New York: Columbia University Press, 1993), 151.
14. Let me supply some evidence for the assertion that all fifteen European Union countries qualify as democracies, according to the criteria I have stipulated. Michael Coppedge and Wolfgang Reinicke attempted to evaluate the degree to which Dahl's "eight institutional guarantees" were present in 137 countries based on their assessment of political conditions as of mid-1985. In their study *all* of the fifteen European Union countries qualified as meeting Dahl's standard for polyarchy. See their "A Scale of Polyarchy," in Raymond D. Gastil (ed.), *Freedom in the World: Political Rights and Civil Liberties, 1987–1988* (New York: Freedom House, 1990), 101–28. Furthermore, the Freedom House evaluates every country in the world annually on a seven point scale for political rights and civil liberties with 1 being the best and 7 being the worst score. For purposes of this essay, if we call a country a democracy that scores no lower than 2 on political rights and 3 on civil liberties, *all* fifteen countries of the European Union have met this criteria for every year since the Coppedge and Reinicke 1985 evaluation. See the annual publication by Gastil listed above. Arend Lijphart, building upon Dahl in his *Democracies: Patterns of Majoritarian and Consensus Government in Twenty-One Countries*

The first thing we should note is that, when one examines the constitutions of the fifteen member countries as of 1990, five of the fifteen, Denmark, Finland, Greece, Sweden, and the United Kingdom (in England and Scotland), had established churches. Norway is not in the European Union but it is also a European democracy with an established church. Let us look at the constitutions, and related quasi-constitutional church–state arrangements in greater detail.[15]

Until 1995 *every* single long-standing West European democracy with a strong Lutheran majority—Sweden, Denmark, Iceland, Finland, and Norway—had an established church. Only Sweden in the last few years has began a process of disestablishing the Lutheran Church. Let me quote from the current Norwegian constitution, which on paper has, from a Weberian perspective, a "caesaropapist" tone to rival Orthodox Christianity.[16]

[Article 2] The Evangelical Lutheran religion shall remain the official religion of the state. The inhabitants professing it are bound to bring up their children in the same.

[Article 4] The King shall at all times profess the Evangelical Lutheran religion and uphold and protect the same.

[Article 12] Half the members of the King's Council shall profess the official religion.

[Article 21] The King after consultation with his Council shall appoint senior ecclesiastical officials.[17]

The Netherlands does not have an established church. However, as a result of a heated conflict between Catholics, Calvinists, and secularizing liberal governments over the role of the church in education, a conflict which at times threatened to create a deep crisis in democracy, the Netherlands in 1917 arrived at a politically negotiated "consociational" formula whereby local communities, if they were overwhelmingly of a specific religious community, could choose to have their local school be a private Calvinist, or a private Catholic,

(New Haven: Yale University Press, 1984), classifies all the countries of the European Union, except for Greece, Spain, and Portugal, as "long standing democracies." However, Linz and Stepan, *Problems of Democratic Transition and Consolidation*, 87–150, offer substantial documentation to advance the argument that since 1984 Greece, Spain, and Portugal have been democracies.

15. The constitutions of all the fifteen states of the European Union (except for the United Kingdom, which does not have a written constitution), both in the original language and in English, complete with any amendments up to 1997, and commentary, are contained in the invaluable nineteen volume work Albert P. Blaustein and Gisbert H. Flanz (eds), *Constitutions of the Countries of the World* (Dobbs Ferry, New York: Oceana Publications, 1985 and updated annually).

16. For Max Weber's discussion of caesaropapism, see his *Economy and Society*, ed. Günther Roth and Claus Wittich (Berkeley: University of California Press, 1978), ii. 1159–63. In 1995 the Synod of the Church of Sweden, responding to proposals for a reform made by the Swedish government and Parliament, began a process that by the year 2000 will lead to substantial disestablishment. See the Revd. Dr Ragnar Persenius, Secretary for the Church, Sweden, "Church and State in Sweden" (http://www.svkyrkan.se/PORVOO/9803/persen.htm).

17. These and all other constitutional articles I will cite are from the translations contained in Blaustein and Flanz (eds.), *Constitutions of the Countries of the World*.

school *and* to receive state support. According to the Dutch political scientist Arend Lijphart, in the 1850s more than three fourths of all elementary school-children in Holland attended public nondenominational schools. One hundred years later, only 28 percent of Dutch children attended such schools, 47 percent were in state supported Catholic private schools, and 27 percent were in state supported Calvinist run private schools.[18] Lijphart, writing in 1975, also noted that in the Netherlands radio and television "are state owned but not state operated. Programming is in the hands of private organizations with large dues-paying membership." Network KRO was in essence Catholic (with 89 percent of its dues-paying members being so). Calvinists made up 75 percent of the dues-paying members of the NCRV network.[19]

Germany and Austria have constitutional provisions in the federal system for local communities to decide on the role of religion in education.[20] Germany does not have an established church, but protestantism and Catholicism—and in some *Länder* (states) the small Jewish community—are recognized as official religions. German taxpayers, unless they elect to pay a 9 percent surcharge to their tax bill in the form of a church tax (*Kirchensteuer*), and thereby officially become a member of the church (*Mitglied der Kirche*), do not have the automatic right to be baptized, married, or buried in their denominational church or, in some cases, even to go to the church hospitals or old age homes which receive state tax support from the *Kirchensteuer*. Access to church run social services are particularly important because, "at the local level, governments that want to set up and operate new hospitals and other publicly funded social services facilities can not proceed unless and until local church authorities have declined to do so."[21] The massive state induced *de facto* subsidies the protestant and Catholic churches receive in Germany have made them, in the judgement of Edinger and Nacos, "the richest churches in the world."[22]

What do contemporary West European constitutions and normal political practice indicate about the allowed role of religious parties in government? Whatever Western analysts may think about the impropriety of religious based parties ruling in a secular democracy such as Turkey, Christian Democratic parties have, of course, frequently ruled in Germany, Austria, Italy, Belgium, and the Netherlands.[23]

18. See the classic by Arend Lijphart, *The Politics of Accommodation: Pluralism and Democracy in the Netherlands*, rev. edn. (Berkeley: University of California Press, 1975), 52.
19. Ibid. 47–51, citation from p. 47.
20. For example, Article 7 of the basic law (the constitution) for the Federal Republic of Germany of 1949 says, "Without prejudice of the state's right of supervision, religious instruction shall be given in accordance with the tenants of the religious communities."
21. See the section entitled "Church, Faith and Politics" in Lewis J. Edinger and Brigitte L. Nacos, *From Bonn to Berlin: German Politics in Transition* (New York: Columbia University Press, 1998), 118–24, and Frederic Spotts, *The Churches and Politics in Germany* (Middletown, Conn.: Wesleyan University Press, 1973), 183–233.
22. Edinger and Nacos, *From Bonn to Berlin*, 119.
23. But, for an analysis of how most of these Christian democratic parties underwent an endogenous process whereby they constructed a political identity (a "self-

The *only* European Union member state whose constitution has any prohibition against political parties using religious affiliations or symbols is Portugal.[24] However, I should make two observations about this apparent Portuguese anomaly. First, the article prohibiting the political party use of any religious symbols in Portugal was drafted in 1976 by a Constituent Assembly under heavy pressure from the revolutionary armed forces movement. The constitution the assembly produced was revised to conform with democratic standards in 1982, but the above article is actually a nondemocratic "residue."[25] Second, there is in Portugal a *de facto* Christian democratic party, the Centro Democrático Social, which operates with full political freedom and which is a member in good standing of all the international Christian democratic organizations.

As we enter the twenty-first century, what is the current status of "separation of church and state" in the Western democracies of the European Union? In the twentieth century probably the two most "hostile" separations of church and state in Western Europe occurred in 1931 in Spain and in 1905 in France. But both countries now have a "friendly" separation of church and state.[26]

Two of the most detailed and authoritative studies of church–state relations in Spain since the 1930s develop a fundamentally similar argument. They argue that the "hostile" separation of church and state in the 1931 constitution contributed to democratic breakdown and civil war and that the "friendly" separation produced in the process of creating the consensually adopted 1978 constitution contributed to democratic consolidation.[27]

The only constitution of a member state of the European Union that explicitly calls its democracy "secular" is France.[28] This definition stems from the hostile separation of church and state in 1905. French politics, for much of the nineteenth century, was embroiled in conflicts between the Jacobean, republican, anticlerical (at times even antireligious) tradition of the French

secularization") which gave them growing autonomy from clerical control, see Stathis N. Kalyvas, *The Rise of Christian Democracy in Europe* (Ithaca: Cornell University Press, 1996), esp. pp. 222–56.

24. Article 47.

25. On why and how the constitution of 1976 was nondemocratic, and its revision in 1982, see Linz and Stepan, *Problems of Democratic Transition*, 123–4.

26. Indeed, Juan J. Linz has suggested that it might be useful to see separation of state and church as varying along a continuum from "hostile" to "friendly" separation of state and church. See his "Der religiöse Gebrauch Politik und/oder der politische Gebrauch der Religion," in H. Maier (ed.), *"Totalitarismus" und "Politische Religionen": Konzepte des Diktaturvergleichs* (Paderborn: Ferdinand Schüningh, 1995), 129–54.

27. See the excellent studies by Victor M. Pérez-Diaz, "The Church and Religion in Contemporary Spain: An Institutional Metamorphosis," in his *The Return of Civil Society: The Emergence of Democratic Spain* (Cambridge, Mass.: Harvard University Press, 1993), 108–83, and Juan J. Linz, "Church and State in Spain: From the Civil War to the Return of Democracy," *Daedalus*, 120 3 (Summer 1991), 159–78. The 1978 Spanish constitution explicitly speaks of the positive contribution that Catholicism and other religions make to the Spanish community.

28. Article 1, 1946 Constitution, and Article 2, 1958 Constitution. In fact, in French the exact word is "laïcité", whose definition itself is intensely debated inside contemporary France, see Guy Haarcher, *La Laïcité* (Paris: Presses Universitaires de France, 1996).

Revolution, which strove for strict separation of church and state, and the anti-Jacobean, proclericalist, indeed ultramontane, Catholic tradition, which strove for an official, state supported church in which the state (democratic or not) was ready to cooperate with the church. The 1905 separation of church and state was a hostile separation that represented the triumph of the Jacobean tradition in that, among other things, religious orders were forbidden to teach, even in private schools.[29] But by 1959, in the most secular country in Western Europe, the Debré Bill allowed state support for teachers in Catholic schools. Indeed, by 1961, 20 percent of the total educational budget in France was for Catholic private schools. France in the 1990s still had a separation of church and state; but, in political terms, it had become a "friendly" separation.[30]

My point is that virtually no Western European democracy now has a rigid or hostile separation of church and state. Indeed, most have arrived at a democratically negotiated freedom of religion from state interference and all of them allow religious groups freedom, not only of private worship, but to organize groups in civil society and political society. The "lesson" from Western Europe, therefore, lies *not* in church–state separation but in the constant political construction and reconstruction of the "twin tolerations." Indeed, it is only in the context of the "twin tolerations" that the concept of "separation of church and state" has a place in the modern vocabulary of West European democracy.

A similar caveat should be borne in mind concerning the concept "secularism." Discursive traditions as dissimilar as the Enlightenment, liberalism, French republicanism, and modernization theory argued, or assumed, that modernity and democracy required secularism. But, from the viewpoint of empirical democratic practice, the concept of secularism must be radically rethought.[31] At the very least, serious analysts must acknowledge, as Tables

29. For the "unfriendly" struggles in the thirty years leading up to the 1905 separation of church and state in France, see William Bosworth, *Catholicism and Crisis in Modern France: French Catholic Groups at the Threshold of the Fifth Republic* (Princeton: Princeton University Press, 1992), 3–43, 279–308, and Sudhir Hazareesingh, "Religion, Clericalism and the Republican State," in his *Political Traditions in Modern France* (Oxford: Oxford University Press, 1994), 98–123.

30. The budget figures for 1961 are from Bosworth, *Catholicism and Crisis in Modern France*, 284. For the much more friendly, but constantly politically argued, negotiated, and crafted question of church–state relations, especially in education, in the early years of the Fifth Republic, see Bernard E. Brown, "Religious Schools and Politics in France," *Midwest Journal of Political Science*, 2 (May 1958), 160–78. The change toward a more friendly separation actually began in the aftermath of the Treaty of Versailles when the French government decided that the newly acquired territory of Alsace-Moselle (where Catholicism and protestantism were both quite strong and had traditionally received many state subsidies in Germany) would not be fully subject to the 1905 legislation concerning separation of church and state because the French state, for reasons of political prudence, agreed to accept the traditional German statutes concerning church–state relations. Indeed, parents in Alsace-Moselle had to ask for a special dispensation for their children to attend a secular school. See Haarcher, *La Laïcité*, 33–5.

31. Fortunately, there is a growing literature that is debating previously widespread assumptions about democracy's need for secularism. For a thoughtful analysis of why the

11.1 and 11.2 make clear, that secularism and separation of church and state have no inherent affinity with democracy, and indeed can be tightly related to nondemocratic forms that violate systematically our twin tolerations. See Tables 11.1 and 11.2.

The categories in Tables 11.1 and 11.2 are not meant to be mutually exclusive and collectively exhaustive. The eight categories depicted are simply meant to convey the range of democratic and nondemocratic state–religious patterns, and to show that there can be democratic and nondemocratic secularism, and that there can be democracies with established churches and democracies with even a "very unfriendly" separation of church and state. One obviously could develop many other categories.[32] However, my central analytic point stands; if we are looking for defining characteristics of a democracy *vis-à-vis* religion, "secularism" and the "separation of church and state" are not an intrinsic part of the core definition, but what we have said about the "twin tolerations" is.

Building upon the rereading we have just done of the empirical context of such phrases as "separation of Church and State" and "secularism," we are in a position to see more rapidly why we should beware of three other major maps of misreading.

Univocality or Multivocality in Religious Systems? Doctrinal Caveats

As a research strategy we should beware of assuming that any religion's doctrine is univocally prodemocratic or antidemocratic. Indeed, I would suggest that a better research strategy is to be on the alert for multivocality. From the view point of the history of ideas, and contributions to democratization paths,

"secularization thesis," as an empirical prediction and a normative prescription, was shared by almost all the founders of modern sociology, see José Casanova's chapter "Secularization, Enlightenment, and Modern Religion" in his *Public Religions in the Modern World* (Chicago: University of Chicago Press, 1994), 11–39. For a trenchant essay about the antidemocratic quality of some arguments that insist on secularism, see John Keane, "The Limits of Secularism," *Times Literary Supplement*, Jan. 9, 1988, 12–13. For a valuable reader that brings together important new statements about secularism by Charles Taylor, "Modes of Secularism," Amartya Sen, "Secularism and its Discontents," and an excellent article by Akeel Bilgrami, "Secularism, Nationalism, and Modernity," that argues about the need in a country such as India for secularism to be socially constructed in such a way that it is "earned," not merely "assumed," as well as articles by Michael J. Sandel, Jean Bauberot, Ashis Nandy, and T. M. Scanlon, see Rajeev Bhargava (ed), *Secularism and its Critics* (Oxford: Oxford University Press, 1998). R. Stephen Warner sparked off a new academic debate about the status of secularism in the United States with his "Work in Progress toward a New Paradigm for the Sociological Study of Religion in the United States," *American Journal of Sociology*, 98 (Mar. 1993), 1044–93.

32. For example, in a nondemocratic system of the subtype where the "state interferes with the necessary degree of autonomy for religion," we could conceive of a situation where the state espouses, but completely controls, an official religion (which is part of its legitimacy claim) even in matters of doctrine, discipline, and public and private worship, and effectively precludes any other religions in its domain.

TABLE 11.1. *The "twin tolerations": varieties of democratic patterns of religious–state relations*

Democratic (and relatively stable) patterns			Democratic (but relatively unstable) pattern
Secular, but religiously friendly, state	Non-secular, but democratically friendly, state	Sociologically spontaneous secularism	Very unfriendly secularism legislated by majority, but reversible by majority
No official religion. Full separation of church and state. No state monies for religious education or organizations	Established church receives state subsidies, and some official religion taught in state schools, (but non-religious students do not have to take religious courses)	Society largely "disenchanted" and religion not an important factor in political life	Antireligious tone in most state regulations (e.g., teaching of religion forbidden in state *and* privately supported schools, no chaplains of any religion allowed in military organizations or state hospitals)
Private religious schools allowed if they conform to normal academic standards	Official religion accorded no constitutional or quasi-constitutional prerogatives to mandate significant policies	Democratically elected officials under no significant formal or informal pressures to comply with religious dictates concerning their public policy decisions	Significant percentage of believers "semiloyal" to regime
Full private and public freedom for all religions as long as they do not violate individual liberties	Citizens can elect to have "church tax" sent to secular institution	All religious groups free to organize civil society and to compete for political power, but have little weight or salience	
Religious organization allowed to minister to their followers inside state organization (e.g., military, state hospitals)	Nonofficial religion allowed full freedom and possibly can receive some state monies		
Religious groups allowed full participation in civil society	All religious groups can participate in civil society		
Organizations and parties related to religious groups allowed to compete for power in political society	All religious groups can compete for power in political society		

TABLE 11.2. *The "twin intolerations": varieties of non-democratic patterns of religious–state relations*

State precludes necessary degree of autonomy for religion in polity		Religious groups preclude necessary degree of autonomy for a democratic government	
Atheistic secularism imposed by the state	Religion controlled by elected government and/or quasi-democratic constitutionally embedded secular procedures	Elected government policies subject to veto by non-elected religious officials	Anti-secularism imposed by theocracy
Right of private worship is violated	Virtually unamendable constitution declares state secular and gives state officials a major role in regulating internal organization and external expression of religion	Constitutional or quasi-constitutional prerogatives accorded to nonelected religious groups to mandate significant policies to the democratically elected authorities	Demos cannot participate in selection of highest religious authorities (and thus the highest political authority does not emanate from, and is not responsible to, democratic procedures)
Right of religious groups to participate in civil society denied	Right of religious groups to participate actively in civil society constitutionally subject to unilateral state control or prohibition	Virtually unamendable constitution mandates the official religion of the state	No permissible area of private or public life allowed that does not conform to dominant religion
Right of religious groups to compete for power in political society denied	Right of organizations or parties related to religious groups to compete for power in political society constitutionally denied	Official religion receives state subsidies	Fusion of religious and political power under religious control
No competitive elections held	Relatively competitive elections normally held	Competitive elections regularly held	
	Right of private worship is respected	Right of private worship is respected	

Western Christianity has certainly been *multivocal* concerning democracy and the twin tolerations. At various times in its history Catholic doctrine has systematically been marshalled to oppose liberalism, the nation-state, tolerance, and democracy. In the name of Catholicism, the Inquisition committed massive human rights violations. Calvinist doctrine in Calvin's Geneva had no space for either inclusive citizenship or any form of representative democracy. Lutheranism, for over 300 years, particularly in northern Germany, theologically and politically accepted caesaropapist state control of religion.[33]

Extrapolating from these particular situations, numerous articles and books were written on the inherent obstacles that Catholicism, or Lutheranism, or Calvinism placed in the way of democracy, because of their antidemocratic doctrines and nondemocratic practices. At other historical moments of course, spiritual and/or political activists in all these religions found, and mobilized, doctrinal elements within their religions to help them craft new practices supportive of tolerance and democratic struggles.

The doctrinal (and intellectual and political) caveat we should take away from this brief discussion should be obvious. When we explore the question of non-Western religions and their relationship to democracy, it would seem appropriate for analysts not to assume univocality, but to explore whether these doctrines contain *multivocal* components that are *usable*, or at least *compatible*, with the political construction of the twin tolerations.

The Fallacy of "Unique Founding Conditions": Methodological Caveats

This fallacy involves the historical analysis of the unique constellation of specific conditions that were present when a distinctly new and powerful phenomenon such as electoral democracy, a powerful civil society relatively independent from the state, or the spirit of capitalism first emerged, and then the assumption that if this *exact set* of conditions is not present, the social invention cannot thrive. The fallacy of course is to confuse the conditions

---

33. On the exclusionary nature of citizenship in Geneva, Michael Walzer writes that Calvin desired that "civil society be integrally composed of all the Christian members of the religious society, and of them alone." On the rejection of any form of representative democracy, Walzer argues, "Calvin never imagined officers...as representatives; he found no human community capable of organizing itself and appointing delegates ...Particular officers were created only by God." See Michael Walzer, *The Revolution of the Saints: A Study in the Origins of Radical Politics* (Cambridge, Mass.: Harvard University Press, 1965), quotes from pp. 55 and 60. In the same book Walzer says that Luther's focus on individual pietistic salvation meant that "the Lutheran saint, in his pursuit of the individual kingdom of heaven, turned away from politics and left the kingdom on earth, as Luther himself wrote, 'to anyone who wants to take it'" (ibid. 26). Of the Reformation, John Rawls correctly notes, "Luther and Calvin were as dogmatic and intolerant as the Roman Church had been." See his *Political Liberalism* (New York: Columbia University Press, 1996), p. xxv.

associated with *invention* of a phenomenon with the possibilities of *replication*, or probably more accurately *reformulation*, under different conditions, of the same general phenomenon. Whatever we may think about Max Weber's thesis in his famous book *The Protestant Ethic and the Spirit of Capitalism*, no one who has followed Korea, Taiwan, or Hong Kong carefully would deny that these polities have created their own form of dynamic capitalism.[34] My point is, we should beware of committing the fallacy of "unique founding conditions" when we examine whether polities strongly influenced by Confucianism, Hinduism, Orthodoxy, or Islam can emulate, or can re-create, using some of their distinctive cultural resources, a form of democracy that would meet, and even surpass, the minimal institutional conditions for a democracy spelled out in the beginning of this essay.

"Take religion off the political agenda": Normative and Empirical Caveats about Rawls

Liberalism, and liberal forms of public reason, or public discourse, have made major contributions to the evolution of modern democracy. However, in elaborate and eloquent formal argumentation liberal political philosophers such as John Rawls and Bruce Ackerman give great weight in the development of a just and liberal society to *liberal arguing* but almost no weight to *democratic bargaining*.[35] Rawls is particularly interested in how a plural society in which the citizens have a variety of socially embedded, reasonable, but deeply opposed comprehensive doctrines can arrive at an overlapping consensus.[36] His normative recommendation is that on major issues of a quasi-constitutional import, individuals should only advance, or be able to advance, their political causes, or arguments, by the use of freestanding conceptions of justice that are not rooted in one of the comprehensive, but opposing, doctrines found in the polity.[37] He thus argues that there are some types of political dispute—such as disputes about religion—that should be taken off the political agenda. He

---

34. Max Weber, in his famous *The Protestant Ethic and the Spirit of Capitalism*, trans. Talcott Parsons (New York: Charles Scribner's Sons, 1958), is at pains not to commit this fallacy. In his introduction he explicitly says he is interested in explaining the special "combination of circumstances" which contributed to the emergence "in Western civilizations" of certain "cultural phenomena." Specifically he is dealing with "the connection of the Spirit of modern economic life with the rational ethics of ascetic Protestantism." However, in his conclusion he correctly insists that a form of diffusion of the spirit of capitalism has occurred that has become independent from its original source. "Since asceticism undertook to remodel the world and to work out its ideals in the world, material goods have gained an increasing and finally an inexorable power over the lives of man . . . Today the spirit of religious asceticism . . . has escaped from the cage. But victorious capitalism, since it rests on mechanical foundations, needs its support no longer" (pp. 13, 127, 181–2).

35. See John Rawls, *Political Liberalism*, and Bruce A. Ackerman, *Social Justice in the Liberal State* (New Haven: Yale University Press, 1980).

36. Rawls, *Political Liberalism*, pp. xviii, 133–72.

37. Ibid. 12.

asserts that "when certain matters are taken off the political agenda, they are no longer regarded as appropriate subjects for political decision by a majority or other plurality votings."[38] *Political Liberalism* leaves democratic activists and theorists with the normative injunction (which carries the weight of obligation) that important public arguments about the place of religion in the polis are only appropriate if they employ, or at least can employ, freestanding conceptions of political justice.

Rawls develops an internally consistent and powerful argument. However, he devotes virtually no attention to the subject of this essay, which is *how* actual polities have consensually and democratically arrived at quasi-constituent agreements to "take religion off the political agenda" of majority decision making. Indeed, if we are interested in political struggles over the role of religion in the polis that arrived at such consensual democratic agreements, it is important to stress that almost none of them empirically, discursively, or even normatively were confined to the Rawlsian liberal normative map.[39]

Politics is about conflict, and democratic politics involves the creation of procedures to manage major conflicts. In many countries that are now long-standing democracies, Western or not, the major conflict for a long period of time was precisely over the place of religion in the polis. In many of these cases the political containment, or neutralization, of religious conflict, was only constructed after long public arguments, and especially political negotiations, in which religion was the dominant item on the political and discursive agenda. In Holland, for example, we have shown how religious conflicts in 1917 were eventually taken off the political agenda of majority decision making only as a result of an extensive bargaining process that ended up in a *democratic—but not liberal—consociational agreement*. In Holland the quasi-constitutional consociational bargain crafted together in 1917 allocated monies, spaces, and mutual vetoes to religious communities with competing comprehensive doctrines concerning many aspects of the educational process, the media, civil society, political society, and indeed, virtually the entire ensemble of Dutch democratic political procedures and practices.

To arrive at such democratic—but not liberal and not secular—procedures as in Holland, there are normally public theological arguments within all the major religious communities where some proponents of the democratic bargain are only able to gain ascendance, or least acquiescence, *within* their religious community for the democratic bargain, by employing religious doctrinal arguments that are *not* conceptually freestanding, but deeply, and

---

38. Ibid. 151.
39. In a private communication with me about this point Bruce Ackerman in Apr. 1999 said that his and Rawls's endeavors are aimed at providing fully developed philosophical arguments for an ideal liberal end state whereas scholars such as Juan J. Linz and myself are concerned with the historically different and prior question of how concrete polities have created the minimal conditions for a democracy.

sometimes uniquely, embedded in their own religious communities' comprehensive doctrine.[40]

One can expect, therefore, that in polities where a significant component of one of the world's major religions may be under the sway of a nondemocratic doctrinally based religious discourse, one of the major tasks of political and spiritual leaders who would like, for whatever reason, to revalue democratic norms in their own religious community will be continually to mount theologically convincing public arguments about the legitimate multivocality of their religion. Such arguments may violate Rawls's requirement for freestanding public reasoning—but they may be vital to the success of the democratization process in a country in the midst of a contestation over the meaning and the appropriateness of democracy. *Liberal arguing* has a place in democracy, but it would empty meaning and history out of political philosophy if we did not leave a place for *democratic bargaining,* and for some forms of nonliberal public argument within religious communities, in such democratic bargaining.

Let us now turn to exploring these general arguments in the contexts of cultures heavily influenced by Confucianism, Islam, and Orthodox Christianity.

Confucianism: Caesar is God?

If one compares Taiwan, South Korea, and Singapore, most scholars of Confucianism would, I believe, acknowledge that there are significant Confucian cultural components in all these countries. They would probably also say that the Confucian legacy was historically somewhat stronger in Taiwan and Korea than in Singapore.[41]

Most scholars of democratization who follow East Asia would, I believe, also acknowledge that in the last five years Taiwan and Korea have held elections that meet Dahl's criteria of the eight minimal guarantees and that also meet the Linz–Stepan additional criteria of a government that increasingly has a democratic constitution and rules within the constitution.[42] In Korea, given

40. For the complicated bargain in Belgium, see Stathis S. Kalyvas, "Democracy and Religious Politics: Evidence from Belgium," *Comparative Political Studies*, 31 (June 1998), 292–320.

41. See e.g., Steve Tsang, "The Confucian Tradition and Democratization," in Yossi Shain and Aharon Klieman (eds.), *Democracy: The Challenges Ahead* (Basingstoke: Macmillan, 1997), 30–47. Indeed Singapore at the height of the Asian Values campaign had to *import* Confucian scholars from abroad in order to reembed Confucianism in the school curriculum.

42. For example, using the previously mentioned annual report of Freedom House, which employs a seven point scale for political rights and civil liberties, we note that in 1973 and 1985 South Korea received a 5 on political rights and a 6 on civil liberties, but a very good 2–2 in 1996. Taiwan scored a 6–5 in 1973, a 5–5 in 1985, but improved to 2–2 in 1996. See Gastil, ed., *Freedom in the World. Political Rights and Civil Liberties, 1996–1997*

the trials and convictions of two former general presidents for gross human rights violations, and the trials and convictions for corruption of some large corporate heads, scholars would also recognize that there has been impressive movement toward a state, and an economic society, that is bound by law, and where political society leaders are more accountable to democratic institutions.

However, when we consider Singapore, in my judgement there is *no* important democratization analyst who could possibly sustain the argument that Singapore even meets half of Dahl's eight minimal guarantees.[43] Thus, if we apply the institutional threshold requirements of a modern democracy, we can say that South Korea and Taiwan are above the threshold and Singapore is below the threshold.

I argued earlier against assuming that any of the world's major religious traditions are univocal. If this argument is right, this means that inside what Huntington calls "kin cultures" we should be on the alert for struggles over meaning, and the attempt to appropriate meaning. When the former prime minister of Singapore Lee Kuan Yew attempted to appropriate "Asian values" as a fundamental part of his regime, he was repeatedly, and correctly, challenged by the new president of Korea, Kim Dae Jung, and the president of Taiwan, Lee Teng-Hui. In essence, in a stylized or paraphrased manner, they both said, "We are democratic. We draw upon some important democratic values found in the Confucian tradition. But *you*, Mr Lee Kuan Yew, do not have a democracy in Singapore and you rationalize it by drawing upon some a-democratic values of Confucianism. We are better democrats, and better Confucians, than you and don't you dare attempt to hijack 'Asian values.' "[44]

(New York: Freedom House, 1997). For substantive details on the democratic transition in South Korea and Taiwan, see Robert A. Scalapino, "Democratizing Dragons: South Korea and Taiwan," *Journal of Democracy*, 4 (July 1993), 70–84, Sang-Yong Choi (ed.), *Democracy in Korea: Its Ideals and Realities* (Seoul: Korean Political Science Association, 1997), and articles on Taiwan and South Korea in the volume edited by Larry Diamond, Marc F. Plattner, Yun-han Chu, and Hung-Mao Tien, *Consolidating Third World Democracies: Regional Challenges* (Baltimore: Johns Hopkins University Press, 1997).

43. For example, in the Freedom House scale, Singapore in 1973 scored a 5–5, and in 1985 a 4–5, in both years better than South Korea and Taiwan. But in 1998 Singapore had gone back to a score of 5–5, substantially lower than both Taiwan and South Korea. A graduate student from Singapore did a paper in one of my seminars exploring the degree to which Singapore satisfied Dahl's eight institutional guarantees and made a convincing and documented case that at most only two of Dahl's eight institutional guarantees were satisfied in the 1996 election. Significantly, as with some comparable students from South Korea and Taiwan I taught in the 1970s or early 1980s, the graduate student decided that it would not be fair to his or her family to pursue this line of inquiry in a doctoral dissertation.

44. For an example of this exchange, see Fareed Zakaria, "Culture is Destiny: A Conversation with Lee Kuan Yew," *Foreign Affairs* (Mar.–Apr. 1994), 109–29, and a response by the new president of Korea, Kim Dae Jung, "Is Culture Destiny? The Myth of Asia's Anti-Democratic Values," *Foreign Affairs* (Nov.–Dec. 1994), 189–94, and the article by the president of Taiwan, Lee Teng-hui, "Chinese Culture and Political Renewal," *Journal of Democracy*, 6 (Oct. 1995), 3–8.

Kim Dae Jung's response succinctly underscores many of the core points of the argument I advanced in the introduction to this essay. He insists that Lee Kwan Yew's version of Asian values is a self-serving rationale for authoritarian rule, and he devotes two pages to citing Confucian and neo-Confucian tenets supportive of democracy, specifically tenets that legitimate dissent. He then talks of "Lee's record of absolute intolerance of dissent" and says Lee's Singapore is a "near totalitarian police state." Kim Dae Jung concluded with an elegant rejection of what I have called the "fallacy of unique founding circumstances." He asserted, "Europeans formalized comprehensive and effective electoral democracy first. The invention of the electoral system is Europe's greatest accomplishment. The fact that this system was developed elsewhere does not mean it will not work in Asia."[45]

Analytically, the South Korean and Taiwan presidents are making normative and empirical distinctions that are crucial to modern democratic theory. At the level of the core defining characteristics of a modern democracy, we must not be relativists. Any country, in any culture, must meet certain institutional and behavioral requirements of the sort I discussed in the introduction to qualify as a democracy.[46] However, we must absolutely also recognize that within the world of democracies there are many subtypes of democracy, with distinctive secondary characteristics; some have a large state, some do not, some accept individual values and reject collective values, some accept individual values *but* also espouse collective values. Many of the secondary values of the Korean and Taiwan democracies, which differentiate them from US, or possibly British, democracy, such as higher saving rates so that the family can look after their own aged, a somewhat more robust role for the state in the economy, and less crime and somewhat greater respect for legal authority, draw upon Confucian values, but none of these "Asian values" in the present political context of a democracy are antidemocratic. Indeed, as Presidents Kim Dae Jung and Lee Teng-hui repeatedly and correctly assert, they are part of the distinctive strength of their subtype of democracy.[47]

45. Kim Dae Jung, "Is Culture Destiny?," 192.
46. Many political activists who are in the Confucian tradition accept this stipulation concerning the universal core minimal requirements for a democracy. For example, Margaret Ng, a Hong Kong democratic activist, in her assessment of the status of the Singapore model in the Asian values debate, explicitly talks of the "Singapore government's undeniably harsh treatment of the opposition." She argues that the basic criteria of what a democracy is "must be universal" and that "every government that claims to be democratic must be measured against these criteria, and beyond a certain degree of deviation, must be declared to be non-democratic." Precisely. See her "Why Asia Needs Democracy," which is her contribution to a symposium, "Hong Kong, Singapore and 'Asian Values,'" *Journal of Democracy*, 8 (Apr. 1997), 19–23, both quotations from p. 21.
47. After accepting the universalism of core aspects of democracy, Kim Dae Jung, in "Is Culture Destiny?," argues that in some ways the "traditional strengths of Asian society can provide for a better democracy" (p. 193). There is absolutely nothing antidemocratic about such an assertion of the positive effect of some Asian values. Indeed, in the new democratic political context some research is finding that high support for Confucian

Let me close this section on Confucianism with some illustrations of the multivocality of its doctrine, and the political appropriation, and now the struggle to reappropriate, meaning. The new translation by Simon Leys of *The Analects of Confucius*, with 100 pages of valuable annotations, correctly points out that imperial and "state Confucianism repeatedly stressed the Confucian precept of *obedience* while obliterating the symmetrical Confucian duty of *disobedience* to a ruler if the ruler deviates from The Way."[48] Some anti-hierarchical Confucian sayings that Simon Leys and new civil society organizations in Korea stress are: "Zila asked how to serve the Prince. The Master said 'Tell him the Truth even if it offends him.' "[49] Or, in furtherance of dissent, there is the Confucian injunction "A righteous man, a man attached to humanity, does not seek life at the expense of humanity; there are instances where he will give his life in order to fulfil his humanity."[50] Xun Zi, one of the great followers of Confucius, built upon the above injunction when he defined a good minister as one who "follows the way, he does not follow the rules."[51]

What of the Confucian legacy and democracy? Clearly, since some authoritarian dynasties, as in Korea, lasted over 500 years, and strove to nurture acquiescence by selectively expressing the obedience components of the Confucian corpus (and by repressing potentially subversive components of the Confucian and neo-Confucian corpus), this legacy of state Confucianism will be diffusely present in new democracies such as Korea and Taiwan for decades to come. But, just as clearly, this legacy has not stopped the emergence of democratic rule in these countries, and indeed some of the most important leaders of political society and civil society in the new democracies of Taiwan and Korea have articulated the "legitimate dissent" and "government accountability" components of the Confucian multivocal legacy to strengthen their struggles to deepen democracy.

---

values, and for deepening democracy, can cluster together and be mutually reinforcing. For example, in Korea one of the more efficacious nongovernmental organizations in the struggle against corruption, for trials for two former military presidents who violated human rights, and for support for the aged was an organization informally called a "pro-Confucian lobby" which used Confucian symbols and dictums in support of the new democratic "way." See the D.Phil. thesis by Bronwen Dalton at Oxford University, "Civil Society and the Social Construction of Corruption in South Korea: A Case Study of the Citizens' Coalition for Economic Justice and its Fight against Corruption," 2000.

48. Simon Leys' translation and annotations of *The Analects of Confucius* (New York: W. W. Norton, 1997). For Leys' discussion of "state Confucianism," see esp. p. 108; for state Confucianism's obliteration of the symmetrical duty of disobedience, see pp. 134–6.

49. Ibid. 136.

50. Ibid. 75.

51. Ibid. 193. For an article that documents the doctrinal legitimation of dissent, and even revolt, against unjust leaders, see Julia Ching, "Human Rights: A Valid Chinese Concept?," in the valuable volume by W. M. Theodore de Bary and Tu Wei-Ming (eds.), *Confucianism and Human Rights* (New York: Columbia University Press, 1998), esp. 72.

Islam: "Free Elections Trap"?

There is an extensive literature arguing that many of the key aspects of democracy are lacking in the Islamic tradition. The lack of dualism between religion and the state is seen as stemming from Muhammad's fusion of military and spiritual authority. The lack of space for democratic public opinion in making laws is seen as deriving from the Korean, wherein God dictated the content of fixed laws to the Prophet Muhammad that a good Islamic polity must follow. The lack of inclusive citizenship is seen as having its origins in interpretations of the Koran which argue that the only true polis in Islam is the fused religious political community of the *umma*, in which there is no legitimate space for other religions in the polity. Certainly with the rise in some countries of Islamic fundamentalism there have been repeated modern assertions by some Islamic activists of all of these doctrinal claims. In the context of the Algerian crisis of 1991–2 this gave rise to intensified scholarly assertions that Islam and democracy were incompatible, and to policy based arguments in leading journals of public opinion in the West against falling into the "Islamic free elections trap." The free elections trap argument was that most people in Islamic cultures are prone to fundamentalism, and thus in essence, if something like Dahl's eight electoral guarantees were allowed, this would lead to the election of governments who would use these democratic freedoms to destroy democracy.[52]

Any human rights activist or democratic theorist must of course acknowledge that there are numerous human rights crimes against individuals that are being committed in some countries in the name of Islam. In Algeria, both the military state and Islamic fundamentalists are slaughtering innocents. Women's rights are being flagrantly violated by the Taliban in Afghanistan. In the name of Islam parts of Sudan are a killing zone. At the aggregate level a recent attempt to document political freedoms and civil rights in 191 countries

52. For examples of the academic literature on the incompatibility of Islam and democracy, see Elie Kedourie, who begins *Democracy and Arab Political Culture* (London: Frank Cass, 1994) with the flat assertion "The idea of democracy is quiet alien to the mind-set of Islam" (p. 1); Professor Amos Perlmutter, "Islam and Democracy Simply aren't Compatible," *International Herald Tribune*, 21 Jan. 1992, 6; and Martin Kramer, "Islam vs. Democracy," *Commentary* (Jan. 1993), 35–42. In the run-up to the Algerian elections there appeared Leslie Gelb's "The Free Elections Trap," *New York Times*, 29 May 1991. This free election trap fear, even in Western liberal circles, is captured by the frequent use of the knowing "joke" about democratic elections in Islamic countries. "Yes, we know, one person, one vote, one time." Huntington never quite says this, but he makes frequent statements in his *The Clash of Civilizations* that give some support to this fear: "Islamic fundamentalists have done well in the few elections that have occurred in Muslim countries and would have come to national power in Algeria if the military had not canceled the 1992 election" (p. 94); "Democratization conflicts with Westernization, and democracy is inherently a parochializing, not a cosmopolitizing, process. Politicians in non-Western societies... fashion what they believe will be the most popular appeals, and these are usually ethnic, nationalist and religious in character" (p. 94); "The general failure of liberal democracy to take hold in Muslim societies... has its source, at least in part, to the inhospitable nature of Islamic culture and society to Western liberal concepts" (p. 114).

in the world concluded that "the Islamic world remains most resistant to the spread of democracy in the world."[53]

It was in the above context that Huntington asserted that the West's problem is "not Islamic fundamentalism but Islam." But, in the Huntingtonian vision of the possible future of Islam there is virtually no analysis of how struggling democratic forces in some key Islamic majority countries might prevail. Indeed, democratic failure is almost "over-determined" in his world of essentialist authoritarian "kin cultures" and unstoppable cultural fault-line wars. How should empirical democratic theorists begin to respond?

I think we should once again begin exploring my hypothesis that all great religious civilizations are multivocal. Certainly, Islamic fundamentalists are attempting to appropriate political Islam. But there are other voices, in the Koran, in scholarly interpretations of the Koran, and among some major contemporary Islamic political leaders.

Within the Koran one of the injunctions most cited by the Islamic democratic leaders, against their nondemocratic Islamic fundamentalist rivals, is that "There shall be no compulsion in Religion."[54] This injunction provides a strong Koranic base for religious tolerance. Indeed, at some moments in history, Islam was noted for its tolerance. Though Huntington completely ignores it, the millet tradition in the Ottoman Empire gave important self-government roles to leaders of four different groups, defined largely as religious communities: the Muslims, the Greeks, the Armenians, and the Jews. Bernard Lewis says of these millets, "the members were subject to the rules and even to the laws of that religion, administered by its own chief."[55] The tolerance for Jews and Christians as "people of the book" thus has a doctrinal basis in Islamic religious tradition. In fact, in some historical periods there was more religious tolerance under Islamic rulers (as in their conquest of Iberia) than in many Christian polities in the same historical period.[56]

Sayyid Qutb, a major theoretician of the Islamic Brotherhood in Egypt, indeed argued against popular sovereignty because the "Sharia is so complete as a legal and moral system that no further legislation is possible."[57] However, in separate places and on separate occasions I have conducted long interviews with four major contemporary Islamic leaders who, with some variations, advanced a quite different set of Islamic doctrines concerning sovereignty, legislation, and democracy. These interviews were with the Indonesians

53. Adrian Karatnychy, "The 1998 Freedom House Survey: The Decline of Illiberal Democracy," *Journal of Democracy* (Jan. 1999), 121.

54. *The Koran*, trans. N. J. Dawood (London: Penguin Books, 1997), 38. This is referred to as Sura (verse) 256.

55. Bernard Lewis, *The Middle East: A Brief History of the Last 2,000 Years* (New York: Scribner, 1995), 321.

56. My Spanish colleague Juan J. Linz has insisted on this point as a comparative historical and political reality.

57. See John L. Esposito and James P. Piscatori, "Democratization and Islam," *Middle East Journal*, 45 3 (Summer 1991), 427–40.

Abdurrahman Wahid and Amien Rais fourteen months before they became, respectively, the president of Indonesia and the chairman of the People's Consultative Assembly after the June 1999 democratic elections; Talgat Tadjuddin, the supreme mufti of Russia, and Rachid Al-Ghannouchi, a major opposition leader in the April 1989 elections in Tunisia, now in exile in London.[58] Five arguments emerged in the interviews.

First, all four of the leaders implicitly rebutted Qutb. They insisted there are four sources of Islamic law. They argued that God's dictates to the Prophet Muhammad are only one of these four and make up probably less than 10 percent of what a modern state would need for *sharia* (Islamic law). Other sources of law can and should, they argued, be developed by the citizens, scholars, jurists, and legislators in a modern law bounded democracy.

Second, they stressed that the Koran has a concept of *shura* ("consultation") which they believe under modern pluralist conditions is best done by consulting the citizens of a polity, both Muslim and non-Muslim, in open competitive elections.

Third, to a person, these four major contemporary Islamic political leaders also mentioned the increasing import of the Islamic concept of *ijtihad* ("independent reasoning"). They argued that, as literacy increases, more people can and will read the Koran, and thus qualify for the right of independent reasoning as Muslims, individuals, and citizens.

Fourth, when the Islamic juridical tradition of *ijma* ("consensus") is combined with the Koranic injunction that "there should be no compulsion in religion," they believe there is space within Islam not only for a majoritarian democracy, but for a version of democracy that respects individual rights and pluralism.

Fifth, none of the four leaders said that religion and the state *needed* to be fused in Islam.[59] Indeed, all but Ghannouchi argued that under modern conditions it would be a mistake. Wahid argued particularly forcefully against an Islamic state. Ghannouchi and Tadjuddin argued at length that the fusion of church and state had actually *not* been the norm in Islam since the ninth century.[60]

58. The interview with Abdurraham Wahid was held in Jakarta on Aug. 15, 1998, and with Amien Rais in Jogjakarta on Aug. 18, 1998. Interviews with Talgat Tadjuddin were held in Oxford on Mar. 10, 1999, and in Baskortostan on Oct. 12, 1999. The interviews with Rachid Al-Ghannouchi were in London on Oct. 11 and 12, 1997.

59. However, Ghannouchi differed from the other three in one extremely important and, from the viewpoint of democratic theory, somewhat disturbing respect. He argued that the ideal form of government would be an Islamic government. He acknowledged that in the modern pluralist world it is extremely difficult to achieve this ideal. Failing this, he argued that it is the obligation of the Muslim community to try to work with allies, from any religion, to establish a just government in a secular democratic system. Earlier in his career, until the mid-1990s, Rais and many of his associates had sometimes advocated an Islamic state.

60. These contemporary Islamic political leaders have historical evidence by some eminent Western scholars on their side. For very convincing historical demonstration

Finally, one of the four, Wahid of Indonesia, said that when properly under-stood and constructed, *sharia*, and Christian concepts of natural law, could well end up being quite similar.[61]

What should we conclude from this brief discussion? It seems valid to con-clude that contemporary Islamic leaders have "usable" elements to draw from in their doctrine, culture, and experience with which to construct a nondemo-cratic vision of a desired future polis. But, there are also other contemporary leaders who have "usable" elements of Islamic doctrine, culture, and experi-ence with which to attempt to support, or construct, a democratic vision of their desired future polis. The tradition is multivocal.[62] However, in the mod-ern context does the empirical evidence nonetheless support the "free election trap" argument? Specifically, should an empirical democratic theorist accept Huntington's argument that the problem "is not Islamic fundamentalism. It is Islam"?

Political activists, journalists, and even professors sometimes misleadingly equate Islam with Arab culture.[63] They then assert correctly that there are no democracies in the Islamic countries of the Middle East. This leaves the false impression there are no Muslims living in democratic political contexts.

From the perspective of democracy, I believe it is useful to say four things at the start to put the issue of Islam and democracy in a more balanced empirical and global perspective. First, there are approximately 1 billion individuals of the Islamic faith in the world.[64] Second, probably only 200 million of the

that after the period of fused military and prophetic rule of Muhammad and the phase of religious expansion "The split between Muslim state and Muslim religious communities came into the open in the ninth century" and that "In the Ottoman Empire the evolution of relations between state and religious elite led to the direct control of the state over religious institutions," see Ira M. Lapidus, "State and Religion in Islamic Societies," *Past and Present*, 151 (May 1996), 3–27, quotations from pp. 15–16. Lapidus's historical evid-ence is consistent with our previous discussion of multivocality in that he argues that since the 10th century, fusion of church and state has never been an unchallenged empirical pattern in Islam and indeed there has always been a contestation between Islamic models (see p. 4).

61. For a more elaborate discussion of many of these concepts such as *sharia*, *shura*, *ijtihad*, and *ijma*, see Dale F. Eickelman and James Piscatori, *Muslim Politics* (Princeton: Princeton University Press, 1996), esp. 46–79, and John L. Esposito and John O. Voll, *Islam and Democracy* (New York: Oxford University Press, 1996), esp. 11–51.

62. Indeed Hossein Modarressi, professor of Islamic law, Department of Near Eastern Studies, Princeton University, who after receiving tenure at Princeton was officially given the status of an Ayatollah in Iran, asserts flatly, "Muslim jurists have differed among themselves on almost every legal question." See his "The Legal Basis for the Validity of the Majority Opinion in Islamic Legislation," in Richard W. Bulliet (ed.), *Under Siege: Islam and Democracy*, Occasional Paper 1 (New York: Middle East Institute, Columbia Univer-sity, 1993), 83.

63. For example, in the first page of his opening discussion of Islam, Huntington mentions the word "Arab" eight times, "tribe" nine times, and *no* South or Southeast Asian Islamic country examples. See Huntington, *The Clash of Civilizations*, 174–5.

64. See ibid., table 4.2, for estimates, as of 1993, of the total population of countries belonging to the world's major civilizations. A somewhat dated but authoritative demo-graphic analysis of the world's Islamic population is found in John R. Weeks, "The Demography of Islamic Nations," *Population Bulletin*, 43 (July 1988), 4–54.

approximately 1 billion Muslims in the world are Arabs. Logically, a subcategory can never stand for the entire category. Third, now that the cold war is over, the Middle East is the area of the world which is most involved in a long standing geomilitary and geopolitical conflict. If peace were crafted in the Middle East, and independence granted to Palestine and supported economically by the West, a number of countries in the Middle East—possibly Tunisia, Jordan, and Lebanon—could resume their experiments with liberalization, Qatar might expand its surprising opening of the media, and antifundamentalist forces in Iran, emboldened by their recent election victories, might be strengthened further in their struggles against theocratic leaders. Fourth, a case could be made that about half of all the world's Muslims, about 435 million people (or over 600 million, if we include Indonesia) live in democracies, near democracies, or intermittent democracies. In many of these polities it is sensible to discuss whether they are democracies, or if they were democracies and experienced democratic breakdown, whether it was due to Islamic politics *per se*, or to other factors, such as the military. In this essay I will only discuss my fourth point, because it is the most controversial, and I believe it will help us examine the "free election trap dilemma" in a more optimistic, and I believe a more globally realistic, manner.

How do I arrive at my figure of 435 million? By looking at Islam in the entire world and including fragile, even intermittent democracies.[65] I thus include the 110 million Muslims in Bangladesh, the 120 million Muslims in Pakistan, and the 65 million Muslims in Turkey. I also include the 120 million Muslims living in India, because I believe they have contributed to Indian democracy and are one of the important voices in the world's multivocal Islamic culture. Finally, if we include the at least 20 million Muslims who live in democratic regimes in areas such as Western Europe, North America, and Australia, we get 435 million. Once again, I believe the inclusion of the Islamic Diaspora is justified because its experience with democracy is important if we are not "essentialists" or "territorialists" about religion, but see Islam as an evolving, constantly changing global culture that is to some degree being "deterritorialized."

The big country that democratization theorists are watching most closely is Indonesia. With its estimated population of 216 million people, roughly 190 million of whom are Muslim, Indonesia is the world's largest Muslim majority country. Obviously, with the worst case of what the economists called "Asian flu"; long-repressed regional demands for decentralization (secession in the cases of East Timor, Acheh, and Irian Jaya); the almost democratically unusable 1945 constitution written during the war of independence; a military organization which has been centrally involved in national politics since the 1940s and which has often exacerbated, or even incited, major communal conflicts, such

---

65. However, at the moment there are no Islamic majority countries with a fully consolidated democracy of the sort Linz and I stipulate in our "Toward Consolidated Democracies" (Ch. 14 in this volume).

as those against Communists and some Chinese in 1965–6, and in East Timor in 1999; no possible transition to democracy will be without great risks and uncertainties. But, will the fact that the country is dominantly Islamic significantly increase the chances of democratic failure or breakdown? I do not think there is strong evidence to support such a presumption.

The thirty-two-year rule of Suharto (1965–98) was a military authoritarian regime that increasingly acquired patrimonial, even "sultanistic," dimensions in the 1990s. However, Islam was never a major part of Suharto's power base. Indeed, most analysts who wrote about the prospect of democracy in Indonesia during the Suharto period did not list Islamic fundamentalists *per se* as a major *obstacle* to democratization.[66]

In any attempt at democratic transition, leadership and organization are extremely important. The two largest, and most influential, Islamic organizations at the start of the possible transition in Indonesia, Nahdatul Ulama (NU), and Muhammadiyah, both with over 25 million members, were led respectively by Abdurrahman Wahid and Amien Rais, whose thinking on religion and democracy I have already discussed. Both leaders in the struggle against Suharto, and during the election campaign of 1999, acted in ways consistent with their democratic and inclusionary arguments.

Amien Rais played a critically constructive role in helping to keep the student protests mobilized, relatively peaceful, and focused on democratic demands. In the aftermath of the fall of Suharto, Amien Rais, after considering leading an existing Islamic political grouping, created a new political party, PAN, which was not explicitly Islamist, and indeed which included non-Muslims in its leadership.[67]

Abdurrahman Wahid also created a new political party, PKB, and throughout the electoral campaign of 1999 argued against an Islamic state, for religious pluralism, and often operated in informal alliances with the most electorally powerful political leader, Megawati Sukarnoputri, and her secular nationalist party, PDI, which includes secular Muslims, Christians, and many non-Muslim minorities.[68] The new president of Indonesia even under the Suharto dictatorship was described by Eickelman and Piscatori as "committed to the idea of a pluralist, democratic, and non-sectarian Indonesia." They added that "Wahid has vigorously argued that religion and politics are separate, and that Islam

66. For example, R. William Liddle, in his "Indonesia's Threefold Crisis," *Journal of Democracy*, 3 (Oct. 1992), 60–74, listed Indonesia's three interrelated crises that negatively affected Indonesia's democratization prospects as (1) the great nondemocratic power of President Suharto, (2) the key role of the military in the looming secession crisis, and (3) nationalism and military repression in East Timor. He said political Islam could be problematic, "though there is evidence that Indonesia's Muslim intellectuals have for the last two decades been quietly forging a new, non-threatening conception of the relationship between state and society in Islam" (pp. 69–70).

67. For an analysis of PAN, PKB, and PDI in the run-up to the June 1999 elections, see R. William Liddle, "Indonesia's Democratic Opening," *Government and Opposition*, 34 (Winter 1999), 94–116.

68. Ibid.

does not incorporate any notion of state."[69] In Indonesia Muslim identities, as Clifford Geertz and others have documented, are far from essentialist, but often moderate, syncretic, and pluralist.[70] Also, much more than in the Middle East, women have a significant degree of personal and career freedom in Indonesia.[71] In this context there was at least some space for a leader like Wahid to attempt to help a transition to democracy by constantly arguing that tolerance was one of the best parts of Indonesia's religious tradition.

Despite interethnic and religious conflicts, often tolerated, and at times even supported (especially in East Timor) by parts of the internally divided armed forces, no Islamic fundamentalist party developed significant mass followings in the year following Suharto's fall. In the freest election in over four decades in Indonesia the two most electorally powerful fundamentalist Islamic parties, PBB and PK, polled 2 percent and 1 percent of the total popular vote respectively in the June 1999 elections.[72]

Democracy in Indonesia is certainly not yet, as in a consolidated democracy, the "only game in town." Outbreaks of religious violence on a number of the

69. See their *Muslim Politics*, 55.

70. There is probably still something in Clifford Geertz's famous phrase (especially for Java) that a common Indonesian, when asked to describe himself, would say: "I am Muslim—but not like the Iranian; in fact I am also part Buddhist, part Hindu, part Christian and part animist." See his *Local Knowledge* (New York: Basic Books, 1983), 226. Geertz has also written, in his *Islam Observed: Religious Development in Morocco and Indonesia* (Chicago: University of Chicago Press, 1971), 12, that "Compared to North Africa, the Middle East, and even Muslim India, whose brand of faith it perhaps most closely resembles, Indonesian Islam has been, at least until recently, remarkably malleable, tentative, syncretistic, and, most significantly of all, multivoiced." Since Geertz made these observations, some currents of the 1979 Iranian Revolution reached Indonesia. However, a 1999 overview of religion in Indonesia advances conclusions broadly similar to Geertz. See Robert W. Hefner, "Religion: Evolving Pluralism," in Donald K. Emmerson (ed.), *Indonesia beyond Suharto: Polity, Economy, Society, Transition* (Armonk, NY: M. E. Sharpe, 1999), 205–36.

71. The party which received the largest number of votes in 1999 was led by a woman, Megawati Sukarnoputri. A quarter of the judges are women. Women are free to veil themselves heavily, or not, and very few do. A majority of the workforce employed in the service sector—58%—are women, compared to 26% in South Asia as a whole, 10% in Turkey, 8% in Egypt, and 7% in Iran. For a well-documented discussion of the constraints, and freedoms, of Islamic women in Indonesia, see Kathryn Robinson, "Women: Difference versus Diversity," in Emmerson (ed.), *Indonesia beyond Suharto*, 237–61.

72. Sociologically, what is impressive is that despite some efforts to exacerbate interethnic and interreligious conflicts, and appeals to fundamentalist Islamic social codes, a public opinion survey conducted by the International Foundation for Electoral Systems found that 87% of the population polled believed that "all groups should have the same rights as citizens." And an Asian Foundation survey found that 61% of the population believed that women should be just as active as men in positions of political leadership. Interestingly, there were no statistically significant differences in this question between males and females, or Muslims and non-Muslims. However, about a third of the respondents in a survey conducted by the Political Science Laboratory of the University of Indonesia and R. William Liddle responded positively to the question: "Should the state be responsible for the implementation of Islamic law?" If the political context deteriorated in Indonesia, there might be more resonance than found in 1998 for more militant Islamic parties.

country's more than 2,000 inhabited islands cause dangerous tensions and breakdowns of law.[73] Nonetheless, against great initial odds, democracy, two years after the fall of Suharto, was still on the agenda in Indonesia.

Let us now turn to Bangladesh, Pakistan, and especially Turkey. All of them of course have, or recently had, military regimes, but in recent times they all at some time have been above or at the threshold of being democracies, so they are important and legitimate subjects for the purposes of this essay. The 1996 election in Bangladesh satisfied all of Dahl's eight institutional guarantees.[74] In fact in that election the government and the Parliament made a major innovation in the repertoire of democratic constitutional engineering when the Parliament consensually passed an amendment to have a neutral caretaker government, called "Chief Advisor," headed by the former chief justice of the Supreme Court, supervise the electoral campaign and the elections themselves.[75] In this context the electoral turnout, at 73 percent (women around 76 percent), was 13 percent higher than in any general election in the history of Bangladesh. Interestingly, the fundamentalist Islamic party, JI, in the freest election in Bangladesh's history trailed far behind three other parties and won only three seats. The JI seems to have polled worst among women in general and especially among women associated with the Gameen "self-help" and "peer monitoring" microenterprise movement.[76] In this revolutionary "peer monitoring" scheme no financial collateral is put up because the community of peers pledge themselves. This innovative "peer monitoring" scheme has a 98 percent loan recovery rate, one of the highest of any

73. See e.g. Seth Mydans, "Religious Warfare on Indonesian Isles Bodes Wide Chaos," *New York Times*, Feb. 9, 2000, 1. However, it is important to note that no nationally prominent political leader has accorded "system blame" on democracy for these outbreaks. Also, when in Feb. 2000 Rais had an unfortunate lapse and made some inflammatory remarks at a mass meeting about the need for Muslim unity in the face of Christian attacks, he was immediately rebuked in the press by prominent Muslims in his own party and by President Wahid. Rais rapidly dissociated himself from such united Muslim appeals.

74. On the Freedom House scale of 1–7, Bangladesh, for the year 1996, received a score of 2 for political rights, the same score as Taiwan and South Korea. However, whereas Taiwan and South Korea received a 2 for civil liberties, Bangladesh, because of problems with rule of law and violence, only received a 4. Countries with major Islamic populations which received a score of 7 on political rights in 1996 included Saudi Arabia, Syria, Iraq, Libya, and Somalia. Countries that received a score of 6 included Algeria, Egypt, Iran, and Lebanon.

75. The most extensive analysis of the constitutional innovation concerning the caretaker government, and of the 1996 election, is the Report of the Non-Governmental Election Observers from South East Asia, *Governance and the Electoral Process in Bangladesh: Parliamentary Elections in 1996* (Colombo: International Center for Ethic Studies, 1996). Bangladesh's democratic performance is especially impressive given its great poverty. Of the 133 countries the World Bank lists by per capita income in dollars, it is the thirteenth lowest, at $220. See *The World Development Report 1996: From Plan to Market* (Oxford University Press for the World Bank, 1996), table 1, and pp. 188–9.

76. In addition to the previously cited *Governance and the Electoral Process in Bangladesh*, see Yasmeen Murshed and Nazim Kamran Choudhury, "Bangladesh's Second Chance," *Journal of Democracy*, 81 (Jan. 1997), 70–82.

World Bank supported schemes in the world, and is part of a women's self-empowering development strategy that is not anti-Islamic, but is a new culturally transforming phenomenon within Islam that opposes, as in recent elections in Iran, hardline Islamic politicians.

Pakistan was founded by Jinnah as an Islamic republic and has some features of Islamic law in its constitution. However, it is important to stress two points. First, the features of Islamic law that are most democratically troubling were imposed under military rule. General Zia, during his period of authoritarian militarism, tried to institutionalize his rule in the late 1970s and early 1980s by using many Islamic symbols and by his claims that he would deepen the Islamic state. But, in his infamous 1984 plebiscite to ratify this authoritarian turn in the name of Islam less than a quarter of the electorate participated. After the fiasco of the plebiscite General Zia, under pressure from all political parties, eventually allowed parliamentary elections. Second, during the recent period of electorally competitive, non-military rule—which was ended by the military coup of October 1999—there had been no significant new impositions of Islamic law on Pakistani citizens, and some curtailment of the reach of Islamic law as the electoral achievements of Islamic fundamentalist parties weakened.

Until the military coup of 1999 there had been five consecutive elections in Pakistan since 1988. Did the results strengthen or weaken the "Islamic free election trap" thesis? Under conditions of growing electorate competitiveness the largest revivalist or fundamentalist Islamic party, IJI, came in second in 1988 and won a plurality in 1990 and 1993. But in 1996 and 1997 all the Islamic fundamentalist parties combined fell to less than 15 percent of the total vote. In the 1997 election, which observers consider the freest and most open of Pakistan's recent elections, Islamic fundamentalist parties only won two seats in the National Assembly.[77] One political analyst observed, "Pakistanis respect the ulema as prayer leaders and theologians, but not as potential [governmental] leaders."[78] In an excellent analytic overview of the relationships of Islamic revivalist parties and competitive elections in Pakistan since independence, S. V. R. Nasr concludes that, far from democratic conditions being a "free election trap," competitive politics "encourages the flowering of the diversity of Muslim political expression and prevents the reduction of the political discourse to revivalism versus secularism."[79] Violent and fundamentalist Islamic groups are active in Pakistan, to be sure. But much of the basis of their support owes more to secret subsidies they receive from Pakistan's notorious

77. For Pakistan's recent elections, see Leo E. Rose and D. Hugh Evans, "Pakistan's Enduring Experiment," *Journal of Democracy*, 81 (Jan. 1997), 83–96, and Mohammed Waseem, "The 1997 Elections in Pakistan," *Electoral Studies*, 17 (Mar. 1998), 129–32.
78. Anwar H. Syed, "Pakistan in 1997: Nawaz Sharif's Second Chance to Govern," *Asian Survey*, 38 (Feb. 1998), 118.
79. S. V. R. Nasr, "Democracy and Islamic Revivalism," *Political Science Quarterly*, 1102 (1995), 279.

Inter-Services Intelligence Agency (ISI) for foreign policy and domestic purposes than from votes they receive in elections.[80]

Huntington's implicit "democratic dilemma," that is, that elections in Islamic majority countries will lead to fundamentalist majorities who in turn will use their electoral freedom to end democracy, gets no support from our analysis of electoral and political behavior in Indonesia, Bangladesh, and Pakistan, the world's first, second, and third largest Islamic countries. Indeed, even in the founding state of Islamic fundamentalism, Iran, the "free election trap thesis" has recently been falsified robustly. Despite the fact that theocratic hardliners control state television, and the Council of Guardians vets all candidates, in the presidential election of 1997, the municipal elections of 1999, and the parliamentary elections of 2000 the antifundamentalist opposition won at least 70 percent of the vote in all three elections. Iran is thus becoming increasingly multivocal. The struggle in Iran precisely pits forces of the "twin tolerations" against forces of "the twin intolerations."[81]

Let me conclude my reflections on Islam and democracy by considering in some detail the undertheorized case of Turkey and our concern for "secularism" and democracy. From June 1996 to June 1997 Turkey had its first democratically elected government in which the senior partner was *de facto* an Islamic party. This party was the Welfare Party led by Prime Minister Necmettin Erbakan. Very rapidly the Welfare Party was accused of violating Turkey's secular constitution. In the wake of these charges and intensifying pressure from the military the Welfare Party resigned, and the Constitutional Court subsequently outlawed the party. From the perspective of my opening analysis about what a democracy is and is not, what is the specific political content of "secularism" in Turkey, and how does it relate to the twin tolerations?

80. See e.g. Sumit Ganguly, "Pakistan's Never Ending Story: Why the October Coup was no Surprise," *Foreign Affairs* (Mar.–Apr. 2000), 2–7. To be sure there have been many unfortunate events in Pakistan, such as Pakistani covert support for the Taliban fundamentalist revolution in Afghanistan, but it would appear that the major source of such support was from the military and intelligence systems acting somewhat autonomously. Recent conflicts with India in Kashmir have a similar origin. Another major source of weakness in the Pakistan polity is violent intra-Islamic strife between different ethnic groups, especially in the Sind.

81. For the 1997 presidential election, see Shaul Bakhash, "Iran's Remarkable Election," *Journal of Democracy* (Jan. 1998), 80–94. Bakhash notes that in the election women and young people played a key mobilizing role against the ruling clerical establishment. President Katami won with "a campaign that stressed the rule of law, tolerance for a multiplicity of views, wider political participation, social justice, and the need to strengthen the institutions of civil society" (p. 81). Despite extensive censorship, and some theocratically led state terrorism, the same antifundamentalist political forces won in Iran's first ever municipal elections in March 1999. See "Iranian Election: Reformers 'Take 70% of Vote,'" *Financial Times*, Mar. 3, 1999, 6. In the parliamentary election of February 2000, despite the fact that the theocratic and authoritarian Council of Guardians had vetoed the candidacies of over seventy of the best known opposition figures, and continued to control television, opposition candidates won twenty-nine of the thirty contested seats in Tehran.

Probably the most prestigious English speaking authority on Turkey is Bernard Lewis, the author of the classic *The Emergence of Modern Turkey*. Lewis is at times contradictory, but his overall thesis is that the main endeavor of Kemal Atatürk's policy toward religion was: "to disestablish [Islam]—to end the power of religion and its exponents in political, social, and cultural affairs, and limit it to matters of belief and worship. In thus reducing Islam to the role of religion in a modern, western nation-state, the Kemalists also made some attempt to give their religion a more modern and more national form."[82]

As a modernization theorist Lewis, in the above quotation, simply assumes that secularism and the nation-state, no matter how achieved, are intrinsic and necessary parts of the path to modernity and democratization. Let me problematize these assumptions. I should first note that the six "arrows" of Kemalism that were officially adopted at the Fourth Grand Congress in 1935 were (1) secularism, (2) nationalism, (3) populism, (4) étatism, (5) republicanism, and (6) revolutionism. *None* of the arrows was democratization. It should also be noted that, given the fact that the Kurdish population in Turkey spoke a different language than the Turks, and constituted at least 15 percent of the population, Turkey in the 1920s, and in the 1990s, was sociologically, if not constitutionally, a multinational state. Atatürk, in his effort to repress Kurdish language and political organization, followed a policy that elsewhere Juan J. Linz and I have called a "nation-state building" strategy. In mononational states, nation-state building and democracy building are complementary logics. But, in multinational states nation-state building and democracy building are normally conflicting logics.[83] Frequent human rights violations by the Turkish state in the recent fifteen-year armed conflict against Kurds in southeast Turkey, unfortunately, underscore this point.

The distinguished democratization theorist, and a specialist on Turkey, Dankwart Rustow was also a major modernization theorist. Like Lewis, Rustow simply does not question how the Kermalist arrows of "secularism" and "nationalism", *in the context of a multinational and culturally Muslim polity*, may be part of an audacious modernization project, but are in significant tension with a democratization project. Indeed, as late as 1988 Darkwart Rustow still asserted that Atatürk, "following the brilliant victory of his nationalist movement, proceeded to build a new structure of government and a Western-style system of popular education and very soon this new Turkish national identity was fully accepted." He further asserts that "Kemal Atatürk's national revolution" and the political and economical changes of his followers "have given Turkey a uniquely favorable climate for the achievement of a stable and thriving democracy."[84]

82. Bernard Lewis, *The Emergence of Modern Turkey*, 2nd edn. (Oxford: Oxford University Press, 1978), 412.
83. See Juan J. Linz and Alfred Stepan, "Toward Consolidated Democracies" (ch. 14 in this volume).
84. Dankwart A. Rustow, "Transitions to Democracy: Turkey's Experience in Historical and Comparative Perspective," in Metin Heper and Ahmet Evin (eds.), *State, Democracy*

With our previous discussion of Western Europe in mind, how accurate is it for the West's greatest authority on Turkey, Bernard Lewis, to say that Atatürk's goals were to "reduce Islam to the role of religion in a modern, western nation-state," and for one of the founders of democratization theory, Dankwart Rustow, to assert that the "new [secular] Turkish national identity was fully [and democratically] accepted?" Let us look at the actual state policies imposed by the Kemalists. Do they violate the twin tolerations?

Nur Yalman, in a telling article called "Some Observations on Secularism in Islam: The Cultural Revolution in Turkey," captures some of the actual qualities of what he calls a Chinese style "cultural revolution" under Kemalism.

Hats with brims are instituted in the place of the fez: the brim would not permit the forehead to touch the ground if any believer could keep his trilby on while praying in the mosques. The veiling of women is forbidden by decree. All religious orders, schools and tariquat are disbanded and abolished as mere receptacles of superstition and inequity. Later, the offices of the Caliph and Seyh-ul Islam, the highest religious offices, are dispensed with. Religious endowments are taken over by the State. Instead of these positions a General Directorate of Religious Affairs is established under the Prime Ministry with firm control over all sunni religious activities. Even more indicative of the Reformer's far-reaching cultural intentions, is the abolition of the Ottoman Arabic script and the adoption of the Latin alphabet. The Islamic calendar is abolished . . . The experience is not a conversion, perhaps (for there is no turning to Christianity), but an anti-conversion, a turning away from Islamic tradition . . . In Turkey the new script has made it very difficult for the new generation to go back even to newspapers of 1920, let alone to the nineteenth century.[85]

A professor of Middle Eastern history at the University of Wisconsin, Kemal H. Karpat, says, "there is no question but that Atatürkism is a strictly state ideology with no claim to reflect the social, cultural or economic ideology of society at large."[86] A Turkish scholar, Binnaz Toprak, who is a specialist on secularism in Turkey, affirms that the Directorate of Religious Affairs in the 1960s, after some religious schooling was allowed, had 52,000 civil servants who directly controlled teachers, textbooks, curriculum, and the precise details of mosque services. He concludes: "The separation of Church and State was never attempted in its Western version as orthodox Islam was put under state control and made subject to state authority."[87]

One often reads or hears allusions to Atatürk's secularism being influenced by, and indeed modeled on, French secularism. However, from the evidence I

and the Military: Turkey in the 1980s (Berlin: Walter de Gruyter, 1988), 239–48, quotations from pp. 241–2 and 246.

85. Nur Yalman, "Some Observations on Secularism in Islam: The Cultural Revolution in Turkey," *Daedalus*, 102 (Winter 1973), 139–68, quotation from pp. 153–4.

86. Kemal H. Karpat, "Military Interventions: Army–Civilian Relations in Turkey before and after 1980," in Heper and Evin (eds.), *State, Democracy and the Military*, 239–48, quotation from pp. 241–2 and 246.

87. Binnaz Toprak, "The State, Politics and Religion in Turkey," in Heper and Evin (eds.), *State, Democracy and the Military*, 119–36, quotation from p. 120.

have given, it should be clear that France in 1905 never assumed this degree of state management of religion. For Western observers to defend Atatürk's version of military controlled religious education as "French type secular democracy" is a complete misreading of secularism in the West, even in France in 1905, much less after 1959, and certainly a misreading of a democratically normal separation of religion and state.[88]

Let us now turn to questions concerning the existing Turkish constitution of 1982. What are its origins and contents? How does it relate to the right of civil society organizations freely to organize themselves, and peacefully to support parties in political society? What is the constitutional position of the National Security Council; specifically, how does it relate to the twin tolerations requirement that democratically elected officials be free to legislate policies, and not be checked by state institutions which are not in any way appointed, or accountable to, democratic procedures?

The current constitution was drafted by a committee vetted by the military during a period of military rule. The final version was revised by the National Security Council. The constitution was approved in a plebiscite, but it was forbidden for anyone to campaign *against* ratification of the constitution.[89] Article 2 reasserts that the Turkish republic is secular. Article 4 says Article 2 can never be changed even by a constitutional amendment. Article 24 reasserts that "education and instruction in religion and ethics shall be under state supervision and control." Article 24 further says, in a key clause that was used to constitutionally ban the Welfare Party, that "No one shall be allowed to exploit or abuse religious systems."

I believe it would be particularly useful if scholars interested in Turkey, religion, and democracy do more research on three key questions for which I will now give tentative answers.

First, did the Welfare Party under Prime Minister Erbakan actually break democratic procedures, as these are normally understood in most long-standing democracies? I am not sure, but I do not think that the case that they did has been proved. If they did, the Welfare Party's coalitional minority government should have been subjected to a parliamentary vote of no confidence, not a military led "soft coup."

---

88. If Turkey actually had either complete separation of religion and state, or complete secularism, it would not need 50,000 civil servants in the Directorate of Religious Affairs to manage religious schooling. The Atatürk tradition is obviously not so much systematically antireligious as it is systematically concerned with controlling religious expression so that it conforms with state goals. For the complexities of "secularism" in Turkey, which probably should be called by its Turkish name *laiklik*, see the excellent chapter "Interpreting Turkey's Secular Model," in Andrew Davison's thought provoking *Secularism and Revivalism in Turkey: A Hermeneutic Reconsideration* (New Haven: Yale University Press, 1998), 134–88.

89. On the context of Turkish constitution making in 1981–2, see Davison, *Secularism and Revivalism in Turkey*, 126. See also William Hale, "Transition to Civilian Governments in Turkey: The Military Perspective," in Herper and Evin (eds.), *State, Democracy and the Military*, 159–75, esp. pp. 166–74.

Second, was the operational definition of "secularism," as used by the military in 1982 and appealed to in the months leading up to the fall of the government in June 1997, more restrictive of the freedom of religious expression of civil society, and the freedom of organization of political society, than is found in long-standing Western democracies? I think that comparative analysis of actual democratic behavior will lead to the conclusion that, Dankwart Rustow or Bernard Lewis notwithstanding, *no* long-standing democracy actually constrains and manages the role of religious expression in civil society and political society as much as Turkey's current constitution does.

Third, was the constitutionally embedded guardian role of the military in the National Security Council to make recommendations that would be given "priority consideration" by the Council of Ministers, and directly to bring public and institutional pressure on the democratically elected government to conform to their recommendations, a violation of democratic civil–military relations as normally practiced by long-standing Western democracies?[90] My first two books were on civil–military relations. I am certain that such military pressures on elected officials, no matter how constitutionally embedded, are a violation of the core institutional definition of democracy that has been advanced in this essay.

If other scholars think I am not at least partially right in my tentative answers to the three questions I have just posed, then in Turkey (as in Pakistan and probably even in Indonesia) military and intelligence organizations, who are not responsible to democratic authority and who often exacerbate ethnic and regional conflict, rather than the religious aspects of civil and political society *per se*, are probably the biggest area to which we must devote our attention as we analyze the prospects for authoritarianism and democracy in these three Muslim majority countries.

It has sometimes been suggested that the question of Islam and democracy involves so many *sui generis* issues that democratization theory does not really apply. I think that my analysis of Indonesia, Bangladesh, Pakistan, Turkey, and even post-1997 Iran, demonstrates the analytic weakness of focusing only on Islam as the principal obstacle to democratization, while neglecting the overall sociopolitical, military, ethnic, economic, and international contexts.[91]

90. Ümit Cizre Sakallioğlu in his "The Anatomy of the Turkish Military's Political Autonomy," *Comparative Politics* (Jan. 1997) argues that "the range and substance of decisions discussed or shaped in the NSC establishes beyond doubt that in the last two decades it has been the most decisive leg of a dual system of executive decision making, the other leg being the council of ministers" (p. 158). Also see George S. Harris, "The Role of the Military in Turkey in the 1980s: Guardians or Decision-Makers," in Herper and Evin (eds.), *State, Democracy and the Military*, 177–200, and Jeremy Salt, "Turkey's Military 'Democracy,'" *Current History* (Feb. 1999), 72–8. These authoritarian elements in the 1982 Turkish constitution became subject to growing criticism by mid-2000 by both the newly elected president of Turkey and the European Union.

91. The economic factors need more study than they have received. In a major forthcoming global study of the economic correlates of democracy Adam Przeworksi *et al.* argue that, given its degree of economic development, the Islamic world has roughly the

Orthodox Christianity: Not a Strong Ally, but a Strong Obstacle?

What can we say about Orthodox Christianity and democracy? As an empirical democratic analyst who has followed resistance movements to nondemocratic rule in communist Europe, I believe one has to acknowledge that Roman Catholicism and protestantism played a more powerful role in recent civil society resistance movements than did Orthodoxy. Why? And what does this mean, and *not* mean, for democracy in countries where Orthodoxy is the most weighty religion? The major explanation for this variance cannot lie in the core religious doctrine of Orthodoxy *per se*, because for their first millennium Roman Catholicism and Orthodox Christianity shared the same theological doctrines. The subsequent Orthodox–Roman Catholic division was fundamentally about papal authority and papal infallibility, not about other doctrinal disputes. The critical differences concerning recent patterns of state resistance in Orthodoxy and Roman Catholicism lies more in their differing organizational forms, and in which parts of their common multivocal tradition have been given the most emphasis, than in doctrine itself.

Let us look comparatively at the question of civil society resistance. Roman Catholicism as a transnational, hierarchical organization can potentially provide material and doctrinal support to a local Catholic church to help it resist state oppression.[92] To the extent that the Catholic Church might resist the state, it could be considered a support for a more robust and autonomous civil society. Empirically, in the resistance stage of democratization, Linz and I analyze in our last book how the Catholic Church played a supportive role in Poland, Lithuania, Chile, Brazil, and, in the last years of Franco, in Spain. Protestantism, with its emphasis on individual conscience and its international networks, can also play a role in supporting civil society's opposition to a repressive state, as in East Germany and in Estonia. In the 1970s and 1980s protestantism, and even more so post-Vatican II Catholicism, chose to give important weight to "the prophetic mission" that calls for individuals to speak out against worldly injustice no matter what the consequences.

percentage of democracies that Przeworski's model, based on economic development, would have predicted. From this perspective the poor, Muslim majority, northwest African country Mali, with its 1998 Freedom House ranking of 3–3, is a democratically "overperforming" country.

92. The resistance of the Catholic Church in Poland has of course been amply documented but even under Stalin, in Lithuania, priests, and often virtually their entire parish, would repeatedly sign individual protests against state policies. See the fascinating documentation in W. Stanley Vardys, *The Catholic Church: Dissent and Nationality in Soviet Lithuania* (Boulder, Colo.: East European Quarterly, distributed by Columbia University Press, 1978). Jane Ellis, in her review of the role of religions in the fifteen Soviet republics, writes: "The strongly Catholic area of Lithuania . . . was virtually the only church in the USSR where bishops, clergy and faithful had remained at one, so there was little need for recrimination over compromises." See her *The Russian Orthodox Church: Triumphalism and Defensiveness* (London: Macmillan Press, 1996), 3.

Concerning civil society and resistance to the state, Orthodox Christianity is often (not always) organizationally and ideologically in a relatively weak position because of what Max Weber called its "caesaropapist" structure, in which the church is a *national* as opposed to a *transnational* organization. In caesaropapist churches the national state often plays a major role in the national church's finances and appointments. Such a national church is not really a relatively autonomous part of civil society because there is a high degree, in Weber's words, of "subordination of priestly to secular power."[93] Indeed, under Stalin the role of secular power in the USSR often meant the *de facto* participation of the KGB in the highest religious counsels of Orthodoxy.

As Max Weber and others have emphasized, Orthodoxy places more stress on liturgy than action, and privileges "quietism" as a response to the world.[94] In the structural context of caesaropapism, and the liturgical context of quietism, the "prophetic" response to injustice, while doctrinally available in Orthodoxy's multivocal tradition, is seldom voiced.[95]

Having acknowledged all of the above, I do not believe that Orthodox Christianity is an inherently antidemocratic force. That is to say, if the leaders of the state and political society are committed to democracy and follow democratic practices, the ceasaropapist structures and the quietist culture should lead to loyal support of democracy by the Orthodox Christian Church, as in Greece since 1975. Bulgaria will be an interesting country to watch in this respect. However, if the leaders of the state and political society are antidemocratic, the democratic opposition in civil society will not normally receive substantial or effective support from a national Orthodox Church.

Let me illustrate these points by discussing the Greek case. Greece, and the Greek part of divided Cyprus, are the only Orthodox majority countries which, for the last five consecutive years, have met all the criteria for a democracy discussed earlier in this essay. Greece from 1967 to 1974 was under

93. For Max Weber's discussion of caesaropapism, see his *Economy and Society*, ed. Gunther Roth and Claus Wittich (Berkeley: University of California Press, 1978), ii. 1159–63, quotation from p. 1161.

94. Weber discusses two contrasting ideal types of route toward religious salvation. One such route he calls "world rejecting." In such a route "concentration upon the actual pursuit of salvation may entail formal withdrawal from the world.... One with such an attitude may regard any participation in these affairs as an acceptance of the world, leading to alienation from God." The other route he calls "inner worldly." In this route "the concentration of human behavior on activities leading to salvation may require participation within the world (or more precisely: within the institutions of the world but in opposition to them).... In this case the world is presented to the religious virtuoso as his responsibility. He may have the obligation to transform the world" (ibid. i. 542). For Weber, the Russian Orthodox monastic traditions inclined more toward the world rejecting route. Massive repression by totalitarian atheistic states under the influence of Stalin also contributed, no doubt, to the selection of quietism in much of Orthodox Europe in recent history. With less state repression, and also probably less state financial support, I expect somewhat less quietism in Orthodoxy's future.

95. Orthodoxy of course is not completely univocal in terms of actions. Empirically, the Orthodox tradition allows for individual protests by religious leaders and their followers. The "Old Believers" in tsarist Russia were a source of some dissent.

authoritarian military rule. What was the role of the Orthodox Church *vis-à-vis* the military dictatorship and the democratic transition? Three points are worth highlighting. First, there were two military juntas, one established in 1967 and one established in November 1973. Within months of the start of both juntas, the juntas had managed to arrange the appointment of a new archbishop to head the Greek Orthodox Church.[96] This would have been impossible in Poland. Second, no past or new scholarly work on the 1967–75 Greek dictatorship accords any significant formal or informal role to Orthodox church resistance to the dictatorship.[97] Third, once democracy was instituted in 1974, except for efforts to preserve some minor church prerogatives, the Orthodox Church did nothing significant to oppose, resist, or stall the eventual consolidation of democracy and has been broadly supportive of the democratic government. Indeed, the Greek Orthodox Church has been much less critical of left-wing democratic governments in Greece than the Polish Catholic Church has been of left-wing democratic governments in Poland.

Greece has an established church. But as we have seen, so does Iceland, Denmark, Finland, Norway, England, and, until 1995, Sweden. From this comparative institutional perspective of long-standing democracies, the democratic task in Greece after 1974 did not require the disestablishment of the church, but the elimination of any nondemocratic domains of church power that restricted democratic politics. The Greek democrats have done this and the Greek Orthodox Church has accepted this. Note, not only does democracy not require a disestablished church, democracy requires, consistent with our thoughts about an unfettered civil society, and the right of believers to express themselves individually and collectively in political society, that no constraints are put on the rights of Orthodox members to argue their case in the public arena. Greek democracies have respected this area of legitimate autonomy of religion. There have been some changes both within state–society relations, and within the Orthodox Church, that has made the "twin tolerations" easier to sustain in the post-1975 world. The constitution crafted in 1975, and ratified in a referendum, is somewhat clearer than the previous Greek constitutions about democratically appropriate areas for state action *vis-à-vis* religion, and for the established church's action *vis-à-vis* other religions and the elected government.[98] Also, within the Orthodox Church, there is growing sentiment that the

96. For details, see Charles A. Frazee, "The Orthodox Church of Greece: The Last Fifteen Years," in John T. A. Koumoulides (ed.), *Hellenic Perspectives: Essays in the History of Greece* (Lanham, Md.: University Press of America, 1980), 145–80.

97. In Dec. 1997 I participated in an international conference in Athens which analyzed the dictatorship thirty years after its inauguration. No scholar I talked to said that new evidence of church resistance has appeared. On democratization and traditional cultural values such as the "quietism" of Orthodoxy, see Nikiforos Diamandouros, *Cultural Dualism and Political Change in Post-Authoritarian Greece*, Instituto Juan March, Madrid, Working Paper 1994/50, esp. pp. 10–12 and the exhaustive n. 14 on pp. 58–9.

98. See A. Baskedis, "Between Partnership and Separation: Relations between Church and State in Greece under the Constitution of 9 June 1975," *Ecumenical Review* (1977), 52–61.

church would be religiously more robust, and more able to play an independent role in civil society, if it were less dependent on the state.[99]

The most important change in the role of the church in Greek politics is that from 1946 to 1949 Greece experienced a civil war and the church opted for an anticommunist exclusionary state for much of the 1946–74 period, not caring whether this state respected democratic procedures or not.[100] Militarily, the Greek civil war ended in 1949; politically, it ended with the creation of a democratic government in 1974; and culturally, it ended with the 1989 coalition between the communists and the conservative New Democracy Party. With the cultural end of the civil war the political salience of the recognized Greek orthodox Church diminished even more, and the "twin tolerations" became more socially embedded in the Greek polis, and in church–state relations.

Conclusion

This essay has touched upon only one of the most contentious issues of our time and has been restricted to Western Christianity, Confucianism, Islam, and Orthodox Christianity. However, today there is not one of the world's major religions that is not internally and externally involved in multivocal struggles over the twin tolerations and the twin intolerations. For Hinduism in India, and Judaism in Israel, religion–state conflicts are now especially politically salient. India and Israel, in the first two decades of their new independence after World War II, were under the political and ideological hegemony of secular political leaders and parties—Mapai in Israel under David Ben-Gurion, and the Congress Party in India under Jawaharlal Nehru. By the 1990s both of these political traditions were challenged by opposition movements which drew some of their support from forces that wanted to redraw the boundaries of the twin tolerations to give a greater place for more fundamentalist, more intolerant visions of the polis.

In Israel the state was originally a nationalist state for the Jewish people, but there are growing demands for it to be a religious as well as a nationalist state.[101]

99. For a spirited analysis of how Orthodoxy is, contra Huntington, consistent with democracy and capable of politically significant internal change, see Elizabeth H. Prodromov, "Paradigms, Power, and Identity: Rediscovering Orthodoxy and Regionalizing Europe," *European Journal of Political Research* 30 (Sept. 1996), 125–54. Also see Sabrina P. Ramet, *Nihil Obstat: Religion, Politics, and Social Changes in East-Central Europe and Russia* (Durham, NC: Duke University Press, 1998).

100. For a historical analysis of the role of the Greek military which contains interesting insights about church–military relations, see Thanos Veremis, *The Military in Greek Politics: From Independence to Democracy* (London: Hurst, 1997).

101. Charles S. Liebman, director of the Argov Center for the Study of the Jewish People at Bar-Ilan University, asserts that "Israeli Judaism [has] undergone a transformation that makes it appear less, rather than more, compatible with the precondition for a

There are also demands to make citizenship for the Arab minority less inclusive, and even to amend the Law of Return so as to give Orthodox rabbis the authority to determine "whom the state of Israel recognizes as a Jew."[102]

In India the Hindu neofundamentalist party the BJP and their associated shock troops in (un)civil society such as the RSS have formed the government with numerous regional parties after the 1998 and 1999 geneal elections. The militant factions of the RSS want eventually to utilize the majority status of Hindus to make India a state that would privilege Hindu values as they inter-pret them.

A major force against the BJP and the RSS is the Gandhian–Nehruvian strand of Hinduism that insists that not only Hinduism, but India, are multivocal, and that the deepest values of Hinduism must respect, and even nurture, the idea of India not as a nation-state of Hindus, but as a diverse, tolerant, civilizational state. Gandhi and Nehru knew that, since India was *de facto* multicultural, multireligious, and multicommunity, "nation-state building" and "democracy building" were conflicting logics.

India is seventeen times poorer than any OECD democracy. The support for democracy in India under such difficult conditions can not be understood without an appreciation of the tremendous power that Gandhi developed by using some traditional Hindu religious values, and styles of action such as satyagraha, in his peaceful struggles for independence, for democracy, for anti-untouchability, and for respect for Muslims. For Gandhi, satyagraha meant "truth force," a form of nonviolent resistance which seeks "the vindica-tion of truth not by infliction of suffering on the opponent but on oneself."[103] For Gandhi, satyagraha was a means to awaken the best in the opponent. Gandhi's goals were to generate widespread recognition of the justice of the cause.[104]

---

stable democratic society." One of the reasons he cites for this change was the growing role in the 1980s and 1990s of neofundamentalist religious parties in the making or breaking of minority governments, either Labor or Likud. Given this context Liebman argues there was a "growing deference of the nonreligious population to the religious elites' definition of Judaism, the Jewish tradition and the Jewish religion." He argues this has implications for the inclusiveness of Israeli democracy because on the basis of virtually all the Israeli public opinion surveys he has studied, even if he controls for education and ethnicity: "The religious Jew is more likely to habor prejudice and less likely to respect the political rights of Arabs [than the nonreligious Jews]." See Charles S. Liebman, "Religion and Democracy in Israel," in Ehud Sprinzak and Larry Diamond (eds.), *Israeli Democracy under Stress* (Boulder, Colo.: Lynne Rienner, 1993), 273–92, quo-tations from pp. 277–8 and 291. In the same volume, see also the Introduction by the editors, pp. 1–20, and the article by Yaron Ezrahi, "Democratic Politics and Culture in Modern Israel: Recent Trends," 255–72.

102. Liebman, "Religion and Democracy in Israel," 284–5.

103. See Suzanne Hoeber Rudolph, "The New Courage: An Essay on Gandhi's Psycho-logy," *World Politics* (Oct. 1963), 98–117, quotation from p. 114.

104. For Gandhi's mobilization of satyagraha and other religious symbols for modern democratic purposes, see Lloyd I. Rudolph and Susanne Hoeber Rudolph, *The Modernity of Tradition: Political Development in India* (Chicago: University of Chicago Press, 1967). For

If India, with its 600 million non-Hindi speakers, with its fourteen languages (each spoken by at least 10 million people), and with its "minority" population of about 120 Muslims, is to remain a democracy, the BJP and the RSS voices of India as a Hindu and Hindi nation-state must be met by an ever stronger Gandhian voice of India as a multireligious, civilizational home to a billion people.[105]

A more complete study of the themes raised by this brief essay would not only discuss religions I have omitted, but would analyze, in much greater detail than I have done, the strange career of the emergence of the twin tolerations in the West. The establishment of state sponsored churches in Scandinavia and Britain, while initially a form of political control of the church, eventually led not only to the twin tolerations, but in the long run also to the "sociologically spontaneous secularization" of the vast part of its citizens. Why?

Liberal scholars might also want to reexamine how illiberal many of the liberal anticlerical movements at times were in France and Spain. What was the political effect of this liberalism from above? In Spain in the early 1930s did liberal and socialist anticlericalism justify the tearing down of walls separating civil cemeteries from Jewish cemeteries? If the 1905 French liberal model of expropriating Jesuit property had been followed in the United States, Georgetown University, and many other Jesuit universities, would have been expropriated. Would this have contributed to the strengthening of a liberal, or an antiliberal, discourse in the United States?

Another important area for further research is the role of the state in generating religious toleration. Scholars, especially sociologists of religion, have focused great attention on society led movements toward tolerance, but at some critical moments state led policies, such as those structured by Emperor Ferdinand I at the Peace of Augsburg of 1555, were crucial for ending society led religious conflicts. Likewise, it was the Ottoman state that crafted the millet system with its extraordinary tolerance for the religious self-government of minority national religious communities. There are many more examples of state led tolerance, as well as state led intolerance, that we need to study.

Finally, even the Western world's most solid construction of a wall separating church and state, the US constitution's First Amendment, which states that the "Congress shall make no law respecting an establishment of religion, or prohibiting the free exercise thereof," is misunderstood by many contemporary US citizens. The amendment did not prohibit the thirteen original states from having *their own established* religions. The First Amendment only prohibited

Gandhi's overall philosophy of conflict, see Joan Bordurant, *The Conquest of Violence: Gandhi's Philosophy of Conflict* (Princeton: Princeton University Press, 1958).

105. For a critical analysis of the BJP and the RSS, see Tapan Bosu *et al.*, *Khaki Shorts and Saffron Flags: A Critique of the Hindu Right* (New Delhi: Orient Longman, 1993). For a discussion of the new crisis of Indian secularism in the post-Nehruvian world and the rise of Hindu fundamentalism that contributed to the 1992 demolition of the Babri Mosque, see Stanley J. Tambiah, "The Crisis of Secularism in India," and Amartya Sen, "Secularism and its Discontents," both in Bhargava (ed.), *Secularism and its Critics*, 418–53, 454–85.

the Congress from establishing one official religion for the United States as a *whole*. In fact, on the eve of the revolution only three of the thirteen colonies—Rhode Island, Pennsylvania, and Delaware—had no provision for an established church. Even after the revolution the South Carolina constitution of 1778 established the "Christian Protestant Religion." Four New England states continued for some time with state subsidized, largely Congregational, churches.[106] The eventual political construction of the West's strongest separation of church and state, and the social emergence of one of the West's most churchgoing, and recently most fundamentalist, populations, is another of the "crooked paths" of toleration and intoleration that needs more study and reflection.

106. For the history of the establishment of churches in America and for debates over the First Amendment, see A. J. Reichley, *Religion in American Public Life* (Washington, DC: Brookings Institution, 1985), 53–167.

III

The Metaframeworks of Democratic Governance and Democratic States

TWELVE

Constitutional Frameworks and Democratic Consolidation: Parliamentarianism versus Presidentialism

with Cindy Skach

Introduction

The struggle to consolidate the new democracies—especially those in Eastern Europe, Latin America, and Asia—has given rise to a wide-ranging debate about the hard choices concerning economic restructuring, economic institutions, and economic markets.[1] A similar debate has focused on democratic *political* institutions and *political* markets. This literature has produced provocative hypotheses about the effects of institutions on democracy. It forms part of the "new institutionalism" literature in comparative politics

---

1. See, e.g., Stephan Haggard and Robert R. Kaufman, eds., *The Politics of Economic Adjustment* (Princeton: Princeton University Press, 1992); Adam Przeworski, *Democracy and the Market: Political and Economic Reforms in Eastern Europe and Latin America* (Cambridge: Cambridge University Press, 1991); and Christopher Clague and Gordon C. Rausser, eds., *The Emergence of Market Economies in Eastern Europe* (Cambridge: Blackwell Press, 1992).

This chapter was first published in *World Politics*, 46 (Oct. 1993), 1–22.
This article grew out of an exchange at a December 1990 meeting in Budapest of the East–South System. Transformations Project, which brought together specialists on Eastern Europe, Southern Europe, and South America. When we were discussing topics for future research and dividing up our collective work, Adam Przeworski lamented that although there were assertions in the literature about the probable impact of different types of institutional arrangements on democratic consolidation, there were no systematic data available. In his notes about the Budapest meeting, Przeworski reiterated that "we seem to know surprisingly little about the effects of the particular institutional arrangements for their effectiveness and their durability. Indeed, the very question whether institutions matter is wide open." See Przeworski, "Notes after the Budapest Meeting" (Chicago: University of Chicago, January 11, 1991), 10. We acknowledge the careful reading and/or comments of Adam Przeworski, Jack Snyder, Douglas Rae, Juan Linz, Michael Alvarez, Martin Gargiulo, Lisa Anderson, Anthony Marx, Gregory Gause, Joel Hellman, and Scott Mainwaring. The normal caveats apply.

that holds as a premise that "political democracy depends not only on economic and social conditions but also on the design of political institutions."[2]

One fundamental political-institutional question that has only recently received serious scholarly attention concerns the impact of different constitutional frameworks on democratic consolidation.[3] Although the topic has been increasingly debated and discussed, little systematic cross-regional evidence has been brought to bear on it. This is unfortunate, because constitutions are essentially "institutional frameworks" that in functioning democracies provide the basic decision rules and incentive systems concerning government formation, the conditions under which governments can continue to rule, and the conditions by which they can be terminated democratically. More than simply one of the many dimensions of a democratic system,[4] constitutions

2. James G. March and Johan P. Olsen, "The New Institutionalism: Organizational Factors in Political Life," *American Political Science Review* 78 (September 1984), 738. For a pioneering early work exemplifying this approach, see Maurice Duverger, *Political Parties* (New York: Wiley, 1954). Other important works that explore the causal relationship between institutions such as electoral systems and political parties, and democratic stability include Giovanni Sartori, *Parties and Party Systems: A Framework for Analysis* (Cambridge: Cambridge University Press, 1976); Douglas Rae, *The Political Consequences of Electoral Laws* (New Haven: Yale University Press, 1967); William H. Riker, *The Theory of Political Coalitions* (New Haven: Yale University Press, 1962); Bernard Grofman and Arend Lijphart, eds., *Electoral Laws and Their Political Consequences* (New York: Agathon, 1986); Rein Taagepera and Matthew Soberg Shugart, *Seats and Votes* (New Haven: Yale University Press, 1989); and Matthew Soberg Shugart and John Carey, *Presidents and Assemblies* (Cambridge: Cambridge University Press, 1992). An important work in the neo-institutionalist literature that focuses on legislatures and structure-induced equilibrium is Kenneth Shepsle, "Institutional Equilibrium and Equilibrium Institutions," in Herbert F. Weisberg, ed., *Political Science: The Science of Politics* (New York: Agathon, 1986). See also Mathew D. McCubbins and Terry Sullivan, eds., *Congress: Structure and Policy* (Cambridge: Cambridge University Press, 1987).

3. There is a growing literature on this question. Much of it is brought together in Juan J. Linz and Arturo Valenzuela, eds., *Presidentialism and Parliamentarianism: Does It Make a Difference?* (Baltimore: Johns Hopkins University Press, forthcoming). However, no article in this valuable collection attempts to gather systematic global quantitative data to address directly the question raised in the title of the book and by Przeworski. Linz first appeared in print on this subject in a brief "Excursus on Presidential and Parliamentary Democracy," in Linz and Alfred Stepan, eds., *The Breakdown of Democratic Regimes* (Baltimore: Johns Hopkins University Press, 1978). His much-cited seminal "underground" paper with the same title as his forthcoming book was first presented at the workshop on "Political Parties in the Southern Cone," Woodrow Wilson International Center, Washington, D.C., 1984; see also idem, "The Perils of Presidentialism," *Journal of Democracy* 1 (Winter 1990). See also Scott Mainwaring, "Presidentialism, Multiparty Systems, and Democracy: The Difficult Equation," *Kellogg Institute Working Paper*, no. 144 (Notre Dame, Ind.: University of Notre Dame, September 1990).

4. We agree with Philippe C. Schmitter's argument that there are many types of democracies and that "consolidation includes a mix of institutions." See Schmitter, "The Consolidation of Democracy and the Choice of Institutions," *East–South System Transformations Working Paper*, no. 7 (Chicago: Department of Political Science, University of Chicago, September 1991), 7. See also Schmitter and Terry Karl, "What Democracy Is . . . and Is Not," *Journal of Democracy* (Summer 1991). The authors list eleven important dimensions that provide a matrix of potential combinations by which political systems can be differently democratic.

create much of the overall system of incentives and organizations within which the other institutions and dimensions found in the many types of democracy are structured and processed.

Study shows that the range of existing constitutional frameworks in the world's long-standing democracies is narrower than one would think.[5] With one exception (Switzerland), every existing democracy today is either presidential (as in the United States), parliamentary (as in most of Western Europe), or a semipresidential hybrid of the two (as in France and Portugal, where there is a directly elected president and a prime minister who must have a majority in the legislature).[6] In this essay we pay particular attention to contrasting what we call "pure parliamentarianism" with "pure presidentialism."[7] Each type has only two fundamental characteristics, and for our purposes of classification these characteristics are necessary and sufficient.

A pure parliamentary regime in a democracy is a system of mutual dependence:

1. The chief executive power must be supported by a majority in the legislature and can fall if it receives a vote of no confidence.
2. The executive power (normally in conjunction with the head of state) has the capacity to dissolve the legislature and call for elections.

5. We realize that any effort to operationalize the concept of "democracy" so that it can be used for purposes of classification of all the countries of the world is inherently difficult. Fortunately there have been two independently designed efforts that attempt this task. One, by Michael Coppedge and Wolfgang Reinicke, attempted to operationalize the eight "institutional guarantees" that Robert Dahl argued were required for a polyarchy. The authors assigned values to 137 countries on a polyarchy scale, based on their assessment of political conditions as of mid-1985. The results are available in Coppedge and Reinicke, "A Measure of Polyarchy" (Paper presented at the Conference on Measuring Democracy, Hoover Institution, Stanford University, May 27–8, 1988); and in idem, "A Scale of Polyarchy," in Raymond D. Gastil, ed., *Freedom in the World: Political Rights and Civil Liberties, 1987–1988* (New York: Freedom House, 1990), 101–28. Robert A. Dahl's seminal discussion of the institutional guarantees needed for polyarchy is found in his *Polyarchy: Participation and Opposition* (New Haven: Yale University Press, 1971), 1–16.
The other effort to operationalize a scale of democracy is the annual Freedom House evaluation of virtually all the countries of the world. The advisory panel in recent years has included such scholars as Seymour Martin Lipset, Giovanni Sartori, and Lucian W. Pye. The value assigned for each year 1973 to 1987 can be found in the above-cited Gastil, 54–65. In this essay, we will call a country a "continuous democracy" if it has received no higher than a scale score of 3 on the Coppedge–Reinicke Polyarchy Scale for 1985 and no higher than a 2.5 averaged score of the ratings for "political rights" and "civil liberties" on the Gastil Democracy Scale, for the 1980–9 period.
6. On the defining characteristics of semipresidentialism, see the seminal article by Maurice Duverger, "A New Political System Model: Semi-Presidential Government," *European Journal of Political Research* 8 (June 1980). See also idem, *Echec au Roi* (Paris: Albin Michel, 1978); and idem, *Le monarchie républicaine* (Paris: R. Laffont, 1974).
7. For a discussion of the semipresidential constitutional framework, its inherent problem of "executive dualism," and the exceptional circumstances that allowed France to manage these problems, see Alfred Stepan and Ezra N. Suleiman, "The French Fifth Republic: A Model for Import? Reflections on Poland and Brazil," in H. E. Chehabi and Alfred Stepan, eds., *Politics, Society and Democracy: Comparative Studies* (Boulder, Colo.: Westview Press, forthcoming), Chapter 13 in this volume.

A pure presidential regime in a democracy is a system of mutual independence:

1. The legislative power has a fixed electoral mandate that is its own source of legitimacy.
2. The chief executive power has a fixed electoral mandate that is its own source of legitimacy.

These necessary and sufficient characteristics are more than classificatory. They are also the constraining conditions within which the vast majority of aspiring democracies must somehow attempt simultaneously to produce major socio-economic changes and to strengthen democratic institutions.[8]

Pure parliamentarianism, as defined here, had been the norm in the democratic world following World War II.[9] However, so far, in the 1980s and 1990s, all the new aspirant democracies in Latin America and Asia (Korea and the Philippines) have chosen pure presidentialism. And to date, of the approximately twenty-five countries that now constitute Eastern Europe and the former Soviet Union, only three—Hungary, the new Czech Republic, and Slovakia—have chosen pure parliamentarianism.[10]

We question the wisdom of this virtual dismissal of the pure parliamentary model by most new democracies and believe that the hasty embrace of presidential models should be reconsidered. In this article we bring evidence in support of the theoretical argument that parliamentary democracies tend to increase the degrees of freedom that facilitate the momentous tasks of economic and social restructuring facing new democracies as they simultaneously attempt to consolidate their democratic institutions.

It is not our purpose in this article to weigh the benefits and the drawbacks of parliamentarianism and presidentialism. Our intention is to report and analyze numerous different sources of data, all of which point in the direction of a much stronger correlation between democratic consolidation and pure parliamentarianism than between democratic consolidation and pure presidential-

8. Alfred Stepan will develop this argument in greater detail in a book he is writing entitled *Democratic Capacities/Democratic Institutions*.

9. For example, in Arend Lijphart's list of the twenty-one continuous democracies of the world since World War II, seventeen were pure parliamentary democracies, two were mixed, one was semipresidential, and only one, the United States, was pure presidential. See Lijphart, *Democracies: Patterns of Majoritarian and Consensus Government in Twenty-one Countries* (New Haven: Yale University Press, 1984), 38.

10. The norm is a directly elected president with very strong *de jure* and *de facto* prerogatives coexisting with a prime minister who needs the support of parliament. As of this writing (April 1993), only Hungary and the newly created Czech Republic and Slovakia had opted for the pure parliamentary constitutional framework. Despite having directly elected presidents, Slovenia, Estonia, and Bulgaria have strong parliamentary features. In Slovakia and Estonia presidents will now be selected by parliament. Bulgaria, however, has moved from an indirectly to a directly elected president. For political, legal, and sociological analyses of constitution making in East European transitions, see the quarterly publication *East European Constitutional Review*, which is part of the Center for the Study of Constitutionalism in Eastern Europe at the University of Chicago. The center was established in 1990 in partnership with the Central European University.

ism. We believe our findings are sufficiently strong to warrant long-range studies that test the probabilistic propositions we indicate.[11]

Constitutional Frameworks: Constructing Relevant Data

We were able to construct a data set about party systems and consolidated democracies. Since we are interested in the lessons about party systems in long-standing consolidated democracies, we include the countries of the Organization of Economic Cooperation and Development (OECD). There were forty-three consolidated democracies in the world between 1979 and 1989.[12] Excluding the "mixed cases" of Switzerland and Finland, there were thirty-four parliamentary democracies, two semipresidential democracies, and only five pure presidential democracies.[13] We used the powerful yet relatively simple formula devised by Markku Laakso and Rein Taagepera to measure the "effective" number of political parties in the legislatures of these forty-one political systems.[14] Of the thirty-four parliamentary democracies, eleven had

11. Duration analysis would be particularly appropriate because it estimates the *conditional* probability of an event taking place (for example, of a democracy "dying," by undergoing military coup), given that the regime has survived for a given period of time as a democracy. This conditional probability is in turn parameterized as a function of exogenous explanatory variables (such as constitutional frameworks). The sign of an estimated coefficient then indicates the direction of the effect of the explanatory variable on the conditional probability of a democracy dying at a given time. Such models allow us to estimate whether democracies exhibit positive or negative "duration dependence": specifically, whether the probability of a democracy dying increases or decreases, respectively, with increases in the duration of the spell. Mike Alvarez, a Ph.D. candidate in political science at the University of Chicago, is creating the data and the appropriate statistical techniques and then implementing this duration analysis as part of his dissertation. Adam Przeworski, too, has embarked on such research. See also Nicholas M. Kiefer, "Economic Duration Data and Hazard Functions," *Journal of Economic Literature* 26 (June 1988).

12. We consider a country to be a "consolidated democracy" if it has received no higher than a scale score of 3 on the Coppedge–Reinicke Polyarchy Scale for 1985 *and* no higher than a 2.5 average of the ratings for "political rights" and "civil liberties" on the Gastil Democracy Scale. Countries that met these joint criteria for every year of the 1979–89 decade are considered "continuous consolidated democracies." See n. 18 herein.

13. Duverger calls Finland semipresidential because the president has significant *de jure* and *de facto* powers; it should be pointed out, however, that from 1925 to 1988 the Finnish president was not so much directly elected as indirectly chosen by party blocs. The candidates normally did not campaign in the country, and though parties put the names of their candidates on the ballot, the electoral college votes were not pledges and often entailed deliberations and multiple balloting, leading Shugart and Carey to conclude that the presidential election system in Finland from 1925 to 1988, "given its party-centered character... was not much different from election in parliament." See Shugart and Carey (n. 2), 212–21, 226–8, quote at 221. We consider Finland to have been a "mixed" constitutional system until 1988.

14. Laakso and Taagepera, " 'Effective' Number of Parties: A Measure with Application to West Europe," *Comparative Political Studies* 12 (April 1979). The formula takes into

between three and seven effective political parties.[15] Both of the semipresidential democracies in this universe had between three and four effective political parties. However, no pure presidential democracy had more than 2.6 effective political parties. These data indicate that consolidated parliamentary and semipresidential democracies can be associated with a large number of parties in their legislatures, whereas consolidated presidential democracies are not associated with the type of multiparty coalitional behavior that facilitates democratic rule in contexts of numerous socioeconomic, ideological, and ethnic cleavages and of numerous parties in the legislature. The currently empty column in Table 12.1 of long-standing presidential democracies with "3.0 or more" effective legislative parties is probably one of the reasons why there are so few continuous presidential democracies.

The Finnish political scientist Tatu Vanhanen published an important study of democratic durability that incorporates the nuances in individual countries' socioeconomic structures. Hence, it provides another data set for testing our hypothesis regarding constitutional frameworks.[16]

Vanhanen constructed a political Index of Democratization (ID) based on (1) the total percentage of the vote received by all parties except the largest vote getter and (2) the total percentage of the population that votes. He has also constructed a socioeconomic Index of Power Resources (IPR) based on six variables: (1) degree of decentralization of nonagricultural economic resources, (2) percentage of total agricultural land owned as family farms, and percentage of population (3) in universities, (4) in cities, (5) that is literate, and (6) that is not employed in agriculture. His major hypothesis is that all countries above his threshold level of 6.5 on his Index of Power Resources "should be democracies," and all countries below his minimum level, 3.5 index points, "should be non-democracies or semi-democracies." He has constructed his indexes for 147 countries for 1980 and 1988.

account each party's relative size in the legislature, as measured by the percentage of seats it holds. The "effective" number of parties is "the number of hypothetical equal-size parties that would have the same total effect on fractionalization of the system as have the actual parties of unequal size." The formula for calculating the effective number of parties (N) is

$$N = \frac{1}{\sum_{i=1}^{n} pi2}$$

where pi = the percentage of total seats held in the legislature by the i-th party.

For each country listed in Table 12.1, we determined the number of seats held in the lower or only house of the legislature at the time of each legislative election between 1979 and 1989. Then, the effective number of political parties (N) was calculated for each of these election years and multiplied by the number of years until the next legislative election.

15. Austria, Ireland, and Iceland have directly elected presidents, but we do not classify them as semipresidential; we concur with Duverger that they are not *de facto* semipresidential since "political practice is parliamentary." See Duverger (n. 6, 1980), 167.

16. See Vanhanen, *The Process of Democratization: A Comparative Study of 147 States, 1980–1988* (New York: Crane Russak, 1990).

TABLE 12.1. A Laakso–Taagepera Index of effective political parties in the legislatures of continuous democracies, 1979–1989[a]

Parliamentary		Semipresidential		Presidential	
3.0 or more parties	Fewer than 3.0 parties	3.0 or more parties	Fewer than 3.0 parties	3.0 or more parties	Fewer than 3.0 parties
	Kiribati[b]				
	Nauru[b]				
	Tuvalu[b]				
	Botswana 1.3				
	St. Vincent 1.4				
	Dominica 1.5				
	Jamaica 1.5				
	Bahamas 1.6				
	Trindidad and Tobago 1.6				
	Barbados 1.7				
	St. Lucia 1.7				USA 1.9
	New Zealand 2.0				
	Canada 2.0				
	UK 2.1				Colombia 2.1
	India 2.1				
	Greece 2.2				Dominican Republic 2.3
	Austria 2.4[c]				
	Australia 2.5				Costa Rica 2.3
	Solomon Islands 2.5				
	Mauritius 2.5				Venezuela 2.6
	Spain 2.7				
	Ireland 2.7[c]				
	Japan 2.9				
West Germany 3.2					
Norway 3.2		France 3.2			
Sweden 3.4					
Luxembourg 3.4					
Israel 3.6		Portugal 3.6			
Netherlands 3.8					
Italy 3.9					
Papua New Guinea 4.0					
Iceland 4.3[c]					
Denmark 5.2					
Belgium 7.0					

Source: See nn. 12, 14 for explanation of the Laakso–Taagepera Index formula, criteria for inclusion into this universe of continuous democracies, and data used to construct this table.

[a] Switzerland and Finland are "mixed" systems with 5.4 and 5.1 "effective" political parties, respectively. See n. 13 for why we classify Finland, until 1988, as a mixed rather than semipresidential regime.

[b] Traditionally in Kiribati, all candidates for the unicameral legislature—the Maneaba—have fought as independents. In 1985 various Maneaba members that were dissatisfied with government policies formed a Christian Democrat opposition grouping. The government grouping then "is generally known as the National Party, although it does not constitute a formal political party." It is more accurate to refer to Kiribati's "parties" as "pro" and "anti" assembly groupings, of which there are a total of two. See J. Denis and Ian Derbyshire, *Political Systems of the World* (Edinburgh: W. and R. Chambers, 1989), 724. This is also true in Tuvalu, where there are no formal political parties, and in Nauru, where there are loosely structured pro-and antigovernment groupings. See Arthur Banks, *Political Handbook of the World* (Binghamton: State University of New York, csa, 1989), 422, 627.

[c] See n. 15 for why Duverger (and we) classify Austria, Ireland, and Iceland as parliamentary rather than presidential regimes.

His hypothesis was broadly confirmed in that 73.6 percent of the countries that were above 6.5 in his IPR qualified as democracies as measured by his Index of Democracy. In his regression analysis with these indexes, Vanhanen found the correlation (r2) between the ID and IPR equal to .707 in 1980 and .709 in 1988. Approximately 76 percent of the 147 country cases tested by Vanhanen had small residuals and deviated from the regression line by less than one standard error of estimate.

However, thirty-six countries in 1980 and thirty-four in 1988 had negative or positive residuals larger than one standard error of estimate. These seventy large-residual cases indicate that about 24 percent of the variance in Vanhanen's regression analysis is unexplained. Vanhanen noted that "large positive residuals indicate that the level of democratization is considerably higher than expected on the basis of the average relationship between ID and IPR [we will call these cases 'democratic overachievers'], and large negative residuals indicate that it is lower than expected [we will call these 'democratic underachievers']." He then asks "how to explain these deviations that contradict my hypothesis? I have not found any general explanation for them."[17]

Vanhanen's unexplained variance—his democratic over-and under-achievers—constitutes a data set with which to test our hypothesis regarding constitutional frameworks. Of the total seventy deviating cases in his 1980 and 1988 studies, fifty-nine occurred in constitutional frameworks we have called "pure parliamentary" or "pure presidential" (thirty-seven and twenty-two cases, respectively). When we analyze democratic underachievers in Vanhanen's set, we find that presidential systems had a democratic underachiever rate 3.4 times greater than did the parliamentary systems. Further, parliamentary systems in Vanhanen's set were 1.8 times more likely than presidential systems to be democratic overachievers. (See Table 12.2.)

Another set of data concerns both comparative capacity to be democratic survivors and vulnerability to military coups. Since we are concerned primarily

TABLE 12.2. Significant "over-" and "under-" democratic achievers:[a] comparison of pure parliamentary and pure presidential systems

	Total countries	Democratic underachievers	Democratic overachievers
Pure parliamentary	37	6 (16.2%)	31 (83.8%)
Pure presidential	22	12 (54.6%)	10 (45.5%)

[a] Based on residuals in Vanhanen's regression analysis with his Index of Power Resources and his Democratic Index for 1980 and 1988.

Source: Vanhanen (n. 16), 75–9, 94–7, presents data for his Index of Democratization and his Index of Power Resources. We determined whether the systems were parliamentary, presidential, or "other" using the references contained in Table 12.5 "Other" includes semipresidential, one-party, and ruling monarchy.

17. Ibid., 84.

with countries that are making some effort to construct democracies, we restrict our analysis to those countries in the world that qualified in the Gastil
Political Rights Scale as democracies for at least one year between 1973 and
1989. Only 77 of the 168 countries in the world met this test. In an attempt to
control for economic development as an intervening variable that might independently influence political stability, we eliminate from this section of our
analysis the twenty-four OECD countries. This leaves a data set of the fifty-three
non-OECD countries that experimented with democracy for at least one year
between 1973 and 1989. Of these, twenty-eight countries were pure
parliamentary, twenty-five were pure presidential, and surprisingly none were
either semipresidential or mixed. Only five of the twenty-five presidential
democracies (20 percent) were democratic for any ten consecutive years in
the 1973–89 period; but seventeen of the twenty-eight pure parliamentary
regimes (61 percent) were democratic for a consecutive ten-year span in the
same period. Parliamentary democracies had a rate of survival more than three
times higher than that of presidential democracies. Pure presidential democracies were also more than twice as likely as pure parliamentary democracies to
experience a military coup. (See Tables 12.3 and 12.4.)

Another source of relevant data concerns the set of countries, ninety-three in
all, that became independent between 1945 and 1979.[18] During the ten-year
period between 1980 and 1989 only fifteen of the ninety-three merit possible

TABLE 12.3.   Universe of the fifty-three non-OECD countries that were
democratic for at least one year between 1973 and 1989 and all the
countries from this set continuously democratic for any ten consecutive
years in this period

	Regime type during democracy		
	Pure parliamentary	Pure presidential	Semipresidential or mixed
Total non-OECD countries democratic for at least one year during 1973–89	28	25	0
Number of countries from above set continuously democratic for ten consecutive years in this period	17	5	0
Democratic survival rate	61%	20%	n.a.

Source: Criteria for inclusion in this universe of countries is based on the Gastil Democracy Scale
and the Coppedge–Reinicke Polyarchy Scale (see n. 5).

18. We use the date of independence since it was usually within one year of independence that new constitutions were drafted and approved in these countries. We exclude
from our analysis those countries that became independent after 1979 because we want
to see which of these countries were then continuously democratic for the ten-year
period 1980–9. This gives us a sample of time between World War II and 1979.

TABLE 12.4.   Percentage of the fifty-three non-OECD countries that were democratic for at least one year in 1973–1989 and experienced a military coup while a democracy[a]

	Regime type at time of coup		
	Pure parliamentary	Pure presidential	Semipresidential or mixed
Total non-OECD countries democratic for at least one year during 1973–89	28	25	0
Number of countries from above set having experienced a military coup while a democracy	5	10	0
Military coup susceptibility rate	18%	40%	n.a.

[a] We define a military coup as an unconstitutional removal of the executive by or with the aid of active-duty members of the domestic armed forces.

Source: Data for incidence of military coups is found in Arthur Banks, *Political Handbook of the World* (Binghamton: State University of New York, csa Publishers, 1989); and Peter J. Taylor, *World Government* (Oxford: Oxford University Press, 1990). For regime type at time of coup, see sources cited in Table 12.5.

classification as continuous democracies. Since we are interested in evolution toward and consolidation of democracy, we examine the regime form that these countries chose at independence. Forty-one countries functioned as parliamentary systems in their first year of independence, thirty-six functioned as presidential systems, three functioned as semipresidential systems, and thirteen functioned as ruling monarchies. At this stage of our research, we are impressed by the fact that no matter what their initial constitutional form, not one of the fifty-two countries in the nonparliamentary categories evolved into a continuous democracy for the 1980–9 sample period, whereas fifteen of the forty-one systems (36 percent) that actually functioned as parliamentary systems in their first year of independence not only evolved into continuous democracies but were the only countries in the entire set to do so. (See Table 12.5.)

If the data in Table 12.5 were strictly numerical observations, the chances of this distribution occurring randomly would be less than one in one thousand. But we realize that the quantification of this qualitative data masks important realities, such as the fact that the classes catch some countries that were always ademocratic or even antidemocratic. We do not rule out the hypothesis that the more democratic countries chose parliamentary systems at independence. Also, the fact that many of the "democratic survivors" are island states and that all but two (Papua New Guinea and Nauru) are former British colonies should be taken into account.[19] We can control for the British colonial legacy,

19. Myron Weiner observes that "most of the smaller, newly independent democracies...are also former British colonies" and puts forth the hypothesis that "tutelary

however, by isolating the fifty former British colonies from our original set of ninety-three. Of the thirty-four from this subset that began independence as parliamentary systems, thirteen (38 percent) evolved into continuous democracies for the 1980–9 period. Of the five former British colonies that began as presidential systems, not one evolved into a democracy for the 1980–9 period.[20] Similarly, not one of the eleven former British colonies that began independence as ruling monarchies evolved into a continuous democracy for 1980–9. This suggests that factors other than British colonial heritage are related to the democratic evolution and durability in these countries. Moreover, the fifteen democratic survivors in our set survived despite challenges such as tribal riots, linguistic conflicts, economic depressions, and/or mutinies. They therefore constitute a set of countries for which the constitutional form may be crucial in explaining democratic durability.

The comparative tendency for different constitutional frameworks to produce legislative majorities can also be ascertained. This is relevant to our central question because majorities help to implement policy programs democratically. Examining evidence from our set of the non-OECD countries that were democratic for at least one year from 1973 to 1987, we note that in presidential democracies the executive's party enjoyed a legislative majority less than half of the time (48 percent of the democratic years). Parliamentary democracies, in sharp contrast, had majorities at least 83 percent of the time. (See Table 12.6.)

A final set of data concerns the duration and reappointment of cabinet ministers in presidential versus parliamentary frameworks. These data relate to the issue of continuity in governance. Some minimal degree of ministerial continuity and/or prior ministerial experience would seem to be helpful in enhancing the political capacity of the government of the day to negotiate with state bureaucracies and with national and transnational corporations. Using a number of recent studies, we have examined all ministerial appointments during the years of democratic rule in Western Europe, the United States, and Latin America between 1950 and 1980. Two major findings emerge. First, the "return ratio" of ministers (that is, the percentage who serve more than once in their careers) is almost three times higher in parliamentary democracies than in

democracy under British colonialism appears to be a significant determinant of democracy in the Third World." See Weiner, "Empirical Democratic Theory," in Myron Weiner and Ergun Özbudun, eds., *Competitive Elections in Developing Countries* (Durham, N.C.: Duke University Press, 1987), esp. 18–23, quote at 19. This question is also addressed by Jorge Domínguez, "The Caribbean Question: Why Has Liberal Democracy (Surprisingly) Flourished?" in Domínguez, ed., *Democracy in the Caribbean: Political, Economic, and Social Perspectives* (Baltimore: Johns Hopkins University Press, 1993). Domínguez discusses how these Caribbean democracies have faced (and survived) severe economic crises. He attributes their democratic stability to the legacy of British institutions (including, but not limited to, the Westminster parliamentary model) and the prodemocratic disposition of the countries' leadership.

20. The five former British colonies that chose presidential systems within one year of independence were Zambia, Cyprus, Malawi, Seychelles, and South Yemen.

TABLE 12.5.   Regime type of the ninety-three countries of the world that became independent between 1945 and 1979 and all the continuous democracies from this set in 1980–1989

Parliamentary $N = 41$	Presidential $N = 36$	Semipresidential $N = 3$	Ruling monarchy $N = 13$
Bahamas	Algeria	Lebanon	Bahrain
Bangladesh	Angola	Senegal	Burundi
Barbados	Benin	Zaire	Cambodia
Botswana	B. Faso		Jordan
Burma	Cameroon		Kuwait
Chad	Cape Verde[b]		Lesotho
Dominica	CAR		Libya
Fiji	Cyprus		Maldives
Gambia	Comoros		Morocco
Ghana[a]	Congo		Oman
Grenada	Djibouti		Qatar
Guyana[a]	Eq. Guinea		Tonga
India	Gabon		UAE
Indonesia	Guinea		
Israel	Guinea Bissau		
Jamaica	Ivory Coast		
Kenya	Korea (S)		
Kiribati	Korea (N)		
Laos	Madagascar		
Malaysia	Malawi		
Malta	Mali		
Mauritius	Mauritania		
Nauru	Mozambique		
Nigeria	Niger		
Pakistan	Philippines		
Papua New Guinea	Rwanda		
St. Lucia	Sao Tomé		
St. Vincent	Seychelles		
Sierra Leone	Syria		
Singapore	Togo		
Solomon Islands	Taiwan		
Somalia	Tunisia		
Sri Lanka[a]	Vietnam (N)		
Sudan	Vietnam (S)		
Suriname	Yemen (S)		
Swaziland	Zambia		
Tanzania			
Trinidad and Tobogo			
Tuvalu			
Uganda			
W. Samoa			

Continuous democracies 1980–1989

$N = 15/41$	$N = 0/36$	$N = 0/3$	$N = 0/13$

Bahamas
Barbados
Botswana
Dominica

India
Israel
Jamaica
Kiribati
Nauru
Papua New Guinea
St. Lucia
St. Vincent
Solomon islands
Trinidad and Tobago
Tuvalu

---

[a] Sri Lanka was certainly and Ghana and Guyana appear to have been parliamentary democracies upon independence in 1948, 1957, and 1966, respectively. In 1960 Ghana changed to a presidential system, and in 1966 it experienced a military coup. The changes to a strong semipresidential system in Sri Lanka (1978) and a presidential system in Guyana (1980) were followed by increased restrictions on political rights and civil liberties. The last years that Sri Lanka and Guyana were classified as democracies on the Gastil Democracy Scale were 1982 and 1973, respectively. Ghana was classified as a democracy on this scale only in 1981–2.

[b] Although Cape Verde became independent in 1975, its first constitution was not promulgated until 1980. For the first five years of independence, Cape Verde appears to have functioned as a presidential system.

Sources: See n. 5 herein for definitions, the Coppedge–Reinicke Polyarchy Scale, and the Gastil Democracy Scale, upon which the table is based. Data for determining regime type at independence are found in Arthur Banks, *Political Handbook of the World* (Binghamton: State University of New York, csa, 1989); Albert P. Blaustein and Gisbert H. Flanz, eds., *Constitutions of the Countries of the World*, vols. 1–19 (Dobbs Ferry, N.Y.: Oceana Publications, 1990); *Keesing's Contemporary Archives; Europa World Yearbook*; Peter J. Taylor, ed., *World Government* (Oxford: Oxford University Press, 1990); Ian Gorvin, ed., *Elections since 1945* (Chicago and London: St. James Press, 1989); and the country studies of the *Area Handbook Series* (Washington, D.C.: Federal Research Division, U.S. Library of Congress, various years).

Results of a Pearson's chi-squared test with this data allow us to reject the null hypothesis that the above distribution is random. The chances of observing this distribution randomly are less than one in one thousand.

---

presidential democracies. Second, the average duration of a minister in any one appointment is almost twice as long in parliamentary democracies as it is in presidential democracies. Even when only those countries with more than twenty-five years of uninterrupted democracy are included in the sample, the findings still hold.[21] The conclusion is inescapable: ministers in presidential democracies have far less experience than their counterparts in parliamentary democracies.

21. See Jean Blondel, *Government Ministers in the Contemporary World* (Beverly Hills, Calif.: Sage, 1985), esp. appendix II, 277–81; Mattei Dogan, *Pathways to Power: Selecting Rulers in Pluralist Democracies* (Boulder, Colo.: Westview Press, 1989); Waldino C. Suárez: "Argentina: Political Transition and Institutional Weakness in Comparative Perspective," in Enrique A. Baloyra, ed., *Comparing New Democracies: Transition and Consolidation in Mediterranean Europe and the Southern Cone* (Boulder, Colo.: Westview Press, 1987); idem, "El gabinete en América Latina: Organización y cambio," *Contribuciones*, no. 1 (January–March 1985); and idem, "El Poder ejecutivo en América Latina: Su capacidad operativa bajo regímenes presidencialistas de gobierno," *Revista de Estudios Políticos*, no. 29 (September–October 1982).

TABLE 12.6.   Total years of presidential and parliamentary democracy of non-OECD countries (1973–87) and total years in which the executives party had a legislative majority

	Total years of democracy[2]	Total democratic years in which executive had a legislative majority	Percentage of democratic years in which executive had a legislative majority[b]
Parliamentary years	208	173	83
Presidential years	122	58	48

[a] Includes all non-OECD countries that qualified as democracies for at least one year during the 1973–87 period, according to the Gastil Polyarchy Scale ten-year evaluation (n. 5). Countries that became independent after 1979 are excluded.

[b] We consider an executive to have had a legislative majority each year in which his or her party held at least 50% of the legislative seats in the country's lower house for parliamentary frameworks and in both houses for presidential frameworks. Coalitional majorities formed after the elections for legislative seats in the parliamentary frameworks are not included here. Therefore, the percentage of parliamentary years in which prime ministers actually governed with legislative majorities is likely to be higher than 83%. The norm in Western Europe, for example, is the coalition, not single-party, legislative majority. See Kaare Strom, *Minority Government and Majority Rule* (Cambridge: Cambridge University Press, 1990).

Source: Data concerning legislative seats and the executives' party affiliations were found in *Keesing's Contemporary Archives*; Ian Govin, *Elections since 1945: A Worldwide Reference Compendium* (Chicago: St. James Press, 1989); Thomas T. Mackie and Richard Rose, *The International Almanac of Electoral History* (London: Macmillan, 1991); *Chronicle of Parliamentary Elections and Developments* (Geneva: International Centre for Parliamentary Documentation, 1973–89).

The Contrasting Logics of Pure Parliamentarianism and Pure Presidentialism

Let us step back from the data for a brief note about the type of statements that can be made about political institutions and democratic consolidation. The status of statements about the impact of institutions is not causally determinative (A causes B) but probabilistic (A tends to be associated with B). For example, Maurice Duverger's well-known observation about electoral systems is a probabilistic proposition: it holds that systems with single-member districts and where a simple plurality wins the seat tend to produce two-party systems, whereas electoral systems with multimember districts and proportional representation tend to produce multiparty systems.[22] The fact that Austria and Canada are exceptions to his proposition is less important than the fact that nineteen of the twenty-one cases of uninterrupted democracy in postwar industrialized countries conform to his proposition.[23]

22. See Duverger (n. 2).
23. For a discussion of Duverger's proposition in the context of modern industrialized democracies, see Arend Lijphart, *Democracies: Patterns of Majoritarian and Consensus Government in Twenty-one Countries* (New Haven: Yale University Press, 1984), 156–9.

A probabilistic proposition in politics is more than a statistical assertion. It entails the identification and explanation of the specific political processes that tend to produce the probabilistic results. And to establish even greater confidence in the proposition, one should examine case studies to explain whether and how the important hypothesized institutional characteristics actually came into play in individual cases.[24]

Whatever the constitutional framework, consolidating democracy outside of the industrialized core of the world is difficult and perilous. The quantitative evidence we have brought to bear on presidentialism and parliamentarianism would assume greater theoretical and political significance if a strong case could be made that the empirically evident propensities we have documented are the logical, indeed the predictable, result of the constitutional frameworks themselves. We believe that such a case can be made.

The essence of pure parliamentarianism is mutual dependence. From this defining condition a series of incentives and decision rules for creating and maintaining single-party or coalitional majorities, minimizing legislative impasses, inhibiting the executive from flouting the constitution, and discouraging political society's support for military coups predictably flows. The essence of pure presidentialism is mutual independence. From this defining (and confining) condition a series of incentives and decision rules for encouraging the emergence of minority governments, discouraging the formation of durable coalitions, maximizing legislative impasses, motivating executives to flout the constitution, and stimulating political society to call periodically for military coups predictably flows. Presidents and legislatures are directly elected and have their own fixed mandates. This mutual independence creates the possibility of a political impasse between the chief executive and the legislative body for which there is no constitutionally available impasse-breaking device.

Here, then, is a paradox. Many new democracies select presidentialism because they believe it to be a strong form of executive government. Yet our data show that between 1973 and 1987 presidential democracies enjoyed legislative majorities less than half of the time. With this relatively low percentage of "supported time" and the fixed mandates of the presidential framework, executives and legislatures in these countries were "stuck" with one another, and executives were condemned to serve out their terms. How often did these executives find it necessary to govern by decree-law—at the edge of constitutionalism—in order to implement the economic restructuring and austerity plans they considered necessary for their development projects?

---

24. There is a growing literature of case studies examining the influence of constitutional frameworks on stability and/or breakdown in developing countries. See, e.g., David M. Lipset, "Papua New Guinea: The Melanesian Ethic and the Spirit of Capitalism, 1975–1986," in Larry Diamond, Juan J. Linz, and Seymour Martin Lipset, eds., *Democracy in Developing Countries: Asia* (Boulder, Colo: Lynne Rienner, 1989), esp. 413. Lipset discusses how the constitutional framework came into play to prevent regime breakdown in Papua New Guinea. See also Dominguez (n. 19).

Our evidence shows that, in contrast to presidentialism, the executive's party in parliamentary democracies enjoyed a majority of seats in the legislature over 83 percent of the time period under study. For the remaining 17 percent of the years, parliamentary executives, motivated by the necessity to survive votes of confidence, formed coalition governments and party alliances in order to attract necessary support. When they were unable to do this, the absence of fixed mandates and the safety devices of the parliamentary institutional framework allowed for calling rapid new elections, the constitutional removal of unpopular, unsupported governments through the vote of no confidence, or simply the withdrawal from the government of a vital coalition partner.

Parliamentarianism entails mutual dependence. The prime minister and his or her government cannot survive without at least the passive support of a legislative majority. The inherent mechanisms of parliamentarianism involved in the mutual dependency relationship—the executive's right to dissolve parliament and the legislature's right to pass a vote of no confidence—are deadlock-breaking devices. These decision rules do not assure that any particular government will be efficient in formulating policies; nor do they assure government stability. But the decision mechanisms available in the parliamentary framework do provide constitutional means for removing deadlocked or inefficient governments (executives and parliaments). The danger that a government without a majority will rule by decree is sharply curtailed by the decision rule that allows the parliamentary majority (or the prime minister's coalition allies or even his or her own party) to call for government reformation.

Why is it logical and predictable that military coups are much more likely in pure presidential constitutional frameworks than in pure parliamentary frameworks? Because, as we discussed above, parliamentary democracies have two decision rules that help resolve crises of the government before they become crises of the regime. First, a government cannot form unless it has acquired at least a "supported minority" in the legislature; second, a government that is perceived to have lost the confidence of the legislature can be voted out of office by the simple political vote of no confidence (or in Germany and Spain by a positive legislative vote for an alternative government). Presidentialism, in sharp contrast, systematically contributes to impasses and democratic breakdown. Because the president and the legislature have separate and fixed mandates, and because presidents more than half of the time find themselves frustrated in the exercise of their power due to their lack of a legislative majority, presidents may often be tempted to bypass the legislature and rule by decree-law. It is extremely difficult to remove even a president who has virtually no consensual support in the country or who is acting unconstitutionally; it usually requires a political–legal–criminal trial (impeachment), whose successful execution requires exceptional majorities.[25] Thus, even when the

25. Schmitter and Karl (n. 4) quite correctly build into their definition of democracy the concept of accountability. But with the exception of the U.S. where a president can be directly relected only once, no president in any other long-standing democracy in the

socioeconomic crises are identical in two countries, the country with the presidential system is more likely to find itself in a crisis of governance and will find it more difficult to solve the crisis before it becomes a regime crisis.[26] Such situations often cause both the president and the opposition to seek military involvement to resolve the crisis in their favor.

Guillermo O'Donnell documented a phenomenon observed in the new Latin American democracies in his extremely interesting (and alarming) article on "delegative democracy," a conceptual opposite of representative democracy.[27] Key characteristics of delegative democracy include (1) presidents who present themselves as being "above" parties, (2) institutions such as congress and the judiciary that are viewed as "a nuisance," with accountability to them considered an unnecessary impediment, (3) a president and his staff who are the alpha and omega of politics, and (4) a president who insulates himself from most existing political institutions and organized interactions and becomes the sole person responsible for "his" policies. We suggest that these characteristics of O'Donnell's delegative democracy are some of the predictable pathologies produced by the multiple logics of the presidential framework. Consider the following: Presidential democracy, due to the logic of its framework, always produces (1) presidents who are directly elected and (2) presidents with fixed terms. Presidential democracy often produces (1) presidents who feel they have a personal mandate and (2) presidents who do not have legislative majorities. Thus, the logic of presidentialism has a strong tendency to produce (1) presidents who adopt a discourse that attacks a key part of political society (the legislature and parties) and (2) presidents who increasingly attempt to rely upon a "state-people" political style and discourse that marginalizes organized groups in political society and civil society. Delegative democracy can no doubt exist in the other constitutional frameworks; however, the multiple logics of pure parliamentarianism seem to work against delegative democracy.

Why are there many enduring multiparty parliamentary democracies but no long-standing presidential ones? In a parliamentary system, the junior political parties that participate in the ruling coalition are institutional members of the government and are often able to negotiate not only the ministers they will receive, but who will be appointed to them. All members of the coalition have an incentive to cooperate if they do not want the government of the day to fall. In these circumstances, democracies with four, five, or six political parties in the legislature can function quite well.

world, once in office, can be held politically accountable by a vote of the citizens' representatives. The accountability mechanism is so extreme and difficult—with the political-legal-criminal trial that needs exceptional majorities (impeachment)—that the accountability principle in presidentialism is weaker than in parliamentarianism.

26. For theoretical differentiation between crises of government and crises of regime, see Juan J. Linz and Alfred Stepan, eds., *The Breakdown of Democratic Regimes* (Baltimore: Johns Hopkins University Press, 1978), esp. 74.

27. See O'Donnell, "Democracia Delegativa?" *Novas Estudos* CEBRAP, no. 31 (October 1991).

There are far fewer incentives for coalitional cooperation in presidentialism. The office of the presidency is nondivisible. The president may select members of the political parties other than his own to serve in the cabinet, but they are selected as individuals, not as members of an enduring and disciplined coalition. Thus, if the president's party (as in President Collor's party in Brazil) has less than 10 percent of the seats in the legislature, he rules with a permanent minority and with weak coalitional incentives. On a vote-by-vote basis, the president may cajole or buy a majority, but repeated purchases of majorities are absolutely inconsistent with the principled austerity plans of restructuring that face most East European and Latin American democracies.

East European or Latin American political leaders who believe that their countries, for historical reasons, are inevitably multiparty in political representation are playing against great odds if they select a presidential system, as the existing evidence demonstrates. Brazil's high party fragmentation, for example, has contributed to a presidential-legislative deadlock that has frozen the lawmaking process in an already fragile democracy. Party fragmentation, the lack of party discipline, and general party underdevelopment in Brazil have been exacerbated by its electoral system, which combines proportional representation with an open list. The 1990 elections yielded 8.5 effective parties in the Brazilian Chamber of Deputies and 6.0 in the Senate.[28] These numbers seem alarmingly high considering that all the long-standing, pure presidential democracies reported in Table 1 had fewer than 2.6 effective political parties.

Moreover, the closer a country approaches the ideal types of "sultanship," "totalitarianism," or early "posttotalitarianism," the "flatter" are their civil and political societies.[29] In these circumstances, adopting the constitutional framework of presidentialism in the period of transition from sultanship, totalitarianism, or early posttotalitarianism reduces the degrees of freedom for an emerging civil and political society to make a midcourse correction, because heads of government have been elected for fixed terms (as in Georgia). In contrast, the Bulgarian transition had significant parliamentary features, which allowed an emerging political society to change the prime minister (and the indirectly elected president) so as to accommodate new demands.

In Poland, where constitutional reformers are flirting with the idea of strengthening the role of the president, party fragmentation is even greater than in Brazil; the effective number of parties in the Polish Sejm after the 1991 legislative elections was 10.8.[30] Most of these parties in the Polish legislature, like those in Brazil, lack clear programs and exist as mere labels for politicians to

28. These numbers were calculated using the Laakso–Taagepera formula and the data reported in *Keesings Record of World Events* (1990); and Arthur S. Banks, ed., *Political Handbook of the World* (Binghamton: csa Publishers, State University of New York, 1991).

29. This argument is developed in Juan J. Linz and Alfred Stepan, "Problems of Democratic Transition and Consolidation: Eastern Europe, Southern Europe and South America" (Book manuscript), pt. 1.

30. This is developed in Stepan and Suleiman (n. 7).

use for election into office.[31] Our data suggest that Poland would be playing against the odds were it to move toward a purely presidential system.

Also flowing from the logic of the constitutional framework are the questions of why ministers serve short terms in presidential democracies and why they are rarely reappointed in their lifetime. Because presidents do not normally enjoy majorities in the legislature, they resort to rapid ministerial rotation as a device in their perpetual search for support on key issues. In parliamentary systems, by contrast, coalitional majorities make such rapid turnover unnecessary. Furthermore, key ministers usually have long and strong associations with their political parties and are often reappointed as government coalitions form and re-form during the life of their careers. In presidential democracies, ministers are strongly associated with a particular president, leave office when the president does, and normally never serve as a minister again in their life.

Conclusion

Let us consider the question that follows from the data. Why does pure parliamentarianism seem to present a more supportive evolutionary framework for consolidating democracy than pure presidentialism? We believe we are now in a position to say that the explanation of why parliamentarianism is a more supportive constitutional framework lies in the following theoretically predictable and empirically observable tendencies: its greater propensity for governments to have majorities to implement their programs; its greater ability to rule in a multiparty setting; its lower propensity for executives to rule at the edge of the constitution and its greater facility at removing a chief executive who does so; its lower susceptibility to military coup; and its greater tendency to provide long party-government careers, which add loyalty and experience to political society.

The analytically separable propensities of parliamentarianism interact to form a mutually supporting system. This system, qua system, increases the degrees of freedom politicians have as they attempt to consolidate democracy. The analytically separable propensities of presidentialism also form a highly interactive system, but they work to impede democratic consolidation.

31. For a discussion of how both the political culture and the institutional structure in Brazil contributed to the country's weak party system, see Scott Mainwaring, "Dilemmas of Multiparty Presidential Democracy: The Case of Brazil," *Kellogg Institute Working Paper* no. 174 (Notre Dame, Ind.: University of Notre Dame, 1992). See also idem, "Politicians, Parties, and Electoral Systems: Brazil in Comparative Perspective," *Comparative Politics* 24 (October 1991); and his forthcoming book on Brazilian political parties.

THIRTEEN

The French Fifth Republic: A Model for Import? Reflections on Poland and Brazil

with Ezra N. Suleiman

Do institutional imports work? Under what conditions do they succeed or fail? Why did the British model of parliamentary government succeed in India, but not in Ghana or Uganda?

These are critical questions, in part because they have enormous practical significance for numerous countries seeking to adopt workable constitutional arrangements, and in part because if we believe that institutions influence or even determine political outcomes, then it becomes incumbent upon us to assess the extent or limits of this influence.

In this article we confine our attention to the possible adoption in Eastern Europe and Latin America of the French semipresidential model. This is not simply a hypothetical case. Many countries in Eastern Europe and Latin America have long been attracted to the success of the semipresidential political system in France because it appears to have succeeded in combining executive authority, parliamentary, government and political stability. Juan Linz maintains that both presidential and semi-presidential systems are highly risk-prone, because they have a built-in potential for clashes between executive and legislative powers, both of which are endowed with legitimacy founded on elections.[1] However, France's semipresidential model appears to have avoided the clash of rival legitimacies while creating a strong executive. For this reason

---

1. See Juan J. Linz, "Presidential or Parliamentary Democracy: Does it Make a Difference?" in Juan J. Linz and Arturo Valenzuela, eds., *The Failure of Presidential Regimes* (Baltimore: Johns Hopkins University Press, forthcoming). Part 2 of this work (thirty-five pages in typescript) is devoted to his reservations about semiparliamentarianism or what he prefers to call a "dual executive." His most extensive empirical discussion is directed to the dual executive in the Weimar Republic. Linz introduces the non-German reading audience to the work he considers the great classic on the problems of semipresidentialism: Werner Kaltefleiter, *Die Funktionen des Staatsoberhauptes in der Parlamentarischen Demokratie* (Cologne: Westdeutscher Verlag, 1970).

This chapter was first published in H. E. Chehabi and Alfred Stepan (eds.), *Politics, Society, and Democracy* (Boulder: Westview Press, 1995), 393–414.

and, to be frank, because of its association with General de Gaulle, the French Fifth Republic has immense appeal in Eastern Europe and in a number of Latin American countries, particularly Chile and Brazil.

This article has three parts. We first examine France to see exactly what the key constitutional features actually are and how and why semipresidentialism has worked reasonably well there. We then explore Poland, which since December 1990 has been *de facto* semipresidential and has encountered grave difficulties with the system. We conclude with some reflections on what other countries such as Brazil should consider as they ponder the relative merits of semipresidential as opposed to parliamentary constitutional formulas.

Presidential Power in France's Fifth Republic

All constitutional arrangements are a reaction to a country's recent history. The Bonn constitution of 1949, reacting both to the Third Reich and to the Weimar Republic, was not overly concerned with creating a strong executive or with the representation of small, extremist, antisystem parties. In France the constitution of the Fifth Republic of 1958 was, above all, intent on avoiding the absence of strong political leadership that had paved the way for nondemocratic authoritarian leaders (Pétain in 1940) and that had failed in decolonization and Algeria. A second, equally important, consideration was to create democratic stability.

How was the combination of democracy, a strong executive, and political stability achieved? If the answer to this question had depended simply on certain provisions in the text of the constitution, the French might be credited with not simply spreading the idea of democracy but also showing how to institute it. Alas, this is not the case.

The question should be divided into two parts: (1) What are the main elements of the French presidential (or semiparliamentary) system? and (2) What is the basis of political stability? By separating for analytic purposes the text that grants powers to the executive from the conditions for political stability, we will avoid the common trap of imputing the latter only to the former.

The main elements of the presidential power within the French semipresidential system are the following:

1. *Popular Election.* The constitution of the Fifth Republic was approved in September 1958. But the political system as we know it came into being as a result of an amendment to the constitution: the referendum of October 26, 1962, that ratified the election of the president of the republic by universal suffrage. After 1965, the date of the first presidential elections in France, the political system was transformed.[2]

2. For a more detailed discussion of the constitutional and political power of the president in the Fifth Republic, see Ezra N. Suleiman, "Presidential Government in

2. *Dissolution of Assembly*. The power to dissolve parliament (Article 12) is a key aspect of presidential leadership in France. The threat of dissolution alone affects the political and policy process. It can be used to renew a president's legitimacy. And, finally, it suggests that the president is both head of state and head of the executive.

3. *Emergency Powers*. As the "guarantor of national independence" and of the integrity of the territory, the president can rule by emergency powers when a threat to national sovereignty and order exists. The power to suspend the constitution is the one that originally raised the greatest fears that the presidential system could lapse into authoritarianism, because Article 16 authorizes the president, without prior approval or any subsequent vote, and without time limits, to rule by emergency powers.

4. *Head of Government*. The president is not only chief of the armed forces, he appoints the prime minister, the ministers in the government ("on the proposal of the prime minister"), and he presides over the Council of Ministers. He directs the government and, through his "arbitration" (Article 5), he is responsible for "the regular functioning of the governmental authorities, as well as the continuity of the state" (Article 5).

5. *Referenda*. The president disposes of the authority to "submit to a referendum any bill dealing with the organization of the public authorities... that without being contrary to the constitution, might affect the functioning of the institutions" (Article 11).

The constitutional powers granted the president are considerable. Yet the relative success of the Fifth Republic has largely derived from the fact that these powers have been used in a very limited way. Article 16 has been invoked on only one occasion, in 1961, when a group of French Army generals rebelled in Algeria. Presidents of the Republic, since de Gaulle resigned following a defeat in a referendum on April 27, 1969, have scarcely used the referendum. Even the power to dissolve the National Assembly has been used with extreme caution: de Gaulle used it twice (1962 and 1968); neither Pompidou nor Giscard d'Estaing had recourse to it; Mitterrand dissolved parliament on two occasions (May 1981 and May 1988), the purpose being to assure himself on both occasions of a majority in the National Assembly.

The careful use of presidential power suggests that democratic stability in France depends more on the president acting as the head of government than on his assuming a posture that elevates him above the governmental and political fray. The use of extraordinary powers (even the calling of the referendum) is considered to be going beyond the bounds of the "normal" func-

France," in Richard Rose and Ezra N. Suleiman, eds., *Presidents and Prime Ministers* (Washington, D.C.: American Enterprise Institute for Policy Research, 1980), pp. 94–138. For an interpretation of the guiding principles of the 1958 constitution by its main author, see Michel Debré, "The Constitution of 1958: Its *Raison Dêtre* and How it Evolved," in William G. Andrews and Stanley Hoffmann, eds., *The Fifth Republic at Twenty* (New York: State University of New York Press, 1980), pp. 11–24.

tioning of institutions. That the dissolution of parliament has occurred only four times—and twice after presidential elections—suggests that even a prerogative that seeks a renewal of legitimacy has been used prudently.

What has Made the System in France Stable?

The political system of the Fifth Republic has not evolved in the manner that the founders of the regime had intended. Originally, the president was to be more like a "republican monarch in a parliamentary regime." The founders intended to put an end to what they saw as the excessively dominant role of parties. They sought a presidency that would be able to govern regardless of party and parliamentary divisions.

In reality, the stability of the Fifth Republic is due as much to the extraconstitutional developments that have accompanied the regime as to the constitutional changes. What has allowed for the stability of the regime?[3]

1. *Majority Parties.* Although a central aim of the founders of the Fifth Republic was to end the *régime des partis* that had characterized the Fourth Republic, the indisputable fact is that the Fifth Republic has owed its stability to the ability of one or another party to secure a majority of seats in the National Assembly. Even when the president's party lost its majority in 1986, the opposition party was able to obtain a majority and so was able to govern.

The swing in the pendulum from presidential to parliamentary forms of government has been made possible and will insure stability as long as the electorate continues to give rise to majority parties. Yet nowhere is it written in the constitution that the political system (whether presidential or parliamentary) depends for its stability on the existence of a party capable of securing a majority of seats in the National Assembly.[4]

2. *The Electoral System.* Electoral systems have generally been used as political weapons in France. The frequent changes in the electoral laws in the Fourth and Fifth Republics indicate that the party in power believes it can affect the outcome by the use of one electoral law as opposed to another.

The electoral system used during the years of the Fifth Republic (except for the 1986 parliamentary elections) has been one that has forced both a regrouping and a bipolar tendency among the political parties. The system in use has been the single-member constituency (winner-take-all) election, but has consisted of two rounds. To advance to the second round in the 1978, 1981, and

---

3. Extraconstitutional developments that have contributed to stability are explored more extensively in Ezra N. Suleiman, "French Presidentialism and Political Stability" in Juan J. Linz and Arturo Valenzuela, eds., *The Crisis of Presidential Regimes.*

4. See Pierre Avril, *Essais sur les partis* (Paris L.G.D.J., 1986); François Boralla, *Les partis politiques dans la France d'aujourd'hui* (Paris: Seuil, 1973); and J. L. Quermonne and C. Changnollaud, *Le Governement de la France sous la Ve République* (Paris: Dalloz, 1991).

1988 parliamentary elections, the electoral law stipulated as a norm that candidates had to have received the support of at least 12.5 per cent of the registered voters.[5] The regrouping and bipolarity occur as a result of the need to support a winning candidate in the second round. The behavior of parties is conditioned by the electoral system that encourages what has been called a *vocation majoritaire.*

3. *Special Governmental Powers to Pass Legislation.* The Fifth Republic has been able to preserve its stability even when the governing party has had a narrow majority. The government neither risks falling nor needs to cease trying to pass legislation when its allies threaten to vote against a bill. The government, lacking a majority, can either withdraw the bill or it can have resource to Article 49.3, which allows the passage of a bill without a vote. The bill is then adopted unless a motion of censure is called within twenty-four hours and then passes.

Article 49.3 has been considered undemocratic since it allows for the passage of legislation without a parliamentary majority on specific bills. On the other hand it does avoid ministerial instability and some have argued it "even constitutes the most incontestable advantage of the Fifth Republic." Article 49.3 gives governments the power to govern in the absence of a definite majority. It is frequently used. Between 1976 and 1987 governments utilized article 49.3 twenty-seven times.[6]

4. *New Formal and Informal Rules in the Legislature.* The legislature in the Third and Fourth Republics had powerful semiautonomous committees, great control over its own procedures, and could pass laws on virtually any subject. However, in the Fifth Republic, the combination of the Organic Law on Parliamentary Procedure, constitutional changes, and increased party discipline have resulted in an entirely new framework of legislative-executive relations.[7] The vote of censure is more difficult, committees have lost most of their blocking power, money bills can not be initiated, and the government has vastly increased control over the timetable and agenda of both houses of parliament. Party discipline is also greater because candidates must be endorsed by a party. The fact that France now *de facto* has the highest electoral threshold in Western Europe is a strong disincentive to rebellious legislators who might consider, as they frequently did in the Fourth Republic, leaving their party and running for office in a new microparty.

5. For an analysis of the Fifth Republic's electoral system, its impact on parties, and its contribution to producing majorities, see Frédéric Bon, *Les élections en France* (Paris: Seuil, 1978), esp. pp. 103–19. See also Nonna Mayer and Pascal Perrineau, *Les Comportements politiques* (Paris: Armand Colin, 1992).

6. Vincent Wright, *The Government and Politics of France* (New York: Homes and Meier, 1989), pp. 139–41.

7. See Ezra N. Suleiman, "Toward the Disciplining of Parties and Legislators: The French Parliamentarism in the Fifth Republic," in Ezra N. Suleiman, ed., *Parliaments and Parliamentarians in Democratic Polities* (New York: Holmes and Meier, 1986), pp. 79–105. Also see the chapter, "The French Parliament: Constitutional Constraints and Potential Power," in Vincent Wright's previously cited *The Government and Politics of France*, pp. 132–55.

Semipresidentialism as a Model

Let us now step away from the details of the French Fifth Republic to discuss semipresidentialism more generally. Maurice Duverger, in his pioneering analysis, labeled governments "semi-presidential" if they meet three conditions: the president is directly elected, the office of the president has significant *de jure* and *de facto* powers, and the prime minister has to enjoy the confidence of the directly elected parliament.[8] Only two of the thirty-seven countries that were continuous democracies during the 1980–9 decade met Duverger's definition— France and Portugal.[9] Austria, Iceland, and Ireland have directly elected presidents and prime ministers who are responsible to a directly elected parliament, but Duverger argues—and we concur—that they are not semipresidential because the president does not have significant *de jure* and *de facto* powers.[10] Duverger and others call Finland semipresidential because the president has significant *de jure* and *de facto* powers, but it should be pointed out that from 1925 to 1988 the Finnish president was not so much directly elected as indirectly chosen by party blocs. The presidential candidates normally did not campaign in the country, and though parties put the names of their candidates on the ballot, the electoral college votes were not pledged and often entailed deliberations and multiple balloting. Shugart and Carey conclude that the presidential election system in Finland from 1925–1988, "given its party-centered character . . . was not much different from election in parliament."[11]

In most countries that discuss the adoption of semipresidentialism the dominant assumption is that (unlike Ireland, Iceland, and Austria) the office of the presidency will have significant *de facto* and *de jure* powers. The assumption is also that (unlike Finland from 1925–1988) there will be a nationwide, intensely contested, direct election campaign for the presidency. These two assumptions make the possibility of constitutional conflict between two electorally legitimated executives the central problem.[12]

8. Maurice Duverger, *Echec au roi* (Paris: Albin Michel, 1978) and his "A New Political System Model: Semi-Presidential Government," in *European Journal of Political Research* 8 (1980): 165–87.
9. See Alfred Stepan and Cindy Skach, "Meta-Institutional Frameworks and Democratic Consolidation," Paper prepared for the Third Meeting of the East–South Transformations Project, January 4–7, 1992, Toledo.
10. "The constitutions of Austria, Ireland and Iceland are semi-presidential. Political practice is parliamentary." See Duverger, "A New Political System Model," p. 167.
11. For a discussion of presidential elections in Finland, see Matthew Soberg Shugart and John M. Carey, *Presidents and Assemblies: Constitutional Design and Electoral Dynamics* (Cambridge: Cambridge University Press, 1992), pp. 212–21 and pp. 226–8, quote from p. 21. On Finland's constitution, and the power relationships between the dual executive offices until 1988, see Jaakko Nousiainen, "Bureaucratic Tradition, Semi-Presidential Rule and Parliamentary Government: The Case of Finland," *European Journal of Political Research* 16, 2 (1988): 229–49.
12. For a comparative analysis of similarities and differences between the semipresidential system of France, Portugal, Ireland, Iceland, Finland, and Austria with an eye for possible import and modification in Latin America see the work by the Chilean

The main theoretical and political worry about semipresidentialism, of course, is precisely the question of deadlock and constitutional conflict between the dual executive. A deadlock can become particularly dangerous if the president has special authority over the security forces and some emergency powers. Theoretically we can posit only two positions whereby this potential for dual executive deadlock and conflict is minimized. If the president is the leader of a party or a party coalition and this coalition wins a clear majority in parliament, there should be no deadlock because the power relationship becomes one of clear constitutional presidential superiority. The only other possible steady state we can posit is one where the prime minister is a party leader, has a single or multiparty majority, and the system can operate in a parliamentary fashion, notwithstanding the president's special prerogatives in the area of defense, internal security, and foreign affairs.

Since the French Fifth Republic is often held up as the example to be emulated, it might be useful to stress again the underanalyzed conditions that have helped French semipresidentialism avoid the potential theoretical problems we believe are intrinsic to the semipresidential formula. As we have seen, for the first twenty-six years of French semipresidentialism the president was a party leader and he was able to lead a party or party coalition that commanded a clear majority in parliament. This yielded the constitutionally sanctioned primacy of the president. There were thus no deadlocks or constitutional conflicts between the prime minister and the president. From March 1986 to May 1988 the president did not control a majority. However, in this period the prime minister did control a majority. The system thus functioned as one where the prime minister was de facto the chief executive. During these twenty-six months, called "cohabitation," there was no deadlock or constitutional conflict.[13] After the 1988 presidential and legislative elections, the president's party and its allies were twenty-four seats short of a formal majority, but were able to rule with the support of the Communists and/or Gaullists, and the system shifted back to one where the president was dominant. The key point is that at no point in the first thirty-four years of French semipresidentialism has there been a time where neither the president nor the prime minister had a working majority. But the potential is there, and it will probably be actualized in the 1990s.

It bears emphasizing that stability is not guaranteed under the Fifth Republic. In its thirty-four year history, this regime has functioned under two forms: the presidential and parliamentary majorities coinciding (hence as a presidential

constitutional lawyer Humberto Nogueira Alcalá, *El régimen semipresidencial ?Una nueva forma de gobierno democrático?* (Santiago: Editorial Andante, 1986).

13. Although Giovanni Sartori correctly stresses that the president retained, and used, his special powers in foreign affairs and defense (he made a point of vetoing the first nomination for Defense Minister sent to him) and insisted on playing his prominant role in these affairs. See Giovanni Sartori, *Seconda Repubblica? Sì, Ma Bene* (Milano: Rizzoli, 1992), pp. 35–41.

system), and the presidential and parliamentary regimes diverging (hence as a parliamentary or cabinet government system).

At least two other scenarios can be envisaged. One involves the existence of a parliamentary majority; the other involves the inability of the electoral outcome to produce a parliamentary majority.

In the first case the parties in the parliamentary majority may refuse to "cohabit" with the president. Considering him to have become delegitimized by the results of the parliamentary elections, the new parliamentary majority may refuse to form a government before the president resigns. Unless the president is able to form a government that has a chance of being supported by the new parliament, a crisis of major propositions is at hand.

In the second case parliamentary elections fail to produce a legislative majority. What is likely to occur in the absence of a party obtaining a majority or in the event of the absence of a dominant party? What alternative exists to the coalition-type governments that characterized the Fourth Republic? In such an event, not an unlikely occurrence, the president would end up trying to form governments capable of governing (at least governing minimally, as coalition governments are wont to do), much as his Fourth Republic predecessor used to do. No constitutional crisis would be entailed; on the other hand political stability—the main argument in favor of the semipresidential system—is no longer assured.

In short, the Fifth Republic has far from exhausted the possibilities (hence probabilities) of how the regime might function at different periods. It has so far experienced only two orderly political systems that are alternates. But the alternation between presidential and parliamentary regimes is scarcely guaranteed, and hardly likely to occur in so orderly a manner the next time around.

Why has Semipresidentialism not Worked in Poland?

Since the direct election of Lech Walesa in December 1990 Poland has been functioning de facto as a semipresidential system. But, the results have been almost diametrically opposite to France. Why?[14]

14. Much of what follows on Poland is based on Alfred Stepan's interviews and observations in Poland, which will be extensively reported and documented in a book tentatively called "Democratic Capacities/Democratic Institutions," and in the chapter, "Poland: 'Authoritarian Communism,' 'Ethical Civil Society,' and 'Ambivalent Political Society'" in Juan J. Linz and Alfred Stepan, *Problems of Democratic Transition and Consolidation: Eastern Europe, Southern Europe, and South America* (Baltimore: Johns Hopkins University Press, forthcoming). Two excellent works that capture some of the specifically political problems of the Polish transition—problems in which semipresidentialism figures prominently—are Jadwiga Staniszkis, *The Dynamics of the Breakthrough in Eastern Europe: The Polish Experience* (Berkeley: University of California Press, 1991); and Jan T. Gross, "Poland: From Civil Society to Political Nation," in Ivo Banac, ed., *Eastern Europe in Revolution* (Ithaca: Cornell University Press, 1992), pp. 56–72.

1. *An Above-Parties President.* Lech Walesa was the only long-standing charismatic leader in Eastern Europe. He chose not to use his great influence and energy by running for a political office, creating a political party in the Sejm, or possibly becoming the first prime minister. Instead, Lech Walesa chose to stay outside of Poland's emerging political society and to remain a moral tribune of civil society. When he eventually did decide to run for an office, he ran as a nonparty candidate for the office of president. As a candidate he articulated the need to maintain the value not of institutionalization but of "spontaneity" and antiformal politics. When democratic consolidation required the authentication of parties and the routinized empowerment of parliament and prime minister, Lech Walesa campaigned as an interventionist president who would be "running around with an ax."[15]

2. *Minority Parties and Governments.* Let us turn now to the question of political parties and their legislative and government producing role. A consolidated democracy requires that a range of political parties not only *represent* interests but seek by coherent programs and organizational activity to aggregate interests. Poland held its first completely competitive elections to both houses of parliament in October 1991, twenty-six months after the formation of the first democratic government. One of the instruments of modern political society to help a few parliamentary parties aggregate interests is the electoral system. In Poland, however, it was decided after a bitter struggle to use proportional representation with no minimum threshold for political parties to have representatives in the nation's legislature.[16] A further factor that hindered aggregation was that Lech Walesa not only maintained his no-party stance but gave ambivalent signs to numerous political groupings that he looked upon them with some favor. For their part, the fragmenting ex-Solidarity groups, by maintaining their claim to be the heirs of the consensual mystique of Solidarity's era, did not articulate programmatic alternatives or seek to become interest-based mass parties.

In this context twenty-nine parties ended up being represented in the Sejm. No party received even 14 per cent of the vote. The four largest parties were strongly polarized and controlled less than 50 per cent of the seats. When we apply the standard Laakso–Taagepera weighted formula for constructing an index of effective political parties in parliament, Poland emerges with an index of 10.8 political parties. In contrast, the two semipresidential systems that combine directly elected presidents with substantial powers, France and Portugal, each have party indexes of 3.2 and 3.6 respectively. In fact, as Table 13.1 makes clear, Poland has substantially more parties than any democracy in the

15. Quoted in Gross, "Poland: From Civil Society to Nation," p. 63.
16. Lech Walesa, in order to encourage larger parties, advocated either a higher threshold or a first-past-the-post electoral system. The former Communists wanted PR because they were worried they would be eliminated with a first-past-the-post. Many of Walesa's former Solidarity allies voted against him to limit his power. See David McQuaid, "The 'War' Over the Election Law," *Report on Eastern Europe* 2, 3 (August 2, 1991): 11–28.

world with ten years' duration. Given these election results the first freely elected parliament of Poland's new democracy found it extremely difficult to form a government.[17] When the government was finally formed after a crisis of almost two months, it still had great difficulty creating a coalition for a program. In the first seven months there were three different prime ministers, none of whom commanded a stable coalitional majority. Relations between the prime minister and the directly elected president became dangerously conflictual, with charges and countercharges of nondemocratic intentions, and even actions.

Conflict and Deadlock between the Dual Executives

A few examples will illustrate the complexity and dangerousness of Poland's constitutional conflict. Soon after the first freely elected parliament met, it received an eight-page document from President Lech Walesa. The president proposed a "little constitution," which he hoped would be ratified quickly and eventually incorporated into the constitution that the parliament hoped to draft, approve, and submit to a referendum. In his "little constitution" Walesa proposed a package whereby the president's power over the prime minister would be increased. The president would have the explicit right to name the prime minister and the right to dismiss the prime minister and the cabinet at his own initiative. The parliament's countervailing right to dismiss a prime minister by a majority vote, on the other hand, would be subject to a presidential veto that could only be overridden by a two-thirds majority.[18]

The parliament was skeptical about the proposal and Walesa eventually withdrew it. However, in numerous forums he indicated he would use the presidential mandate to fight for his policy views. For example, he went to his original base at Gdansk and proclaimed, "I will make demands in the name of the masses who elected me. I am returning to the masses. I will not accept responsibility for what the government does, but I will be with you."[19] In April, after a series of conflicts with the prime minister over who had the right to appoint key officials in the Defense Ministry, Walesa went on national television to declare he would petition the Sejm "for greater rights for the

17. For the election results and the difficulty in forming a government, see David McQuaid, "The Parliamentary Elections: A Postmortem," *Report on Eastern Europe* (November 8, 1991): 15–21; and Louisa Vinton, "Impasse Reached on Talks on New Government," *Report on Eastern Europe* (November 29, 1992): 19–25.

18. Walesa's five-page proposal was contained in a December 3, 1991, letter to the president of the Sejm, Wieslaw Chrzanowski. A copy of the letter and the proposal are now available in the liberary of the Sejm. For some details of the letter see Louisa Vinton, "Five-Party Coalition Gains Strength, Walesa Proposes 'Little Constitution,'" *Report on Eastern Europe* (December 6, 1991): 7–8.

19. Cited in *RFE/RL Research Report* (January 17, 1992): 15.

TABLE 13.1. *A Laakso–Taagepera Index of "effective" political parties in the legislatures of the parliamentary, semipresidential, and presidential continuous democracies, 1979–1989*

Parliamentary		Semipresidential		Presidential	
3.0 or more parties	Fewer than 3.0 parties	3.0 or more parties	Fewer than 3.0 parties	3.0 or more parties	Fewer than 3.0 parties
	Kiribati[a]				USA 1.9
	Nauru[a]				Colombia 2.1
	Tuvalu[a]				Dominican Rep. 2.3
	Botswana 1.3				
	St. Vincent 1.4				
	Dominica 1.5				
	Jamaica 1.5				
	Bahamas 1.6				
	Trinidad & Tobago 1.6				
	Barbados 1.7				
	St. Lucia 1.7				
	New Zealand 2.0				
	Canada 2.0				
	UK 2.1				
	India 2.1				
	Greece 2.2				

Costa Rica 2.3

Venezuela 2.6

Austria 2.4
Australia 2.5
Solomons 2.5
Mauritius 2.5
Ireland 2.7
Spain 2.7
Japan 2.9

France 3.2

Portugal 3.6

West Germany 3.2
Norway 3.2
Sweden 3.4
Luxembourg 3.4
Israel 3.6
Netherlands 3.8
Italy 3.9
Papua New Guinea 4.0
Iceland 4.3
Denmark 5.2
Belgium 7.0

Poland 10.8[b]

Brazil 8.5[b]

[a] Given the absence of formal parties, there are less than two "political groupings." Switzerland and Finland are "mixed" systems with 5.4 and 5.1 effective parties, respectively.

[b] Poland and Brazil were not democracies in the 1979–89 time period. They are included merely to show how exceptionally high their "effective" number of political parties was when they became electoral democracies in 1991 and 1989, respectively.

Source: See Table 12.1.

president, whereby the prime minister would be subordinate to the president, just like the French system.... After the experience we have been through, we probably all agree that the only situation for Poland is an above-party government, a government we will form out of specialists."[20]

Two of his previously close supporters voiced worries about a breakdown of democracy initiated by actions from the Belvedere, the presidential palace. Jadwiga Staniszkis, who had worked for Walesa's election as president, wrote about the problem of combining presidential bonapartism and executive dualism: "Poland does not yet see the breakdown of democracy, but it may be on the brink of it.... There is mounting evidence of a coming executive coup (against the politicians)."[21] Jaroslaw Kaczyski, chairman of the Center Alliance, had been Walesa's presidential chief of staff. However, in answer to a reporter's question, "Does the Belvedere really constitute the worst threat to democracy?" he answered, "It is the political arrangement by which one of the power centers remains practically outside any control but itself controls all the others, which constitutes a threat. After all, by sending his draft constitution to the Sejm, the president showed his hand. He wanted all power for himself."[22]

In fact, President Walesa did not "control all" the other power centers and he did not attempt an executive coup. But at the very least these events indicate that Polish "semipresidentialism" contributed to great constitutional and intragovernment conflicts that were impeding, rather than helping, the consolidation of democracy.

From his part, the first prime minister selected by the democratically elected parliament, Jan Olszewski, waged a series of campaigns against the president. These included two acts of great constitutional ambiguity: the releasing, without prior discussion and evaluation, to the Sejm of a list of sixty-four supposed "collaborators" and the mobilization of the special police. For these acts the prime minister was voted out of office and a senate committee recommended a criminal investigation.[23]

Eroding Public Support for Democratic Institutions

At the height of the conflict between the president, the prime minister, and the Sejm in May 1992, Polish public opinion had a more disfavourable opinion towards these three key elected components of political society than they did toward any other major organization in Poland. Indeed there was a popular

20. Quoted in *FBIS-EEU*, April 30, 1992, p. 14.
21. See Jadwiga Staniszkis, "Continuity and Change in Post-Communist Europe," The Hague, Netherlands Institute of International Relations, June 1992, p. 27.
22. Interview in *East European Reporter* (March–April 1992): 51.
23. This paragraph is based on discussion of Stepan with members of the Sejm's Constitutional Commission, July 22–6, 1992, in Warsaw.

Polish saying to the effect that anyone who got caught in the "Bermuda Triangle" between the warring president, prime minister, and Sejm would be injured. In contrast, the three most popular institutions were the armed forces, police, and the Ombudsman, because they were seen as giving service to the citizens and were not involved in the "Bermuda Triangle" conflict. See Table 13.2.

The Polish Center for the Study of Public Opinion did not design any questions explicitly exploring antidemocratic sentiment in 1989–91. However, in the midst of the political crisis of May 1992, it conducted a poll concerning which, if any, emergency measures, ranging from the right of the government (or the president) to rule by decree to a ban on democracy, were acceptable (see Table 13.3). This is open to various interpretations. However, if one calls those who would approve of a "law of strong hand and ban on democracy" antidemocratic, 30 per cent of those polled were antidemocractic. If one calls those who answered "difficult to say" ambivalent democrats, we could say that 44 per cent of the Polish population in May 1992 expressed antidemocratic or ambivalent democratic opinions. However, when in late July 1992 a more consensual prime minister was appointed, and there were signs that the conflict within the "Bermuda Triangle" had diminished, the question was repeated again, and nondemocrats dropped from 30 per cent to 25 per cent. Also, since the most probable form of emergency government that could emerge in Poland would be one led by the president, it was significant that the polls revealed a growing percentage of Polish respondents who replied that they were more in favor of a rule whereby the prime minister responded to the parliament than to the president—that is to say, a standard parliamentary form of government.

By August 1992 a still divided Sejm selected Hanna Suchocka, Poland's third prime minister in four months. She argued that it was impossible to govern if the president and prime minister were at odds and thus supported a modified version of Walesa's "short constitution." She concluded that therefore the president's "constitutional rights" should be respected. She thus gave her

TABLE 13.2. Disapproval rate of major political institutions, February 1990, October 1991, May 1992 (%)

	February 1990	October 1991	May 1992
Lower chamber of legislature	14	54	60
Government and ministers	14	48	53
President	n.a.	43	52
Catholic Church	12	25	44
Local authorities	n.a.	33	33
Police	n.a.	21	21
Armed forces	15	10	12
Ombudsman	n.a.	9	10

Source: Centrum Bodania Opini Spolecznej (Center for the Study of Public Opinion, CBOS). Data and translation provided by the director, Lena Kolarska-Bobínska.

TABLE 13.3.   Support for a range of emergency measures in Poland, May 1–3, 1992 (%)

	Strongly approving	Rather approving	Rather disapproving	Strongly disapproving	Difficult to say
"Law of strong hand and ban on democracy"	11	19	19	37	14
"Government can rule by decree"	10	35	16	15	24
"President can rule by decree"	9	24	17	30	20
"Significant limitations on right to strike"	14	29	21	21	15
"Creation of new government with president as prime minister"	14	18	14	29	25
"Call for general strike"	7	20	21	41	11

Source: Centrum Bodania Spolecznej (Center for the Study of Public Opinion, CBOS).

support to the normalization of the special powers of the president, which had their origins in the round-table pact. The Sejm accepted her recommendation—without any of the special conditions that allowed semipresidentialism to work well in France—and Poland went a step further toward making "executive-dualism" a permanent part of Poland's fragile democracy. Due to party fragmentation, and dualistic deadlock, Poland's effort to advance toward a balanced budget and a mixed economy had stalled, and the most heroic transition in Eastern Europe faced severe political as well as economic problems.[24]

Final Reflections

The obvious lesson from France is that semipresidentialism without electoral reform, party changes, and special laws governing legislative functions would not have produced the efficacy and legitimacy that the French Fifth Republic achieved. The less obvious lesson is that, even with these changes, should the French electorate not continue to produce governments with majorities,

24. The *Economist Intelligence Unit* Country Report No. 3 (1992) for Poland reported that "though the real economy proved surprisingly resilient to the lack of political steer, key developments were seriously delayed. Perhaps most important here was the sheer immobility of the mass privatisation programme where nothing happened for a good six months, so further eroding Poland's credibility in the West," p. 6.

cabinet instability could well reappear and the dual executive problem could emerge. Comparative evidence demonstrates the difficulty of producing majorities: in 1992 only two countries in Western Europe, Portugal and United Kingdom have produced single-party majorities in two consecutive elections. The lesson of Poland is that if a country is considering adopting semipresidentialism in its strong French form—a directly elected president who comes to office after winning an intense campaign throughout the country and has substantial powers—political leaders need to introduce simultaneously a package of complementary reforms.

Brazil will have a plebiscite about the adoption of parliamentarism in April 1993. If the parliamentary option is selected there will be intense discussions in the legislature about different semipresidential or parliamentary options. Many legislators currently favor a variant close to the French Fifth Republic. But of the major new democracies in the world only Poland has a higher party index than Brazil (8.5), and Brazil's parties are even less disciplined than Poland's (see Table 13.4). Brazil's party laws now provide lucrative incentives for "rent-seeking" behavior by political entrepreneurs who create miniparties precisely so they can generate "rent" by loaning out their party label on television time. Brazil's electoral laws also provide numerous rational incentives for antiparty choices.[25] One major indicator of this antiparty behavior is the fact that during the 1987–90 Brazilian Congress, almost one-third of the 559 deputies had switched parties since their November 1986 election to office.[26]

25. Fortunately in recent years a high-quality literature has focused on these problems and discussed plausible political engineering proposals. The pioneer in this field has been Bolívar Lamounier. Many of his reflections are brought together in his *Partidos e Utopias: O Brasil no limiar dos anos 90* (São Paulo: Edições Loyola, 1989). Also see Bolívar Lamounier, ed., *De Geisel a Collor: O Balanço da Transição* (São Paulo: Sumaré, 1990). Also see Lamounier's "O Modelo Institucional dos Anos Trinta e a Presente Crise Brasileira," paper prepared for an international conference he organized entitled "Seminário Parlamentarismo ou Presidencialismo: Perspectivas Sobre a Reorganização Institucional Brasileira," March 1992, São Paulo. At the same conference a valuable paper was given by António Octávio Cintra, "Algumas Idéias Para a Engenharia Institucional da Consolidação Democrática." For extensive documentation of Brazil's unparalleled package of incentives for anti-party behavior, see Scott Mainwaring, "Politicians, Parties, and Electoral Systems: Brazil in Comparative Perspective," *Comparative Politics* (October 1991): 21–43. In a recent work Mainwaring argues that "Brazilian presidents have developed a supra-and antiparty tradition. This tradition can be seen as a 'rational' response of presidents to the dilemmas they face." He goes on to stress that "it is not only personalities and political culture, but also political structures that explain why presidents have acted against parties." See his "Dilemmas of Multiparty Presidential Democracy: The Case of Brazil" (University of Notre Dame: Kellogg Institute Working Paper No. 174, May 1992), pp. 24 and 29, respectively. On the problems that Brazil's political culture and institutional structure pose for democracy, see Scott Mainwaring, Guillermo O'Donnell, and J. Samuel Valenzuela, eds., *Issues in Democratic Consolidation: The New South American Democracies in Comparative Perspective* (Notre Dame: University of Notre Dame Press, 1992), especially pp. 42–50.

26. See Scott Mainwaring, "Politicians, Parties, and Electoral Systems: Brazil in Comparative Perspective," *Comparative Politics* (October 1991): 28. Mainwaring also documents how Brazilian federalism has contributed to antiparty behavior. In a survey he conducted in 1988 regarding deputies' and senators' allegiances to their states and

TABLE 13.4.   "Effective" number of political parties in the Brazilian Congress, 1990 elections

Party	Number of seats in House	Number of seats in Senate
PMDB	109	26
PFL	92	14
PDT	41	5
PRN	41	4
PDS	40	4
PSDB	37	10
PT	34	1
PTB	33	6
PDC	21	3
PL	15	–
PSB	12	2
PCdoB	5	–
PCB	3	–
PRS	4	–
PSC	5	–
PTR	2	–
PST	2	1
PMN	1	1
PSD	1	1
Independents	–	4
total	498	81

Note: "Effective" number of political parties in the House = 8.5; "effective" number of political parties in the Senate = 6.0. The formula for the "effective" number of political parties is $N = 1/\sum_{i=1}^{n} pi^2$ where pi = percentage of seats held in the legislature by the i-th party. See Markku Laakso and Rein Taagepera, "Effective Number of Parties: A Measure with Application to West Europe," *Comparative Political Studies* 12,1 (April 1979): 3–27.

Source: *Keesing's Record of World Events* (London: Longman, 1990); and Arthur S. Banks, ed., *Political Handbook of the World: 1991* (Binghamton, N.Y.: CSA Publishers, 1991). This table is reproduced from Alfred Stepan and Cindy Skach, "Meta-Institutional Frameworks and Democratic Consolidation," paper prepared for the Third Meeting of the East–South Transformations Project, January 4–7, 1992, Toledo, Spain.

Obviously, for a country like Brazil changes in the electoral law, such as a "closed" as opposed to an "open" list, would increase party discipline. A requirement that a party receive a minimum of five percent of the national vote before it can win seats in the national parliament, allocated by proportional representation and/or single member first-past-the-post elections, would reduce the number of parties. As it stands now, parties need only obtain the electoral quotient (the number of votes divided by the number of seats) in the national parliament. Therefore, parties forming a coalition before elections could win seats in the national legislature with as little as 0.04 per cent of the

districts, 49.5 per cent of the congressmen polled stated that they would support their state (rather than their party) if there were to be a conflict between the needs of their state and those of their party. Only 31.3% said they would vote with their party. See Scott Mainwaring, "Politicians, Parties, and Electoral Systems," previously cited, pp. 32–3.

vote.[27] In order to avoid "governor's parties" that get a large vote, but all in one state, there probably should be some requirement that a party receive at least 1 per cent in three different states. Party law changes, such as an increase in the number of seats a party needs to have the status of a parliamentary group with agenda privileges and representation on committees, or to gain free access to television, would also produce fewer and more disciplined parties.

But our final judgment is that semipresidentialism, as Juan Linz has argued, is a more risk-prone system than the modern parliamentarianism that has evolved in Europe in countries other than France after World War II. For, no matter what electoral and party laws are made, direct presidential elections in the era of television always present the danger that a populist, antiparty candidate like Brazil's Collor, Peru's Fujimori, Poland's Tyminski, or the USA's Perot might win the presidency. In contrast, the multiple logics of parliamentarianism virtually preclude the emergence of such figures as heads of party-based governments. Also, semipresidentialism inherently entails the possibility of deadlocked government and constitutional conflict between the dual executive if voters do not produce majorities. If there ever is a constitutional conflict between the dual executive, the fact that the president and prime minister share powers in the areas of defense might put the military in a *deliberative* role that is not healthy for fragile new democracies. A majority prime minister in conflict with a president who has special emergency powers and a special relationship to the military is a risk-prone arrangement. Furthermore, semipresentialism always produces presidents with a fixed term, who, regardless of how incompetent, criminal, or unconstitutional they might ever become, can only be removed via the difficult and dangerous procedure of an impeachment.[28]

27. Scott Mainwaring, Ibid., p. 43 n. 7, makes this point using a hypothetical example of a party coalition.

28. Though a detailed consideration is beyond the scope of this chapter, we believe that much rethinking needs to be done about the implicit comparison between the presumed inefficiency of parliamentarism in the Third and Fourth Republics versus the efficacy of the semipresidentialism of the Fifth Republic. Between 1877 and 1958 parliaments frequently brought down governments, but governments virtually never dissolved parliaments. This severe asymmetry has led many modern analysts to see the Third and Fourth Republics not as standard parliamentarism but as an "Assembly Regime." In fact, the real comparative choice for the Brazils of the world is not between the Assembly Regime of the Third and Fourth Republics and semipresidentialism. The real choice is between modern French semipresidentialism or modern parliamentarism of the German sort, with such features as a constructive vote of no-confidence and a mixed electoral system that combines majority single-member districts and PR seats with a significant threshold for parliamentary representation.

A further historical note about the Fourth Republic: France's economic development during the period was extremely impressive and cabinet coalition-formation labored under the fact that, after 1947, France had the largest and probably most Stalinist Communist party in Western Europe that was not considered coalition material. The problem of putting together a "winning" but "connected" coalition was further aggravated by the strategy of the Gaullists, which was to participate in parliamentary elections but not in cabinets. In fact, to use a classic Linzian concept, the Gaullists, the Communists, and the Pujadists throughout the Fourth Republic had strong antisystem qualities, and were at

Let us conclude with our final worries about presidential and prime minister-ial relations in France and Brazil. The French political system is vastly complic-ated by the existence of a president and a prime minister. When the two are of the same political party there may be enormous rivalry or, in the absence of rivalry, the president becomes the head of the government. When the two depend on different electoral majorities, the prime minister functions as head of the government while the president is shunned to the sidelines. The poten-tial for considerable conflict exists, far more than existed in France between 1986 and 1988. The president remains head of the armed forces, has to sign treaties, has to approve nominations to public enterprises, the civil service, and even the government, and his signature for the implementation of decrees remains necessary. A conflict of major proportions between the president and the government is a possibility that needs to be considered. For one has to consider a situation that entails the opposition capturing a legislative majority, hence directing the government and capable of governing (even with the aid of an Article 49.3, should its majority dwindle as a result of some of its coalition partners departing), while the president remains in office and continues to be head of the armed forces. Brazil needs, in other words, to consider not only the conflicts that have so far manifested themselves in the Fifth Republic but also the potential conflicts that may yet arise and, most important, how those conflicts are likely to develop and to be resolved in the Brazilian context.

best "semi-loyal" democrats. Any system—parliamentary, semipresidential, or presiden-tial—would have faced extreme problems of efficacy and legitimacy under such condi-tions. A final historical note about the Fifth Republic is that the greatest achievement of de Gaulle was his resolution of the Algerian crisis. He accomplished this while still invested by the parliament as a prime minister with majority support. From May 1958 to October 1958 de Gaulle was a prime minister. He only became president in October 1958.

FOURTEEN

Toward Consolidated Democracies

with Juan J. Linz

It is necessary to begin by saying a few words about three minimal conditions that must obtain before there can be any possibility of speaking of democratic consolidation. First, in a modern polity, free and authoritative elections cannot be held, winners cannot exercise the monopoly of legitimate force, and citizens cannot effectively have their rights protected by a rule of law unless a state exists. In some parts of the world, conflicts about the authority and domain of the *polis* and the identities and loyalties of the *demos* are so intense that no state exists. No state, no democracy.

Second, democracy cannot be thought of as consolidated until a democratic transition has been brought to completion. A necessary but by no means sufficient condition for the completion of a democratic transition is the holding of free and contested elections (on the basis of broadly inclusive voter eligibility) that meet the seven institutional requirements for elections in a polyarchy that Robert A. Dahl has set forth.[1] Such elections are not sufficient, however, to complete a democratic transition. In many cases (e.g., Chile as of 1996) in which free and contested elections have been held, the government resulting from elections like these lacks the *de jure* as well as *de facto* power to determine policy in many significant areas because the executive, legislative, and judicial powers are still decisively constrained by an interlocking set of "reserve domains," military "prerogatives," or "authoritarian enclaves."[2]

1. See Robert A. Dahl, *Polyarchy: Participation and Opposition* (New Haven: Yale University Press, 1971), 3.
2. We document the incomplete status of the Chilean democratic transition in chapter 13 of our book. For military prerogatives, see Alfred Stepan, *Rethinking Military Politics: Brazil and the Southern Cone* (Princeton: Princeton University Press, 1988), 68–127. For the electoralist fallacy in Central America, see Terry Lynn Karl, "The Hybrid Regimes of Central America," *Journal of Democracy* 6 (July 1995): 72–86. Dahl in his *Polyarchy* has

This chapter was first published in the *Journal of Democracy*, 72 (Apr. 1996), 14–33.
This essay is largely drawn from excerpts from *Problems of Democratic Transition and Consolidation: Southern Europe, South America, and Post-communist Europe* (Baltimore: Johns Hopkins University Press, 1996). Interested readers can find more detailed documentation, analysis, and references there. We thank the Ford Foundation and the Carnegie Corporation of New York for help in our research.

Third, no regime should be called a democracy unless its rulers govern democratically. If freely elected executives (no matter what the magnitude of their majority) infringe the constitution, violate the rights of individuals and minorities, impinge upon the legitimate functions of the legislature, and thus fail to rule within the bounds of a state of law, their regimes are not democracies.

In sum, when we talk about the consolidation of democracy, we are not dealing with liberalized nondemocratic regimes, or with pseudodemocracies, or with hybrid democracies where some democratic institutions coexist with nondemocratic institutions outside the control of the democratic state. Only democracies can become consolidated democracies.

Let us now turn to examining how, and when, new political systems that meet the three minimal conditions of "stateness," a completed democratic transition, and a government that rules democratically can be considered consolidated democracies.[3]

In most cases after a democratic transition is completed, there are still many tasks that need to be accomplished, conditions that must be established, and attitudes and habits that must be cultivated before democracy can be regarded as consolidated. What, then, are the characteristics of a consolidated democracy? Many scholars, in advancing definitions of consolidated democracy, enumerate all the regime characteristics that would improve the overall quality of democracy. We favor, instead, a narrower definition of democratic consolidation, but one that nonetheless combines behavioral, attitudinal, and constitutional dimensions. Essentially, by a "consolidated democracy" we mean a political regime in which democracy as a complex system of institutions, rules, and patterned incentives and disincentives has become, in a phrase, "the only game in town."[4]

an eighth institutional guarantee, which does not address elections as such, but rather the requirement that "[Institutions] for making government policies [should] depend on votes and other expressions of preference" (p. 3). This addresses our concern about reserve domains.

3. Some readers have accused our work—and other studies of democratic transition and consolidation—of being teleological. If this means advocating a single end-state democracy, we decidedly do not share such a view. If, however, teleological means (as the *Oxford English Dictionary* says) "a view that developments are due to the purpose or design that is served by them," our analysis is in part teleological, for we do not believe that structural factors *per se* lead to democracy and its consolidation. Social actors (and in some measure particular leaders) must also act purposefully to achieve a change of regime leading to some form of governing that can be considered democratic. The design of democracy that these actors pursue may be different from the one resulting from their actions, but without action whose intent is to create "a" democracy (rather than the particular institutionalized form that results), a transition to and consolidation of democracy are difficult to conceive. The processes that we are studying do, therefore, involve a "teleological" element that does not exclude important structural factors (or many unpredictable events). In addition, there is not a single motive but a variety of motives for pursuing democracy (as we define it) as a goal.

4. For other discussions about the concept of democratic consolidation, see Scott Mainwaring, Guillermo O'Donnell, and J. Samuel Valenzuela, eds., *Issues in Democratic*

Behaviorally, democracy becomes the only game in town when no significant political group seriously attempts to overthrow the democratic regime or to promote domestic or international violence in order to secede from the state. When this situation obtains, the behavior of the newly elected government that has emerged from the democratic transition is no longer dominated by the problem of how to avoid democratic breakdown. (Exceptionally, the democratic process can be used to achieve secession, creating separate states that can be democracies.) Attitudinally, democracy becomes the only game in town when, even in the face of severe political and economic crises, the overwhelming majority of the people believe that any further political change must emerge from within the parameters of democratic procedures. Constitutionally, democracy becomes the only game in town when all of the actors in the polity become habituated to the fact that political conflict within the state will be resolved according to established norms, and that violations of these norms are likely to be both ineffective and costly. In short, with consolidation, democracy becomes routinized and deeply internalized in social, institutional, and even psychological life, as well as in political calculations for achieving success.

Our working definition of a consolidated democracy is then as follows: *Behaviorally*, a democratic regime in a territory is consolidated when no significant national, social, economic, political, or institutional actors spend significant resources attempting to achieve their objectives by creating a nondemocratic regime or by seceding from the state. *Attitudinally*, a democratic regime is consolidated when a strong majority of public opinion, even in the midst of major economic problems and deep dissatisfaction with incumbents, holds the belief that democratic procedures and institutions are the most appropriate way to govern collective life, and when support for antisystem alternatives is quite small or more-or-less isolated from prodemocratic forces. *Constitutionally*, a democratic regime is consolidated when governmental and nongovernmental forces alike become subject to, and habituated to, the resolution of conflict within the bounds of the specific laws, procedures, and institutions sanctioned by the new democratic process.

We must add two important caveats. First, when we say a regime is a consolidated democracy, we do not preclude the possibility that at some future time it could break down. Such a breakdown, however, would be related not to weaknesses or problems specific to the historic process of democratic consolidation, but to a new dynamic in which the democratic regime cannot solve a set of problems, a nondemocratic alternative gains significant supporters, and former democratic regime loyalists begin to behave in a constitutionally disloyal or semiloyal manner.[5]

Consolidation: The New South American Democracies in Comparative Perspective (Notre Dame: University of Notre Dame Press, 1992).

5. In essence, this means that the literature on democratic breakdown, such as that found in Juan J. Linz and Alfred Stepan, eds., *The Breakdown of Democratic Regimes*

Our second caveat is that we do not want to imply that there is only one type of consolidated democracy. An exciting new area of research is concerned with precisely this issue—the varieties of consolidated democracies. We also do not want to imply that consolidated democracies could not continue to improve their quality by raising the minimal economic plateau upon which all citizens stand, and by deepening popular participation in the political and social life of the country. Within the category of consolidated democracies there is a continuum from low-quality to high-quality democracies. Improving the quality of consolidated democracies is an urgent political and intellectual task, but our goal in this essay, though related, is a different one. As we are living in a period in which an unprecedented number of countries have completed democratic transitions and are attempting to consolidate democracies, it is politically and conceptually important that we understand the specific tasks of "crafting" democratic consolidation. Unfortunately, too much of the discussion of the current "wave" of democratization focuses almost solely on elections or on the presumed democratizing potential of market mechanisms. Democratic consolidation, however, requires much more than elections and markets.

Crafting and Conditions

In addition to a functioning state, five other interconnected and mutually reinforcing conditions must be present, or be crafted, in order for a democracy to be consolidated. First, the conditions must exist for the development of a free and lively *civil society*. Second, there must be a relatively autonomous *political society*. Third, throughout the territory of the state all major political actors, especially the government and the state apparatus, must be effectively subjected to a *rule of law* that protects individual freedoms and associational life. Fourth, there must be a *state bureaucracy* that is usable by the new democratic government. Fifth, there must be an institutionalized *economic society*. Let us explain what is involved in crafting this interrelated set of conditions.

By "civil society," we refer to that arena of the polity where self-organizing and relatively autonomous groups, movements, and individuals attempt to articulate values, to create associations and solidarities, and to advance their interests. Civil society can include manifold social movements (e.g., women's groups, neighborhood associations, religious groupings, and intellectual

(Baltimore: Johns Hopkins University Press, 1978), would be much more directly relevant to analyzing such a phenomenon than this essay or related books on democratic transition and consolidation. This is not a criticism of the transition literature; rather, our point is that the democratic-transition and democratic-breakdown literatures need to be integrated into the overall literature on modern democratic theory. From the perspective of such an integrated theory, the "breakdown of a consolidated democracy" is not an oxymoron.

organizations), as well as associations from all social strata (such as trade unions, entrepreneurial groups, and professional associations).

By "political society," we mean that arena in which political actors compete for the legitimate right to exercise control over public power and the state apparatus. Civil society by itself can destroy a nondemocratic regime, but democratic consolidation (or even a full democratic transition) must involve political society. Democratic consolidation requires that citizens develop an appreciation for the core institutions of a democratic political society—political parties, legislatures, elections, electoral rules, political leadership, and interparty alliances.

It is important to stress not only the difference between civil society and political society, but also their complementarity, which is not always recognized. One of these two arenas is frequently neglected in favor of the other. Worse, within the democratic community, champions of either civil society or political society all too often adopt a discourse and a set of practices that are implicitly inimical to the normal development of the other.

In the recent struggles against the nondemocratic regimes of Eastern Europe and Latin America, a discourse was constructed that emphasized "civil society versus the state"—a dichotomy that has a long philosophical genealogy. More importantly for our purposes, it was also politically useful to those democratic movements emerging in states where explicitly political organizations were forbidden or extremely weak. In many countries, civil society was rightly considered to be the hero of democratic resistance and transition.

The problem arises at the moment of democratic transition. Democratic leaders of political society quite often argue that civil society, having played its historic role, should be demobilized so as to allow for the development of normal democratic politics. Such an argument is not only bad democratic theory, it is also bad democratic politics. A robust civil society, with the capacity to generate political alternatives and to monitor government and state, can help start transitions, help resist reversals, help push transitions to their completion, and help consolidate and deepen democracy. At all stages of the democratization process, therefore, a lively and independent civil society is invaluable.

But we should also consider how to recognize (and thus help overcome) the false opposition sometimes drawn between civil society and political society. The danger posed for the development of political society by civil society is that normative preferences and styles of organization perfectly appropriate to civil society might be taken to be the desirable—or indeed the only legitimate—style of organization for political society. For example, many civil society leaders view "internal conflict" and "division" within the democratic forces with moral antipathy. "Institutional routinization," "intermediaries," and "compromise" within politics are often spoken of pejoratively. But each of the above terms refers to an indispensable practice of political society in a consolidated democracy. Democratic consolidation requires political parties, one of whose primary tasks is precisely to aggregate and represent differences between democrats. Consolidation requires that habituation to the norms and procedures of democratic conflict-regulation be developed. A high degrèe of institutional routinization is a key part of such a process. Intermediation between the state and civil society, and the structuring of compromise, are likewise legitimate and necessary tasks of political society. In short, political society—informed, pressured, and periodically renewed by civil society—must somehow achieve a workable agreement on the myriad ways in which democratic power will be crafted and exercised.

The Need for a *Rechtsstaat*

To achieve a consolidated democracy, the necessary degree of autonomy of civil and political society must be embedded in, and supported by, our third arena, the rule of law. All significant actors—especially the democratic government and the state apparatus—must be held accountable to, and become habituated to, the rule of law. For the types of civil society and political society we have just described, a rule of law animated by a spirit of constitutionalism is an indispensable condition. Constitutionalism, which should not be confused with majoritarianism, entails a relatively strong consensus regarding the constitution, and especially a commitment to "self-binding" procedures of governance that can be altered only by exceptional majorities. It also requires a clear hierarchy of laws, interpreted by an independent judicial system and supported by a strong legal culture in civil society.[6]

The emergence of a *Rechtsstaat*—a state of law, or perhaps more accurately a state subject to law—was one of the major accomplishments of nineteenth-century liberalism (long before full democratization) in continental Europe and to some extent in Japan. A *Rechtsstaat* meant that the government and the state apparatus would be subject to the law, that areas of discretionary power would be defined and increasingly limited, and that citizens could turn to courts to defend themselves against the state and its officials. The modern *Rechtsstaat* is fundamental in making democratization possible, since without it citizens would not be able to exercise their political rights with full freedom and independence.

A state of law is particularly crucial for the consolidation of democracy. It is the most important continuous and routine way in which the elected government and the state administration are subjected to a network of laws, courts, semiautonomous review and control agencies, and civil-society norms that not only check the state's illegal tendencies but also embed it in an interconnecting

---

6. On the relationships between constitutionalism, democracy, legal culture, and "self-bindingness," see Jon Elster and Rune Slagstad, eds., *Constitutionalism and Democracy* (Cambridge: Cambridge University Press, 1988), 1–18.

web of mechanisms requiring transparency and accountability. Freely elected governments can, but do not necessarily, create such a state of law. The consolidation of democracy, however, requires such a law-bound, constraint-embedded state. Indeed, the more that all the institutions of the state function according to the principle of the state of law, the higher the quality of democracy and the better the society.

Constitutionalism and the rule of law must determine the offices to be filled by election, the procedures to elect those officeholders, and the definition of and limits to their power in order for people to be willing to participate in, and to accept the outcomes of, the democratic game. This may pose a problem if the rules, even if enacted by a majority, are so unfair or poorly crafted and so difficult to change democratically that they are unacceptable to a large number of citizens. For example, an electoral law that gives 80 percent of the seats in parliament to a party that wins less than 50 percent of the vote, or an ideologically loaded constitution that is extremely difficult to amend, is not likely to be conducive to democratic consolidation.

Finally, a democracy in which a single leader enjoys, or thinks he or she enjoys, a "democratic" legitimacy that allows him or her to ignore, dismiss, or alter other institutions—the legislature, the courts, the constitutional limits of power—does not fit our conception of rule of law in a democratic regime. The formal or informal institutionalization of such a system is not likely to result in a consolidated democracy unless such discretion is checked.

Some presidential democracies—with their tendency toward populist, plebiscitarian, "delegative" characteristics, together with a fixed term of office and a "no-reelection" rule that excludes accountability before the electorate—encourage nonconstitutional or anticonstitutional behavior that threatens the rule of law, often democracy itself, and certainly democratic consolidation. A prime minister who develops similar tendencies toward abuse of power is more likely than a president to be checked by other institutions: votes of no confidence by the opposition, or the loss of support by members of his own party. Early elections are a legal vehicle available in parliamentarianism—but unavailable in presidentialism—to help solve crises generated by such abusive leadership.

A Usable Bureaucracy

These three conditions—a lively and independent civil society; a political society with sufficient autonomy and a working consensus about procedures of governance; and constitutionalism and a rule of law—are virtually definitional prerequisites of a consolidated democracy. However, these conditions are much more likely to be satisfied where there are also found a bureaucracy usable by democratic leaders and an institutionalized economic society.

Democracy is a form of governance in which the rights of citizens are guaranteed and protected. To protect the rights of its citizens and to deliver other basic services that citizens demand, a democratic government needs to be able to exercise effectively its claim to a monopoly of the legitimate use of force in its territory. Even if the state had no other functions than these, it would have to tax compulsorily in order to pay for police officers, judges, and basic services. A modern democracy, therefore, needs the effective capacity to command, to regulate, and to extract tax revenues. For this, it needs a functioning state with a bureaucracy considered usable by the new democratic government.

In many territories of the world today—especially in parts of the former Soviet Union—no adequately functioning state exists. Insufficient taxing capacity on the part of the state or a weak normative and bureaucratic "presence" in much of its territory, such that citizens cannot effectively demand that their rights be respected or receive any basic entitlements, is also a great problem in many countries in Latin America, including Brazil. The question of the usability of the state bureaucracy by the new democratic regime also emerges in countries such as Chile, where the outgoing nondemocratic regime was able to give tenure to many key members of the state bureaucracy in politically sensitive areas such as justice and education. Important questions about the usability of the state bureaucracy by new democrats inevitably emerge in cases where the distinction between the communist party and the state had been virtually obliterated (as in much of postcommunist Europe), and the party is now out of power.

Economic Society

The final supportive condition for a consolidated democracy concerns the economy, an arena that we believe should be called "economic society." We use this phrase to call attention to two claims that we believe are theoretically and empirically sound. First, there has never been, and there cannot be, a consolidated democracy that has a command economy (except perhaps in wartime). Second, there has never been, and almost certainly will never be, a modern consolidated democracy with a pure market economy. Modern consolidated democracies require a set of sociopolitically crafted and accepted norms, institutions, and regulations—what we call "economic society"—that mediate between the state and the market.

No empirical evidence has ever been adduced to indicate that a polity meeting our definition of a consolidated democracy has ever existed with a command economy. Is there a theoretical reason to explain such a universal empirical outcome? We think so. On theoretical grounds, our assumption is that at least a nontrivial degree of market autonomy and of ownership diversity in the economy is necessary to produce the independence and liveliness of civil society that allow it to make its contribution to a democracy. Similarly, if all property is in the hands of the state, along with all decisions about pricing, labor, supply, and distribution, the relative autonomy of political society required for a consolidated democracy could not exist.[7]

But why are completely free markets unable to coexist with modern consolidated democracies? Empirically, serious studies of modern polities repeatedly verify the existence of significant degrees of market intervention and state ownership in all consolidated democracies.[8] Theoretically, there are at least three reasons why this should be so. First, notwithstanding certain ideologically extreme but surprisingly prevalent neoliberal claims about the self-sufficiency of the market, pure market economies could neither come into being nor be maintained without a degree of state regulation. Markets require legally enforced contracts, the issuance of money, regulated standards for weights and measures, and the protection of property, both public and private. These requirements dictate a role for the state in the economy. Second, even the best of markets experience "market failures" that must be corrected if the market is to function well.[9] No less an advocate of the "invisible hand" of the market than Adam Smith acknowledged that the state is necessary to perform certain functions. In a crucial but neglected passage in the *Wealth of Nations*, Adam Smith identified three important tasks of the state:

First, the duty of protecting the society from the violence and invasion of other independent societies; secondly, the duty of protecting, as far as possible, every member of the society from the injustice or oppression of every other member of it, or the duty of establishing an exact administration of justice; and, thirdly, the duty of erecting and maintaining certain public works and certain public institutions which it can never be for the interest of any individual, or small number of individuals, to erect and maintain; because the profit could never repay the expense to any individual or small number of individuals, though it may frequently do much more than repay it to a great society.[10]

Finally, and most importantly, democracy entails free public contestation concerning governmental priorities and policies. If a democracy never produced policies that generated government-mandated public goods in the areas of education, health, and transportation, and never provided some economic safety net for its citizens and some alleviation of gross economic inequality, democracy would not be sustainable. Theoretically, of course, it would be

7. Robert A. Dahl, in a similar argument, talks about two arrows of causation that produce this result; see his "Why All Democratic Countries Have Mixed Economies," in John Chapman and Ian Shapiro, eds., *Democratic Community, Nomos XXXV* (New York: New York University Press, 1993), 259–82.

8. See, for example, John R. Freeman, *Democracies and Market: The Politics of Mixed Economies* (Ithaca, N.Y.: Cornell University Press, 1989).

9. For an excellent analysis of inevitable market failures, see Peter Murrell, "Can Neoclassical Economics Underpin the Reform of Centrally Planned Economies?" *Journal of Economic Perspectives* 5 (1991): 59–76.

10. Adam Smith, *The Wealth of Nations*, 2 vols. (London: J.M. Dent and Sons, Everyman's Library, 1910), 2:180–1.

antidemocratic to take such public policies off the agenda of legitimate public contestation. Thus, even in the extreme hypothetical case of a democracy that began with a pure market economy, the very working of a modern democracy (and a modern advanced capitalist economy) would lead to the transformation of that pure market economy into a mixed economy, or that set of norms, regulations, policies, and institutions which we call "economic society."[11]

Any way we analyze the problem, democratic consolidation requires the institutionalization of a politically regulated market. This requires an economic society, which in turn requires an effective state. Even a goal such as narrowing the scope of public ownership (i.e., privatization) in an orderly and legal way is almost certainly carried out more effectively by a stronger state than by a weaker one. Economic deterioration due to the state's inability to carry out needed regulatory functions greatly compounds the problems of economic reform and democratization.[12]

In summary, a modern consolidated democracy can be conceived of as comprising five major interrelated arenas, each of which, to function properly, must have its own primary organizing principle. Rightly understood, democracy is more than a regime; it is an interacting system. No single arena in such a system can function properly without some support from another arena, or often from all of the remaining arenas. For example, civil society in a democracy needs the support of a rule of law that guarantees to people their right of association, and needs the support of a state apparatus that will effectively impose legal sanctions on those who would illegally attempt to deny others that right. Furthermore, each arena in the democratic system has an impact on other arenas. For example, political society manages the governmental bureaucracy and produces the overall regulatory framework that guides and contains economic society. In a consolidated democracy, therefore, there are constant mediations among the five principal arenas, each of which is influenced by the others.

Two Surmountable Obstacles

Two of the most widely cited obstacles to democratic consolidation are the dangers posed by ethnic conflict in multinational states and by disappointed

11. Robert A. Dahl's line of reasoning follows a similar development. See his "Why All Democratic Countries Have Mixed Economies," cited in note 7 above, 259–82.

12. In postcommunist Europe, the Czech Republic and Hungary are well on the way to becoming institutionalized economic societies. In sharp contrast, in Ukraine and Russia the writ of the state does not extend far enough for us to speak of an economic society. The consequences of the lack of an economic society are manifest everywhere. For example, Russia, with a population 15 times larger than Hungary's and with vastly more raw materials, only received 3.6 billion dollars of direct foreign investment in 1992–3, whereas Hungary received 9 billion dollars of direct foreign investment in the same two years.

popular hopes for economic improvement in states undergoing simultaneous political and economic reform. These are real problems. Democratic theorists and crafters alike must recognize that there is often more than one "awakened nation" present in the state, and that there can be prolonged economic reversals after democratic transition begins. Nonetheless, we are convinced, on both theoretical and empirical grounds, that democracy can still make significant strides toward consolidation under such conditions. We are furthermore convinced that if democratic theorists conceptualize what such obstacles mean and do not mean, this may lessen the dangers of democratic disenchantment and help to identify obstacle-reducing paths. That is our task in the rest of this essay.

Under what empirical conditions do "nation-states" and "democratization" form complementary logics? Under what conditions do they form conflicting logics? If they form conflicting logics, what types of practices and institutions will make democratic consolidation most, or least, likely?

Many political thinkers and activists assume that Weberian states, nation-states, and democracy cohere as part of the very grammar of modern polities. In a world where France, Germany, Portugal, Greece, and Japan are all Weberian states, nation-states, and democracies, such an assumption may seem justified. Yet in many countries that are not yet consolidated democracies, a nation-state policy often has a different logic than a democratic policy. By a nation-state policy we mean one in which the leaders of the state pursue what Rogers Brubaker calls "nationalizing state policies" aimed at increasing cultural homogeneity. Consciously or unconsciously, the leaders send messages that the state should be "of and for" the nation.[13] In the constitutions they write and in the politics they practice, the dominant nation's language becomes the only official language and occasionally the only acceptable language for state business and for education; the religion of the nation is privileged (even if it is not necessarily made the official religion); and the culture of the dominant nation is privileged in state symbols (such as the flag, national anthem, and even eligibility for some types of military service) and in state-controlled means of socialization (such as radio, television, and textbooks). By contrast, democratic policies in the state-making process are those that emphasize a broad and inclusive citizenship that accords equal individual rights to all.

Under what empirical conditions are the logics of state policies aimed at nation-building congruent with those aimed at crafting democracy? Empirically, conflicts between these different policies are reduced when almost all of the residents of a state identify with one subjective idea of the nation, and when that nation is virtually coextensive with the state. These conditions are met only if there is no significant irredenta outside the state's boundaries, if

---

13. See Rogers Brubaker's "National Minorities, Nationalizing States, and External National Homelands in the New Europe," *Daedalus* 124 (Spring 1995): 107–32.

there is only one nation existing (or awakened) in the state, and if there is little cultural diversity within the state. In these circumstances (and, we will argue, virtually *only* in these circumstances) leaders of the government can simultaneously pursue democratization policies and nation-state policies. This congruence between the *polis* and the *demos* facilitates the creation of a democratic nation-state; it also virtually eliminates all problems of "stateness" and should thus be considered a supportive condition for democratic consolidation. Under modern circumstances, however, very few states will begin a possible democratic transition with a high degree of national homogeneity. This lack of homogeneity tends to exacerbate problems of "stateness."

Democracy is characterized not by subjects but by citizens; thus a democratic transition often puts the question of the relation between *polis* and *demos* at the center of politics. From all that has been said thus far, three assertions can be made. First, the greater the extent to which the population of a state is composed of a plurality of national, linguistic, religious, or cultural societies, the more complex politics becomes, since an agreement on the fundamentals of a democracy will be more difficult. Second, while this does not mean that consolidating democracy in multinational or multicultural states is impossible, it does mean that especially careful political crafting of democratic norms, practices, and institutions is required. Third, some methods of dealing with the problems of "stateness" are inherently incompatible with democracy.

Clear thinking on this subject demands that we call into question some facile assumptions. One of the most dangerous ideas for democracy is that "every state should strive to become a nation-state and every nation should become a state." In fact, it is probably impossible for half of the territories in the world that are not now democratic ever to become both "nation-states" and "consolidated democracies," as we have defined these terms. One of the reasons for this is that many existing nondemocratic states are multinational, multilingual, and multicultural. To make them "nation-states" by democratic means would be extremely difficult. In structurally embedded multicultural settings, virtually the only democratic way to create a homogeneous nation-state is through voluntary cultural assimilation, voluntary exit, or peaceful creation and voluntary acceptance of new territorial boundaries. These are empirically and democratically difficult measures, and hence are exceedingly rare.

The other possibilities for creating a homogeneous nation-state in such settings involve subtle (or not-so-subtle) sanctions against those not speaking the language, wearing the attire, or practicing the religion of the titular nation. Under modern circumstances—where all significant groups have writers and intellectuals who disseminate national cultures, where communication systems have greatly increased the possibility for migrants to remain continuously connected to their home cultures, and where modern democratic norms accept a degree of multiculturalism—such sanctions, even if not formally antidemocratic, would probably not be conducive to democratic crafting.[14] If the titular nation actually wants a truly homogeneous nation-state, a variant of "ethnic cleansing" is too often a temptation.

Another difficulty in the way of building nation-states that are also democracies derives from the manner in which humanity is spatially distributed across the globe. One building block for nations is language. But as Ernest Gellner observed, there are possibly as many as eight thousand languages (not counting important dialects) currently spoken in the world.[15] Even if we assume that only one out of every ten languages is a base for a "reasonably effective" nationalism, there could be as many as eight hundred viable national communities.[16] But cultural, linguistic, and religious groups are not neatly segmented into eight thousand or eight hundred nationalities, each occupying reasonably well-defined territories. On the contrary, these groups are profoundly intermixed and overlapping.

We are not arguing against democratically crafted "velvet divorces." We should note, however, that relatively clear cultural boundaries facilitate such territorial separations. Latvia would like to be a nation-state, but in none of its seven most-populous cities is Latvian spoken by a majority of the residents. In Tallinn, the capital of Estonia, barely half the people of this aspiring nation-state speak Estonian. For these and many other countries, no simple territorial division or "velvet divorce" is available.[17]

Democracy and Multinational States

Some analysts were happy when the separate nationalities of the USSR became 15 republics, all based on "titular nationalities," on the assumption that democratic nation-states might emerge. In fact, many political leaders in these republics sounded extreme nationalist (rather than democratic) themes in the first elections. One possible formula for diminishing conflict between

---

14. See, for example, the outstanding monograph by Eugen Weber, *Peasants into Frenchmen: The Modernization of Rural France, 1870–1914* (Stanford: Stanford University Press, 1976), which analyzes in extensive detail the wide repertoire of nation-state mandated policies in the schools, the civil service, and the military that were systematically designed to repress and eliminate multilingualism and multiculturalism and to create a nation-state. From today's perspective, similar endeavors of modern states appear far from admirable and represent a cost that many of us would not like to pay. However, it is not just a question of how we evaluate such efforts of state-based nation-building, but of how feasible these efforts are in the contemporary context.

15. See Ernest Gellner, *Nations and Nationalism* (Ithaca, N.Y.: Cornell University Press, 1983), 44.

16. This conjecture is developed by Gellner in *Nations*, 44–5.

17. See the excellent, and sobering, book by Anatol Lieven, *The Baltic Revolution: Estonia, Latvia, Lithuania and the Path to Independence* (New Haven: Yale University Press, 1993), 434.

titular nationalities and "migrants" is what David Laitin calls the "competitive-assimilation game." That is, it becomes in the best interests of some working-class migrants to assimilate in order to enhance the life chances of their children in the new environment. This may happen to Spanish working-class migrants in culturally and economically vibrant Catalonia, but is it likely to occur among Russians in Central Asia? In 1989 in Almaty, the capital of Kazakhstan, Russians constituted 59 percent of the population, and the Kazakhs, the titular nationality, only 22.5 percent. Less than 1 percent of the Russians spoke the titular language. In Bishkek, the capital of Kyrgyzstan, the comparable percentages were virtually identical. In such contexts, shaped by settler colonialism, it is utterly implausible that a nation-state would emerge voluntarily through a process of competitive assimilation.[18]

So how can democracy possibly be achieved in multinational states? We have a strong hypothesis about how *not* to consolidate democracy in multinational settings. The greater the percentage of people in a given state who either were born there or arrived without perceiving themselves as foreign citizens, and who are subsequently denied citizenship in the state (when their life chances would be hurt by such denial), the more unlikely it is that this state will consolidate democracy. Phrased more positively, our hypothesis is that in a multinational, multicultural setting, the chances of consolidating democracy are increased by state policies that grant inclusive and equal citizenship and give all citizens a common "roof" of state-mandated and state-enforced individual rights.

Such multinational states also have an even greater need than other polities to explore a variety of nonmajoritarian, nonplebiscitarian formulas. For example, if there are strong geographic concentrations of different groups within the state, federalism might be an option worth exploring. The state and the society might also allow a variety of publicly supported communal institutions—such as media and schools in different languages, symbolic recognition of cultural diversity, a variety of legally accepted marriage codes, legal and political tolerance for parties representing different communities, and a whole array of political procedures and devices that Arend Lijphart has described as "consociational democracy."[19] Typically, proportional representation, rather than large single-member districts with first-past-the-post elections, can facilitate representation of geographically dispersed minorities. Some strict adherents to the tradition of political liberalism, with its focus on universalism and individual rights, oppose any form of collective rights. But we believe that in a multinational, multicultural society and state, combining collective rights

---

18. For David Laitin's analysis of what he calls a "migrant competitive-assimilation game" in Catalonia, and his analysis of a possible "colonial-settler game" in the Central Asian republics of the former Soviet Union, see his "The Four Nationality Games and Soviet Politics," *Journal of Soviet Nationalities* 2 (Spring 1991): 1–37.

19. See Arend Lijphart's seminal article "Consociational Democracy," *World Politics* 21 (January 1969): 207–25.

for nationalities or minorities with individual rights fully protected by the state is the least-conflictual solution.[20]

Where transitions occur in the context of a nondemocratic, multinational federal system, the crafting of democratic federalism should probably begin with elections at the federal level, so as to generate a legitimate framework for later deliberations on how to decentralize the polity democratically. If the first competitive elections are regional, the elections will tend to favor regional nationalists, and ethnocracies rather than democracies may well emerge.[21] However, the specific ways of structuring political life in multinational settings need to be contextualized in each country. Along these lines, we believe that it is time to reevaluate some past experiments with nonterritorial autonomy such as the kinds of partially self-governing ethnic or religious communities exemplified by the Jewish Kabal of the Polish-Lithuanian Common wealth, the millets of the Ottoman Empire, or the "national curias" of the late Hapsburg Empire. These mechanisms will not eliminate conflict in multinational states, but they may moderate conflict and help make both the state and democracy more viable.

We also believe that some conceptual, political, and normative attention should be given to the possibility of "state-nations." We call "state-nations" those multicultural or even multinational states that nonetheless still manage to engender strong identification and loyalty from their diverse citizens. The United States is such a multicultural and increasingly multilingual country; Switzerland is another. Neither is strictly speaking a "nation-state," but we believe both could now be called "state-nations." Under Jawaharlal Nehru, India made significant gains in managing multinational tensions by the skillful and consensual use of numerous consociational practices. Through this process India became, in the 1950s and early 1960s, a democratic "state-nation"; but if Hindu nationalists win power in the 1990s and attempt to turn India (with its 115 million Muslims) into a Hindu nation-state, communal violence would almost certainly increase and Indian democracy would be gravely threatened.

Multiple Identities

Let us conclude with a word about "political identities." Many writings on nationalism have focused on "primordial" identities and the need for

20. For interesting arguments that some notion of group rights is, in fact, necessary to the very definition of some types of individual rights and necessary to the advancement of universal norms in rights, see the work by the Oxford philosopher Joseph Raz, *The Morality of Freedom* (Oxford: Oxford University Press, 1986), 165–217. Also see Will Kymlicka, *Multicultural Citizenship: A Liberal Theory of Minority Rights* (Oxford: Oxford University Press, 1995), 107–30.

21. We develop this point in greater detail in our "Political Identities and Electoral Sequences: Spain, the Soviet Union and Yugoslavia," *Daedalus* 121 (Spring 1992): 123–39;

people to choose between mutually exclusive identities. Our research into political identities, however, has shown two things. First, political identities are not fixed or "primordial" in the *Oxford English Dictionary's* sense of "existing at (or from) the very beginning." Rather, they are highly changeable and socially constructed. Second, if nationalist politicians (or social scientists and census-takers with crude dichotomous categories) do not force polarization, many people may prefer to define themselves as having multiple and complementary identities.[22] In fact, along with a common political "roof" of state-protected rights for inclusive and equal citizenship, the human capacity for multiple and complementary identities is one of the key factors that makes democracy in multinational states possible. Because political identities are not fixed and permanent, the quality of democratic leadership is particularly important. Multiple and complementary political identities can be nurtured by political leadership, as can polarized and conflictual political identities. Before the conscious use of "ethnic cleansing" as a strategy to construct nation-states in the former Yugoslavia, Sarajevo was a multinational city whose citizens had multiple identities and one of the world's highest interfaith-marriage rates.

Our central proposition is that, if successful democratic consolidation is the goal, would-be crafters of democracy must take into careful consideration the particular mix of nations, cultures, and awakened political identities present in the territory. Some kinds of democracy are possible with one type of *polis*, but virtually impossible if political elites attempt to build another type of *polis*. Political elites in a multinational territory could initiate "nationalizing policies" that might not violate human rights or the Council of Europe's norms for democracy, but would have the effect, in each of the five arenas of the polity, of greatly diminishing the chances of democratic consolidation.

An example of such "nationalizing policies" in each of five arenas would be the following: In the arena of civil society, schooling and mass media could be restricted to the official language. In the arena of political society, nationalizing citizenship laws could lead to a significant overrepresentation of the dominant nationality in elected offices. In the arena of the rule of law, the legal system could subtly privilege a whole range of nationalizing customs, practices, and

and in our *Problems of Democratic Transition and Consolidation* in the chapters on Spain, on "stateness" in the USSR, and on Russian speakers' changing identities in Estonia and Latvia.

22. In our *Problems of Democratic Transition and Consolidation*, we show how in Catalonia in 1982, when respondents were given the opportunity to self-locate their identities on a questionnaire offering the following five possibilities—"Spanish," "more Spanish than Catalan," "equally Spanish and Catalan," "more Catalan than Spanish," or "Catalan"—the most-chosen category, among respondents with both parents born in Catalonia, as well as among respondents with neither parent born in Catalonia, was the multiple and complementary category "equally Spanish and Catalan." We also show how identities in Catalonia were becoming more polarized and conflict-ridden before democratic devolution.

institutions. In the arena of the state bureaucracy, a rapid changeover to one official language could decrease other nationalities' participation in, and access to, state services. Finally, in the arena of economic society, the titular nationality, as the presumed "owners" of the nation-state, could be given special or even exclusive rights to land redistribution (or voucher distribution, if there was privatization). In contrast, if the real goal is democratic consolidation, a democratizing strategy would require less majoritarian and more consensual policies in each of the above arenas.

A final point to stress concerns timing. Potentially difficult democratic outcomes may be achievable only if some preemptive policies and decisions are argued for, negotiated, and implemented by political leaders. If the opportunity for such ameliorative policies is lost, the range of available space for manœuvre will be narrowed, and a dynamic of societal conflict will likely intensify until democratic consolidation becomes increasingly difficult, and eventually impossible.

Problems of Simultaneous Reform

The widely held view that market reform and privatization can legitimate new democracies is based on the dubious assumption that economic improvement can be achieved simultaneously with the installation and legitimation of democratic institutions. We believe that, in countries with imploded command economies, democratic polities can and must be installed and legitimized by a variety of other appeals before the possible benefits of a market economy fully materialize. Many analysts and political advisors dismiss the case for giving priority to state restructuring because they assume that, due to people's demands for material improvements, economic and political gains must not only be pursued but occur simultaneously. Some even argue that simultaneous economic and political reforms are necessary, but that such simultaneity is impossible.[23]

We can call the two opposing perspectives about the relationship between economics and democratization the "tightly coupled" hypothesis and the "loosely coupled" hypothesis. By "loosely coupled," we do not mean that there is no relationship between economic and political perceptions, only that the relationship is not necessarily one-to-one. For at least a medium-range time horizon, people can make independent, and even opposite, assessments about political and economic trends. We further believe that when people's

23. The title of a widely disseminated article by Jon Elster captures this perspective; see "The Necessity and Impossibility of Simultaneous Economic and Political Reform," in Douglas Greenberg, Stanley N. Katz, Melanie Beth Oliviero, and Steven C. Wheatley, eds., *Constitutionalism and Democracy: Transitions in the Contemporary World* (Oxford: Oxford University Press, 1993), 267–74.

assessments about politics are positive, they can provide a valuable cushion for painful economic restructuring.[24] Let us look at the evidence concerning the relationship between economic growth and democratization in the first five years of postcommunist Europe. Certainly, if we look only at relatively hard economic data, none of the 27 countries in postcommunist Europe except Poland experienced positive growth in 1992. Indeed, in 1993 all postcommunist countries were still well below their 1989 industrial output levels.[25]

If we look at subjective impressions of economic well-being in six East Central European countries, the mean positive rating (on a + 100 to a −100 scale) among those polled between November 1993 and March 1994 was 60.2 for the communist economic system, but was only 37.3 for the postcommunist economic system—a drop of almost 23 points. The tightly coupled hypothesis would predict that attitudes toward the political system would also drop steeply, even if not by the full 23 points. What does the evidence show? The mean positive ranking of the communist political system was 45.7. Thus a one-to-one correlation between the political and economic evaluations would have yielded a positive evaluation of the political system of 22.6. Yet the mean positive ranking for the postcommunist political system, far from falling, rose to 61.5—or 38.9 points higher than a "perfectly coupled" hypothesis would have predicted.[26]

How can we explain such incongruence? First of all, human beings are capable of making separate and correct judgements about a basket of economic goods (which may be deteriorating) and a basket of political goods (which may be improving). In fact, in the same survey the respondents judged that, in important areas directly affected by the democratic political system, their life experiences and chances had overwhelmingly improved, even though they also asserted that their own personal household economic situations had worsened.[27]

We do not believe such incongruence can last forever; it does indicate, however, that in a radical transformation like that occurring in East Central Europe, the deterioration of the economy does not necessarily translate into rapid erosion of support for the political system. The perceived legitimacy of the political system has given democratic institutions in East Central Europe an important degree of insulation from the perceived inefficacy of the new economic system. Indeed, most people in East Central Europe in 1994 had a fairly long time horizon and expressed optimism that by 1999 the performance of

24. The voters might, due to negative economic performance, vote incumbents out of office, but the overall economic policies of their successors might well continue to be roughly the same. Poland in 1993–5, and Hungary in 1994–5 come to mind.

25. See our *Problems of Democratic Transition and Consolidation.*

26. See Richard Rose and Christian Haerfer, "New Democracies Barometer III: Learning from What is Happening," *Studies in Public Policy* No. 230 (1994), questions 22–3, 32–3. Percentages rounded off.

27. Rose and Haerfer, "New Democracies," questions 26, 35, 36, 39, 40, and 42.

both the new democracy and the new economic system would improve significantly.[28]

Thus the evidence in East Central Europe is strongly in favor of the argument that deferred gratification and confidence in the future are possible even when there is an acknowledged lag in economic improvement. Simultaneity of rapid political and economic results is indeed extremely difficult, but fortunately the citizens of East Central Europe did not perceive it as necessary.

Democracy and the Quality of Life

While we believe that it is a good thing for democracies to be consolidated, we should make it clear that consolidation does not necessarily entail either a high-quality democracy or a high-quality society. Democratic institutions—however important—are only one set of public institutions affecting citizens' lives. The courts, the central bank, the police, the armed forces, certain independent regulatory agencies, public-service agencies, and public hospitals are not governed democratically, and their officials are not elected by the citizens. Even in established democracies, not all of these institutions are controlled by elected officials, although many are overseen by them. These institutions operate, however, in a legal framework created by elected bodies and thereby derive their authority from them.

In view of all this, the quality of public life is in great measure a reflection not simply of the democratic or nondemocratic character of the regime, but of the quality of those other institutions.

Policy decisions by democratic governments and legislators certainly affect the quality of life, particularly in the long run, but no democracy can assure the presence of reputable bankers, entrepreneurs with initiative, physicians devoted to their patients, competent professors, creative scholars and artists, or even honest judges. The overall quality of a society is only in small part a function of democracy (or, for that matter, a function of nondemocratic regimes). Yet all of those dimensions of society affect the satisfaction of its citizens, including their satisfaction with the government and even with democracy itself. The feeling that democracy is to blame for all sorts of other problems is likely to be particularly acute in societies in which the distinctive contributions of democracy to the quality of life are not well understood and perhaps not highly valued. The more that democrats suggest that the achievement of democratic politics will bring the attainment of all those other goods, the greater will be the eventual disenchantment.

There are problems specific to the functioning of the state, and particularly to democratic institutions and political processes, that allow us to speak of the

28. Rose and Haerfer, "New Democracies," questions 24, 26, 35, 36, 39, 40, 42, and 34.

quality of democracy separately from the quality of society. Our assumption is that the quality of democracy can contribute positively or negatively to the quality of society, but that the two should not be confused. We as scholars should, in our research, explore both dimensions of the overall quality of life.

FIFTEEN

Toward a New Comparative Politics of Federalism, (Multi)Nationalism, and Democracy: Beyond Rikerian Federalism

Introduction

The subject of this article is the role of federalism in the functioning, and occasionally even the making or breaking, of democracies. Federalism has never been more crucial for the study of democracy and comparative politics. If our unit of analysis is the total number of people who live in long-standing democracies, the majority of them live in federal systems.[1] If our unit of analysis is relatively long-standing (if often troubled) multinational and multilingual democracies, *all* the polities that fall most clearly into this category are federal.[2] However, *all* the territorial fragmentation of postcommunist Europe occurred in three multinational, formally federal, systems. It is crucial that we analyze and explain these two sharply different patterns. Finally, if we turn our attention to two major, recent democratizing efforts, in Brazil and Russia, any

---

1. This is of course largely a function of the size of federal democracies. The most populous democracy in North America, the United States of America, is federal. The most populous democracy in Western Europe, the Federal Rikerlic of Germany, is federal. The most populous democracy in Asia, indeed in the world, India, is federal. Other long-standing federal democracies include Australia, Austria, Belgium, Canada, Spain, and Switzerland.

2. These countries are Belgium, Canada, India, and Spain. Switzerland is, of course, a federal democracy, but I will discuss my reservations about calling it "multinational" later in this article. Many major polities that are not now democracies, should they ever become so on their existing territories, would be multinational. Countries in this category include Burma, Malaysia, China, and until recently, Indonesia and Nigeria. To become democracies most of these countries would probably have to craft workable federal systems. The debates about deepening integration in the European Union, and the "democratic deficit" are, of course, debates about multinational federalism.

serious analysis of their democratic prospects involves an analysis of the difficulties presented by their distinctive federal systems.[3]

Yet despite the centrality of federalism to a very large number of politics in the world, the existing political science literature on federalism does not, in my judgement, help us sufficiently in the tasks of comparative analysis.

In this article I endeavor to show how we might begin to make federalism a more powerful conceptual and empirical category for a truly comparative analysis of politics by developing three themes. First, I show that the democracy, federalism, and nationalism literatures have been developed in relatively mutual isolation and that we can only make more meaningful and powerful statements about comparative federalism if we relate the three literatures to each other. Second, I demonstrate that all federal systems constrain the lawmaking capacity of the democratically elected legislators at the center. However, I argue that it is analytically and politically fruitful to study democratic federal systems as existing along a "demos constraining" to "demos enabling" continuum.[4] I also make a strong case that at *all* points in the continuum federal institutions can have a great impact on policy. I cannot develop these arguments without addressing the most influential political scientist who has written on federalism, the late William H. Riker. Riker's classic and still influential arguments about federalism stand in fundamental opposition to those I advance in this article. Third, I construct and operationalize the analytic framework of the demos constraining – demos enabling continuum, by evaluating four propositions about federalism, using data from India, Germany, Spain, the United States, and Brazil.

Riker, Federalism, and Political Science

There are a number of major analysts of federalism. Two of the most prominent are K. C. Wheare, an influential constitutionalist, and Daniel J. Elazar, the founder of the journal devoted to federalism *Publius*.[5] But the analyst who

3. See my "Russian Federalism in Comparative Perspective" *Post-Soviet Affairs*, 16 2 (Apr.–June 2000), 133–76, and my "Brazil's Decentralized Federalism: Bringing Government Closer to the Citizens?," *Daedalus*, 129 2 (Spring 2000), 145–69.

4. By "demos" I simply mean *all* the citizens of the polity. "Demos constraining" is not meant to imply that "a majority" always exists or is always right. I believe that in some federations, especially multinational or multicultural federations, there can be a role for nonmajoritarian consociational practices which are consensually agreed upon by both the demos at the center and the "demoi" of the subunits of federation. One of the major purposes of this paper is precisely to assess how different types of democratic federal systems are "demos constraining" whereas some have important "demos enabling" characteristics.

5. See Kenneth C. Wheare, *Federal Government* (Oxford: Oxford University Press, 1946). This book was last reprinted in 1990. Daniel J. Elazar has written or edited nearly fifteen

has most affected political science approaches to federalism is William H. Riker, and we can not progress too far without either building upon his arguments, or showing good reasons to refine or even reject his arguments. Riker, of course, is one of the intellectual founders of rational choice theory in political science; he made enduring contributions to coalition theory, most notably in his seminal work on "minimum winning coalitions," and contributed to many other areas of political science. Indeed, according to a recent attempt to construct criteria for a political science hall of fame for the 1954–94 period, Riker emerged at the top of two important indices.[6]

One of the central themes in Riker's work was federalism. For thirty years he was probably the major figure in the subfield. In 1964 he wrote *Federalism: Origin, Operation, Significance*, which discussed the United States, and briefly, every contemporary federal system in the world.[7] In 1975, as the leading political scientist in the area of federalism, he contributed a very boldly argued, long article on the subject for the classic, eight volume *Handbook of Political Science*, edited by Fred Greenstein and Nelson Polsby.[8] In 1987 he brought together most of his writings on United States' federalism in his book *The Development of American Federalism*.[9] In 1995, just before his death, he was invited as the leading comparativist in the subfield to write the theoretical introduction to a volume written by European scholars on the federal future of the European Union.[10] Riker's thoughts on federalism were directly related to his normative and empirical concerns about how to avoid the dangers of democratic populism. Indeed, his theory of individual choice and theory of democracy are brought together in his *Liberalism against Populism: A Confrontation between the Theory of Democracy and the Theory of Social Choice*.[11]

books that relate to federalism. For political scientists his most influential book is *Exploring Federalism* (Tuscaloosa: University of Alabama Press, 1987).

6. Riker published sixteen articles in the *American Political Science Review* in this period, more than any other political scientist. He also led a political science journal citation index in this period. Riker is prominent not just in the judgement of United States political scientists. Robert E. Goodin and Hans-Dieter Klingemann, from Australia and Germany respectively, recently edited the massive *The New Handbook of Political Science*. In this handbook Riker is listed as one of the "integrators" of political science in the world, and receives twenty-four references in the index, whereas Wheare received one, and Elazar none. See A. H. Miller, C. Tien, and A. A. Peebler, "The American Political Science Review Hall of Fame: Assessments and Implications for an Evolving Discipline," *P. S.: Political Science & Politics* (Mar. 1996), 73–83, and Robert E. Goodin and Hans-Dieter Klingemann (eds), *The New Handbook of Political Science* (Oxford: Oxford University Press, 1996), 40–1 and the index to their book.

7. William H. Riker, *Federalism: Origin, Operation, Significance* (Boston: Little Brown, 1964).

8. William H. Riker, "Federalism," in Fred Greenstein and Nelson W. Polsby (eds), *Handbook of Political Science* (Reading, Mass.: Addison-Wesley, 1975), v. 93–172.

9. William H. Riker, *The Development of American Federalism* (Boston: Kluwer Academic Publishers, 1987), 17–42.

10. William H. Riker, "European Federalism: The Lessons of Past Experience," in J. J. Hesse and V. Wright (eds), *Federalizing Europe? The Costs, Benefits, and Preconditions of Federal Political Systems* (Oxford: Oxford University Press, 1996), 9–24.

11. (Prospect Heights, Ill.: Waveland Press, 1982).

My goal in this article is not to provide a systematic review of the entire Rikerian federalist framework, but rather to argue that the building blocks of a more powerful approach to the comparative study of federalism, multinationalism, and democracy necessarily require serious consideration of some key analytic, historical, normative, and policy dimensions which are either not found, or are misleading, in the Rikerian framework.

In a book length project Juan Linz and I shall develop (and integrate) our thoughts on the interrelationship of democratization, federalism, and nationalism in much greater detail.[12] Here, in this brief introduction to my article, I indicate some of the most crucial distinctions that I believe must be made.

Federalism in Democratic and Nondemocratic Systems

A fundamental distinction should be made between a democratic system which is federal, and a nondemocratic system with federal features. In a strict sense, only a system that is a constitutional democracy can provide *credible guarantees* and the institutionally embedded mechanisms that help ensure that the lawmaking prerogatives of the subunits will be respected. In a democracy the specificities of the federal formula that has been constitutionally adopted will routinely structure many political processes, such as how the most important laws are adopted at the center and in the subunits, and how the jurisdictional boundaries between the center and the subunits will be adjudicated and maintained. However, in a nondemocratic system, federalism may or may not structure significantly such political processes.

If one accepts, as Linz and I do, Robert A. Dahl's definition of a federal system, then in a very strict sense only a democracy can be a federal system.[13] This is so because, for Dahl, federalism is "a system in which some matters are exclusively *within* the competence of certain local units—cantons, states, provinces—and are constitutionally *beyond* the scope of the authority of the national government; and where certain other matters are constitutionally outside the scope of the authority of the smaller units."[14] Only a system that is a democracy can build the relatively autonomous constitutional, legislative,

---

12. This project, of five or six years' duration, will result in our jointly authored book *Federalism, Democracy and Nation*. Also see Juan J. Linz, "Democracy, Multinationalism and Federalism," Paper presented at IPSA, Aug. 17–22, 1997.

13. Late imperial Germany had a fairly strong rule of law, and was a federation, but very important aspects of how power was formed and exercised were still nondemocratic.

14. Robert A. Dahl, "Federalism and the Democratic Process," in his *Democracy, Identity and Equality* (Oslo: Norwegian University Press, 1986), 114–26, citation from p. 114; emphasis in the original.

and judicial systems necessary to meet the Dahlian requirements for a federation. My focus in this paper, then, is on federalism *in a democracy*, and all that this entails.

This is not of course to deny that in some circumstances the federal features of some nondemocratic polities may not become extremely important; for example, during the period of high Stalinism in the USSR the party-state under Stalin's direction determined policy. This was so, notwithstanding the extensive range of sovereign rights, including "the right freely to secede from the USSR" (Article 72, 1977), that were given in the constitution to the Soviet republics. However, when the party-state began to weaken in the late 1980s, and a decree of electoral competitiveness was introduced into the federal subunits at the republican level, the same Soviet federal features, in the *new* political context, provided great "resource mobilization" opportunities for republican level elites to reconstitute their power bases by emphasizing the sovereignty claims of their republics.[15]

If we are to make progress as comparativists, we need to analyze the difference in how democratic and nondemocratic federal political systems function politically. Some of the most important works on federalism do not make this distinction. For example, William H. Riker, in his much cited 1975 article on federalism, lists Canada, the USA, Yugoslavia, and the USSR as meeting his criteria for federal systems. Indeed, Riker classifies the USA and Yugoslavia as the same subtype, "centralized federalism."[16] Binding together Yugoslavia and the United States into the same analytic category obfuscated, of course, the much more meaningful way in which the power structures and political dynamics of the two polities were fundamentally different. For example, precisely because Yugoslavia was not a democracy, its "quasi-federal system" could function peacefully as long as the party-state played the key steering role. Once elections begun to breathe some life into the inert and incomplete federal system, it fragmented.

This point is of wider significance for the comparative analysis of federalism. If one excludes the German case as being "one nation in two states," then there were eight nondemocratic states in communist Europe in 1989. Five were unitary and three had some quasi-federal features. The five unitary states are still five unitary states. However, the three quasi-federal states are now twenty-three independent countries, many of them nondemocratic majoritarian ethnocracies.

---

15. See "The Problem of 'Stateness' and Transition: The USSR and Russia," in Juan J. Linz and Alfred Stepan, *Problems of Democratic Transition and Consolidation: Southern Europe, South America and Post-Communist Europe* (Baltimore: Johns Hopkins University Press, 1996), 365–400. Indeed, throughout the nondemocratic period of Brazilian 20th century history, 1930–45 and 1964–85, federalism remained of some political importance. In Mexico federalism played an important role in the death throes of one of the world's longest reigning nondemocratic party systems.

16. Riker, "Federalism," v. 93–172.

"Coming Together," "Holding Together," and "Putting Together" Federations: Origins, Purposes, and Structures

Another major distinction that must be made is between federations whose initial purpose is to "come together" versus those whose purpose is to "hold together." The idea of a "coming together" federation of course is that based on the US model. In Philadelphia in 1787 previously sovereign units made what William Riker calls a "federal bargain." For Riker, the two necessary conditions for a federal bargain, which he asserts *all* long-standing federations have actually met (and he included the USSR and India as long-standing federations), are (1) that there exists a group of individual polities, all of which have strong identities and substantial sovereignty, and (2) as a group they perceive that they face external threats, which can be lessened if they agree to pool their sovereignty and make a federation.[17] The nature of the bargain is that even the least powerful members of the new federation, given their strong identity and their strong sovereignty, will attempt to keep as much of their identity and sovereignty as possible. The strongest members of the new federation, as part of the bargain, agree to accept a continuing high degree of political autonomy among the smaller or less powerful members, as the price they pay for improving their own security by creating the federation. For the classic confederations that agreed to become federations, the United States of America and Switzerland, Riker's argument is powerful.

However, as comparativists, we must recognize that some of the most important federations in the world emerged from a completely different historical and political logic. India in late 1948, Belgium in 1969, and Spain in 1975 were all political systems with strong *unitary* features. Nevertheless, political leaders in all these three multinational polities arrived at the constitutional decision that the best way to "hold together" in a democracy would be to *devolve power* and to turn their threatened polities into federations. The 1950 Indian constitution, the 1978 Spanish constitution, and the 1993 Belgian constitution are all federal.[18] To supplement Riker's version of federation formation, which

17. For William H. Riker's discussion of the two necessary conditions for a federal bargain, see ibid. v. 92–117, 128–31.
18. Numerous references on the origins of India's "holding together" federation to follow. For Belgium's shift from a unitary state to a federal system with consociational characteristics, see Liesbeth Hooghe, "Belgium: From Regionalism to Federalism," *Regional Politics and Policy*, 3 (Autumn 1993), 44–69; Robert Senelle, "The Reform of the Belgian State," in Joachim Jens Hesse and Vincent Wright (eds.), *Federalizing Europe? The Costs, Benefits and Preconditions of Federal Political Systems* (Oxford: Oxford University Press, 1996), 266–324; and Wilfried Swenden: "Belgium: A Federal State in Search of a Nation," Paper prepared for a Conference on Democracy, Nationalism, and Federalism at All Souls College, University of Oxford, June 5–8, 1997. For analysis of the process by which Spain was transformed from a unitary state to a federal state, see Juan J. Linz, "Spanish Democracy and the Estado de las Autonomías," in Robert A. Goldwin, Art Kaufman, and William A. Schambra (eds) *Forging Unity out of Diversity: The Approach of*

I will call a "coming together" ideal type, I therefore suggest that we create a supplementary ideal type of federation formation that I will call "holding together."

The origins of "holding together" federation formation, and consequently the characteristic political structures that are crafted in a "holding together" federation, are quite different than those found in Riker's "coming together" federations.

A good example is the creation of federalism in India. The chairman of the drafting committee of the Indian constitution, B. R. Ambedkar, when he presented the draft constitution for the consideration of the members of the Constituent Assembly, was very explicit that the Indian constitution was designed to maintain the unity of India. He argued that the Indian constitution was guided by principles and mechanisms that were thus fundamentally different from those found in the United States constitution. In his address to the Constituent Assembly Ambedkar assumed that India was already a diverse polity with substantial unity, but that to maintain this unity, under democratic conditions, a federation would be useful. Ambedkar told the members of the Assembly that

The use of the word Union is deliberate . . . The Drafting Committee wanted to make it clear that though India was to be a federation, *the Federation was not the result of an agreement by the States to join in a Federation* and that the Federation not being the result of an agreement no State has the right to secede from it . . . Though the country and the people may be divided into different States for convenience of administration the country is one integral whole, its people a single people living under a single imperium derived from a single source.[19]

Mohit Bhattacharya in a careful review of the mindset of the founding fathers points out that by the time Ambedkar presented the draft to the Constituent Assembly in November 1948, both the partition between Pakistan and India, and the somewhat reluctant and occasionally even coerced integration of virtually all the 568 princely states, had already occurred. Therefore, the strong bargaining power of units with a great deal of sovereignty, crucial to Rikerian views of "coming together" federalism, in essence no longer existed when Ambedkar presented his draft constitution.[20] Bhattacharya's reading of

Eight Nations (Washington, D.C.: American Institute for Public Policy Research, 1989), 260–326; and Robert Agronoff, "Asymmetrical and Symmetrical Federalism in Spain: An Examination of Intergovernmental Policy," in Bertus de Villiers (ed.), *Evaluating Federal Systems* (Pretoria: Juta, 1994), 61–89.

19. Ambedkar's speech is found in its entirety in India, *Constituent Assembly Debates* (New Delhi, 1951), ii. 31–44; my italics.

20. To be sure if the partition had not occurred, and if the Muslim territories that are now Pakistan and Bangladesh had sent representatives to the Constituent Assembly, a very different bargaining context would have predominated. In such a context the bargaining power of the princely states, especially the Muslim ruled princely states in central India such as Hyderabad, would also have been augmented. Once the violent partition began however, both the Congress Party leaders in the Constituent Assembly, and the last British vice'roy, Lord Mountbatten, felt that a new geopolitical situation

the Constituent Assembly papers is that the central motivation in the minds of the constitution drafters was to hold the center together.

What ultimately emerged was a "devolutionary federation" as a fundamentally unitary state devolved powers on the units through a long process of evolution ... [Once] the problem of integration of the Princely States had disappeared after partition, the "federal situation" itself had virtually evaporated with it ... The bargaining situation disappeared ... The architects of the Constitution were sensitive pragmatists. Their attention was focused on ... the central authority that would hold the nation together.[21]

If we include nonvoluntary, nondemocratic federation formation (a category that Riker does not contemplate), we would need to supplement "coming together" and "holding together" federation formation with a third ideal type, which I will call "putting together." Let us see why this would be useful.

Riker has famously argued that the USSR in 1921–2 had the same two fundamental bargaining conditions (a felt need for security in a larger unit but a continuing sense of strong regional identities) as that found in the thirteen American states or the Swiss cantons. In his section on the formation of Soviet federalism in 1922, Riker wrote, "If one looks at the circumstances of its origin it is just like all the other federations here discussed, in that both bargaining conditions are clearly present ... There is a universally feared threat and there is a sense of provincial loyalty owing to differences of ideology, so that both the bargaining conditions were satisfied at the time that the Union of Soviet Socialist Republics was planned."[22] However, the fact is that some of the units, such as Georgia, Armenia, Azerbaijan, and the Ukraine, did not receive much international support for their independence and were integrated by a significant degree of military force into the USSR in the 1920s (to say nothing of Latvia, Estonia, and Lithuania, which were militarily "integrated" in 1940). All these countries were experiencing substantial popular pressures to become mononational "nation-states" when they were integrated into the USSR as "union republics." It distorts history, theory, and language to say that in 1921–2 Georgian, Armenian, Azerbaijan, and Ukrainian bargaining preferences and bargaining capabilities were "just like" the states of the USA in

existed. In this new context the Nehru government actually used military force to integrate the largest princely state, Hyderabad, in Sept. 1948. Mountbatten, on numerous informal and formal occasions, let the princely states inside India's new borders know that they no longer had a strong bargaining position. He urged them to join the Indian union and said that if they did not, the United Kingdom would not let them join the British Commonwealth as independent states. Two key books that shed light on the weak bargaining power of the princely states after partition are V. P. Menon, *Integration of the Indian States* (Madras: Orient Longman, 1956), and Ian Copland, *The Princes of India in the Endgame of Empire, 1917–1947* (Cambridge: Cambridge University Press, 1997).

21. Mohit Bhattacharya, "The Mind of the Founding Fathers," in Nirmal Mukarji and Balveer Arora (eds.), *Federalism in India: Origins and Development* (New Delhi: Vikas, 1992), 81–102, quotations from pp. 101–2.

22. Riker, "Federalism," v. 122.

1787, or the cantons of Switzerland in 1848.[23] We need the ideal type of "putting together."

Riker suggests that all long-standing federations, including the USSR and India, were in his "coming together" pattern. I suggest it is analytically more useful to use at least three ideal types of federation formation. The actual historical analysis of the process of federation formation in a particular country, such as Canada, might even require simultaneous attention to all three ideal types. See Table 15.1.

Democratic Federalism in Multinational and Mononational Contexts: Questions of Identity and Asymmetry

The third fundamental concern of the new research agenda on democratic federalism should be nationalism, and especially federalism in multicultural and multinational polities. Just as we comparativists have to work on the relationship of federalism to democracy, we have to work on the relationship of nationalism (and multinationalism) to democracy. By 1986, three years before the Berlin wall came down, two new important bodies of literature were in place that should have helped us to think carefully about the difficult relationship between democratization and (multi)nationalism. Ernest Gellner published his magisterial *Nations and Nationalism* in 1983, the same year that saw the publication of another modern classic on nationalism, Benedict Anderson's *Imagined Communities: Reflections on the Origin and Spread of Nationalism*.[24] By 1986 the four volume work edited by Guillermo O'Donnell, Philippe C. Schmitter, and Laurence Whitehead *Transitions from Authoritarian Rule* was released and immediately created the field of "transitology."[25]

23. Modern historical accounts of the 1921–2 period would almost certainly place more emphasis on nationalist resistance in countries such as Georgia, and the correlation of military force, especially the Red Army's capacity to conquer Georgia, Armenia, Azerbaijan, and Ukraine, in the absence of international military and diplomatic support for their continued independence. For the Georgia case, see Ronald Grigor Suny, *The Revenge of the Past: Nationalism, Revolution and the Collapse of the Soviet Union* (Stanford, Calif.: Stanford University Press, 1993). For the international military balance of power that allowed Soviet military integration efforts to be decisive, see Alexander J. Motyl, *Sovietology, Rationality and Nationality: Coming to Grips with Nationalism in the USSR* (New York: Columbia University Press, 1990), esp. 103–18. For the crucial role of the Red Armies in inducing "bargains," see Richard Pipes, *The Formation of the Soviet Union: Communism and Nationalism, 1917–1923* (Cambridge, Mass.: Harvard University Press, 1954), esp. 193–240.

24. Ernest Gellner, *Nations and Nationalism* (Oxford: Blackwell, 1983), and Benedict Anderson, *Imagined Communities: Reflections on the Origin and Spread of Nationalism* (London: New Left Books, 1983).

25. *Transitions from Authoritarian Rule: Prospects for Democracy* (Baltimore: Johns Hopkins University Press, 1986). The four paperback volumes, published separately, were

TABLE 15.1. *"Coming together," "holding together," and "putting together" ideal types of federation formation*

"Coming together"	"Holding together"	"Putting together"
Largely voluntary bargain by relatively autonomous units to come together so that by pooling sovignty but retaining their identity they can increase their security	Largely a consensual parliamentary decision to attempt to hold together a unitary state by creating a multinational federal system	Heavily coercive effort by a centralizing power to put together a multinational state, some units of which had been independent states
Close to ideal type:	India 1950	USSR 1922
USA 1787	Spain 1978	
Switzerland 1848	Belgium 1993	
Australia 1901		
Further from ideal type:		
Canada[a] 1867		
Germany[b] 1870, 1919, 1949		
Austria[c] 1918		
Brazil[d] 1891		

[a] Most English speaking provinces followed a "coming together" pattern. But British conquest of French Canada in 1759 had elements of "putting together" federalism. Furthermore, in 1867 the British government told the English Canadians that the best way to "hold together" Canada would be to create a federation, which would give French speaking Canada a variety of constitutionally imbedded prerogatives of the sort now associated with asymmetrical federalism.

[b] In 1870 Prussia was hegemonic power in empire but all units tied together by German language and growing spirit of German nationalism. Federation formed in 1870 mainly by nonelected hereditary rulers. In 1949 most traditional boundaries had been changed by the Allied occupational powers.

[c] With only one dissenting vote in the Constituent Assembly, Article 1 of the 1918 Constitution of the Republic of Austria stated that Austria was a part of Germany. But later the post-First World War Treaty of St Germain forbade Austrian unification with Germany. Sovereignty was thus "imposed" on Austria as a separate state, and Article 1 was revoked reluctantly.

[d] Most Brazilian states were not unhappy about the Brazilian Federal Republic being created in 1889. However, Brazil was an independent state and unitary empire from 1822 to 1889 and the military, after the coup overthrowing the emperor, unilaterally announced in their "Proclamation of the Republic" that the federation was formed and that the military would use force to ensure the unity of the federation. When the first federal constitution was constructed during the Constituent Assembly of 1890–1, the state of São Paulo (supported by their ally Minas Gerais) was the hegemonic political and economic force.

What strikes me now as amazing is that these two bodies of literature, which in retrospect should have learned so much from each other, were virtually separate and noncommunicating discourses. In the four volumes on democratic transitions, nationalism is never thematized as a major issue, or even given one separate chapter. Indeed, the word "nationalism" only appears in the index of one of the four volumes, that on southern Europe, and the reader is only referred to one page on Spain, one page on Portugal, and two pages on Greece. The name of Ernest Gellner does not appear in the index of any of the four volumes, nor does the name of Benedict Anderson. As the author of one of the comparative articles in this series, I of course must share responsibility for this omission.

For their part, on the other hand, neither Gellner in *Nations and Nationalism*, nor Anderson in *Imagined Communities*, in any way thematized democracy, and indeed the word did not enter into the index of either book.

In my judgement one of the most urgent problems facing modern democratic theorists and practitioners is how to reconcile nationalism and democracy, especially in multinational settings. Federalism (along with some consociational practices) is often one of the potentially attractive (but also potentially dangerous) political formulas those wishing to craft democracy in multinational policies must consider. Obviously, the two previously noncommunicating discourses of democratization and nationalism must come into constant dialogue with each other, especially if we are to address systematically the possibilities of multinational democratic federalism.[26]

Now that we have shown how, for comparative analysis, our three key political and conceptual concerns—democracy, federalism, and nationalism—stand in necessary relationship to each other, let me briefly illustrate two of the many questions about democratic federalism that can best be approached by using all three concepts in a closely connected framework.

Let us look first at the need in democratic federalism, especially if the demos is multinational, for multiple and complementary identities. If federalism is to be a useful concept to employ in the comparative analysis of democracy, we will have to develop the implications of the minimal Dahlian requirements of democratic federalism for political identities and loyalties. Democratic political systems probably should not be called federal systems unless they meet two criteria. First, within the state there must exist some territorial political subunits whose electorate is exclusively drawn from citizens of the subunit *and* which have areas of legal and policy making autonomy and sovereignty that are constitutionally guaranteed. Second, there must be a statewide political

devoted to general theoretical concerns, southern Europe, Latin America, and comparative perspectives.

26. Juan J. Linz and I first began to address this problem in our chapter "Stateness, Nationalism and Democratization," in *Problems of Democratic Transition and Consolidation*, 16–32. Also see chs. 19 and 20 in the same book. Also see my "Modern Multinational Democracies: Transcending a Gellnerian Oxymoron" (ch. 9 in this volume).

unit, which contains a legislature elected by the statewide population, and which has some law and policy making areas that are constitutionally guaranteed to fall within the sovereignty of this statewide body.

If one accepts these arguments, it also follows that in a robust democratic federal political system, the more citizens feel a sense of allegiance to both of the democratically legitimated sovereignties, each with its constitutionally guaranteed scope of action, the more democratically secure the federation. Ideally, therefore, citizens within a democratic federation should have *dual* but *complementary* political identities. This is so because, as members of a territorial subunit, if they and the elected leaders of the subunit do not feel that the center provides some goods, security, or identities that they consider valuable, and which are *not* available from the subunit alone, then their loyalty to the center will be weak. Potentially they will provide a constituency for the politics of secession. At the very least, they might provide a constituency for a politics of alienation, or a sense of exploitation, neither of which will help democratic consolidation. Likewise, if many citizens of the federal state and leaders of the center feel that the federal system entails few benefits, but imposes many political and economic costs, *and* that the costs of intervention (or encouraged exit) are relatively low, the democratic federation will be endangered.

Federalism is a potentially attractive formula for some types of multinational polities, but the politics of building and maintaining dual and complementary identities needs more thought and research. Public opinion surveys are a particularly promising tool in exploring the political circumstances in which loyalty to a "state-nation" at the center can grow, while loyalty to a nonsecessionist but nonetheless nationalist subunit also grows.[27]

Another area where it is crucial to simultaneously employ concepts of democracy, multinationalism, and federalism is when we analyze the question of symmetrical federalism and asymmetrical federalism. There are two legitimate uses of the word "asymmetrical" in the study of federalism. The first refers largely to socioeconomic asymmetry and its implications for bargaining within the federation. Steven L. Solnick is doing important work in this area.[28] The second legitimate use of the word "asymmetrical" in the study of federalism refers to constitutionally embedded differences between the legal status and prerogatives of different subunits within the same federation. In this section I

27. In the Linz–Stepan volume *Federalism, Democracy and Nation* we will develop this argument with survey data on political identities in numerous countries. In the survey data, we will document emerging patterns of conflictual identity polarization in some polities, as well as documenting the emergence of multiple and complementary identities in others.

28. See his "The Political Economy of Russian Federalism: A Framework for Analysis," *Problems of Post-Communism*, 43/8 (1996), 13–25. A key article in the socio-economic asymmetry approach to federalism is Charles D. Tarlton, "Symmetry and Asymmetry as Elements of Federalism: A Theoretical Speculation," *Journal of Politics*, 27/4 (1965), 861–4.

am mainly concerned with *constitutional* asymmetry, but I will also discuss *a-constitutional* asymmetry, and *anticonstitutional* asymmetry.

Let us first try to make a distinction between multinational and mononational states. I call a state multinational if (1) it has territorially based different linguistic identities that are often compounded with ethnic and/or religious and/or cultural identities, and (2) there are significant political groups who would like to build political sovereignties, or an independent state or states, around these territorially based differences. If we use this definition of multinational states, of the eleven federal states with at least ten years of democratic rule at the moment, Canada, Spain, Belgium, and India are multinational. Democratic federations that may be multicultural, and which may have significant indigenous populations, but which are not multinational as I have defined the term, are Austria, Australia, the USA, Germany, Argentina, and Brazil. Paradoxically, the country that is the most difficult to classify as to whether its is actually multinational or not is Switzerland. Many analysts refer of course to Switzerland as multinational, because most of the cantons are (exclusively) French, German, or Italian speaking. However, part of the argument against calling Switzerland multinational is that protestant and Catholic differences are linguistically crosscutting rather than compounding. Most importantly, none of the parties that have been in the "magic formula" four party power sharing coalition that has ruled Switzerland since 1958 is built around a single language, and no significant party advocates secession from what Linz and I prefer to call the "state-nation" (rather than the "multinational state") of Switzerland.

If we employ the definitions I have just advanced, we can create, for analytic purposes, a dichotomy between multinational states and mononational states. We can also divide these states into (largely) constitutionally symmetrical federal states, and (largely) constitutionally asymmetrical federal states. This gives us the standard foursquare figure depicted in Figure 15.2.

Regardless of how one classifies Switzerland, a powerful pattern is clear. *All* (or all but one) of the long-standing multinational federal democracies are constitutionally asymmetrical. *All* (or all but one) of the long-standing mononational federal democracies are constitutionally symmetrical. Therefore, in itself the fact that Russia, as a multinational federal state, is asymmetrical does not make it a democratic exception. In this respect Russia conforms to the democratic norm.

What is an exception to democracy, however, is the fact that Russia has forty-six a-constitutional, bilateral treaties that were negotiated and signed by the chief executive of Russia, and the chief executive of one of the eighty-nine constituent members of the Russian federation, without being signed, or even shown, to the Russian Parliament. This is procedurally exceptional in a democratic federation. A further unconformity (indeed gross incompatibility) with democracy is that many of the bilateral treaties were also substantively exceptional for a democratic federation because they contained passages or

Constitution

	Symmetrical	Asymmetrical
Mononational	Austria Germany Australia USA Argentina Brazil Swizerland(state-nation?)	
Multinational	or Switzerland (multinational?)	India Belgium Canada Spain (Russia; but not a democracy)

FIG. 15.1.   Constitutional–legal arrangements of entire universe of federal systems
that have been democracies since 1988

agreements that were in violation of the federal constitution (and sometimes even of the constitutions of the signatory republics). This compounded further the already profoundly anticonstitutional quality of Russian politics owing to the fact that many of the eighty-nine members of the Russian federation wrote and passed their own constitutions, or statutes, which contradicted parts of the federal constitution.[29] For what is not, and what is, exceptional about Russia's asymmetrical federalism, see Table 15.2.

If we had not made a distinction between democratic and nondemocratic federations, and between mononational and multinational federations, we would not have been able to identify the powerful and significant patterns revealed in Figure 15.1 and Table 15.2. Once these patterns are established, a new research agenda emerges for comparativists, especially the question of whether Spain, India, Belgium, and Canada could "hold together" as democratic polities if they were either unitary states or symmetrical federal states.

Rethinking the Normative Basis in Favor of Majority-Limiting Federalism: The Multiple Values Required for Consolidating Democratic Federalism

The distinction between "coming together federalism" and "holding together federalism" opens the way for a reexamination of a major normative issue. An

---

29. For more detail, see my "Russian Federalism in Comparative Perspective."

TABLE 15.2. *Range of symmetrical and asymmetrical federal systems*

Constitutionally largely symmetrical	Some asymmetrical differences constitutionally embedded and implemented	Major asymmetrical differences constitutionally embedded, extraconstitutionally negotiated, and/or anticonstitutionally exercised
USA Australia Switzerland Germany Austria Brazil	Spain. Different autonomies have different prerogatives that are constitutionally embedded. All new arrangements must be public and be approved by both chambers of parliament. Both center and autonomies subject to binding decisions by Constitutional Court India. Federacy relationship with Jammu Kashmir and numerous special linguistic and tribal arrangements Belgium. Extensive constitutional provisions for different linguistic communities and use of consociational and nonterritorial representation arrangements. Special status of Brussels and the small German speaking territory Canada. French speaking Quebec has a number of prerogatives the English speaking provinces do not have in such areas as education, law, and immigration policy	Russia. Constitutionally, republics have higher status as members of the Russian federation than do "territories," "regions," "federal cities," "autonomous regions," and "autonomous areas." All these classifications stem from Soviet federalism Extraconstitutionally, private treaties are negotiated between the executive of the center and the executives of the subunits, often with special prerogatives or dispensations, that were not voted upon by the Parliament or even widely known before they were signed Anticonstitutionally, numerous provisions of the constitutions or statutes of the eighty-nine subjects of the federation are in contradiction with the 1993 Russian constitution. The Constitutional Court often does not make a ruling, and when it does make a ruling, it often is not implemented. No "common legal space" in Russia

implicit, and often explicit, normative argument for federalism is that it protects individual rights against a too powerful center or even a "tyranny of the majority." William Riker is explicit about the fact that, for him, one of the most attractive aspects of federalism is that it contributes to a limited government which is a check on populist majorities. "The populist ideal requires that rules move swiftly and surely to embody in law the popular decision on an electoral platform."[30] Riker espoused normatively a multicameral legislature precisely because he believes it helps to limit populist majorities. Riker was happy to draw attention to the fact that in the United States the multicameral legislature is "really three houses: the president, Senate and House of Representatives based on different divisions of the people into constituencies. The different constituencies have typically kept the interests of rulers separate."[31] For Riker, the second great contribution of US style federalism to limited government is the division of authority between national and local governments, and especially its fragmenting effect on parties. "This is the famous American federalism; copied over half the world. The constitutional restraint is not, however, the legal division of duties between central and local governments but rather the resultant localization of political parties that renders national leadership of them impossible."[32] For Riker, the beneficial constraints that US federalism promotes are that "Multi-cameralism and federalism have enforced localism in parties, and this in turn has forced rulers to persuade rather than to control. The total effect is that policy does not change either rapidly or sharply enough to hurt anyone very badly."[33]

But in multinational federations, especially in fragile new democracies, is it always normatively desirable or politically useful to have such a "localization of political parties" that it renders politywide leadership impossible? It is by no means clear. Consider, for example, the role of statewide parties in "founding elections" in multinational federal polities. In the founding elections in Nigeria in 1959 the polis was divided into a Northern Region, a Western Region, and an Eastern Region. In each of these regions, an ethnically based regional party won control of its regional legislature. In the federal legislature there were virtually no elected representatives of statewide parties. This situation directly contributed to intense political conflict emerging out of the compounding cleavages of ethnoterritorial regionalism, and eventually to the civil war over the Biafran secessionist attempt. In Yugoslavia the first competitive elections were at the republican level and were all won by regional and ethnic nationalist parties. The Yugoslav civil wars occurred before a single statewide election was held. In contrast in Spain statewide and provincial elections were held simultaneously. Statewide parties formed the central government *and* twelve of the fourteen subunit governments. In India, after the simultaneous elections for the center and the subunits, the statewide Congress Party formed the

---

30. Riker, *Liberalism against Populism*, 247.
31. Ibid. 250.   32. Ibid.   33. Ibid. 253.

government at the center *and* in all of the states. Clearly, if the goal is the consolidation of democracy in a multicultural or multinational polity, a strong case can be made that the existence of statewide parties is useful.

The role of statewide parties would seem to be especially important if the primary purpose is to "hold together" a federation in a form that reconciles cultural diversity with policy making efficacy. Such a reconciliation is, of course, precisely what the Indian Constituent Assembly was striving to create. To quote Ambedkar again: "The...Constitution has sought to forge means and methods whereby India will have Federation and at the same time will have uniformity in all basic matters which are essential to maintain the unity of the country. The means adopted by the Constitution are three: (1) a single judiciary; (2) uniformity in fundamental laws, civil and criminal, and (3) a common All-India Civil Service to man important posts."[34]

Let us now directly address some critical normative and conceptual issues about democracy and my use of the phrases "demos constraining" or "demos enabling."[35] If one takes democratic consolidation as a desired normative goal, and if one recognizes the empirical reality that such consolidation is often not achieved, then it is useful to think deeply about what mix of values might, in a probabilistic sense, be associated with promoting, or inhibiting, democratic consolidation. In my judgement democratic consolidation is helped if three core values—liberty, equality, and efficacy—are all addressed in such a way that none are neglected, and all reinforce one another.

Liberty of individual citizens is clearly a positive value. In a democracy this implies that the majority, however constituted, should not impose policies on minorities that violate individual rights. Constitutionalism and the rule of law are major democratic institutions that help to preserve liberty and individual rights. For many liberal thinkers, especially in the US tradition, federalism is often presented as playing a key role, for some thinkers *the* key role, in constraining the "tyranny of the majority."

Another value in modern democracies is the *equality* of the citizens in a polity, the equality of the members of the demos. In a minimal sense this means "one citizen, one vote." In a more expanded sense equality could also mean that the demos assumes some commitment to raise all individual citizens to a shared core of basic rights and well-being.

Finally, if a democracy is to persist, and if new democracies are to be consolidated, the institutions of governance should be crafted is such a way as to enable the demos of the overall polity, and the demoi of the subunits, to be governed with an acceptable degree of *efficacy*. Efficacy as a value (unlike

34. Ambedkar's remarks are in India, *Constituent Assembly Debates*.
35. In an earlier version of this article I used the phrase "majority constraining" instead of "demos constraining." Scott Mainwaring and Gerry Mackie raised a number of conceptual issues about my use of the term "majority constraining," for which I thank them.

liberty) is not uniquely related to democracy. Nondemocratic regimes can aspire to efficacy. But, if we understand democracy as a set of lived, valued, and historically precarious institutions, there are reasons to believe that a democratic polity with very low efficacy is *less* likely to endure than a democracy with moderate or high efficacy. Principled democrats should not, therefore, if possible, craft institutions of governance for the demos and the demoi that make efficacy especially difficult.

If one accepts that "liberty," "equality," and "efficacy" are *all* important for a high quality democracy, how should these three values relate to each other in democratic federalism? A strong tradition in US liberal thought gives a privileged place to federalism's contribution to liberty. As we have seen, Riker is a member of this tradition. Some theorists who are particularly interested in preventing "the tyranny of the majority" entertain ideas not only of "supermajorities" but even of legislative unanimity in multiple legislatures.[36] This of course in theory would help preclude a tyranny of the majority.

For some fundamental and controversial constitutional issues it is a great advantage if consensual, near unanimous, agreements can be achieved. However, theoretically and empirically, a "unanimity rule," or even a strict supermajority requirement for routine governmental decision making, is in strong tension with the values of efficacy and equality. The requirement of supermajorities makes legislation much more difficult to pass and gives minorities great blocking power.[37] Indeed, in an extreme demos constraining form of federalism, legislators possibly representing less than 10 percent of the electorate might constitute what I would call a "blocking win-set." That is, they control sufficient votes to stop the status quo from being changed if they do not want it changed. In such circumstances these legislators, even if they were programmatically in favor of legislation, might be structurally tempted to exploit their blocking win-set position to get rent seeking rewards. Clearly, small blocking win-sets that are constitutionally embedded in a democratic federal system also raise serious questions about the equality of one citizen one vote.

Politically therefore, constitutionally embedded blocking win-sets can potentially raise acute questions about the efficacious and legitimate functioning of democracy. For example, there might be a prolonged period in a country during which a strong majority of the political leaders, and a strong majority of the electorate in the country, believe that major changes are necessary. But, if

36. For a useful discussion of this normative dimension of US political thought, see Robert E. Goodin, "Institutionalizing the Public Interest: The Defense of Deadlock and Beyond," *American Political Science Review*, 90 (June 1996), 331–43.

37. If supermajorities were to be a requirement for *all* decisions in a federal system, then some "starting points" might be much better than others. For example, if the starting point entailed great inequality (such as US slavery based in the South) it would raise more potential problems than in a federal system with a starting point of widely diffused social and economic equalities.

the federation has been crafted to facilitate win-sets of blocking vetoes by small minorities, the efficacy and legitimacy of that democracy could be eroded by such demos constraining federal features. If many citizens believe that a popular government with popular policies is being blocked via the very institutions of democracy itself (such as in an extreme variety of demos constraining federalism) it is possible that this situation could create a context in which most of the legislation is not actually stopped, but is passed, with diffuse public support, by executive decree. Such a situation may be good or bad for efficacy. However, it is certainly not conducive to democratic consolidation, which is best advanced if the passage of major rules is done inside, not outside, democratic legislative processes.[38]

Federalism as a Demos Constraining – Demos Enabling Continuum

Riker argues that the fundamental structure of modern federalism is what he calls "centralized federalism." Riker sees the United States not only as the origin of this model, but as the modal form of federalism. I argue that it is much more empirically useful for a comparativist to approach democratic federalism as a continuum from least demos constraining to most demos constraining. In this alternative conceptual approach the United States emerges, not as the modal

---

38. Two possible arguments against the thesis that I will advance in this paper—that Brazil is an extreme outlier on the "demos constraining continuum"—is that the democratic reforming president Fernando Henrique Cardoso (1995–) is seldom in fact blocked from implementing new measures because (1) he uses presidential decree powers, and (2) most of the nondecree legislation he formally proposes to Congress actually passes. For an impressive argumentation, and documentation, of this position, see Angelina Cheibub Figueiredo and Fernando Limongi, "Medidas Provisórias: Abdicação ou Delegação?," *Novos Estudos*, 47 (Mar. 1997), 127–54. I do not challenge any of the data in their meticulous and valuable study. However, I would like to make two observations. First, the fact that President Cardoso, who would like to consolidate the institutions of democracy in Brazil, has to pass so much legislation that is popularly supported and is crucial for the efficacy of government, via decrees, is an unfortunate way to advance the democratic values of liberty, equality, and efficacy. Under a less able and democratically committed president the demos constraining element of Brazilian federalism might contribute to what Guillermo O'Donnell calls "delegative democracy." The second observation I would like to make is methodological (and extremely political). Political leaders only have so much political capital and resources. They also know how to count. If a powerful minority win-set opposes many of their preferred policy proposals, they will be parsimonious in the measures they will attempt to get by this formidable blocking winset. From this methodological perspective what is more important? The fact that *most* of the measures that the president proposes to the Congress actually gets passed, or the fact that *most* of the measures that the president would like to pass he decides not to propose formally to the Congress because of what he sees as blocking win-sets? Based on my interviews with cabinet ministers at the beginning of the Cardoso administration, and twice later, at two year intervals, I believe that the latter sequence is the more politically significant.

type of modern federalism, but as an extreme outlier at the demos constraining end of the continuum. Let me develop my argument.

Until 1787 the only form of federalism in the world, according to Riker, was "decentralized federalism." Riker argues that in 1787 the founding fathers "invented centralized federalism."[39] Throughout his writings Riker stresses the theme that "it is the centralized form of federation that the world finds attractive."[40] For Riker, all modern federal systems are derived from the US model, and he often presents the US model as the norm.

Riker urges the reader to accept the implicit dichotomy "decentralized federalism" versus "centralized federalism." But, I urge the reader to see what Riker calls decentralized federalism as a variety of "alliances" or "confederations" in which the fundamental characteristic was that the sovereignty of the members of an alliance or a confederation was not constitutionally constrained. Members were situationally constrained, but only as long as each sovereign member judged it was in their interest to act collectively. In some cases before Philadelphia in 1787 what Riker calls "decentralized federalism" did require a unanimous vote. But, analytically, a decision rule requiring unanimity is of course consistent with the absolute sovereignty of the individual members, because no decision can be made against their interest.

Riker is right that something new emerged in Philadelphia. What emerged was a formula to *constrain constitutionally* all units of the federation in such a way that exit would be constitutionally impossible or extremely difficult. Also, unanimity was not required for compulsory decisions. If there is a dichotomy, therefore, it is between alliances and confederations on the one hand, and federations on the other. If the reader accepts this revision of the Rikerian dichotomy, then we are ready for the next step.

All democratic federations, *qua* federations, are *center constraining*. Instead of "centralized federalism" being conceived of as standing in dichotomous opposition to "decentralized federalism," I suggest that it is analytically more fruitful to conceive of democratic federalism as forming a *continuum that runs from high demos constraining to demos enabling*. The framework of a continuum opens up the analytic and historical category of federalism to a range of empirical and conceptual distinctions that are not possible if we simply lump all federal systems into the single category of "centralized federalism." For example, I will show that, far from the United States' version of "centralized federalism" being the federal norm, it is an extreme "outlier" on the demos constraining end of the continuum that I will construct. In fact, as I shall demonstrate later, of the main federal systems in the world, only Brazil has a potential to block the democratic majority at the center comparable to the majority blocking potential of the United States. Germany, rather than being ruled out of the category of federal systems because it deviates from the US norm, as K. C. Wheare

---

39. William H. Riker, "The Invention of Centralized Federalism," in his *The Development of American Federalism*, 17–42.
40. Riker, "Federalism," 10.

suggested, is actually much closer to the center (the norm) on the federal continuum. India, the survival of whose democratic political system cannot be understood without analyzing its federal component, but which Wheare called only "quasi-federal" because it deviated so much from the United States, is at the least demos constraining end of the continuum, extremely far from the United States. In the conceptual terms of our discussion, India in the 1980s and 1990s shared only two characteristics with the United States: it was federal and democratic.

Why are *all* democratic federations inherently center constraining? For four reasons. The first reason is conceptual and constitutional with empirical consequences. Robert A. Dahl's definition succinctly captured the dual sovereignty dimension of federalism that constitutionally constrains the demos at the center[41] If we accept Dahl's definition, we must accept that all democratic federations, *qua* federations, are center, and even to some extent, demos constraining. Consider federalism's impact on agendas. Democracies normally have an open agenda. That is, within the formulas prescribed by the constitution, there are no policy areas where the democratic majority in the polis can not make laws. This is one of the reasons why Adam Przeworski talks of democracy as a form of "institutionalized uncertainty."[42] However, unlike a unitary democratic system, in all federal systems the demos at the center must accept a *closed agenda* in that some issue areas are constitutionally beyond their lawmaking powers.[43]

The second way in which all democratic federations constrain the demos is that the demos is diffused, not only into many demoi, but also into various authority structures. The demos is constrained vertically, as Dahl's argument makes clear. In addition the demos is also constrained horizontally. At the center there are two lawmaking legislatures. One legislature, the lower chamber, represents the principle of the population, and can come close to the pure democratic equality of one person, one vote. But the upper chamber represents the principle of territory. The ideological discourse of territorial equality (one unit, one vote) can mask *massive inequality* (a citizen's vote in a small state can count for more than a hundred votes in a large state).

The third way in which all democratic federations constrain the demos relates to the constitution. All democratic constitutions should be "self-binding," in that they should be (optimally) difficult to change.[44] In an extreme case of a constitution that is extremely difficult to change, a democratic

41. Robert A. Dahl, "Federalism and the Democratic Process," 114–26, citation from p. 114; emphasis in the original.
42. Adam Prezworski, "Some Problems in the Study of the Transition to Democracy," in O'Donnell *et al.* (eds.), *Transitions from Authoritarian Rule: Comparative Perspectives* (Baltimore: Johns Hopkins University Press, 1986), 47–63, esp. 58–60.
43. Robert A. Dahl, *Democracy and its Critics* (New Haven: Yale University Press, 1989), 135–52 and 193–212.
44. Jon Elster and Rune Slagstad (eds.), *Constitutions and Democracy* (Cambridge: Cambridge University Press, 1988), 8–14.

question could be raised about whether one generation of democrats should bind for ever future generations of democrats. The more areas that are stipulated as being constitutionally *beyond* the democratic center in a federal system, the broader the range of policy areas in which future generations at the center must produce supermajorities in order to be able to legislate. Hypothetically, it is possible that at some time in the future the overwhelming majority of people in *all* the subunits might want to become a unitary state. However, the constitution's framing generation may have explicitly precluded any amendment that would change the fundamental nature of the federal system. In that case the only option would be to write a new constitution.[45]

Most political changes are not as extreme as the hypothetical case just referred to, but changing the rules of the game of a federation are exceptionally difficult. From the perspective either of game theory, or of legislative behavior, the hardest rules to change are decision rules which structurally favor a group whose positive vote is nevertheless needed to change those rules. A vote in the upper chamber to make a highly unequal federal system less demos constraining is such a vote.[46]

The fourth reason why all democratic federations are demos constraining follows from the previous three. Constitutions in democratic federations are necessarily more complex than constitutions in unitary democracies. Potential policy issues in areas such as the environment, welfare, legislation, health, and research are constantly being socially and economically reconstructed. The boundaries of what is consensually a subunit government concern, or a central government concern, are in continual flux. Boundary adjudication is therefore more essential, and more difficult, in a federal than in a unitary system. Thus, another major political actor that does not owe its lawmaking authority to periodic checks by the demos, or even the demoi, the judiciary, is normally empowered to play a bigger role in a federal system that it does in a unitary system.

For all the reasons I have just analyzed, all democratic federations are thus inherently demos constraining. However, as I shall document later, democratic federations can and do vary immensely in the degree to which they are demos constraining. In fact some federations are constructed in such a way as to be, within the limits of federalism, demos enabling. The analytical weakness of Riker's concept of the fundamental dichtomy between "decentralized federalism" and "centralized federalism" is that it makes it difficult to see and evaluate the great variation within what he calls "centralized federalism." Later in this

45. See e.g. Article 79 of the German Basic Law (Constitution), which says: "Amendments of this basic law affecting the division of the federation into *Länder* [or] the participation on principle of the *Länder* in legislation . . . shall be inadmissible."

46. The last line of Article 5 of the US constitution stipulates that "No state, without its Consent, shall be deprived of its equal Suffrage in the Senate." Some constitutional lawyers argue that Article 5 makes the massive malrepresentation of two senators per state, regardless of the size of the populations of the states, beyond revocation by a majority, a supermajority, or even a constitutional amendment.

article I operationalize my concept of a federalist continuum, and demonstrate how it opens up a more fruitful approach to the empirical, and even the normative, comparative analysis of federalism.

Federalism and the Potential for a Structurally Induced Policy Status Quo

The last major Rikerian thesis I want to examine concerns policy. The argument Riker makes appears paradoxical. Despite his normative argument in favor of federalism because of its majority blocking tendency to fragment parties, he argues that federal institutions, by themselves, have *no* policy impact. I argue, on the contrary, that federal institutions matter. Matter a lot. What is the structure of Riker's argument?

Riker sees individual preferences as being the driving force behind social choice. From this premise Riker argues that, if an aggregate of individuals believe that any particular set of institutions such as federal institutions contribute to policy outcomes they do not like, it is relatively easy for them to change those institutions, and to change policy. This line of argumentation is what leads Riker to the seemingly peculiar position of being the world's most prestigious academic authority on federalism *and* asserting that the object of his scientific observation is actually a powerless chimera. Let me quote at some length Riker's words on why federal institutions do not matter:

It is difficult to escape the conclusion that the accidents of federalism (i.e. the constitutional and administrative details) do not make any difference at all. They simply provide a standard of style for federal countries that differ somewhat from the standard for unitary ones. In federal countries, it is often necessary to go through the form of showing that a government has legal authority to do what it wants to do. But of course, if it really wants to do it, the authority is always there. Lawyers, especially constitutional lawyers, have a little more work in a federation than in a unitary system; otherwise there is not much difference.[47]

No matter how useful the fiction of federalism is in creating new government, one should not overlook the fact that it is a fiction. In the study of federal governments, therefore, it is always appropriate to go behind the fiction to study the real forces in a political system.[48]

What counts is not the rather trivial constitutional structure but rather the political and economic culture ... Federalism is at most an intervening and relatively unimportant variable.[49]

Federalism makes no particular difference for public policy.[50]

47. Riker, "Federalism," 144.
48. Riker, "Six Books in Search of a Subject, or, Does Federalism Exist and Does it Matter?," *Comparative Politics* (Oct. 1969), 146.
49. Ibid., 144–5.
50. Riker, "Federalism," 143 n. 23.

One of the reasons for the strange death of federalism in modern democratic theory is that the major theorist of federalism killed it. The reasoning behind such Rikerian judgements are that he sees collective decisions and policies as being fundamentally derived from an aggregate of individual preferences. In a stylized manner we can say that Riker sees aggregated tastes as inherently unstable and as essentially incoherent. Democracy entails a "preference induced disequilibrium." Tastes make demands. Institutions ultimately translate tastes into policies. Thus tastes are the fundamental explanation of policy outcomes. It is from the context of this logic that Riker asserts that federal institutions are "at most an intervening and relatively unimportant variable."

In some of his writings, to be sure, Riker acknowledges that institutions might matter, but the central thrust of his argument is that tastes matter more than institutions. For Riker, "institutions are probably best seen as *congealed tastes*... If institutions are congealed tastes and if tastes lack equilibria, then also do institutions, except for short-run events."[51]

Tastes do matter, but so do institutions. In some instances a democracy can break down or slide into civil war in the short term. In US history a case could possibly be made that "in the short term" (say in the twenty years leading up to the first shot being fired) the highly demos constraining quality of US federal institutions contributed to the civil war.

As Kenneth Shepsle and Barry Weingast convincingly argue, part of the force of Riker's argument comes from the dual assumption that individuals do not have fixed tastes or agendas, and that the institutions they are in do not have bounded contexts which structure incentives.[52] If these two assumptions hold, then if the aggregate of individuals in a legislature actually have a preference for a policy measure, they can easily pass relevant legislation. But, as Shepsle and Weingast go on to demonstrate, *neither* of these assumptions is warranted in the study of legislatures. They show how, for example, even in the US House of Representatives institutional issues such as bureaucratic routines, decision rules, seniority on important committees, and the rule that any law passed must be superior, in the judgement of the gatekeepers, to the status quo often produce a "structurally induced equilibrium." Shepsle and Weingast show how such institutionally structured decision systems can have a strong impact on policy. The status quo often prevails, not because of individual tastes, but because of the specific institutional structures of the Congress, and also

---

51. Riker, "Implications for the Disequilibrium of Majority Rule for the Study of Institutions," *American Political Science Review*, 74 (1980), 432–47, quotation from p. 445; my italics.

52. For a pioneering evaluation of these methodological issues, see two articles by Kenneth A. Shepsle and Barry R. Weingast, who show how institutions can help frame, and reframe, incentive structures. See their "The Institutional Foundations of Committee Power," *American Political Science Review*, 81 (Jan. 1987), 85–104, and their "Structure Induced Equilibrium and Legislative Choice," *Public Choice*, 37 (1981), 503–19.

because congressmen come into this institutional setting not from completely unbounded but from bounded contexts. The overall context within which individual congressmen actually function has something to do with the regional interest groups that send them, and which will help defeat or reelect them, in less than two years. Correctly understood, the vectors of new institutionalism, and the vectors of individual rational choice, may actually point in the same direction in the case of many federal systems, namely the status quo.

If this can happen in the US House of Representatives, which has close to near proportional representation in terms of one person, one vote, one does not have to be a "new institutionalist" to be sensitive to the policy implications of federalism in a country like Brazil, where the Senate's prerogatives place it at the extreme end of the demos constraining continuum, and where the constituencies and governors that help send members to the Senate have their own agendas and control resources that the senators value.[53] Brazil is a struggling new democracy with one of the world's worst income distributions. In 1996 the majority of the population continually expressed strong preferences for reforms, and President Cardoso, who also backed reforms, ended the year with extremely high approval ratings. Nevertheless, neither the "tastes" of the citizens nor the preferences of the president were able to produce many reforms. In the Brazilian upper chamber a group of senators who represent less than 9 percent of the electorate can produce a "win-set" to block major legislative reform. If the institutions of the equally apportioned US House of Representatives can produce structurally induced equilibria, Brazilian federalism, which has an extremely malapportioned upper house *and* an extremely malapportioned lower house, can certainly help contribute to the continuation of a structurally induced status quo. No serious analyst of Brazil, after carefully studying the consequences of the decision rules and the prerogatives of the Senate, the states, and the governors, could sustain an argument that federalism is a relatively unimportant intervening variable.

---

53. In a private communication David Fleischer (professor of political science at the University of Brasília) estimates that roughly 40% of Brazilian federal senators have been governors (many more than once) and that many of the senators aspire to be governors. Almost no US senators were once governors *and* aspire to return as governors. For powerful documentation that the career paths of federal deputies and senators in Brazil are heavily oriented toward, and influenced by, their states, see Scott Mainwaring and David Samuels, "Bringing the States Back In: Federalism and Democracy in Contemporary Brazil," Paper prepared for the Conference on Democracy and Federalism, All Souls College, Oxford University June 5–8, 1997; and David Samuels and Fernando Luiz Abrução, "The New Politics of the Governors: Subnational Politics and the Brazilian Transition to Democracy," Paper prepared for the Aug. 1997 meeting of the International Political Science Association, Seoul. They estimate that in the 1991–4 legislature approximately 35% of the sitting deputies either exhibited a preference, or actually gave up their seat, for a state level executive or electoral post.

Operationalizing the Demos Constraining – Demos Enabling Continuum

If I have raised empirical and normative questions about the Rikerian framework, it is now incumbent upon me to attempt to operationalize my concept of a demos constraining continuum, and to use it for the comparative analysis of politics in democratic federal systems.

Democratic federal systems can vary significantly on a number of constitutionally embedded practices and decision making formulas that go against the general democratic principle of "one person, one vote." There can also be extremely important paraconstitutional patterns of political behavior that mitigate or exacerbate limits on the ability of a politywide majority to make policy. While each of the above individual factors has some impact on the rule making capacity of the demos, what is of most importance is how these factors interact with one another in such a way as to impede systematically a potential majority's capacity to alter the status quo or to facilitate (within the limits of the constitutionally guaranteed areas of subunit rights) the capacity of a majority to create politywide decisions they deem necessary for the quality of democracy and efficacious policy making. In this article I give special attention to four variables, three of them constitutionally embedded, and one, among the most important, a paraconstitutional practice of political parties. The four variables, and the associated propositions concerning their demos constraining potential in federal systems, are the following:

Variable 1: The degree of overrepresentation in the territorial chamber

Proposition: The greater the overrepresentation of the less populous states (and thus the underrepresentation of the more populous states) the greater the demos-constraining potential of the senate.

Variable 2: The "policy scope" of the territorial chamber

Proposition: The greater the "policy scope" of the chamber that represents the principle of territory, the greater the potential to limit the lawmaking powers of the chamber that represents the principle of population.

Variable 3: The degree to which policy making is constitutionally allocated to super majorities or to subunits of the federation

Proposition: The greater the amount of policy making competencies that are constitutionally prescribed as requiring super majorities or as being beyond the lawmaking powers of the central government, the greater the demos is constrained.

Variable 4: The degree to which the party system is politywide in its orientation and incentive systems

Proposition: The more political parties are disciplined parties whose incentive systems, especially concerning nominations, privileges politywide interests over provincial and local interests, the more politywide parties can mitigate the inherent demos limiting characteristics of federalism.

Variable 1: The Degree of Overrepresentation in the Territorial Chamber

All federations have a legislative chamber that represents the specific territories of the subunits that constitute the federation (hereafter called the senate, the territorial chamber, or the upper house) and one legislative chamber that represents the people as a whole (hereafter called the lower house). As measured by the democratic principle of "one person, one vote," all upper houses to some degree violate the democratic principle of equality. However, what is not often recognized is that there can be, and is, enormous variation in the degree of inequality in which small states are overrepresented in federal upper houses.

The most widely known example and emulated model of democratic federalism is that drafted in 1787 in Philadelphia. But the US model has a number of characteristics that are not essential to democratic federalism. Indeed, a case can be made that the US model, *qua* model, should be open to debate, negotiation, and challenge. One problematic characteristic of the US model relates to the composition of the upper federal chamber.

The rationale of second chambers in federations is that they pay particular attention to issues of special relevance to the subunits of the federation. Not as a point of principle, but rather as part of the historical "grand compromise" between the big and small states, the representatives of the big states in 1787–8 made two major concessions which violated formal democratic equality.[54] First, they gave the small states equal representation or, more accurately, *massive overrepresentation* in the upper chamber. Second, with less awareness of the implications, they made the *policy scope* of both houses basically the same. These two decisions, which I call "disproportionate representation" and "symmetrical policy scope," are a fundamental part of the US federal formula. But should they necessarily be a part of modern democratic federalism? Let us first restrict our attention to variable 1, the composition of the upper chamber.

Within existing democratic federal systems some states are overrepresented by more than a factor of 100. Such massive overrepresentation is not a necessary feature of democratic federalism. If an ethnic or cultural minority in a federation were overrepresented by such a drastic number in the upper chamber, and if the chamber had a policy scope equal to that of the more democratically elected house, this would almost certainly create problems of allegiance

54. For an excellent discussion of how and why these compromises were made, see Elaine K. Swift, *The Making of an American Senate: Reconstitutive Change in Congress, 1787–1841* (Ann Arbor: University of Michigan Press, 1996), 1–94. Also see Riker, *The Development of American Federalism*, 17–42.

to the federation by some leaders at the center, especially in a multinational federation.

How great is the variation of overrepresentation in modern democratic federal systems? The democratic federal system with the least overrepresentation is Belgium, with a Gini-coefficient of overrepresentation of only 0.015.[55] India is 0.10, Germany is 0.32. But the US has a Gini-coefficient of overrepresentation in the second chamber of 0.49, while Brazil is close at 0.52.

What are the actual empirical patterns behind such differences in the Gini-coefficient of inequality of representation in the upper chamber? In Austria, for example, which is only slightly less proportional than Belgium, there are nine states (*Länder*). Each state is represented in the federal chamber, but the total number of representatives is allocated almost according to population as follows: Vienna, 12 seats; Lower Austria, 12; Upper Austria, 10; Carinthia, 4; Tyrol, 5; Burgenland and Vorarlberg, 3 each.[56]

In Germany the 1949 Basic Law (Bonn Constitution) stipulates that the subunits (or *Länder*) of the federation will get between three to six votes in the upper chamber (Bundesrat): "Each *Land* shall have at least three votes; *Länder* with more than two million inhabitants shall have four, *Länder* with more than six million inhabitants five, and *Länder* with more than seven million inhabitants six votes."[57] The smallest *Land*, Bremen, in 1993 had a population of 686,000 and was allocated three votes in the upper house. The largest *Land*, North Rhine-Westphalia, had a population of 17,679,000 and was allocated six votes in the upper house.[58] Thus, one vote in Bremen was worth thirteen votes in North Rhine-Westphalia.

The United States and Brazil have the same decision rule concerning votes in the upper chamber; each state, no matter the population, receives an equal amount of senate seats (two in the USA and three in Brazil). In the United States the state with the smallest population in 1990 was Wyoming, with 453,588 people, and the state with the largest population was California, with 29,760,021.[59] Thus, one vote in Wyoming was worth sixty-six votes in California.

---

55. The Gini Index of Inequality simply measures the degree of inequality among variables, where an index value of zero denotes complete equality and an index value approaching the theoretical maximum of 1.0 denotes complete inequality (which would mean here that one state has all the representatives). See Arend Lijphart, *Democracies: Patterns of Majoritarian and Consensus Government in Twenty-One Countries* (New Haven: Yale University Press, 1984), 173–5.

56. See "Austria, the Constitution," in *Europa World Book 1990* (London: Europa Publications, 1990), 405.

57. S. E. Finer, Vernon Bogdanor, and Bernard Rudden, *Comparing Constitutions* (Oxford: Oxford University Press, 1995), 150; trans. from Article 51, para. 20 of the Bonn Constitution.

58. See "Germany," in *Europa World Year Book 1995* (London: Europa Publications, 1995), i. 1293.

59. *Whitaker's Almanack* (London: I. Whitaker, 1997).

Brazil is even more demos constraining than the United States. The smallest state in Brazil in 1991 was Roraima, with a population of 215,790, and the largest state was São Paulo, with a population of 31,192,818.[60] Thus one vote cast in Roraima has 144 times as much weight as a vote cast in São Paulo.

The demos constraining nature of Brazil's federalism is in fact even more extreme if we consider the lower house. For purposes of brevity I will not treat representation in the lower house as a separate variable. However, I should note that the rhetorical and political power of the need to represent territory (as opposed to population, i.e., "one person, one vote") is so strong in Brazil that every state, no matter how small, receives a "floor" of eight deputies in the House of Representatives, and no state, no matter how populous, can receive more than the "ceiling" of seventy deputies. If there were perfect proportionality in Brazil, Roraima would receive one deputy and São Paulo close to 115 deputies. As it is, Roraima receives eight deputies and São Paulo only seventy.[61]

On our demos constraining continuum, therefore, it is clear that on variable 1 Belgium, Austria, and India are at the low end. Germany is near the center, and the United States, Brazil, and Argentina are the most demos constraining. See Table 15.3.

Variable 2: The Policy Scope of the Territorial Chamber

There is no sense in having a federation unless the subunits can play some role in making, or at the very least reviewing, laws that directly affect how the federation works. This is particularly true for multinational or multicultural federations. Lawmaking powers concerning cultural issues such as language, religion, or education are among the most important reasons for the very existence of such multinational federations.

However, federal legislative systems differ greatly as to what politywide competences are accorded to the upper house. The US House of Representatives has greater prerogatives than the Senate in originating money bills, and thus some analysts believe its powers are greater than the Senate's. However, a case could be made that in some important respects the unrepresentative Senate has even greater powers than the House of Representatives (which is reapportioned every decade to reflect population changes). In the creation of Supreme Court justices, for instance, the president nominates, the Senate denies or confirms the nominations, and the House of Representatives is constitutionally marginalized. The same holds true for all major posts in the executive branch. The

60. *Europa World Year Book 1995*, 618, and Daniel J. Elazar *et al.*, *Federal Systems of the World* (Harlow: Longman, 1994), 44.

61. For a discussion of this serious problem of malapportionement in the lower house, see the excellent book by Scott P. Mainwaring, *Rethinking Party Systems in the Third Wave of Democratization: The Case of Brazil* (Stanford, Calif.: Stanford University Press, 1999), esp. ch. 5. The estimate of 115 deputies for São Paulo in 1997 is by Professor David Fleischer, from the University of Brasília, a specialist on the Brazilian legislature.

TABLE 15.3. *A continuum of the degree of overrepresentation in the upper houses of twelve modern federal democracies*

Gini Index of Inequality[a]		Ratio of best represented to worst represented federal unit (on basis of population)		Percentage of seats of best represented decile	
Belgium	.015	Austria	1.5/1	Belgium	10.8
Austria	.05	Belgium	2/1	Austria	11.9
India	.10	Spain	10/1	India	15.4
Spain	.31	India	11/1	Spain	23.7
Germany	.32	Germany	13/1	Germany	24.0
Canada	.34	Australia	13/1	Australia	28.7
Australia	.36	Canada	21/1	Canada	33.4
Russia	.43	Switzerland	40/1	Russia	35.0
Switzerland	.45	USA	66/1	Switzerland	38.4
USA	.49	Argentina	85/1	USA	39.7
Brazil	.52	Brazil	144/1	Brazil	41.3
Argentina	.61	Russia	370/1	Argentina	44.8

Note: The status of Russia as a democracy is the most questionable of the twelve countries in the table. The Russian data are included for comparative purposes. This table was prepared with the help of Wilfried Swenden, as part of the Stepan–Swenden federal data bank. We are grateful to Cindy Skach and Jeff Kahn for having provided us with the data on India and Russia respectively. Other data were taken from *Whitaker's Almanack* (London: I. Whitaker, 1997); *The Europa World Year Book 1995* (London: Europa Publications, 1995); and Daniel J. Elazar *et al.*, *Federal Systems of the World* (Harlow: Longman, 1994). For the constitutional provisions on second chambers, see S. E. Finer, Vernon Bogdanor, and Bernard Rudden, *Comparing Constitutions* (Oxford: Oxford University Press, 1995); and A. P. Blaustein and G. H. Flanz (eds.), *Constitutions of the Countries of the World* (Dobbs Ferry, NY: Oceana Publications, 1991–).

[a] The formula is: $G = 1 + 1/n - 2ny(y1 + 2y2 + 3y3 + \ldots + nyn$, with n = number of units, y = mean percentage of seats. In case one uses deciles as units y is automatically 10; so is n. y1, y2, y3, ...yn stands for the percentage of seats that corresponds to each of the deciles. The Gini-coefficient equals zero if the composition of the upper chamber is fully proportional, and equals one if one subunit has all the votes in the second chamber. Arend Lijphart was among the first authors to use the Gini-coefficient as a measure of inequality for the composition of second chambers. See Arend Lijphart, *Democracies: Patterns of Majoritarian and Consensus Government in Twenty-One Countries* (New Haven: Yale University Press, 1984), 174.

secretary, deputy secretary, and all assistant secretaries of all cabinet rank departments must be confirmed by the Senate. Likewise for such positions as the directors of the Central Intelligence Agency, National Security Council, Federal Bureau of Investigation, and many other major government agencies.

Brazil in theory follows the US constitutional formula of power symmetry between the two houses. The lower house, as in the United States, has greater authority in originating money bills. Also, unless the Senate votes against an entire bill, the House of Representatives can alter any changes the Senate makes to a bill without a conference. However, the Senate has twelve areas where it has exclusive competence. For example, the Senate directly appoints two thirds of the judges that review federal expenditures, and has the right to deny or confirm the other third. The Senate has exclusive competence to authorize state borrowing, and can override a negative opinion of the Central Bank. The

Senate has exclusive competence to approve the central administration's foreign borrowing levels. In Brazil there is *no* policy area that is beyond the policy making competence of the Senate, but there are many key policy areas that are the exclusive lawmaking prerogatives of the Senate.

In Brazil the interaction of variables 1 and 2 means that states that represent only 13 percent of the total electorate have 51 percent of the votes in the Senate. This small group of senators thus has to be treated with deference, patronage, and logrolling because it is a group that can, theoretically, block policies supported by senators representing 87 percent of the population.

The US model of "symmetry of policy scope" is not of course the only model. Indeed, the US model is once again at the extreme end of the demos constraining continuum. It is important to emphasize that neither democratic theory nor modern democratic practice requires that a chamber with massive disproportionality be given policy making powers equal to that of the proportional chamber. For example, I have not seen a serious charge that the second chamber in Germany, the Bundesrat, is treated unfairly or undemocratically because of its limited scope. The close-to-proportional first chamber, the Bundestag, which represents all the voters of Germany, has the *exclusive* power to elect and dismiss the chancellor. Germany's famous "constructive vote of no confidence" is only voted upon in the lower chamber.[62] Likewise, originally the second chamber's consent was not needed for approximately 60 percent of the statutes passed by the lower chamber.[63] The upper chamber's right to cast a "suspensive veto," and thus to force a proposed statute to be considered by a joint committee, is of growing importance owing to divided majorities in the lower and upper chambers. However, in the thirteen legislative periods between 1949 to 1998 the highest refusal rate on consent bills was only 2.5 percent. During the 1953–8 session and the 1983–7 sessions the upper chamber did not effectively veto a single bill.[64]

This difference in policy scope between the US model and what eventually became the German federal model was absolutely understood—and resisted—by the American Occupation authorities during the drafting of the Bonn constitution. According to the eminent scholar of political institutions Herman Finer, the Americans were "convinced of the desirability of a weak federal authority. They were persuaded by the kind of arguments for federalism and the separation of powers needed in the nascent U.S.A. in 1788, namely, to keep

62. See Articles 63 and 67 of the German Basic Law.
63. Nearly fifty years after the creation of the Basic Law the Bundesrat today has to consent to approximately 55–65% of all federal legislation in a normal legislative session. This increase in the consent ratio of total legislation was partly to compensate for the fact that German federalism became somewhat more "centralized" and "administrative" in character over the years. Another significant factor in increasing the consent ratio was that the *Länder* won the right to vote upon many issues relating to federal integration into the European Union.
64. See the meticulous Oxford University D.Phil. by Wilfried Swenden, "Federalism and Second Chambers: Regional Representation in Parliamentary Federations," 2000, ch. 6.

government weak for the sake of a durable and democratic (that is, atomized) system. This caused the S.P.D. [the German Social Democratic Party] to go into opposition." Eventually the SPD prevailed over American objections and "secured that, broadly speaking, the second chamber should not be of the dominant state-powerful type over the lower chamber."[65]

So German federalism is less disproportionate than US federalism, and less symmetrical in policy scope than US federalism. On both dimensions, therefore, a case can be made that German federalism is more formally (and I believe substantively) democratic.[66]

Spain is less demos constraining than Germany. As in Germany, the lower chamber, the Cortes, has exclusive competence over the two most important politywide issues, the power to authorize the formation of the government, and to vote a "constructive motion of no confidence." However, the upper chamber has even less scope than in Germany to veto legislation passed by the lower chamber.

The most important power the Spanish upper chamber has is the capacity to block an armed intervention of the central government in one of the autonomous provinces. Since such intervention is of direct relevance for the nature of the federation, it is correct that the territorial chamber has special powers in this respect. The constitution is very carefully crafted in this respect, as we will see when we discuss variable 3.

At the lowest end of the demos constraining scale of territorial chambers are countries such as India, Spain, and Belgium. They are so low, indeed, that some analysts might even argue that the territorial chambers are too weak for these countries to be considered federations. However, if one accepts the fundamental Dahlian definition of a federation as involving powers of the subunits that are constitutionally *beyond* the power of the center, Spain and Belgium are clearly federal, because of variable 3 (to be discussed shortly), concerning the power of the subunits, which in Spain and Belgium are quite substantial. As a paper by the Belgian political scientist Wilfried Swenden makes clear, one of the most distinctive aspects about Belgian federalism is that it is a multinational and multicultural polity that combines substantial federal and consociational characteristics. On the Gini index Belgium's upper house is the closest to pure proportional representation in the Stepan–Swenden database. However, the Belgian Senate has to consent to constitutional amendments and international treaties, and all legislation affecting the structure of federal

65. Herman Finer, *Governments of Greater European Powers: A Comparative Study of the Governments and Political Culture of Great Britain, France, Germany and the Soviet Union* (London: Methuen, 1956), quotation from p. 690; emphasis in the original.

66. On German federalism, and more specifically on the German constitutional concept known as *Bundestreue* (often translated as "federal trust" or "comity"), see Bertus de Villiers, *Bundestreue: The Soul of an Intergovernmental Partnership: Comparative Analysis of the Principles Underlying Bundestreue in the Federal Republic of Germany, Switzerland and Belgium*, Konrad-Adenauer Stiftung Occasional Papers (Johannesburg: RSA, Mar. 1995).

institutions and the judicial organization of the country. But amendments to the constitution or all legislation that substantially affects the federal structure or the linguistic statute of the Communities require special majorities. All constitutional amendments require a two-thirds majority in both houses. Significantly, all legislation or constitutional amendments relating to linguistic matters not only require an overall two-thirds parliamentary majority, but also a majority within each linguistic group in Parliament. It should be noted that on such occasions, both houses are split according to linguistic lines. Critics have therefore argued that there is no need for a strong federal bicameral system, since this technique of so-called "special majorities" likewise applies to the lower house.[67]

Constitutionally, the Spanish and Indian upper houses, like Germany's play no role in votes of confidence or no confidence. However, unlike Germany, the Spanish and Indian upper chambers have no significant lawmaking role in the federation.[68] In fact they are close to a revisionary chamber, like the House of Lords in the United Kingdom. In one important area, however, the Spanish upper chamber plays a crucial role in preserving the autonomy of the subunits. This area concerns the right of the center to use armed force to impose "order" on a subunit. All democracies have some provisions for emergency laws. The key question is whether the emergency provisions are written in an explicit enough manner that such powers actually can only be implemented with the consent of the legislature, for specific purposes agreed to by the legislature, and only for finite periods determined by the legislature. In a federation this is an area where it is absolutely appropriate for the upper chamber to play a central role, because armed interventions by the center in the subunits involve a fundamental aspect of the federation *qua* federation.

Federal interventions are discussed in Article 155 of the Spanish constitution. Interventions can only occur after four conditions are satisfied. First, the government must come to a legal determination that some subunit has violated the constitution, or is not upholding the constitution. Second, the central government must convey this legal determination in writing to the subunit and ask for a response. Third, if the government considers the response of the subunit to be inadequate, it can ask the upper chamber to vote for federal intervention. Fourth, no intervention can occur unless the upper chamber approves by an absolute majority. Given this clear set of guidelines, time for

67. See Swenden, "Belgium: A Federal State in Search of a Nation."
68. The Indian upper chamber at the center, the Council of States, does have some, if not many, blocking powers. For example, Article 249 stipulates that the Parliament cannot legislate with respect to an issue that has been allocated as a prerogative of the state legislative assemblies unless two thirds of the members present and voting in the Council of States approve. Also, Article 368 stipulates that constitutional amendments cannot be passed unless an absolute majority of the members of the Council of States approve, and that two thirds of those present and voting in the Council of States approve. The article also stipulates that such a parliamentary approved amendment must be ratified by not less than one half of the state legislatures.

mutual adjustments and bargaining is built into the process. In the first nineteen years of the Spanish constitution *no* intervention under Article 155 ever occurred. In my judgement it is probably correct to say that the upper house plays an appropriate demos constraining role *vis-à-vis* federal interventions.

In India it is probably also correct to say that the constitutional formula concerning federal interventions does not sufficiently constrain a government in possession of a majority. The constitutional article that is relevant is Article 356. This article simply says that the Council of Ministers (the cabinet) can instruct the president to ask for an intervention (called "president's rule"), which would dissolve a provincial legislature and government and put the province under the direct rule of the center. The only requirement for such an intervention is that the governor (a nonelected official appointed by the center) indicates that the government of the province "can not be carried on in accordance with the provisions of the constitution." No vote authorizing federal intervention is needed in either the upper or the lower house for the first sixty days of intervention. After two months the upper house and the lower house must formally vote a renewal for six months or the intervention must cease. Thus the upper chamber does have the constitutional power to curtail a federal intervention. But the constitutional provisions on intervention are so loose, and the Congress Party in the past so often had such politywide party majorities and discipline (variable 5), that "president's rule" happened frequently, even under the democratic and consociational rule of Nehru. In fact, between 1947 and 1997 president's rule was implemented over 100 times and affected every state.

However, a combination of factors, including recent court decisions which have begun to insist that the central government at least publish the explicit grounds for intervention, the increasing frequency of minority governments at the center, and the growing coalitional weight of provincial parties, has made the employment of president's rule more difficult and controversial.[69] If we restrict our analysis only to the majority constraining features of the upper house, a case could be made that the federal dimension of Indian democracy might be enhanced if an absolute majority of the upper house were required *before* president's rule could be implemented. The recent court decisions are also probably right to insist that the central government explicitly documents why an intervention is called for.

69. For the history and recent evolution of president's rule in India, two useful articles are Ved Marwah, "Use and Abuse of Emergency Powers: The Indian Experience," and Agit Mozoomdar, "The Supreme Court and President's Rule," both in the valuable volume by Balveer Arora and Douglas V. Verney (eds), *Multiple Identities in a Single State: Indian Federalism in Comparative Perspective* (New Delhi: Konark Publishers, 1995), 136–59 and 160–8. I will develop this point further when I write up the results of my Apr. 1997 trip to India in which I discussed Article 356 with the former chief justice of the Supreme Court and the former chief minister of Kerala, who had Article 356 used against him. Both the former chief justice and the former chief minister believe that Article 356 can, and should, be used more sparingly.

Unlike variable 1, namely the principle of representation of the upper house, variable 2, concerning the legislative competencies of the upper house, does not lend itself to quantification. However, I believe sufficient qualitative evidence has been given to allow us to place the five countries I have discussed along a demos constraining continuum for the variable. See Table 15.4.

Variable 3: The Degree to which Policy Making is Constitutionally Allocated to Supermajorities or to Subunits of the Federation

This is a complex variable that contains three closely related but analytically distinct components. The first component concerns the amount of potential legislative issues that are embedded in the constitution and that require exceptional lawmaking majorities. The second component concerns which powers are constitutionally given to the subunits and which to the center. The third component concerns whether, if the constitution is silent on an issue, the presumption is that residual lawmaking power resides with the center or with the subunits.

If the constitution is relatively parsimonious, or even when detailed is devoted to principles, most laws can be passed with simple majorities. Depending on variable 2, these votes may or may not involve the upper house. However, the above three components may interrelate in such a way that senators, representing less than 8 percent of the total electorate, might have a blocking veto over an extensive degree of legislation, and could conceivably thwart a majority again and again. This is a question not only of democratic theory but of democratic practice. If a minority can use its blocking power to defend a status quo that democratic theorists, constitutional analysts, public opinion, and the majority of politicians believe should be changed, then this is dangerous for democracy. Such a situation could create a climate of widespread "semiloyalty" to democracy itself, and/or lead to a context supportive of what Guillermo O'Donnell calls "delegative democracy," in which presidents rule via exceptional measures in the name of efficacy, but to the harm of the full democratic process.[70]

This variable also concerns the amount of policy making authority reserved for the center and that reserved for the subunits. Democratic federations vary greatly concerning how much lawmaking authority is permanently given to the subunits, and how much is reserved for the center. Here an important distinction must be made. A polity can *decentralize administration* and *transfer most of the budget* to the subunits in areas such as health, law enforcement, and welfare, but *reserve for the central legislators the right to pass basic legislation*

70. Guillermo O'Donnell, "Delegative Democracy," *Journal of Democracy*, 51 (Jan. 1994), 55–69. For the concept of "semiloyalty" and how it contributes to democratic breakdown, see Juan J. Linz, *The Breakdown of Democratic Regimes: Crisis, Breakdown and Reequilibration* (Baltimore: Johns Hopkins University Press, 1978).

TABLE 15.4. *Continuum of the upper chamber's constitutional prerogatives to constrain a majority at the center*

Least constraining				Most constraining
India	Spain	Germany	United States of America	Brazil
Virtually only a revisionary chamber	Major power is Article 155 of the constitution, which precludes intervention by the center unless it has received the absolute majority approval of the upper house	Upper chamber plays no role in constructive vote of no confidence. This is the exclusive competence of the lower chamber. Only can play a potential veto role in approximately 65% of the total legislative agenda that directly relates to centre–subunit issues	Extensive capacity to block a democratic majority. The unrepresentative chamber has the same voting rights on all legislation as the "one person, one vote" chamber	Excessive for the efficacious and legitimate functioning of democratic government
The upper chamber has no constitutional powers to protect subunit autonomy against a sixty day central intervention. Upper chamber has capacity to review or deny President's rule only after sixty days	Plays no role in constructive vote of no confidence or normal legislation	Relatively slight capacity to block a potential majority of the lower chamber. Even in the years when the upper chamber was controlled by a different majority than the majority of the lower chamber, the upper chamber sustained less than 3% of its vetoes	Senate has exclusive competence to confirm or deny all major judicial and administrative appointments. A chair of a committee can at times be a "win-set" of one	The extremely disproportional upper chamber must approve all legislation. The Senate has twelve areas where they have exclusive lawmaking prerogatives
	Largely a revisionary chamber	Upper chamber plays almost no role in confirming or denying major administrative appointments	A "win-set" of senators representing only 15% of the total electorate can block ordinary legislation	A "win-set" of senators representing 13% of the total electorate can block ordinary legislation supported by senators representing 87% of the population

and carry out authoritative oversight in these areas. Or, the polity could give the subunits exclusive lawmaking and taxing powers in these areas, whether or not they contribute to overall citizen equality and well-being in the federation.

Once again, Brazilian federalism is the most demos constraining in all these matters. A frustrated former minister of planning, Dr José Serra, the distinguished economist and a senator who received more votes than any senator in Brazil's history, says of the Brazilian constitution of 1988 that "it is not really a constitution, but a social, political, and economic law."[71] An extraordinary amount of issues, such as the exact details of retirement plans, foreign and state ownership, special tax schemes for regional development projects, fixed percentages of tax allocations to the center, states, and municipalities, and numerous other items, are embedded in the 1988 constitution.[72] They are thus beyond the scope of ordinary majority legislation. To pass an amendment in any of these areas requires a 60 percent positive vote of *all* members, whether they are present or not, twice, in both houses. In a context of a country the size of a continent, where average nonattendance even at the Constituent Assembly was over 30 percent, this is an extremely arduous task. To be sure this is an easier constitutional amendment process than in the United States, but the US constitution is much more parsimonious than that of Brazil.

Even if we assume 100 percent legislative attendance—which would cost the government an extraordinary amount of lobbying and costly side payments— the minimum "win-set" for blocking any law that is constitutionally embedded is simply the negative vote of senators who represent 8 percent of Brazil's total electorate.[73] The influence of what Carl Friedrich called the "law of anticipated response" comes into play in such a situation. The Brazilian situation is thus a clear instance of what Shepsle and Weingast call "structurally induced equilibrium." Since all players are aware of the blocking potential of a small minority, many potential policy initiatives, even if they are backed by a

71. Interview with the author in São Paulo, Dec. 2, 1996 and repeated in a public talk at the University of London, Feb. 1997.

72. In my "Brazil's Decentralized Federalism" I attempt to explain why this occurred. The short answer is that the constitution of 1988 was constructed after a long period (1964–85) of direct military rule that greatly curtailed the power of the states. In the newly democratizing atmosphere of the constituent assembly a discourse predominated in which the more all rights were explicitly spelled out, and the more power was devolved to states and municipalities, the more democratic Brazil would be. Also, the interests of the federal center were not strongly represented in the constituent assembly because Brazil had not had a directly elected president since 1960. However, governors, who had been directly elected since 1982, had great moral and political power in the constituent assembly, and the decentralized constitution, which transferred a significant amount of Brazil's total tax revenue from the center to the states and municipalities, served many of their political, financial, and tax interests.

73. I arrive at the calculation in the following way; more than 40% of the votes needed to block a constitutional reform are held by senators who represent only 8% of the Brazilian population.

majority of Congress and by public opinion, are taken off the agenda.[74] Even when the issue is not taken off the policy agenda, the cost of passing reform legislation is often extremely high in terms of logrolling and special regional payments. For a country like Brazil, which as late as 1993 had an inflation rate of over 2,000 percent per annum, such a pattern of "structurally induced" nonactions, and/or highly costly actions, puts enormous constraints on the central government's capacity to carry out coherent fiscal planning and to implement needed reform.

The other component of what is constitutionally embedded in Brazil concerns the powers of the states and municipalities. Until recently twenty-four of Brazil's twenty-seven states had their own state banks and frequently issued loans to themselves. The only federal body that had to approve outside bonds was the territorial chamber, the Senate. States also, until November 1996, had the power to tax exports. The cost of getting the Congress to approve a law abolishing state taxes on exports is estimated as 0.5 percent of Brazil's GNP in 1997.

The final component of subunit authority concerns residual lawmaking authority. The presumption in Brazil is that, if the constitution is silent on an issue, residual lawmaking authority rests with the subunits.[75] In Brazil the interaction of variables 1, 2, and 3 creates an extremely high majority blocking potential, and places Brazil, once again, on the extreme of the continuum we are examining.

The United States shares with Brazil the presumption that, for those areas that are not defined in the constitution, residual sovereignty resides with the states, a presumption which is, in itself, demos constraining. However, the political impact of what is in the constitution is substantially less constraining in the United States than in Brazil, because the US constitution is more parsimonious, and among other things there are no banks owned by the states.

Germany's constitution is much less demos constraining than that of the United States. A very large area of lawmaking authority is explicitly given to the federal center. Much legislation is also concurrent, and thus shared by the center and the subunits. Moreover, the constitution is explicit, and therefore reduces the power of courts to make law, by the eight words contained in Article 31: "federal law shall take precedence over Land law." Articles 72–4 also make clear the wide range of areas where the federal law can, if the lower house so wants, prevail.

One of the innovations in the practice of German federalism is that, while the majority in the lower chamber at the center retains the constitutional right

74. This point was repeatedly emphasized to me in interviews I held in Nov. and Dec. 1996 with numerous central government officials including the ministers of finance and of state administration, the former planning minister, and President Cardoso.

75. For a pioneering analysis of the 1988 constitution and the powers of the governors, see Fernando Luiz Abrucio, *Os Barões da federação: Os Governadores* (Universidade de São Paulo: Tese de Mestrado, 1996).

to pass laws, and to exercise oversight, public expenditures of German subnational units, as a percentage of GDP, are greater than in the United States. Also, most of the federal programs are directly administered by *Länder* officials, whereas in the United States many federal programs are administered by federal employees. In conceptual and political terms, therefore, we can say that in Germany the lower chamber at the center retains more lawmaking power than in the United States, but decentralizes more administration. The key point is that a polity can decentralize, without the demos at the center constitutionally yielding lawmaking and oversight authority.

The most significant part of Spain's federalism is the vertical dimension. Spain's system of *autonomías* is an "asymmetrical federalism," in the sense that some provinces, such as Catalonia and the Basque Country, negotiated, via the statues of autonomy arrangements, greater prerogatives than other autonomous provinces. These prerogatives are embedded in statues with constitutional standing. From the perspective of game theory Spain's asymmetrical federalism has created an iterative bargaining game. For example, a nationalist political leader may control a nationalist party based in one province whose votes are needed to put together a governmental majority at the center. This situation would therefore give the province the bargaining power, *de facto*, to renegotiate the terms of the statutes of autonomy. Spanish asymmetrical federal bargaining games so far have been constructed *within* the constitution.

Russian federalism is also asymmetrical; however, many of the iterative bargaining games are *outside* the constitution. Russia's federal bargaining games are therefore often harmful to democratic consolidation because subunits unilaterally redraft their own constitutions, often in ways that violate the constitution of the Russian federation.

The Indian constitution retains residual power at the center, but it is a constitution that in many respects helps India's multinational federalism. For example, the constitution allows the majority at the center, and clusters of linguistic minorities in the subunits, to work together to create, under parliamentary authority, new linguistic states with great facility.[76] This capacity has been extremely important in "holding together" India's polity in a democratic

76. For the judicious multifactorial approach that guided what became the world's largest redrawing of linguistic, social, environmental, and political boundaries, see Government of India, Home Department, *Report of the States Reorganization Commission* (New Delhi: Government of India Press, 1955). For an analysis of the politics of language in India, see Paul R. Brass, *Language, Religion and Politics in North India* (London: Cambridge University Press, 1974). To get an understanding of the secessionist tensions that were building up in the Tamil areas of the south before the "holding together" linguistic devolution, see Margurite Ross Barnett, *The Politics of Cultural Nationalism in South India* (Princeton: Princeton University Press, 1976). There was also mobilizations and protests in the non-Hindi speaking south in favor of English being retained as an official language for communications within the Indian union. See e.g. Duncan B. Forrester, "The Madras Anti-Hindi Agitation, 1965," *Pacific Affairs*, 39 (Spring 1966), 19–36. As a result of the politics of democratic federalism English as well as Hindi were retained.

way. Precisely because the members of the Constituent Assembly knew that the most controversial issue surrounding Indian unity was language policy, and that there was a desire on the part of many delegates eventually to reorganize the states along more linguistic lines, the language of the constitution was extremely *demos enabling*. Future parliaments were given rights to redraw state boundaries completely. Article 3 of the constitution was categorical. With a simple majority "Parliament may by law (a) form a state by separation of territory from any state or by uniting two or more states... (b) diminish the area of any state... (c) alter the name of any state." In a true "coming together" federation the sovereign states would obviously have been able to bargain successfully for a much more demos constraining constitution to protect states' rights.

The 1991 census indicated that India has more than 3,000 mother tongues which are legally recognized. There are thirty-three different languages, each of which is spoken by at least 1 million people. In a relatively consensual manner, most of the boundaries of the states in India were redrawn between 1956 and 1966, and later a process of creating new tribal states in the northeast was begun.

In political terms, it is probably fair to say that the survival of India as the world's largest multicultural, multinational democracy was greatly facilitated by the constitutional structure of the federal system. India's demos enabling federal structure allowed the majority at the center to respond to minority demands from states for greater linguistic and cultural autonomy. If India had been a unitary state (or had had a US style demos constraining federal structure), neither the demos, nor the regional demoi, would have had this constitutional flexibility available to them. For how the continuum concerning variable 3 can be presented, see Table 15.5.

Variable 4: The Degree to which the Party System is Politywide in its Orientation and Incentive Systems

A federal system by definition has executives and legislatures elected in each of the constituent units. These executives and legislatures necessarily have some control over budgets and laws. Structurally and empirically, therefore, federalism *per se* is a system of patronage, power, and prestige that can challenge the power and authority of politywide parties. Such challenges are present in a systematically lesser degree in a unitary than in a federal political system. Some analysts infer from this that the relative absence of ideology and strong disciplined parties in the United States is produced fundamentally by the federal system.[77] This happens to be true for the United States, but it is *not* true of all federal systems. Let us see why.

---

77. David Truman, "Federalism and the Party System," in Arthur W. Macmahon (ed.), *Federalism: Mature and Emergent* (Garden City, NY: Doubleday, 1955), 115–36.

TABLE 15.5. *The constitutional allocation of policy making to super majorities and to subunits of the federation*

Least ⟶ Most

India	Germany	Spain	United States	Brazil
Does not constrain majorities	Slightly majority constraining	Major constraints on majority at the center derives from the statues of autonomy	Strongly majority constraining	Extremely majority constraining
Capacity to respond to minority desires to redraw the linguistic boundaries of states	Federal law explicitly given precedent over *Land* law	Occasional iterative, within constitution, bargaining process if center needs votes of provincial party during process of government formation	Constitution is extremely difficult to amend but is parsimonious, so vast majority of legislation can be passed as ordinary legislation	1988 constitution so extensive that much ordinary legislation can only be passed by the exceptional majorities required for constitutional amendments
Probably should constrain the ease by which the majority can intervene in states	Wide areas where lawmaking powers are either explicitly given to the center or concurrent responsibilities	Any asymmetrical provincial powers must be voted upon and approved by Parliament at the center	Power is horizontally shared at the center between three branches. Power is vertically devolved and shared in "marble cake" federalism between the federal and the state governments	States and municipalities had such extreme control over export taxes and banking that central government's fiscal and trade policy in 1989–96 was impeded. Some centralization of tax and bank policies in 1995–9, but extremely costly to the center
Since 1994 Supreme Court decisions give somewhat more protection to subunits from the imposition of "president's rule" from the center	More tax money is spent by the *Länder* and local authorities than by the center. Many federal programs are decentralized so as to be administered by the *Länder* while lawmaking and policy oversight remains the prerogative of the center	Residual power with center	Residual power with states	Residual power with states
Residual power with center	Most powers are concurrent, but residual powers are with the *Länder*			

Some federal party systems, for a variety of reasons, often produce a majority (coalitional or single party) at the center. Such a coalition may also have polity-wide discipline and a strong politywide organizational infrastructure that creates incentives for disciplined allegiance to politywide parties. In such cases the party system in itself can act as a centralizing, majority producing force inside a mononational federation, as in Germany since 1949, or even in a multicultural, multilingual federation, as in India from 1947 until 1967.

There are many countervailing factors, including ideology, that can contribute to such politywide unity despite the inherent fragmenting pressures found in all federations. For example, if there are no primary elections; if there is either a closed list proportional representation (in which parties rank the candidates), or a single member district in which the politywide party selects the party nominees; if the politywide party provides the vast majority of campaign funding for its nominees; and if the system is parliamentary, there will be a strong set of structural and rational choice incentives—despite federalism—to produce disciplined politywide parties.

In sharp contrast, if the political system has either an open list PR system or a single member district with primaries; if the candidates must raise almost all their money independently of the politywide parties; and if the system is presidential, then there are very few structural or rational choice incentives to produce politywide party unity. The United States, and even more so Brazil, are systems of this latter sort.[78]

But Brazil and the United States are "state-nations." The situation is potentially more complicated (and democratically dangerous) if the polity is a multinational state and there are no disciplined statewide parties. In Russia, for example, 103 of the 171 members of the Federal Council in 1997 belonged to no party at all.[79] In the Yugoslavian and Soviet multinational polities the first competitive elections for executive power were held not in the center, but in the provinces. The fact that there were virtually no politywide parties in the USSR or Yugoslavia contributed to state disintegration in both countries.[80] In contrast, in the federal "state-nation" of Brazil the fact that, in the democratic transition process, direct elections for governor were held in 1982, but not for the presidency until 1989, contributed to the center and demos constraining nature of the 1988 constitution and the increased decentralization of Brazil's fiscal resources, but it did *not* endanger Brazil's territorial unity.

Spain is a multinational federal polity that contains strong politywide parties with some small but significant provincial parties. Linz and I have argued elsewhere that the fact that the first competitive free elections after the death

78. See Mainwaring, *Rethinking Party Systems in the Third Wave of Party Democratization*. Brazil scores near the top on a wide range of indicators concerning party fragmentation or indiscipline.

79. John Barber, "Opposition in Russia," *Government and Opposition*, 324 (Autumn 1997), 608.

80. Juan J. Linz and Alfred Stepan, "Political Identities and Electoral Sequences: Spain, Soviet Union and Yugoslavia," *Daedalus*, 1212 (Spring 1992), 510–22, Chapter 10 in this volume.

of Franco were politywide contributed to the creation of strong politywide parties, even in Catalonia and the Basque Country.[81] However, Catalonia, the province with the strongest autonomy movement, is governed by a regional national party coalition. A regional nationalist party is also strong in the Basque Country. This is a fundamental feature of Spain's "asymmetrical federalism," and it contributes to the iterative bargaining games that occur if no party at the center has a majority.[82]

Russia, like Spain, is a case of asymmetrical federalism, but, as we have seen, it differs from Spain in some very important, and democratically dangerous, respects. Spain is a parliamentary system, and since 1983 after each general parliamentary election a party has achieved a majority or "supported minority" position, and the leader of that party has become the prime minister.

The prime minister is the head of the party, and works hard to maintain politywide party discipline. But in Russia the system is semipresidential of the "superpresidential" sort. The president's mandate comes from a direct election and is therefore independent of whether he has a majority in parliament or not. In fact, President Yeltsin, as president, never belonged to any political party, never campaigned for political parties in the parliamentary elections, and never, between January 1992 and July 1998, had anything close to a majority in the lower house. Many of the candidates for the Duma and the governorships ran as "independents." Like Spain, Russia's asymmetrical federalism has produced an iterative bargaining game, but a variety that is more impeding of democratic consolidation than that of Spain. The first move in the bargaining game by many Russian subunits is to issue unilaterally their own constitution or statutes, which often violates the federal constitution.[83] For the continuum of how parties do, or do not, mitigate the demos constraining features of a federation, see Table 15.6.

Concluding Reflections

Federal institutions matter for policy at *all* points on the demos constraining–demos enabling continuum. Likewise, whether a federation has constitutionally symmetrical or asymmetrical competences for each state is of great import for matters of policy. At the demos constraining end Brazilian senators who represent as little as 8 percent of the electorate have more seats in the Senate than senators who represent more than 90 percent of the electorate. At

81. Ibid.
82. In the Mar. 2000 parliamentary elections, however, the ruling party (People's Party) won an absolute majority and thus was able to form a government without having to make significant bargains with regional nationalist parties.
83. See my "Russian Federalism in Comparative Perspective."

TABLE 15.6. *The degree to which party system empowers majority by creating polity-wide programmatic discipline*

Most   Least

India (1947–67)	Germany	Spain	USA	India (1991–)	Brazil
Politywide Congress Party always had a strong majority at the center and controlled vast majority of states where it played a major but not coercive role in nominations	Strong politywide parties control almost all the seats in the lower and upper chamber and exercise rigid discipline on their members. Ideological tradition of trust and mutual aid (*Bundestreue*). When one party, or a "closely connected" coalition of parties, controls both chambers, the majority is strongly empowered. However, if the party or coalition that controls the lower chamber does not control the upper chamber, they are less empowered	Disciplined politywide parties control most of lower house, which is key policy making chamber. But owing to Spain's asymmetrical multinational federalism, there exist strong provincial parties who are able to negotiate for special status when no party has a majority at the center	Primary system and self-financing make local and state influence more important than politywide influences for most nominations and elections. Polsby calls the USA a system with "100 state parties flying two banners." Nomination system for president, and single member plurality districts, contribute to two party system, as does *de facto* anti-third party state level legislation. In federal legislature a two party system is encouraged by the rules of the Congressional Committee which privilege the two major parties. Party discipline grew in the democratic party with the end of the Dixicrates in the 1960s and in the Republican Party owing to emergence of the neoconservatives with Reagan	No party at the center has had a majority. Majority of states controlled by a regional party. Thirteen parties, most of them regional, but no longer separatist, formed the government at the center in 1996–7, twenty-three in 1999. However, India's "regional" parties are becoming in some sense more "centric-regional" than purely regional because they constituted the bulk of the governing coalition at the center in 1996–7 and contributed to the BJP led government coalition in 1998–9 and 1999–	Nominations fundamentally controlled at state and municipal level. Most of campaigns are self-financed. Extremely high Pedersen party volatility index (50%). Large number of parties. Laakso-Taagepera index of around 8. Almost a third of congressmen newly elected to 1992–6 Congress changed parties "State-nation," so no separatist parties but many state delegations to the center have strong regional policy agendas

the demos enabling end of the continuum federalism has a policy impact, especially in "holding together," multinational, asymmetrical federal systems. A unitary system, or a demos constraining, constitutionally symmetrical federal system could not have made as many, and as rapid, linguistic boundary adjustments as were made in India. Likewise, such a system would not have at its disposal the vast repertoire of federal policies that allow the multicultural, multilinguistic, multireligious Indian polity of a billion people to "hold together." The use of creative federalizing devices in India seems simultaneously, in almost all states, to respond to diversity, while reducing secessionist tendencies to small minorities. Democratic federal devolution of power, and the granting of group specific rights, has not been a slippery slope to secession, or to the violation of individual rights, as liberal rights theorists often fear.[84] Once Tamil speakers were given a state, English was retained as a language of the union, and a regional party won control of the state legislature, thus the issue of Tamil secession became a nonissue.[85] Democratic elections and devolution in Punjab in the late 1990s also made violent Sikh secessionist movements almost a nonissue.[86] It appears that India is more decentralized, and more "a state-nation" with a civilizational culture in the late 1990s, than ever before. Multiple and complementary identities which were not the norm for some important Tamil-speaking political leaders in India in the 1950s, or for significant number of Sikhs in Punjab in the 1980s, are now the norm in both areas.[87] Such processes are worth pondering as we develop a new research agenda on democratic federalism, in multinational as well as mononational states.

84. For pioneering treatments of the issue of collective rights versus individual rights and liberal theorists' hostility to the former, see the book by the philosopher Will Kymlicka, *Multicultural Citizenship: A Liberal Theory of Minority-Rights* (Oxford: Clarendon Press, 1995). For a powerful argument by a distinguished legal theorist that group rights are often a precondition of individual rights, see Joseph Raz, *The Morality of Freedom* (Oxford: Clarendon Press, 1986), 193–216. For a political and philosophically acute discussion of these issues in India, see Rajeev Bhargava, "Secularism, Democracy and Rights," in Mehdi Arslan and Jannaki Rayan (eds.), *Communalism in India* (Delhi: Manohav, 1994), 61–73.

85. In contrast, if the unitary but multinational state of Sri Lanka, after independence, had crafted a "holding together" federation, with a Tamil-speaking state in the northern part of the country, the now almost unmanageable issue of ethnic violence and democratic breakdown may well never have become an issue. For a compelling analysis of the political construction of polarized identities in Sri Lanka, see Sumantra Bose, "State Crises and Nationalities Conflict in Sri Lanka and Yugoslavia," *Comparative Political Studies*, 28 (Apr. 1995), 87–116.

86. Valuable data on loyalties and identities supportive of democracy in India is contained in a soon to be published survey designed by V. B. Singh and Yogendra Yadev of the Center for the Study of Developing Societies in Delhi. Preliminary results are contained in *India Today* (Aug. 31, 1996), 36–53.

87. See Sanjay Kumar, "Punjab: A Vote for Change," and Ranbir Singh, "Politics in Punjab: Restoration of Accommodation Model," both in *Politics in India* (Apr. 1997), 39–40, 37–9. In this overall context of multiple and complementary identities, and the fact that 23 parties are in the ruling coalition in the year 2000, the power of the Hindu fundamentalist party, BJP, is culturally and politically constrained.

Spain's "holding together," asymmetrical federalism produces an iterative bargaining game, but also helps produce a system of multiple but complementary identities. In 1991 in Catalonia 73 percent of the population were proud to be Spanish, 82 percent proud to be Catalan, and 83 percent were in favor of increased movement toward confederal formulas in Europe within the European Community.[88]

Let me conclude with three caveats that have implications for future research. First, some advocates of federalism favor federal, as opposed to unitary, governments because they believe they contribute to liberty, subsidiarity, and democracy. I have seen no systematic evidence to support such presumptions, but they clearly need to be researched. Other scholars and activists argue that, unless a polity is very large, or very multinational, federal institutions are neither necessary, nor even useful. Once again, such claims need to be researched, but on grounds of legitimacy, efficacy, and equality, this argument would appear, prima facie, to be a reasonable position.

My second caveat is that, while it may be true that all democracies that are strongly multinational are federal and asymmetrical, some federal practices can be potentially dangerous, especially during moments of transformation in multinational, nondemocratic polities. As we have already discussed, the three formally federal states of communist Europe fragmented with substantial bloodshed into twenty-three independent countries, many of them ethnocracies. Our research agenda on multinational federalism needs to focus on what political practices and incentives contribute to multiple and complementary identities, civic peace, and democracy, and which practices and incentives contribute to polarizing identities, fratricide, and ethnocracies.

My final caveat is that while I have argued, contra Riker, that federal institutions "do matter," such institutions can of course change over time. Of the four variables I have discussed in this article, the most amenable to change is the role of political parties and their impact on federal institutions. As Table 15.6 makes clear, India from 1947 to 1967 was normally ruled at the center, and in the states, by the Congress Party. But, since 1996 the three non-Congress ruling coalitions have contained between thirteen and twenty-three parties, many of them with a strong base in one, or only a few, states. This factor in itself has altered the political and socioeconomic federal balance in the direction of growing powers for states *vis-à-vis* the center. In Germany in the mid-1990s parties that were in opposition to the governing coalition at the center came to control a majority of the *Länder* and thus to control a majority in the upper house. *De facto*, even without a constitutional change, the relative weight of the upper chamber in German federalism increased in this period. Power changes of this sort occur routinely in federal systems. Nonetheless, many decision rules and institutional routines that affect power relations in federal

88. Linz and Stepan, *Problems of Democratic Transition*, 102.

systems are constitutionally embedded—like variables 1, 2, and 3 discussed in this article—and therefore require supermajorities to change.

Thus, even though preferences may change, there are many consequential, structurally induced regularities in the different types of democratic federal system, and we must devise better strategies to learn more about such regularities.

Index

Page numbers in **bold** refer to figures, and those in *italic* to tables.